robert von neumann

the design and creation of jewelry

third edition

krause publications

700 E. State Street • Iola, WI 54990-0001
Telephone: 715/445-2214

Copyright © 1961, 1972, 1982 by Robert von Neumann
Third Edition   All Rights Reserved
Published in Iola, Wisconsin, 54990 by Krause Publications
and simultaneously in Canada by VNR Publishers,
1410 Birchmount Road, Scarborough, Ontario M1P 2E7
Designed by Arlene Putterman
Manufactured in the United States of America

Library of Congress Cataloging in Publication Data

Von Neumann, Robert.
   The design and creation of jewelry.

   Bibliography: p. 308
   Includes index.
   1. Jewelry making. I. Title.
TS740.V6 1982   739.27   80-70258
ISBN 0-8019-7066-0   AACR2
ISBN 0-8019-7067-9 (pbk.)

    13 14 15 16 17 18 19 20 21   5 4 3 2 1 0 9 8

the
design
and
creation
of jewelry

contents

8
stimulants for the mind's eye   276

appendix   295

supply sources for tools and materials   305

bibliography   308

index   312

preface

The significant increase in both the creation and the use of jewelry in the past few decades restates a truth that is many thousands of years old: man needs personal adornment.

After inventing the tools for defense and food gathering, earliest man exercised his total ability in the creation of objects to be worn and to be beautiful to his eye. The discovery of metals started a tradition of transforming the raw materials of metal, stone, and glass into objects of richness and delight that continues to grow and expand to this day.

The technology of metalworking has become complex. Though many of the tools of the jeweler today are identical to those in use two thousand years ago, a constantly expanding refinement of techniques and materials has resulted in a body of information almost as varied as a science. Where in the past an apprentice might have started to absorb the knowledge of a craft at a very early age, virtually all present-day craftsmen begin their concentrations only after years of general schooling. The difficulty in arriving at a total knowledge of working a material has re-sulted in many abbreviations of older, more time-consuming techniques. However, even with the increased use of time and energy-saving devices, there is much that only painstaking experience can teach.

There have been several excellent books written on the subject of jewelry making. Each has attempted—as far as is possible—to establish a simulation of the apprentice-master relationship. This is, of course, tremendously difficult since to put into words clearly enough the act of doing is almost impossible. It would take volumes to describe every action of hand and mind used in the design and creation of jewelry.

In writing such a book, the author has attempted to describe only his personal experiences with the art of jewelry making. These experiences have occurred in the creation of his own work and in helping to solve the problems of his students. As far as possible, the author has avoided including information about which he has no personal knowledge, and in a field as varied and complex as jewelry making there are always avenues of expression and technique which have not been explored. Where these are touched upon, the author wishes only to excite interest in the reader to explore these directions as fully as possible and to come to independent conclusions. In addition, sections of this book dealing with technical processes and specialized equipment have been written with the hope that the equipment will be simple and inexpensive enough for the artist-jeweler to construct and use it in the workshop.

The value of a book written on this basis is that, for those who have already had experience in jewelry making, there is much information to be used in making comparisons of technique and practice. For those who have not yet started, the information is functional without establishing restrictions of expression.

The creation of jewelry has unique aspects different from any other art form. It has one function—to be decorative. The definition of decoration can and should be as personal as the imagination can be. Jewelry can be as freely experimental as any art form but, perhaps more than other art forms, it needs an underlying foundation of craftsmanship to be completely valid. Describing this combination of factors—the freedom to invent and explore coupled with a thorough knowledge of technical factors—has been the goal of the author in writing this book.

Robert von Neumann

acknowledgments

Without the constant cooperation of my colleagues in the field of jewelry making and the yearly stimulation of vital and interested students, this book could not have been attempted. Special thanks to Dennis French, Christine Johnson, Julia Manheim, John Paul Miller, Barbara Minor, Eleanor Moty, Ronald H. Pearson, Eugene and Hiroko Sato Pijanowski, Wendy Ramshaw, Francis Stephen, Elizabeth Treskow, Deborah Weintrob and J. Fred Woell for allowing me to demonstrate the great variety and beauty of today's jewelry through photographs of their work.

the
design
and
creation
of jewelry

materials and tools

• metals and alloys

The materials of jewelry making are quite varied. Traditionally, metals of many kinds, gemstones, wood, ivory, bone, and vitreous enamels have been used in the creation of personal ornament. The development of new materials—the plastics—and technological advances in metallurgy have resulted in an ever-increasing range of expressive possibilities.

Perhaps the basic material in jewelry making has always been metal. Almost all of the commonly available metals—platinum, gold, silver, copper, iron, and so forth—have been used in jewelry making at one time or another.

Gold and silver especially have long been prized in jewelry because they enhance the preciousness of fine design and workmanship.

Metals for jewelry making can be obtained in many shapes and forms. In addition, many have been developed into alloys, each having its special quality and use. The jewelry maker today can purchase a sheet of metal of desired dimension and thickness from a refiner, even specifying that it be soft or hard. Wire of a number of shapes and a great range of diameters can also be purchased, but many craftsmen prefer to draw wire to required dimensions when needed by using drawplates.

Metals can also be purchased as small bars, ingots or nuggets to be used in casting or forging.

Before describing the important aspects of a number of metals used in jewelry making, the system of measurement should be explained. Nonferrous metals—those not containing iron or steel—are measured in the United States by the Brown and Sharpe or American Standard gauge systems. A sheet of metal or a section of wire is measured in its thickness by inserting it into an appropriate numbered slot in the gauge plate. (See Figs. 1–1 and 1–2.)

When ordering sheet or wire from a supplier, it is necessary to state all of the dimensions: *length, width,* and *thickness (gauge)*. When ordering by weight (precious metals are weighed by the troy weight system), it is still necessary to state *width* and *gauge* or, if wire, *gauge* and *shape*.

fig. 1–1

fig. 1–2

MAJOR NONFERROUS METALS FOR JEWELRY MAKING

SILVER (AG)

Melting Points:

Fine silver   1761°F
Sterling silver 1640°F

For a number of excellent reasons silver is most often used for hand-wrought jewelry. Fine silver, the correct term for pure, unalloyed silver, is the whitest of all metals, has the greatest luster, and—next to fine gold—is the most malleable and ductile of all metals. It is so malleable that it can be beaten into thin sheets or *leaves*

0.00025 millimeter (mm.) thick. At this point silver readily transmits light.

Silver is so ductile that 1 gram (G.), a piece as large as a pea, can be drawn out as a wire more than one mile long.

Hammering, bending, or compressing silver between steel rollers hardens it, but careful heating to the correct temperature quickly softens it once more. This last process, called *annealing,* will be described in Chapter 3.

Fine silver is too soft for most jewelry purposes except when used as a base for enameling. Because of its softness, other metals (usually copper in small amounts) are generally added to silver to form a stronger alloy. This alloy of copper and fine silver is called *sterling* silver if the proportions consist of 925 parts fine silver and 75 parts copper per thousand parts. Although other metals can be used, this amount of copper has been found to give silver the necessary toughness without reducing its ductility and malleability too much. In addition, the copper allows silver to be colored in controlled ways—a process that often enriches the surface quality of silver objects.

There are many other silver alloys, some of which are in use today, whereas others are found only in antique metalwork. U.S. silver coins consist of ninety parts fine silver and ten parts copper. Much old jewelry used an alloy of eighty parts fine silver and twenty parts copper. This alloy is close to that of medium and hard silver solder, so the repair of work that is not stamped "sterling" can be very risky.

A very high melting-point silver alloy (2246° F) consists of 66.7 parts fine silver and 33.3 parts platinum.

The gauges of sterling silver illustrated in Fig. 1–3 show some of the practical uses for sheet-form silver.

Sterling silver wire can be found in all standard gauges, although those shown in Fig. 1–4 are used most commonly by jewelry makers.

materials and tools

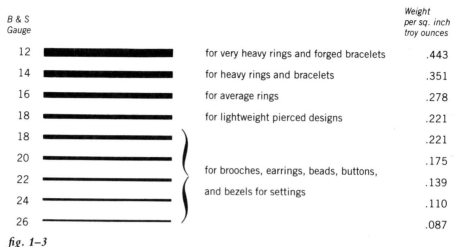

B & S Gauge		Weight per sq. inch troy ounces
12	for very heavy rings and forged bracelets	.443
14	for heavy rings and bracelets	.351
16	for average rings	.278
18	for lightweight pierced designs	.221
18		.221
20		.175
22	for brooches, earrings, beads, buttons, and bezels for settings	.139
24		.110
26		.087

fig. 1–3
Courtesy, Handy & Harman

GOLD (AU)

Melting Points:

Range from 1380° F to 2732° F

Gold is a dense, lustrous yellow metal, the most malleable and ductile of all metals. In its pure (*fine*) state, 1 G. can be drawn into a length of wire two miles long. It can be beaten into a sheet so thin that 1 ounce (oz.) may be spread over three hundred square feet (sq. ft.).

Pure gold, like fine silver, is too soft for most practical purposes. It has thus been alloyed with a number of other metals to form alloys that vary considerably in color, hardness, malleability, and melting point.

Silver added to gold reduces the depth of the yellow color and forms a greenish alloy when used in larger amounts. Copper deepens the yellow of pure gold, making it both redder and harder.

The triple alloy of gold, copper, and silver is very malleable and close to the color of pure gold. Alloys containing platinum, or palladium, form the white golds often used in the setting of precious gems. White golds are usually harder and more

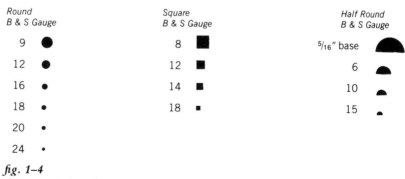

fig. 1–4
Courtesy, Handy & Harman

durable than other alloys of gold and thus lend themselves well to the delicate, though strong, settings required for faceted stones.

Zinc and nickel are two other metals commonly alloyed with gold to create new characteristics. As in the case of sterling silver, the legal proportions for gold must be accurate before an article can be stamped with a *karat* value.

Pure or fine gold is considered to be 24 karats of fineness. Alloy golds may be 22, 20, 18, 14, 12, or 10 karats, or even less. For example, 18K. gold is an alloy of eighteen parts pure gold plus six parts of another metal; 12K. gold is only half gold; and alloys below 10K. cannot be stamped legally with the *karat* or quality stamp.

The finest and more expensive hand-wrought work in gold is usually of 18K. quality. It has a somewhat richer quality and oxidizes less than other usable karats. But 14K. golds are of good color and, being less expensive, are most often used in jewelry making.

Karat golds in general require more force in working than does sterling silver, but a jewelry maker can easily adjust to this difference.

Sheet and wire of karat golds can be purchased in the same forms as sterling or fine silver. It is important to remember, however, that gold is heavier than sterling silver. A silver ring reproduced in 14K. gold might be 26% heavier, and in 18K. gold as much as 50% heavier. This could have great bearing on the size and design of work in gold, which is probably more successful when handled with lightness and delicacy.

Some of the more interesting gold alloys are:

	Melting Point
Standard (British) Gold	1382° F
92 Au + 8 Cu	
Pale Yellow Gold	
92 Au + 0–8 Ag + 0–8.3 Fe	

	Melting Point
14K. Yellow Gold	
58 Au + 14–28 Cu + 4–28 Ag	
18K. Yellow Gold	
75 Au + 10–20 Ag + 5–15 Cu	
Dark Red Gold	1832° F
50 Au + 50 Cu	
White Gold	
75–85 Au + 8–10 Ni + 2–9 Zn	
Platinum Gold	2732° F
60 Au + 40 Pt	
Palladium Gold	2309° F
90 Au + 10 Pd	
Blue Gold	2129° F
75 Au + 25 Fe	
Gray Gold	
86 Au + 38–46 Cu + 12–20 Ag	
Purple Gold (Roberts-Austin)	1382° F
79 Au + 21 Al	

For Japanese alloys of gold, see Chapter 5.

COPPER (CU)

Melting Point: 1981° F

Copper has been in use since 8000 B.C. Since it is often found in its pure state, since it is quite malleable and durable, and because of its rich red color, early man found immediate decorative and functional uses for this metal.

The natural rich brown *patina* that copper developed with use has always been highly prized by Japanese metalworkers, and it could be utilized more in our own contemporary expression.

Copper's tendency toward rapid oxidation and sulfurization may be controlled by the addition of other metals to form alloys with a great range of characteristics. Many of these alloys may be used in jewelry making. The most important are:

BRASS

Melting Points:

Range from 930° F to 2075° F

Brass is basically an alloy of copper and zinc. The color can be bright yellow, a greenish yellow, or the reddish yellow of bronze and it can be very decorative when combined with the white of silver and the red of copper. Even though the melting point of so-called standard brass is over 1700° F, it has a tendency to collapse into silver when soldered to it at a much lower temperature.

Some brass alloys are:

	Melting Point
Yellow Brass	1724° F
67 Cu + 33 Zn	
Red Brass	2066° F to 2102° F
85–90 Cu + 10–15 Zn	

BRONZE

Melting Points:

Range from 572° F to 1926° F

Basically an alloy of copper and tin, bronze is a versatile metal that can be made to be as soft as pure copper or as hard as some steels. In color it ranges from a warm red-yellow through gold to dark brown.

Aluminum bronzes—alloys of copper and aluminum plus small amounts of other nonferrous metals—have high tensile strength and clean casting qualities, and they are acid- and oxide-resistant. Melting points of these alloys range from 1130° F to 1926° F.

Phosphor bronzes—alloys of copper, tin, phosphorus, and zinc—are true bronzes to which small amounts of phosphorus have been added as deoxidizers and strengtheners. They are very hard, springy alloys. Other bronze alloys are:

Reddish Yellow
   84.42 Cu + 11.8 Zn + 4.30 Sn
Orange Yellow
   83.00 Cu + 12.00 Zn + 5.00 Sn
Coinage Bronze
   95.00 Cu + 1.00 Zn + 4.00 Sn

Hardware Bronze
   89.00 Cu + 9.00 Zn + 2.00 Pb

NICKEL SILVER

Melting Point: 1959° F

Nickel silver contains no silver at all, consisting of approximately 60% copper, 20% nickel, and 20% zinc.

Nickel silver is a strong, ductile alloy that is resistant to oxidation even at high temperatures. It has a slightly yellowish-gray quality, which makes it less rich in color than silver.

MONEL METAL

Monel metal is an alloy of 29% copper, 68½% nickel, 1% iron, and 1% manganese, with trace amounts of silicon, sulfur, and carbon.

Monel metal is a rather dark gray alloy of considerable strength and great oxidation resistance.

A few other copper-base alloys are still in use:

	Melting Point
German Silver	
46.00 Cu + 34.00 Zn	
+ 20.00 Ni	
Nickel Coinage, U.S.A.	2201° F
75.00 Cu + 25.00 Ni	
Chinese Silver	
58.00 Cu + 17.50 Zn	
+ 11.50 Ni + 11.00 Co	
+ 2.00 Ag	

PEWTER

Melting Points: From 500° F

Pewter is quite soft in most forms and is easily formed by repoussé and smithing techniques. Once an alloy of lead and tin alone, more modern alloys of pewter consist of a combination of copper, tin, and antimony. Pewter's low melting point requires the use of soft solders, which lack strength and precision for fine work.

Several common tin-based alloys are:

| | |

Standard Pewter
  85.00 Sn + 6.80 Cu
  + 6.00 Bi + 1.70 Sb
Britannia Metal   437° F
  90.00 to 91.00 Sn + 7.00 to
  8.00 Sb
White Metal
  82.00 Sn + 12.00 Sb + 6.00 Cu

PLATINUM AND PALLADIUM

Melting Points:

Platinum (Pt)	3224° F
Palladium (Pd)	2831° F

Working the expensive white metals platinum and palladium requires specialized equipment and techniques. To generate the heat required to solder these metals (a platinum solder made up of 70.00 Ag + 30.00 Pt melts at 2120° F), the jewelry maker must use an oxygen-acetylene welding torch. When using very small flames, work is sometimes welded with such torches.

Platinum, often hardened further with the addition of iridium, is used commonly for delicate settings of faceted stones such as diamonds. Palladium is often used, alloyed with platinum, as a basic metal for very expensive jewelry. Although very strong, neither metal has the warm brightness of silver, and both are most often used in settings of gemstones.

SOLDERING COPPER OR COPPER-BASED ALLOYS

There is one major difficulty in combining metals such as silver and copper during soldering. Hard solder used in much jewelry making is a light-colored alloy of silver, copper, and zinc. Since it is light in color, a misplaced piece of solder or an overabundance of solder can easily form an unsightly blemish on a darker metal. Consequently, greater than usual care must be exercised in placing solder accurately and in heating it during soldering.

Another difficulty in soldering copper and its alloys is that the metal quickly forms an oxide scale or surface coating after being heated. This often prevents solder from melting or flowing. This can be avoided by careful but rapid heating—prolonged heating increases oxide formation—and a heavier than usual flux application prior to heating.

Copper, brass, and bronze can be given a high luster by buffing, a warm matte tone by brushing, or a rich patina of black, brown, green, or green-blue by the application of various chemicals. The application of color to metal is described in Chapters 2 and 5.

FERROUS AND OTHER METALS

IRON, STEEL, AND ALUMINUM

Although iron, steel, and aluminum can be used in jewelry making, they often present problems in work techniques that make them less functional than the previous metals.

Iron and steel are difficult to combine by soldering in a precise or delicate manner. Much stronger joins are made in these metals by welding or brazing, both techniques being somewhat coarse for jewelry making.

Aluminum, in addition to having a rather unpleasant lack of weight and substance, is even more difficult to solder well. Recent developments in solder alloys and fluxes for aluminum have resulted in improved strength and durability in joins, but they do not lend themselves to more precise jewelry soldering needs.

Often the inherent restrictions in metals and other materials force the imaginative designer-craftsman into new paths of experimentation. Therefore, all materials should be examined as potential media and none discarded merely because of a traditional lack of interest in them.

● enamels

Vitreous enamel, a form of fused glass, has long been combined with metal as a decorative art form. Like glass, it is hard, brilliant, and permanent. Colors have not lost intensity and richness in the thousands of years since they were first fused to metal.

As early as 500 B.C. the Greeks had already known much about the technology and use of enamels, and this knowledge spread north and east until it found fertile ground in Europe, China, and Japan, where enameling eventually developed as an important art form in itself.

Enamel is composed of a basic flux or *frit,* which is colorless, and various metallic oxides, which give it color or opacity.

By combining a number of oxides in a great variety of proportions, hundreds of colors have now been developed. In addition, clear or translucent colored enamels vary in hue and intensity depending on the thickness of a layer as well as on the metal to which they have been fused by heat. Today, enamels are used not only on all of the traditional metals (such as gold, silver, copper, and alloys of these metals), but also on iron, steel, and aluminum.

Enamels can be purchased already ground and graded to specific particle sizes. These graded sizes are used in a number of enamel applications, such as painting, dipping, spraying, inlaying, screening, and sifting.

Enamels can also be purchased in lump form, after which they may be ground in an agate or mullite mortar to the particle size desired. Enamels tend to decompose slowly when stored as ground particles, but they last much longer in lump form.

Enamels can be transparent, translucent, opalescent, or opaque. Combinations of colors having these qualities may be used to create depth and variety in design.

Enamel surfaces after fusion to metal range from glassy brightness to matte softness.

A number of traditional application techniques are readily adaptable to the experimental approach of contemporary jewelry. These techniques, both historical and contemporary, are described in Chapter 4.

● precious and semiprecious gems

Gems have always been considered an important element in jewelry. The rarity of a richly colored stone, its brilliance when polished, and its effective accenting of a form in metal have all combined to make a gem precious.

In earliest times the most colorful stones that could be worked easily were of greatest value. In Egypt, where jewelry performed an unusually important function in society, gems such as turquoise, lapis lazuli, carnelian, agate, and coral were used lavishly in necklaces, head ornaments, and bracelets. As the skill of gem cutting—*lapidary*—developed, harder materials such as quartz, amethyst, ruby, sapphire, and diamond were introduced into jewelry.

Today, hundreds of gem materials can be purchased in the form of shaped and polished gems, or the craftsperson can shape them to his own purpose, beginning with raw materials.

The setting of gems in metal and the basic lapidary techniques are described in Chapter 4.

● wood

Although not widely used in jewelry in the past, wood is finding ever greater ap-

The jewelry and other small metal objects of
Central and South America, Africa, Asia, and
Europe reflect not only the religious and the social
values of these ornaments, but also a great delight
in the forms of living things. In almost all
instances, the shapes of animals, birds, fish,
insects, and man himself have been enriched,
reorganized, and imaginatively interpreted.

The skill with which artisans of early cultures
fabricated ornaments in gold, silver, and jewels is
impressive when one considers the simple tools
and materials known to them. Though most of the
intricate work was first modeled in wax and then
cast in the ciré-perdue process, many cultures
knew and practiced the intricacies of soldering,
forming, and stone cutting.

The Portuguese in West Africa and the Spaniards
in Central and South America wrote glowing
accounts of the delicacy and the richness of the
ornaments found there. It was difficult for them to
believe that people they considered to be simple
and savage in other respects could have produced
work of such sophistication that it rivaled some of
the best of the European Renaissance.

For the contemporary artist-designer, work of
these cultures is significant in the great variety of
form interpretation—from the most naturalistic to
the utmost in expressionism.

1

2

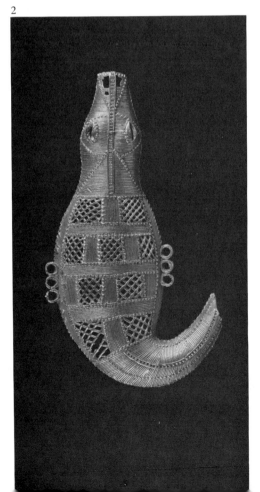

8

materials and tools

1 Christ medallion, from the Guelph Treasure, German (Frankish), 8th century; gold and cloisonné enamel. *The Cleveland Museum of Art, J. H. Wade Collection*

2 Gold crocodile, Ivory Coast; lost wax casting. *The Cleveland Museum of Art, John L. Severance Collection*

3 Gold figure, Chibcha Culture, Colombia; lost wax casting. *The Cleveland Museum of Art, Mr. and Mrs. Henry Humphreys Memorial*

4 Gold mask, embossed, Mochica Culture, Peru. *The Cleveland Museum of Art, Mr. and Mrs. Henry Humphreys Memorial*

3

4

1

2

Never in history has the art of the jeweler
assumed such importance to society as it did during
the 14th to the 18th centuries in Europe. Both
men and women of the aristocracy and the
wealthy merchant class adorned themselves with
garlands of gold chains encrusted with rubies,
pearls, and sapphires. Each hand wore several
rings—often several on each finger. Medallions of
gold and jewels were sewn to clothing of rich
velvets, silks, and furs, and the need for
displaying ever new, ever more impressive jewels
had goldsmiths and silversmiths by the hundreds
working to their highest capacity.

During the 15th and 16th centuries especially, the
skills of cloisonné, champlèvé, plique-à-jour,
and grisaille enameling were highly developed as
decorative enrichments of jewelry. The cutting,
polishing, and setting of gems became a major
industry, as well as establishing shapes and uses
still popular today.

10

materials and tools

1 A goldsmith's shop, c. 1576; copper engraving by Delaune. *The Bettmann Archive*

2 Pendant representing Europa and the Bull in gold, gems, baroque pearl, and enamel; in the style of Benvenuto Cellini; Italian, 16th century. *The National Galley of Art, Washington, D. C., Widener Collection, 1942*

3 Pendant representing a centaur in gold, gems, baroque pearls, and enamel; Italian School, 16th century. *The National Gallery of Art, Washington, D. C., Widener Collection, 1942*

4 Pendant representing a triton in gold, gems, baroque pearls, and enamel; Italian School, 16th century. *The National Gallery of Art, Washington, D. C., Widener Collection, 1942*

5 Pendant representing a mermaid, in gold, gems, baroque pearls, and enamel; in the style of Benvenuto Cellini; Italian, 16th century. *The National Gallery of Art, Washington, D. C., Widener Collection, 1942*

3

4

5

plication in contemporary jewelry design. It has been used as a frame or background for metal forms, as an alternation with metal in repetitive forms, or as a sculptural element independent of other materials. It can also be inlaid into metal or have metal imbedded into its surface.

The tropics of the world supply the craftsman with a number of rare and handsome woods. These can be purchased in small amounts from firms dealing in materials for fine cabinet work. Such woods as ebony, cocobolo, zebra wood, snake wood, amaranth, and rosewood are all beautiful enough and durable enough to be used as a precious material.

Some of our native hardwoods—birch, black walnut, cherry, and oak—are often locally available. All hardwoods, those of a close and compact grain, can be worked with virtually the same tools used in metalworking.

The processes of cutting, forming, fastening, and finishing wood for jewelry are described in Chapter 4.

• plastics

Of all materials available to the jewelry designer-craftsman today, none contains as much potential as the plastics. Almost unknown before the twentieth century, plastics offer today's craftsman a real challenge in use and interpretation.

Since plastics can be used as solids, semisolids, or liquids, the range of interpretative possibilities is unlimited.

Using standard metalworking tools and equipment, the craftsman can saw, file, carve, grind, drill, and polish plastics such as Lucite, Plexiglas, Delrin, and nylon. It is also possible to cast specific shapes and imbed or enclose decorative materials of other kinds in the slow-hardening liquid polyester and epoxy plastics.

Plastics are manufactured in a range of colors, but they can also be dyed by the craftsman himself.

Plastic materials are so versatile that the great danger lies in the conscious simulation of other, perhaps more difficult to work materials. True honesty of workmanship exploits a material only in directions that are basic to that material. To create mineral or wood imitations in plastic, for example, is fraudulent and not deserving of the jewelry maker's time or effort.

Techniques for plastic are described in Chapter 4.

• additional materials

History provides us with a number of other materials that, with the freedom of expression characteristic of contemporary design, can be interpreted in fresh and exciting ways.

Shells, seeds, bamboo and other reeds, and even insects were used by early or primitive craftsmen where metal or stone was not available or not known. Shells can be drilled and polished by using metalworking tools and techniques. Seeds can be drilled, set as gems, or cut into sections for repetition of shape. Reed and bamboo, because of their tubular rigidity and varied surface textures and colors, can be used in necklaces and bracelets in countless ways.

Insects, whole or in part, can be fused into plastic and used as central or repeated motifs. The hard bodies of domestic and tropical beetles, colorful and intriguing in shape, may be set as gems are set.

These materials are not the only ones that can be used in jewelry making by any means. In the search for creative expression, an imaginative designer-craftsman will discover countless new and fresh applications. In this sense the designer is a true creator.

• jewelry findings

Pieces of jewelry must be attached to mechanical fittings—*findings*—so that they can be worn. The means of applying findings to jewelry will be described specifically at other points in this text.

A great variety of shapes and qualities in findings is available to the craftsman, and it often requires discrimination to decide which might be best in a design. There are several degrees of quality in findings, and often the same shape and function can be found in both cheap and expensive materials. The least expensive findings are made of yellow or white metal-plated brass or nickel. Because these do not wear well and often become soft in soldering, they should not be used in fine jewelry. For a small increase in cost, it is best to use sterling silver findings for silver jewelry and karat gold findings for gold jewelry.

Findings are manufactured for virtually every purpose, and often they are quite well designed. Even so, many craftsmen prefer to design and construct a finding for a specific piece of jewelry, feeling that it will be better integrated with the piece.

FOR EARRINGS

1. Standard screw type.
2. Screw type with link.
3. Screw type with dome.
4. Clip.
5. Wire with link, for pierced ears.

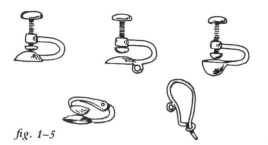

fig. 1–5

FOR PINS AND BROOCHES

1. Side opening catch, joint and pinstem with fixed rivet.
2. Side opening catch, joint with soft-soldering patch. Pinstem with loose rivet.

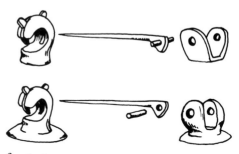

fig. 1–6

FOR NECKLACES AND BRACELETS

1. Spring ring.
2. Round jump ring.
3. Oval jump ring
4. Foldover catch.
5. Box catch.

fig. 1–7

13

FOR TIE TACKS

1. Tie tack with holding spur.

fig. 1–8

FOR CUFF LINKS

1. Cuff link back with separate rivet and joint.

fig. 1–9

• tools and equipment for the workshop

It is interesting that creative man had, at an early time, designed the tools of his arts so well that many have not changed in shape and function to this day. Of course modern technology has improved the quality of the tools, and mass production has made a tremendous variety available to the craftsman who had to make his own in past ages, but the functional aspect has changed very little.

The tools of the designer-craftsman need not be complex or great in number.

The Indian silversmiths and jewelers of the American Southwest practice great economy in their work. The hardware store supplies a ball-peen hammer, a few large and small files, and sandpaper. A blowtorch supplies heat, and an electric motor speeds the polishing operation.

Although the work is often simple in concept, it reflects the fact that a workshop full of expensive gadgets is not of primary importance in jewelry making. What *is* important is that the right tools for the work at hand be chosen with care.

As in all purchases, it is foolish economy to buy the least expensive of several makes of a tool. Cheap pliers mar the materials they work on and often break under normal pressure. Files that are poorly made are rough and uneven in cutting surface. Saw frames can break under the tension necessary to insert a blade.

A sense of confidence in a tool is a value that can be seen in the finished object. In addition, there is great aesthetic pleasure in handling a well-designed and beautifully made tool, and it becomes a pleasure to maintain it in good condition.

The following lists of tools are divided into four categories.

The first lists basic equipment. Without this equipment the designer-craftsman will be hampered in his explorations of techniques and materials.

The second list includes additional small tools that are not of primary necessity in the beginning, but later become necessary to the organization of a complete workshop.

The third list includes the items of large equipment basic to the workshop. In some cases, their greatest contribution comes in the saving of time. One can be sure, contrary to a romantic nineteenth-century philosophy, that the levelheaded craftsmen of earlier times would have found these economies worthwhile had they been available.

The fourth list contains additional large

equipment that might complete a well-organized workshop. In some cases, the high cost of these tools may prohibit their purchase by the individual craftsman. It is worthwhile investigating local recreation and school workshop facilities. Often these areas make machinery and space available to interested individuals or groups.

The catalogs and price lists of the better jewelry tool and supply houses often illustrate a complete range of tools and materials available. The names and addresses of the major supply companies are listed in the back of the book. Local hardware stores are also good sources, except for the highly specialized tools of the craft.

LIST 1—BASIC SMALL TOOLS

FOR SAWING, CUTTING, AND FILING

1. Jeweler's saw frame, 5″, adjustable
2. Jeweler's saw blades: Nos. 1 and 2 for average work; nos. 2/0 and 3/0 for fine work
3. Assorted needle files, No. 1 or No. 2 cut, 5½″ length: round, half-round, crossing, barrette, square, knife
4. Large hand files, 6″ cutting length, No. 1 or No. 2 cut, wooden handles: flat, half-round, round, triangle,
5. Riffler files: No. 7, flat and curved; no. 10, spoon, half-round and curved; no. 17, pointed, half-round; no. 5, knife
6. File brush
7. Jeweler's bench pin or V-board and clamp
8. Jeweler's shears: plate shears with scissors handle or Brown's jeweler's shears
9. Diagonal nippers
10. Hand drill
11. Drill bits—graduated sizes
12. Ring clamp
13. Beeswax
14. Center punches and scribes
15. Small smooth-jawed bench vise
16. Scotch stones

FOR FORMING

1. Pliers with smooth, polished jaws: round-nose, chain, flat-nose, half-round, rivet-setting
2. Chasing hammer with convex polished head
3. Scraper, hollow
4. Burnisher, straight, curved, with narrow 2″ blade
5. Lead block
6. Steel block, polished
7. Hardwood blocks: solid maple or scored maple
8. Wood mallet, curved and flat end
9. Ring mandrel with graduated sizes

FOR DECORATING

1. Chasing tools
2. Potassium sulfide (liver of sulfur)
3. Other chemicals for patination

FOR SOLDERING

Editor's Note: Use of asbestos sheets, pads, rings, and linings is *not* recommended. Asbestos is a known carcinogen; its use is not entirely safe under any circumstances, although a respirator equipped with a cartridge which filters asbestos dust provides some reduction in risk, according to the Occupational Safety and Health Administration. Firebrick, pumice lumps in an annealing pan, or charcoal or magnesium blocks are suitable wherever the instructions call for a heatproof sheet, ring, pad, or block. It is rather more problematic to find an altogether satisfactory substitute for casting-flask linings: two of the available products are Nomex and Castart, and other new compounds specifically developed to replace asbestos are rapidly becoming available. The author cannot recommend these untried substitutes; the jeweler must experiment with casting inexpensive materials until he finds the most successful solution.

1. Tweezers, smooth and polished: fine-pointed and crosslock

2. Small brushes for flux and solder application
3. Binding wire
4. Heatproof sheet
5. Charcoal or other heatproof block or ring
6. Solder: silver solder in sheets, strips, or wire; gold solder in sheets, strips, or wire; lead solder wire
7. Silver solder flux, either paste or liquid
8. Lead solder flux
9. Pickle pan or jar with cover. Can be copper, glass, or stoneware
10. Pickle tongs
11. Pointer
12. Yellow ocher to protect solder joins
13. Soldering unit: gas-air or acetylene; mouth blow pipe and gas; or propane gas in self-contained unit
14. Sulfuric and nitric acid or Sparex pickling compound
15. Flint striker

FOR BUFFING AND POLISHING

1. Emery paper, at least two sizes, Nos. 1 and 3/0
2. Buffing sticks and boxwood pegs
3. Rouge cloth
4. Abrasives: tripoli, pumice, rouge

MISCELLANEOUS TOOLS

1. Steel rule
2. Scribe
3. Compass

LIST 2—SUPPLEMENTARY SMALL TOOLS

FOR SAWING AND CUTTING

1. Jeweler's saw frame, 8″, adjustable
2. Scorer, small

FOR FORMING

1. Dapping block and dapping punches
2. Steel bending block
3. Bezel mandrels: oval, square, and round

4. Small stakes
5. Large stakes and holder
6. Smithing hammers
7. Pitch bowl
8. Gem pusher, square, round
9. Beading tools
10. Seating drills and burrs
11. Plastic mallet
12. Rubber mallet
13. Horn mallet
14. Bracelet mandrel

FOR DECORATING

1. Engraving burins
2. Arkansas stone
3. Oilstone
4. Sealing wax
5. Additional chasing tools
6. Matting tools
7. Acid resist for etching
8. Pyrex glass tray

FOR SOLDERING

1. Locking tweezers with holding stand
2. Heat-resistant ring–soldering mandrel

FOR BUFFING AND POLISHING

1. Buffing and polishing wheels of cotton, muslin, wool, etc.: stitched, unstitched, lead center, goblet
2. Felt buffing wheels
3. Felt and emery ring-buffing mandrels
4. Flexible-shaft machine
5. Buffing and grinding equipment for the flexible-shaft machine

MISCELLANEOUS

1. Gem holder
2. Draw plate: round hole, square hole, half round hole
3. Drawing tongs
4. Gauge plate
5. Set of ring sizes
6. Jeweler's loupe
7. Stamps: hallmark (maker's name or sign); sterling; 14K and 18K (for gold); assorted numbers; assorted letters

materials and tools

8. Slide caliper—inches and millimeters
9. Hand reamer
10. Washout brushes
11. Jeweler's screw plate for threading holes and wire

LIST 3—BASIC LARGE TOOLS

FOR SAWING AND CUTTING

1. Bench shears, 4″ blade
2. Small drill press with electric motor

FOR FORMING

1. Additional stakes
2. Additional mandrels for bracelets, etc.
3. Large vise
4. Centrifugal casting equipment: machine, casting flasks, sprue formers, sprue pins, crucibles and crucible tongs, casting wax—bars, sheet, and wire, and casting flux

FOR DECORATING

1. Enameling kiln and equipment: trivets, sieves, spatulas, Carborundum stones, cloisonné wire, gold and silver leaf, assorted ground and lump enamels
2. Plating machine and equipment
3. Electroforming equipment

FOR SOLDERING

1. Pumice pans, rotating

FOR BUFFING AND POLISHING

1. Polishing machine with hoods and dust collection

LIST 4—SUPPLEMENTARY LARGE TOOLS

1. Jig saw, electric
2. Belt sanding machine
3. Rolling mill
4. Lapidary equipment: cabochon unit with saw, grinding wheels, sanding and polishing discs, facet-cutting machine

5. Jeweler's workbench

The ideal workbench is designed specifically for jewelry making, but an ordinary table or desk will do if it is sturdy enough. The workbench should be located near a water source, good light, and good ventilation. Soldering and pickling can be done at the bench unless large pieces are made. In that case, a fire- and acid-proof work area should be designed containing adequate fume-venting facilities.

• organization of the workshop

Though it is possible to make jewelry in virtually any space large enough to hold a table or a desk, it is far better to have space designed specially for this activity. An ideal room has, in addition to good traffic space, the following assets:

GOOD LIGHTING

Good lighting can be incandescent in the form of adjustable lamps for each work area (i.e., construction, soldering, pickling, buffing). Fluorescent fixtures are adequate, but they place a greater strain on the eyes when working with small objects.

WATER

A convenient source of hot and cold water is almost imperative for washing work after pickling in acid and after buffing and polishing.

ADEQUATE ELECTRICITY

Since much equipment is motor-driven or uses heavy current loads in heating elements, an adequate 220-volt line should be laid in. Enough wall or baseboard outlets should be supplied so that overloads on extension cords are prevented.

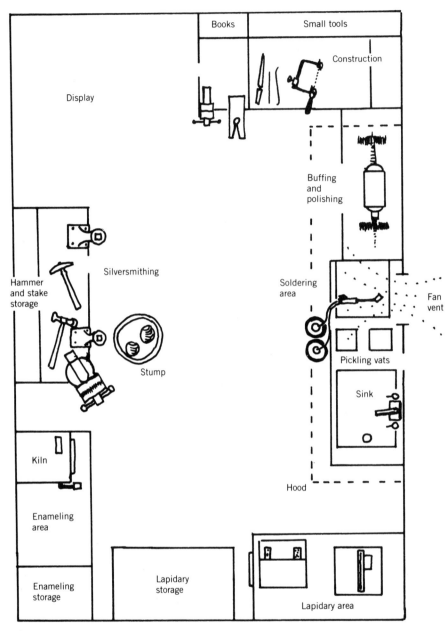

Books

Small tools

Construction

Display

Buffing
and
polishing

Silversmithing

Hammer
and stake
storage

Soldering
area

Fan
vent

Stump

Pickling vats

Sink

Kiln

Hood

Enameling
area

Enameling
storage

Lapidary
storage

Lapidary area

fig. 1–10

VENTILATION

At best, a hood should be placed over a common soldering, annealing, and pickling area. This should have a fan strong enough to pull out dangerous fumes and gases quickly. Lacking this, there should be good window ventilation.

PROPER WALL, CEILING, AND FLOOR SURFACES

Since much metal work requires considerable hammering, it is wise to soundproof walls and ceilings as well as possible. If cleanliness is to be considered, these surfaces should be washable as well as light in color in order to increase total lightness in the room.

The floor should be able to withstand the moving of heavy objects and the occasional spilling of water or acids. Painted concrete or industrial tile is adequate.

STORAGE SPACE

Built-in or spatial cabinets for tool, material, and chemical storage should be designed for ease of use and maintenance, and for safety. It might be well to provide locks where children and others might create a safety problem. (See Fig. 1–10.)

2   basic techniques

Each craftsman, having worked with his craft over a period of time, finds that it is always possible to modify—even to change radically—the methods used by other craftsmen of the past and of the present. The steps of construction in metal and other materials outlined in this and following chapters are the result of experience in teaching jewelry making and in personal jewelry work. They describe *one* way—but never the *only* way—of working.

Perhaps, at times, the description of a process may seem unnecessarily complex. In attempting to establish a more complete understanding of the logic of an approach, detailed analysis is not only necessary but also justification for such a book as this. Actually to participate quite closely in the development of a process is the most ideal learning situation. Descriptions must always fall short of such participation, but when they are developed in detail, this unfortunate gap may be reduced somewhat.

Again, the description of a given approach to a problem, whether of design or of construction, represents only one craftsman's experience and is not to be taken as aesthetic law.

● drawing and transferring a design to metal

When making the preliminary sketches for a piece of jewelry, always anticipate problems in the actual construction. Keep in mind, while designing, such factors as ultimate size, weight, and strength. Know your materials well enough to avoid designing forms that may not survive construction or wear.

If you choose a metal that is rather soft and easily bent, avoid designing shapes that project away from a supporting surface. *This is especially important when using wire.*

The placement and types of findings should be planned for at this stage so that they will function well, will be safe when worn, and will not interfere with the unity of the design.

Preliminary sketches may be complex in showing several views of a piece. They may indicate textures accurately and plan areas to be oxidized. They may be rendered accurately to show dimensions and surface reflections. On the other hand, a sketch may be no more than a simple linear indication of shapes and forms.

One of the real pleasures in designing freely for personal satisfaction comes in allowing the tools, materials—even chance—to dictate some of the decisions. Often a texture or shape that effectively adds to the original design concept comes about during construction. Remain flexible in attitude. In avoiding an arbitrary narrowness in designing one can make of the purely mechanical—and often time-consuming—construction of jewelry a constantly interesting and challenging experience.

Once the sketch has been made, there are several ways in which its parts may be transferred to the working metal:

1. Many designer-craftsmen resketch directly on the metal. A freely evolved design might even benefit by having been interpreted just once more!
2. The back of the paper design might be blacked in with a soft lead pencil and the design transferred by drawing over the lines when placed over the metal. If the design is drawn on tracing paper, it is possible to see the shape and the limits of the sheet of metal beneath it. This allows an economical placement of the design and reduces waste.
3. A similar transfer technique is to place carbon paper between the sketch and the metal. This may make a rather heavy dark line, which might blur or hide small details in the sketch.
4. A highly professional but more time-consuming technique consists of cleaning the surface of the metal to free it of greasy film. A thin layer of Chinese white tempera is painted on and allowed to dry. A carbon or pencil-rubbed impression then shows up very well after transfer.

After any of the foregoing procedures, it is wise to use a pointed scribe to scratch lightly over the pencil or carbon lines, for during sawing the latter might be rubbed off in handling. Make the scratches light since chance and a change of mind might dictate a new direction later, at which time a deep scratch would be difficult to remove.

5. If you want to be precise and accurate, the sketch may be cut out of the paper and rubber-cemented directly to the metal. For a good join allow a layer of cement to become almost dry on both paper and metal before joining them. In this way the saw will cut through both the paper design and the metal at the same time.

• sawing and piercing

MATERIALS

Jeweler's saw frame
Jeweler's saw blades
Beeswax
Bench pin, V clamp or vise

A skillful craftsman with a good saw can approximate with a saw cut what can be done with a pencil line. By following a few basic rules, and with practice, it is possible to cut out any shape desired. The saw may be used to cut out simple basic forms or to create the most complex linear pattern.

In selecting a saw for metal sawing, make sure that the clamps holding the blade ends fit together smoothly. Be sure also that the frame is adjustable so that it may be easily lengthened or shortened. Select a saw frame that is 4″ to 5″ deep for average cutting. A deeper saw frame, though more versatile, is much less easily controlled while sawing because of the poor weight balance. If necessary, purchase an extra saw frame 6″ or more deep, from the blade to the back of the frame, for cutting deeply into a sheet of metal. (See Fig. 2–1.)

The blades to be used should be the best available. Generally, those made in Switzerland and Germany give the best quality

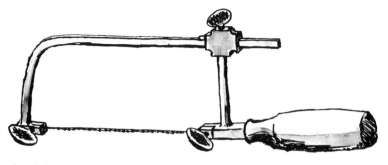

fig. 2–1

for the cost. Blades vary in size; an "8/0" is very fine and a "14" very coarse. For general work, a "1" or a "2" will do very well. A "2/0" or a "3/0" is useful for delicate linear work, but they break easily if not controlled at all times.

Beeswax is used to lubricate the blade, thus reducing wear and speeding the sawing operation, but, if applied too often, beeswax tends to clog the saw teeth and thus reduces the efficiency of sawing. Excess wax may be brushed out of saw teeth with a bristle brush.

Many jeweler's benches come equipped with a slot holding a hardwood pin into which a *V* has been cut. This *bench pin* forms a support for the sheet of metal while you are sawing horizontally. (See Fig. 2–2.)

For workbenches without the above equipment, a *V board and clamp* may be purchased for the same purpose or a hard-wood board might be cut to shape and fastened with a *C* clamp. The circle at the end of the *V* cut enables delicate sawing of small pieces while furnishing support at the necessary points. (See Fig. 2–3.)

A small bench or machinist's vise may also be used if precautions are taken to protect the sawed metal from excessive jaw pressure or marring due to rough jaw surfaces. Many craftsmen line the vise jaw faces with smooth hardwood, leather, or sheet cork.

ATTACHING THE BLADE

Attaching the blade properly is important! Being made of fine tool steel, jeweler's blades are brittle and should be handled accordingly.

Step 1. Loosen the jaw nuts on both ends of the frame.

Step 2. Insert the blade all the way into the top jaw nut. Make sure that the saw teeth face *away* from the frame back and angle *toward* the handle. Tighten the top jaw nut.

Step 3. Brace the end of the saw frame against the bench so that the frame back hangs down and the handle faces you. (See Fig. 2–4.)

Step 4. Make sure that the loose end of the saw blade almost but not quite reaches the bottom jaw nut. This added length is necessary when compressing the frame.

fig. 2–2

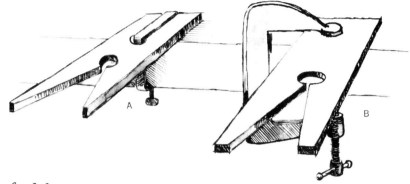

fig. 2–3

Compress the frame by pressing it against the bench and, while compressed, insert the loose blade end, tighten it into place, and release pressure slowly. If pressure is released too quickly, the sudden strain may snap the blade. The blade should be rigid and give a "pinging" sound when plucked.

STARTING THE SAW CUT

When starting a cut from the edge of a sheet of metal, the blade tends to stick or skid from place to place. This may be avoided by starting a groove in the edge by a few upward strokes of the blade. The actual cutting takes place on the down stroke, but a few strokes in the other direction help at the start.

SAWING

There are basically three aspects of sawing that should be mastered to prevent excessive blade breakage. The first rule is that *the blade must be kept perpendicular to the*

fig. 2–4

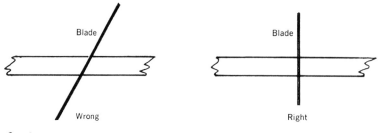

fig. 2–5

sawing surface of the metal at all times. (See Fig. 2–5.) If the blade is at an angle, it becomes pinched when making a curved cut or when it is withdrawn from an incomplete cut. Pinching breaks the brittle and tightly strung blade.

The second rule is to *avoid excessive forward or downward pressure while moving the saw.* The weight of the hand is enough to draw the blade through anything but the thickest and toughest metal. In addition, there is a natural forward motion to the saw stroke, so it is unnecessary to push the blade forward with each stroke. Take it easy! Don't saw too fast—you lose control—and always use as many of the cutting teeth of the blade as possible with each stroke.

The third thing to keep in mind is to *use no force when backing out of a cut.* The blade must come out the way it went in. Pinching at this point breaks many blades. If the saw blade is deep in an intricate passage of lines, it might be best simply to release the bottom end of the blade, pull it out of the metal, and reset it again.

It is possible to saw the most intricate arabesques as well as sharp and precise angular shapes. When an angle of any degree is desired, one merely saws forward on one leg of the angle to the apex or point of turning, pauses at that point while continuing to saw up and down without forward motion, and slowly turns the entire saw frame to the desired degree of angle. Once the new angle has been reached, the saw may again travel forward.

In sawing curves of any degree the same action takes place. The saw frame is slowly turned in the desired direction while sawing up and down and forward. Some craftsmen keep the saw in one forward position while moving the metal about. Others move both saw and metal as necessary. One soon evolves the most natural technique for the job.

PIERCING

When it is necessary to cut out a hole or a negative shape from the interior of a sheet of metal, a somewhat different start is made. After the sketch is transferred to the metal, a small indentation is punched at some appropriate point on the inside of that shape. This dent acts as a start for a small (No. 60) drill bit. The bit drills the hole through which the saw blade is inserted.

Important! When using a punch, always place the metal on a *flat metal* surface, such as an anvil or a bench block. If the punching takes place over wood or some other soft surface, the metal around the indentation will be bent and depressed. This sort of blemish is difficult to remove.

After the saw blade is inserted through the drilled hole, the blade is set again as before and sawing may proceed. When the saw arrives at the drilled hole again, the blade is released and the cut-out metal removed. (See Fig. 2–6.)

In all sawing it is wise to saw on the *waste side* of a sketch line so that if the saw

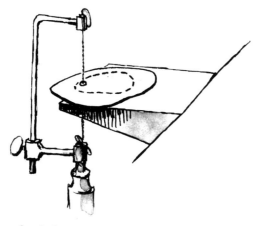

fig. 2–6

cuts irregularly the mistakes may be remedied by filing and will not infringe on the planned proportion of the design.

BLADE BREAKAGE

Often, when a blade breaks, fairly large sections of the cutting teeth remain intact. By making the saw frame shorter, these fragments may still be used. Since the toothed portion is more brittle than the ends, the blade is liable to break more easily the second time so that it will be necessary to be more careful in sawing.

Saw blades do wear out. When the teeth are dulled to the point where extra force must be used in cutting, it is best to replace the blade. Extra pressure decreases control, so nothing is gained by this economy.

● filing, scraping, stoning, and burnishing

MATERIALS

Large hand files: round, half-round, flat, all No. 2 cut
Needle files: round, half-round, triangular, bird-tongue, knife, flat, slitting, crochet, joint-finishing, barrette, equaling, square, all No. 2 cut
Riffler files
Hollow scraper
Burnisher, curved or straight
Scotch stone

FILING

There is always a correct file to use for the job at hand. Some files are limited to one kind of work, while others may be used interchangeably. In all filing an efficient stroke of the file surface over the metal is important. To file incorrectly wastes time and energy and often causes more trouble than it solves.

Basically, an efficient cutting stroke consists of filing from the tip of the file to the handle. (See Fig. 2–7.) Many craftsmen develop the habit of filing from tip to handle, lifting the file from the metal

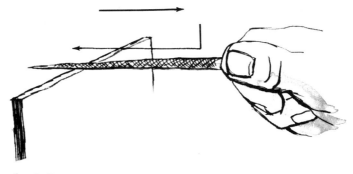

fig. 2–7

1 Pendant; silver, pierced and filed

2 Pendants; silver, and silver and ebony, pierced and filed

3 Pin, Stan Fuka; silver, pierced and filed

4 Bracelet; silver, pierced and filed

5 Pin and pendant; silver, pierced and filed

6 Pins, Pat Monigold; silver, pierced and filed

All student work was done by undergraduates at the University of Illinois

1

2

3

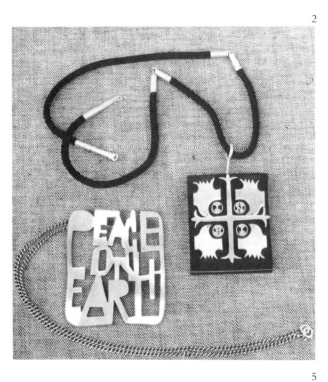

4

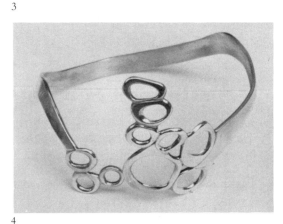

5

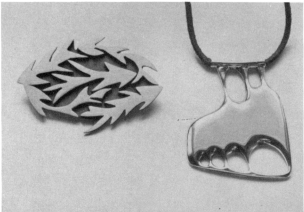

6

surface at the end of each stroke. Others leave the file in contact but allow it to slide *lightly* back to the tip. Pressure is then again applied on the cutting stroke.

Since filing is used most often for refining or correcting sawed edges, an economy of motion should be developed to do this well and quickly.

Filing along an edge in line with the edge causes the file to slip off to the side. Filing away high spots only where they occur causes too many depressions that also must be removed. It is best to file at a diagonal to the filing surface with a long, even, sliding stroke. If this eventually causes rough parallel grooves in the filing surface, you can remove them by filing from a new tangent. This slanted sliding stroke should cover the greatest distance possible, and it may be used on either convex or concave surfaces. (See Fig. 2–8.)

Of course, the correct file shape is important here. For concave edges a half-round, bird-tongue, or round file should be used. For convex edges any of the several flat-sided files will work well.

Using the sliding stroke efficiently results in filing many high spots with each stroke and rapidly arriving at a clean, even edge or bevel.

While being filed, work may be held in the hand, in a ring clamp, or in a vise.

When holding metal by the hand alone, it is necessary to brace it against the workbench edge or some part of the bench pin. It is possible to design a wooden projection fastened to the bench as a firm, easily approached support.

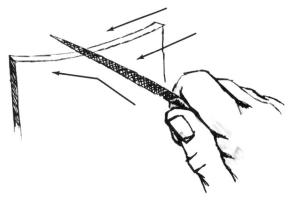

fig. 2–8

At times the sections of metal to be filed are either too small or too fragile to be held by hand. A ring clamp makes an ideal and safe holder for this purpose. The work should be placed far enough into the jaws of the ring clamp to prevent bending or breaking with the pressure of filing. Again, firm bracing of the ring clamp against the bench is necessary. (See Fig. 2–9.)

At times several edges, too large for the ring clamp, must be filed simultaneously. Or again, a rather large single edge must be filed with great precision in preparation for a soldering join. Here the vise—with suitably protected jaws—becomes necessary. With work held in a vise, both hands are free to guide the file accurately over edges or surfaces. It is possible to cement several pieces of metal together so that all can be sawed and filed simultaneously. If epoxy cement is used for strength, the pieces can be separated later by heating the

fig. 2–9

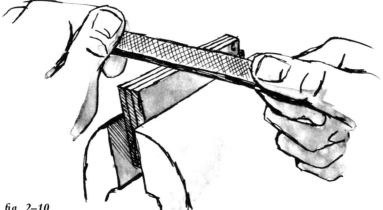

fig. 2–10

metal until the cement has burned to ash. (See Fig. 2–10.)

When to use a large hand file or a smaller needle file is a question that only circumstances can answer. In general, it is more efficient to use a large file for large outside edges, whether straight or curved. A needle file may be used to further refine the work of the large file after the bulk of the filing is done.

The decision to bevel (angle or round off) an edge is best determined by the design. One design (perhaps one in which sharp crispness and angularity are emphasized) might have all edges at right angles to the flat surface. Another, perhaps more curvilinear design might profit more by a softening of the edges. It is always amazing how great the illusion of three-dimensionality can be when edges are beveled in a variety of ways.

By beveling an edge one creates a greater variety of reflections in the final polished work. This technique might enhance its richness. In addition, the sculptured quality beveling lends to a design removes it quite effectively from the feeling of stamped-out mass-produced jewelry. It affords the craftsman one more element of critical choice when deciding where and how far to alter an edge.

As a matter of craftsmanship, it is well to soften the edges of the reverse side of a piece of jewelry. In this way it feels good to the hand and reminds one that good craftsmanship does not end with only the visible surfaces.

Some of the needle files, in having a specific shape, have a function that should be exploited. As an example, the barrette file is smooth on two top surfaces and on its edges. This enables it to file close to an angle without cutting into the angle and causing additional work.

The round or rattail file may be used for enlarging drilled holes or in altering the shape of a drilled hole for decorative purposes.

The knife file is ideal for refining deep notches and angles, whereas the triangular file may best be used for filing sharp notches and lines across a surface. Fig. 2–11 shows where on a piece of metal various files would be most efficiently used.

One of the pleasures of jewelry making is that each process is usually slow enough so that you can plan the next step while occupied with the first. This habit pattern develops a time- and energy-saving technique, and it soon comes with experience.

Since files in jewelry making are often used on different materials, they often be-

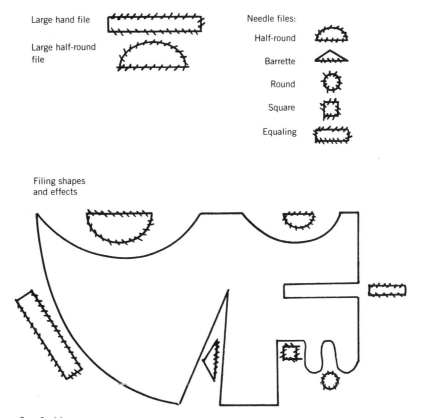

Large hand file

Large half-round file

Needle files:

Half-round

Barrette

Round

Square

Equaling

Filing shapes and effects

fig. 2–11

come clogged with wood dust or metal particles. A file brush, preferably one with fiber bristles on one side and steel bristles on the other, is used to brush out most particles, and a narrow pointed scribe or pin may be used to pry out soft metal particles. It helps to dust the file with chalk. This does not prevent good cutting but leaves little space for other particles to become imbedded.

If a file is used on lead or lead solder, it should either be cleaned meticulously after use or set aside for this purpose in the future. A particle of lead that comes in contact with a high-temperature soldering process on silver or other metals will eat into that metal and make it impossible to repair without great effort. Always keep lead away from silver soldering operations!

SCRAPING

The process of scraping actually carves away the metal. A scraper may be used, if you have strength and control, to cut angles or bevels on edges or to form depressions on flat surfaces. Most often this tool is used to remove excess and unwanted solder. With care, the solder lump can be shaved away until the clean metal is exposed. After scraping, the surface usually must be further refined by filing, stoning, or sanding, but it is quite a bit faster to do the scraping first.

The scraper should be kept very sharp

by honing it on a fine oilstone. Then the tip should be plunged into a large cork when not in use.

The scraping technique demands that the cutting edge be parallel with the surface to be scraped, for a higher angle would cause a "chatter" that forms ridges and makes the surface rough. (See Fig. 2–12.)

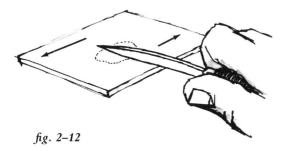

fig. 2–12

STONING

In places where a file or a scraper will not fit easily, or where a design is too delicate for their use, a scotch stone becomes practical.

Scotch stones—also called "Water of Ayr" and "Tam-o-shanter" stones—come in a variety of lengths and dimensions. For general use a stone ¼″ square and 5″ long is ideal. For stoning in narrow, restricted areas, the stone may be filed or ground to the necessary shape and kept to that shape by further filing or grinding.

Stoning should be done under flowing water or in a pan of water. If the stone and the metal are dry, the metal particles will soon clog the stone. It is best to stone an area larger than the spot where solder or roughness must be removed. But don't replace a lump of solder with an equally unsightly hollow! Since the stone is quite smooth and also rather soft, considerable pressure is needed for effective stoning. A sharp jet of water or a little brushing will remove loose stone and metal particles after stoning. Check the stoned area often during the process by wiping away the residue.

BURNISHING

A burnisher is a highly polished, hard steel tool with a handle. The blade is usually a pointed ellipse in section and may be curved or straight. A blade length of 3″ to 4″ is ideal for jewelry purposes, but of the two shapes the straight burnisher is the more easily controlled. Burnishers should be stored in a wrapping of chamois and kept highly polished at all times.

The burnisher has two basic uses in jewelry making. The first is to smooth and give a high polish to beveled edges where other polishing techniques would not be practical. The second use is for removal of deep scratches and pits on surfaces. In burnishing out a scratch always rub the blade in the direction of the scratch. If rubbed across the scratch, a dip could result, which might be worse than the original blemish. (See Fig. 2–13.)

Considerable controlled pressure is necessary in burnishing since the surface of the metal is actually moved and compressed to fill in scratches and pits.

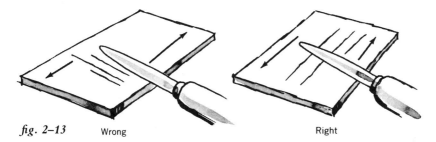

fig. 2–13   Wrong   Right

Burnish over a large enough area to avoid forming a depression. A drop of light oil helps in moving the burnisher. Emery paper may be used to remove burnishing marks.

Another use for the burnisher is to press a bezel around a gemstone. This will be described in detail in Chapter 4.

A *word of caution:* The high polish and considerable pressure on the burnisher can cause it to slip. This often creates a deep scratch, which is much harder to remove. Use short, controlled rubbing strokes and use your free hand as a support and guide when possible.

• finishing

Finishing is the most important technique mentioned so far since it determines the final quality of the piece.

There are many forms of abrasive cloth and paper, but one or two types usually suffice. A fine and a fairly coarse emery paper have proved to be effective and economical.

In one brand, Behr-Manning, sizes Nos. 1 and 3/0, fulfill most needs. The No. 1 emery, being sharp and quite coarse, is used to remove file marks, scraper marks, scotch-stone marks, surface scratches and pits (if not too large), and minor beveling. If carefully handled, it may be used to give an overall matte finish to the work.

The No. 3/0 emery paper is used primarily to refine the surface left by No. 1 emery paper and to clean surfaces of oxides, oil films, and fingerprints in preparation for soldering.

Both types of emery paper should be used in small pieces. A piece 2″ square, folded in half so that the rough surfaces are on the outside, is more efficient than a large sheet. Folding the paper prevents it from slipping between your fingers and the metal during the pressure of sanding.

Here again, considerable pressure should be applied for effective sanding.

Smaller pieces can be folded, rolled, or wound around an appropriate needle file in order to reach narrow and difficult areas.

To prevent deep parallel scratches, rub in several directions during sanding.

Do not discard worn pieces of emery too quickly! They might be useful for a finer sanding later.

• cutting techniques (bobbing)
MATERIALS

Hand-buffing sticks
Cutting wheels
Electric motor
Cutting compounds: Pumice, powdered emery, Lea compound C, tripoli

The craftsman need not use an electric polishing or cutting machine to bring metal work to a desired finish. For centuries, before electricity, rubbing with coarse or fine powders by hand or with leather achieved highly reflective and rich surfaces.

The cutting or bobbing operation consists of removing the marks of previous tool use (such as filing, burnishing, and sanding) by hard rubbing with a sharp but uniformly small-particled substance. This may be done by moistening a material like pumice to make a paste and using thumb and fingers for rubbing to a smooth finish.

A faster, more efficient method is to use a wooden hand-buffing stick, half of which is covered with felt or leather. These sticks can be purchased, or a strip of the proper material can be glued to a suitable flat stick. In making the buff, you can design it for a specific purpose—i.e., thin and narrow for tight angles, round and tapered for small concave surfaces, sculptured to fit a special form.

Since water-moistened pumice would fall away from such a tool before much cutting could be done, tripoli can be used. Tripoli consists of a fine siliceous ooze in powder form mixed with tallow or wax and pressed into blocks or bars. The tallow enables the abrasive to adhere to the rubbing surface.

In hand bobbing considerable pressure must be used, and you should avoid moving in one direction too long. Otherwise, you may end up with an unwanted groove.

Emery, an impure form of corundum (the mineral from which sapphires and rubies are made) comes in the same forms as tripoli and can be used in the same manner. This is one of the oldest abrasive materials used by man.

In machine bobbing, the use of wheels of various materials attached to the spindle of an electric motor may save in time and effort, but an inexperienced worker might also bob away more metal than planned.

There are a great variety of wheel types available. Some do only one type of work well, whereas others might do several.

Wood—Used for cutting primarily with emery or pumice as the abrasive. Special shapes can be formed to accommodate a specific need.

Leather—These wheels, while expensive, outlast cloth or felt wheels and hold the cutting compound better. The best wheels are of buffalo or walrus hide.

Felt—Available in a number of hardnesses, and it can be used with most compounds. Felt wheels are used most often on angular edges and small planes. However, it is quite easy to cut grooves in the metal if the wheel is improperly positioned while cutting.

Cloth—These wheels come in a variety of shapes, materials, and diameters. Some are nothing more than a number of disks fastened by a metal grommet in the center; others may be stitched and glued to give firmness to the shape. They may be made of cotton, muslin, or wool. Abrasives can be used with cloth wheels

either dry (as tripoli) or moist (as in a pumice paste). By varying diameters and motor speeds a variety of bobbing actions can be achieved.

Brushes—Also available in a variety of materials and shapes. The bristles may be of fiber (Tampico brushes), pig bristle, or a plastic such as nylon. A Tampico brush used with activated pumice at slow motor speeds produces a faster cutting action than any other type of wheel.

Wheel mandrels—Mandrels are used to bob or polish the insides of pieces of jewelry such as rings or bracelets. They may be made of hard felt or of wood with a slot to hold a covering of emery paper, or of emery stone. Emery paper of various grits is also constructed as a hollow cone to fit over a cone-shaped wood spindle and adhered by centrifugal force.

After constant use with tripoli and other cake abrasives, the surface of a bobbing wheel might become so matted that it may cut inefficiently and unevenly. Excess abrasive may be removed by holding a coarse file or hacksaw blade against the rotating wheel. Or the wheels may be washed in a solution of one quart of hot water to which one tablespoon of ammonia and a little salt have been added. The addition of a liquid detergent helps dissolve the binding medium. The wheel can be spun dry after washing.

Effective cutting, buffing, or polishing depends as much on motor speed (rpm) as it does on the type of wheel or abrasive used. The larger the wheel diameter, the greater the speed at its working edge.

The surface speed, the rate of travel of the wheel surface past a given point, can be calculated by this formula:

Surface speed = Circumference of wheel in inches × rpm ÷ 12

The following are recommended motor speeds for a variety of wheels.

For leather or felt: 2,000 to 2,500 rpm
For muslin or flannel: 3,000 to 4,000 rpm
For bristle: 1,250 to 1,750 rpm

An ideal motor arrangement is one in which the wheel area is housed in an open-fronted hood with some means of vacuuming dust particles into a container. Lacking this, a simple hood for protection may be made of galvanized sheet metal and a pan with 1″ of water with a little detergent placed under the wheel. This collects a great deal of the waste. (See Fig. 2–14.)

fig. 2–14
Courtesy, Allcraft Tool & Supply Co., Inc.

The steps involved in safe and effective cutting are simple but important:

Step 1. Place the wheel on the revolving spindle for quick centering.

Step 2. Apply abrasive to the revolving wheel.

Step 3. Hold the work securely in both hands if possible. If the wheel catches a projection on its down swing, the work may be torn from the hand, causing damage both to the user and the work. The backdrop or hood is necessary since a piece of metal might be spun away from the wheel with great force. Always work with the wheel rotating forward and down. Apply the metal piece to a point below the horizontal median of the wheel. At this point the wheel rotates *away* from the work, so the work should be angled to accommodate this. Press the work against the wheel enough to notice and feel the cutting action. Light pressure is ineffective.

Step 4. Move the work constantly! If it is allowed to remain in one position too long, excessive cutting might remove detail and change the shape. Cross-buff for a uniform surface.

Step 5. Stop occasionally to reapply abrasive and to check progress. A piece of cleansing tissue can be used to wipe away abrasive waste. If the piece heats up through friction, it may be dipped into a pan of water occasionally. Small pieces too difficult to hold by hand and that would heat up too quickly may be held in a ring clamp. A word of caution: Chain or other articulated forms must be firmly wrapped around or tacked to a board to prevent being fouled in the wheel.

Step 6. Clean all traces of bobbing compounds from work. If left in cracks or seams, they may cause scratches during the final polishing process.

TRUMMING

Trumming is an ancient method for bobbing and polishing delicate or intricate areas too small for hand or machine work. A small cord, preferably of nylon for long wear, is held by one end in a vise. The other end is held in the hand, pulled tight, and rubbed with an abrasive. The cord is then placed through or into the opening of the design and again stretched. Cutting or polishing is achieved by moving the work back and forth along the string with pressure.

• stamping

After all parts are sawed out, filed, sanded, and bobbed, but *before* soldering starts, metals such as silver, gold, and platinum may be stamped with marks identifying quality, maker (hallmark), or the word "Handwrought." Stamping later in the process of working the piece might be difficult or impossible without marring the design.

Most craftsmen today purchase such stamps as "Sterling," "14K.," "18K.," "Platinum," and "Handwrought." These come in a number of sizes, and all but "Handwrought" must be stamped on work claiming to use that metal if it is to be sold. There are strict domestic and international laws governing this practice.

A hallmark can be made of soft tool steel by engraving, carving, or filing the design and then case hardening the stamp, or a stamp designed by the craftsman can be purchased.

Number stamps and letter stamps are also available in various sizes.

The work to be stamped is placed on a *polished steel* surface and one or more blows with a hammer used to indent the end of the stamp into the softer metal. Care must be exercised so that the stamp does not move between hammer blows.

The slight blemish on the reverse of the point stamped can be removed by sanding or stoning.

Be sure to place the mark where future soldering of shapes or findings will not cover it!

● hard soldering sterling silver and other nonferrous metals

There are two basic soldering techniques to be used with sterling silver. Soldering done at temperatures above 1000° F. is called "hard soldering," while soldering done at temperatures below 1000° F. is called "soft soldering." The materials, the steps, and even the principles are totally different and cannot be interchanged.

MATERIALS

Solder
Flux
Flux brush
Charcoal block, magnesium block, pyrofax coil
Tweezers: pointed and locking
Pointer
Iron binding wire
Torch: gas + air, acetylene, propane, or mouth blowpipe
Emery paper
Pumice
Brush

There are five sequences in accurate soldering. Each is as important as the next, and performing any of them carelessly can result in failure. The steps in sequence are:

Step 1. Fitting: Making a tight, even join between surfaces to be soldered.
Step 2. Cleaning: Removing surface films of grease, oil, or oxide.
Step 3. Fluxing: Applying liquid or paste flux to all areas in sufficient amounts to prevent oxidation during heating.
Step 4. Solder placement: Placing the correct solder in the right places and in the right amounts.
Step 5. Heating: Using torches or blowpipes in a manner that quickly and safely causes solder to melt and flow.

STEP 1. FITTING

Surfaces and edges to be soldered together must fit closely along their entire length and breadth. Since flowing solder is attracted by capillary action to a junction of surfaces (but will *not* bridge gaps or irregularities) the close fitting of a join cannot be neglected.

In the soldering of two flat surfaces, both must be free of warping or dents. Large dents must be removed by careful hammering with a *wood* or *plastic* hammer over

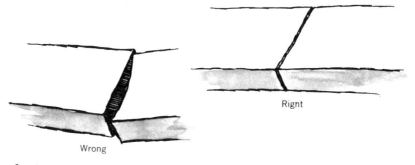

Right

Wrong

fig. 2–15

a smooth flat surface. Smaller dents can be removed by filing or stoning.

Warped metal can be flattened in the same manner or, if thin enough, corrected by hand. Sight along several edges to check final flatness.

Wire often develops kinks in shaping, and these are best removed by hand through bending and counterbending. Remember, solder flows along a join easily, but it cannot bridge sections out of contact with each other.

Joining ends in a butt join is simple if the ends meet tightly and evenly over their entire length. (See Fig. 2–15.) A butt join can be strengthened if both ends are beveled in order to increase the surface to be soldered. (See Fig. 2–16.)

If a warp in sheet metal or a kink in wire is very slight, the softening effect of heating might cause the piece to drop into position. This can be aided by pressure with a pointer or tweezers just as the solder begins to flow. Do not remove heat while doing this, since the solder "freezes" al-

most immediately and will not flow between the new contacts.

It is far better to make an initial proper fitting than to depend on the foregoing. If done unskillfully, press fitting heated metal may shatter wire or sheet, or the parts may move completely out of position.

STEP 2. CLEANING

Solder will not flow over or onto a dirty surface. All traces of fingerprints, cutting or buffing compounds, and oxidation *must* be removed.

Chemical cleaning is most effective, but it is also time consuming. In this process oils and greases are burned off by heating the metal to a dull red. Oxides are then removed by acid pickling and the work is then washed thoroughly. If there are small hollow spaces where acid pickle collects, the acid must be neutralized by boiling the work in a solution of 1 tbsp. baking soda to 1 cup water. After rinsing, work may

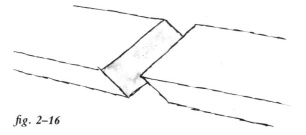

fig. 2–16

1

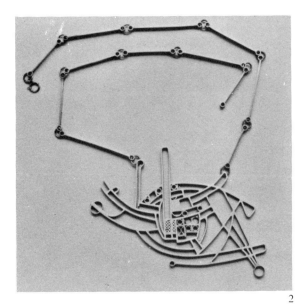

2

3

4

1 Pendants; silver

2 Necklace, Peter Haythornthwaite; silver wire and tubing

3 Pins; silver

4 Pins and pendant; silver

5 Pendant; oxidized silver

6 Pin; silver, formed, bent with wire legs

7 Pin; silver with overlay and wire

8 Haircomb; bronze, repoussé; 2″ wide

9 Buckle, Greg Fensterman; bronze; 3⅛″ wide

10 Buckle; brass, sandblasted; 3″ wide

11 Buckle, back view

All student work was done
by undergraduates at
the University of Illinois

5 6   7

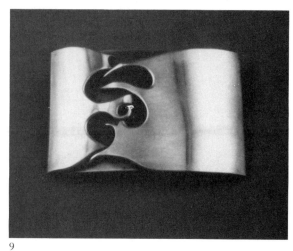

8 9

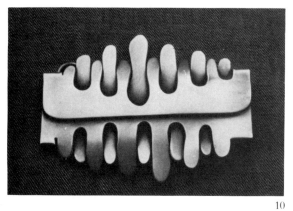

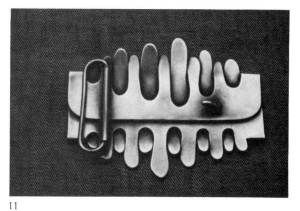

10 11

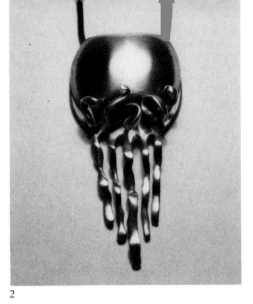

1 2

3

4

1 Pendant, Susan Grubb; oxidized silver

2 Pendant, Karen Cahill; bronze; 2½″ long

3 Pin, Jane Standebach; silver sheet and wire

4 Brooch, Dennis Ryan; bronze repoussé; 2½″ long

5 Pendant, Jan MacNeil; copper and silver, sandblasted

6 Buckle, Robert McHenry; mixed metals, goldstone; 3″ wide

7 Pin; bronze and sandblasted silver

8 "Leaping Bull" pin; silver, 3″ wide

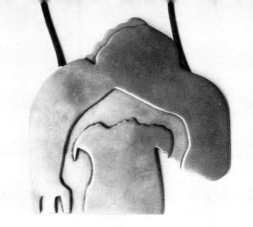

*All student work was done
by undergraduates at
the University of Illinois*

5

6

7   8

   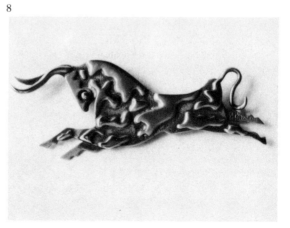

be kept under water to prevent oxidation. It then should be handled with tweezers to prevent new fingerprints.

A faster, and almost as effective, cleaning process involves brushing the work with moist pumice and a bristle brush. Work can also be cleaned by sanding it with a *clean* piece of emery paper. For most purposes the last is adequate for removing all dirt. A clean surface is bright and allows flux to be spread evenly without forming drops and pools.

Sanding wire after bending it into shape is difficult, so bending must be done with clean fingers or with pliers. If wire is to be soldered to a flat surface, it might be possible to sand its contacting edges clean on a flat sheet of emery paper.

STEP 3. FLUXING

Hard solder flux may be boric acid, borax, or a prepared liquid or paste combining several fluxing ingredients. A lump of borax can be rubbed to a paste by adding a little water to a slate dish designed for this purpose. This is the fluxing technique used by some of the finest jewelers of the past. Today it is more efficient to use one of the several patented mixtures, since they have greater fluxing and cleaning action. Some fluxes can also be used as temperature indicators.

It is important that *all* surfaces to be soldered are completely covered with flux. Each piece of solder should also be fluxed. This can be done by putting the solder fragments into place with a flux-moistened brush.

To prevent excessive cuprous and cupric oxides from forming on sterling silver and other copper-based alloys, flux all surfaces except the bottom of the work. Since this is in contact with charcoal, the oxides do not form so easily.

The action of flux is to prevent oxides from forming when metal is heated. Borax, or fluxes containing borax, become fluid and glasslike around 1200° F and thus prevent oxides or dissolve oxides as they form.

Prolonged high heat breaks down the protecting qualities of fluxes to the point that they will no longer absorb oxides, and they may even pull away from the surface entirely. This is why heating must be done quickly and only enough to cause solder flow.

STEP 4. SOLDER PLACEMENT

Hard solder is usually an alloy of the metal on which it is used, with small amounts of other metals added. Thus silver solder is an alloy of silver, copper, and zinc in varying amounts. By combining metals a new metal is formed that usually has a lower melting point than the metals used to form the alloy.

Unfortunately there are no *hard* solders for copper, bronze, brass, or nickel silver that match in color. Since silver-based hard solder is light in color—especially the "Hard" and "IT" forms—great care must be taken to avoid excessive soldering or inaccurate use. (Soldering gold and gold alloys will be discussed later in this chapter.)

If more than one soldering is needed to complete a piece, different solders can be used with melting points that are successively lower. In most cases, however, a single type of solder such as "Easy" can be used, even with several solderings, if careful fitting and bracing is used to prevent collapse should the old solder remelt.

Handy and Harman supplies this list of melting points for its silver solders:

	Fluid at
"Easy" solder (for most simple soldering)	1325° F
"Medium" solder (for first or second solderings, or for multiple soldering operations)	1390° F
"Hard" solder (for first or second solderings, or for multiple soldering operations)	1425° F

"IT" solder (only for joins requiring great strength)

Fluid at

1460° F

Remember that sterling silver begins to break down at 1500° F and becomes liquid at 1640° F. Fine silver is liquid at 1761° F. Silver solder comes in sheets, wires, sticks, strips, or powder form. For jewelry purposes, sheets or strips are the most practical.

The sheet or strip is cut into small pieces, or *paillons*. Since it is usually better to use several small, easily heated pieces rather than one large piece at a given point, these *paillons* should be about 1/16" square. Even smaller pieces must be used when soldering fine wire or small shot. Scissors or jeweler's shears are used to "fringe" the edge of a sheet of solder for a depth of about 1/2". The cuts are 1/16" apart, and the pieces are formed by making a right-angle cut 1/16" wide across the fringe. (See Fig. 2–17.)

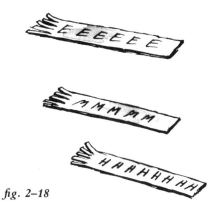

fig. 2–18

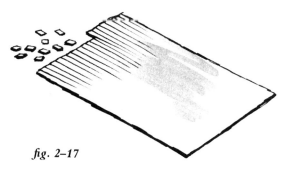

fig. 2–17

Place the index finger along the side of the scissors to prevent the solder from flying around during cutting.

To prevent mixing solder pieces of different melting points, each solder should have a separate, labeled container. In addition, each sheet or strip should be scratched with the initial of the solder type to prevent confusion. (See Fig. 2–18.) The *paillons* should always be much thinner than the work to be soldered. Usually 28 to 30 B & S gauge is thin enough, but it may

be rolled or hammered thinner if necessary.

Solder should be placed only where, in flowing, it will make a good join. Use only enough to do the job. Too much solder causes difficulty in melting, as well as blemishes. If excess solder flows off a join onto a visible surface, it may prevent future evenness of coloring and will have to be removed by stoning. Excessive solder while soldering wire might prevent some of the solder from flowing at all.

SOLDERING FLAT SURFACES

After determining which piece will be on top, and after thoroughly cleaning and fluxing all surfaces, place the solder on the *reverse* of the top piece; this ensures that all solder will be covered correctly. The solder should be positioned 1/8" to 1/4" apart around the outside edge of the top piece, with an additional three or four pieces in the middle if the surface is large. (See Fig. 2–19.)

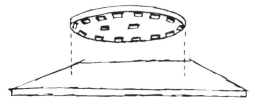

fig. 2–19

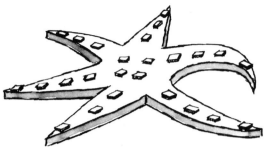

fig. 2-20

Before lifting the top piece with tweezers, allow the flux to dry for a moment. This will prevent the solder from falling off or moving while it is upside down. The *paillons* should be picked up and put into place with a flux-moistened brush tip. Choose an inexpensive small, pointed brush—one accidental application of solder to a hot piece of metal and the bristles are gone!

If the top piece of metal has long projections, make sure that solder is placed at every tip. If these projections are narrow, do not place *paillons* all around the edges but only down the center of the projection. (See Fig. 2-20.)

On small overlaid pieces it might be best to premelt the solder onto the undersurfaces. This reduces the chance for a position shift at the moment of melting in the usual technique. (See Fig. 2-21.) Unless it is overheated, solder can be remelted several times without seriously reducing its flow qualities. Each heating, however, tends to change the alloy proportions and makes remelting more difficult.

On flat to flat or slightly curved surfaces soldered horizontally, it is not necessary to use binding wire to hold the work in position. Gravity will keep even small pieces in position, and the wire binding will become too loose to do much good once the solder flows.

The two surfaces should be separated only by *paillons*. Be very sure that no foreign matter is between surfaces or the work will not come together when the solder flows! (See Fig. 2-22.)

It is possible to solder two or more layers together in one operation, but when they are stacked too high, it is difficult to heat all of the pieces evenly. The top surfaces may be too close to melting, while the bottom piece is many degrees cooler.

The work should now be placed on a

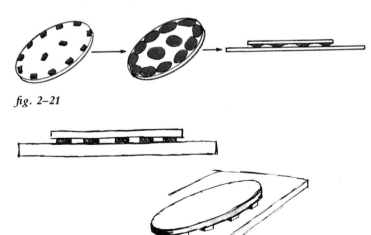

fig. 2-21

fig. 2-22

charcoal or heat resistant block, firebrick, or Carborundum grains and again checked for alignment. All displaced solder should be put back into place or removed. Heat-resistant materials, such as charcoal, retain and reflect heat, thus speeding the soldering operation. In addition, charcoal tends to prevent oxidation where metal touches it. Such materials as hard brick, sheet rock, and stone are unsuitable since they dissipate so much heat that quick, even heating of metal is impossible.

STEP 5. HEATING

Before describing the correct application of heat, it might be well to explain torch and flame qualities and how they should be used.

GAS-AIR TORCHES

In established workshops and in many schools, torches are fed by a combination of gas and compressed air. The gases may be manufactured illuminating gas, natural gas, or propane. Special tips may be needed in each case since a tip for illuminating gas would not form an adequate flame when used with natural gas. Air pressure may be supplied by a foot bellows or by a mo-

tor-driven compressor. The torches, then, have two adjustable inlets for gas and air, and by changing their proportions a number of flame sizes and types can be obtained. Most torches also have a variety of tips available that form flames ranging from large soft flames to small pointed flames.

With a gas-air torch the most effective flame for soldering pieces 1″ in diameter is about 5″ long, is soft at the tip, and might have a *little* yellow at the end of an otherwise blue flame. Too much yellow—a reducing flame—is too soft for concentration of heat, and it might deposit unburned soot particles on the work, which could prevent solder flow. A too-yellow flame also lacks the heat necessary for quick soldering.

A flame that is a hard, pointed blue—an oxidizing flame—is even more dangerous. Far from melting solder quickly, it causes heavy deposits of cuprous and cupric oxides on sterling silver and other copper-containing metals, as well as on the solder itself. This quickly prevents all solder flow. Being small-pointed, this flame also may overheat small areas instead of uniformly heating the whole unit. (See Fig. 2–23.)

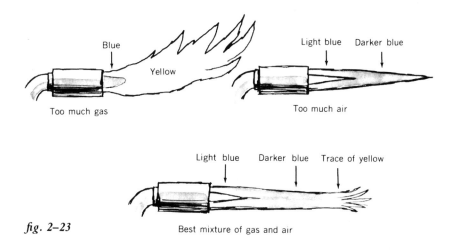

fig. 2–23   Best mixture of gas and air

43

When soldering small units such as chain links or filigree, the flame size should be smaller while using the correct gas–air mixture. Generally, the last inch of the flame should touch the metal surfaces.

ACETYLENE TORCHES

Self-contained pressure tanks of acetylene are available in sets consisting of a tank, hose, pressure gauge and valve, and an adjustable torchhead. (See Fig. 2–24.)

fig. 2–24
Courtesy of Swest, Inc.

Acetylene gas has the advantage of forming a clean, quick-heating flame, and this can be used large or very small for a variety of soldering purposes. Being self-contained, it can be moved from place to place for use in several areas of the workshop. The initial cost is high, since the tank is bought outright or leased, but with normal use a full tank of gas lasts for quite a long time and may be exchanged for a refill at low cost.

Since the gas mixes with air at the torch tip without being able to be adjusted, only the flame length can be varied, although tips of different sizes and shapes are available.

A No. 1 tip in the Prest-O-Lite unit is good for jewelry work.

PROPANE CANISTER TORCHES

Small, self-contained, and disposable cans of pressurized propane gas are available with a reusable torch attachment. These are adequate for small jewelry work, but for prolonged heating or work on large pieces they do not last long enough to be economical.

The flame is not very adjustable, but it is clean and hot. Propane torches are good for the beginner since they often cost less than ten dollars.

BUNSEN BURNERS OR ALCOHOL BURNERS

For many years craftsmen have used a brass mouth blowpipe through which air is blown, deflecting and concentrating the flame of a gas Bunsen burner or alcohol flame. By these means a small, hot, and carefully controlled flame can be focused closely when delicate work is being soldered. An alcohol burner and blowpipe can be used for soldering small gold or silver areas even when other torches are available. The flame is too small, however, to function well on work larger than 2″ in diameter.

In areas where manufactured illuminating gas is still available for cooking and heating, a torch similar to the blowpipe is both inexpensive and effective. It consists simply of a length of hose, one end attached to a gas jet (such as for the burner of a kitchen stove) and the other to a mouth blowpipe. The gas enters the pipe through an interior pipe and mixes with air at the tip. With such a torch it is simple to adjust the size, the heat, and the duration of the flame.

With practice inhaling through the nose and using the cheeks as a pressure chamber, it is possible to maintain a very even air supply and a steady flame. For many years the author used such a torch for all soldering and regrets that he now lives where it cannot be used, since it will not work well with natural gas.

A gas-mouth blowpipe can also be used at the kitchen stove, with a sheet of asbestos providing a safe soldering area over the burner.

Various small alcohol and chemical tablet torches are available, but they do not supply enough of the right kind of heat to be practical. Electric soldering guns or irons are used only for soft (lead) soldering and even for this purpose cannot be used delicately in jewelry making.

Electric arc soldering machines are too expensive and limited in the type of work they can do to warrant purchase by the jeweler-craftsman. For most conditions, the author prefers the self-contained acetylene torch and considers it to be a worthwhile investment.

Correct heat application, with any of these torches, is obtained as follows:

The flame should first be rotated around the *outside* edge of the fluxed work without touching the metal itself. Metal heated too quickly makes even dry flux boil or foam, causing the solder or the metal pieces to move. When this occurs, both the pieces and the solder must be moved back into position quickly. Always have a pair of pointed tweezers or a pointed steel rod in hand for this purpose. A section of coathanger wire, sharpened at one end, works well. If, upon cooling, the displaced pieces stick, the whole unit should be heated again slightly to remelt the flux, since cooled flux may hold solder and work securely.

The best indication that foaming has stopped is the formation of a white crust on fluxed surfaces. Once the crust is formed, the work may be heated directly.

The *entire* metal area *must* be brought to solder flow temperature as a unit. If heat is concentrated at one point, the surrounding metal will dissipate it, prolonging or even preventing solder flow. Move the torch slowly back and forth or around the entire area until the solder begins to melt.

There are several ways to determine correct solder flow temperature. Some fluxes, such as Handy and Harman Paste Flux, become clear and liquid at 1100° F. When this happens, you know that only a few hundred degrees more of heat will cause the solder to melt.

With experience the color of the metal itself becomes an accurate guide. Many craftsmen solder in subdued light so that they can better see the medium dark red glow, indicating that the solder should be flowing. Often it is possible to see the solder melt and flow, as in soldering wire, but when *paillons* are hidden between two pieces, it is best to watch for: (1) a drop of the top piece as solder changes from solid to liquid; (2) after a little additional heat a bright seam of molten solder showing at an edge.

If this seam is not noticed and if, through inexperience, the color of metal gives no indication that solder should be flowing, solder flow may often be incomplete. This often happens when soldering overlaid work. The top piece has become hot enough to attract the solder beneath it, causing it to flow to this surface. The top piece has dropped so that it seems to be together—only to fall apart when pickled, or even later on. To prevent this, always heat for a few seconds longer after seeing the top piece drop. This may very well bring some of the molten solder to the edge for a sure indication.

A number of things can cause soldering failures:

1. *Incomplete solder melting.* Cure: After careful pickling, all work is refluxed, solder added where necessary (if any has fallen off), and heat reapplied.

2. *Solder balling and refusing to melt.* Cause: Metal surfaces may be dirty with grease, oil, or oxides. Solder may be dirty. Excessive preheating may cause oxides or flux to be supercharged with oxides, thus no longer absorbing or preventing oxidation. Too much heat concentration may cause metal to cool in unheated areas. An incorrect flame (too much or too little air) may cause soot or oxides. Another cause is heating too slowly, even if the correct temperature is finally reached (flux can prevent and absorb only so much oxidation). Prolonged high heat causes trouble, as does incomplete solder contact. Since solder flows to the *hottest* area as well as to a *junction* of surfaces, it should be in contact with junctions, and generally heat should be directed toward them.

3. *Foreign matter.* Through accident or carelessness, particles of charcoal or metal filings might remain between two surfaces, preventing them from coming together when solder flows. Always check for dirt and use *only* what you know to be solder.

4. *Accidental use of wrong solder.* If solders of different melting points are not kept in separate, labeled containers, it is easy to mistake a high melting solder with a medium or low solder. Delicate work can be melted completely before the mistake is even suspected!

5. *Careless use of whiting or yellow ocher.* Both of these substances (their proper use to be described later), when accidentally mixed with flux, can completely prevent solder flow. Keep fluxed areas separate from those painted with these materials!

6. *Poor fitting of parts.* This causes most difficulties, since the solder cannot bridge gaps between surfaces or flow along wire when it is not completely in contact with its support. Although it is sometimes possible to press a warped sheet or wire into place *while applying heat,* great damage may result if work becomes too hot while doing so. Remember, most metals become brittle at high temperatures and can be shattered by forcing them. Be sure of correct fitting from the outset.

7. *Moving of parts before or after solder flow.* As mentioned, if parts move before solder has begun to flow, they can be pushed back into position. After doing so be sure that all solder is also in position, since a blemish caused by misplaced solder is very visible and difficult to remove.

   If work moves just as solder melts (this often happens due to capillary attraction when soldering very small pieces close to each other), it is best to use tweezers or a pointer to move them while the solder is still fluid. Do not remove heat, since this will cause the solder to solidify immediately, making remelting quite difficult. If a moved piece refuses to be repositioned, do not heat more than once. Continued high heat causes a stronger joining, as well as burning away some of the zinc in the solder. This causes it to melt at an even higher temperature. It is best to pickle work carefully, to wash off pickle carefully (making sure that no acid remains between the surfaces to be soldered), and again to reflux thoroughly. If heat is now applied correctly, the pieces *may* be moved into position, but usually it is more difficult to remelt solder that has once been fluid.

   It is inevitable that, upon moving a piece to a new position, a solder scar, or "ghost," appears where solder has melted originally. This must be removed by abrasives or it will leave a roughness that will be difficult to hide or color in the finishing process.

After solder has melted satisfactorily, the piece may be dropped into pickle while still hot or, if allowed to cool, may be boiled in pickle until clean. If dropped cold into cold pickle, it will eventually be cleaned of oxides, but this might take some time, depending on the strength of the solution.

Since it is possible to solder many times on the same piece, it is very important that oxides formed during one heating are all removed before the next heating. It is, of course, necessary to reflux everything carefully before each soldering! Be sure that no pumice or other abrasives work into areas to be soldered.

As a check list for successful soldering, remember to have:

1. Close-fitting joins
2. Clean surfaces
3. Careful fluxing
4. The right amount, placement, and type of solder
5. Removal of foreign objects
6. Careful but quick preheating
7. Even heat over the entire metal area
8. Enough heat to cause complete solder flow
9. Correct pickling or cleaning *and* re-fluxing between solderings

In general, the rules of hard soldering apply equally to soldering flat sheet to flat sheet, curved metal to curved metal, edges to edges, wire to flat metal, wire to wire, grains to flat metal, or grains to wire.

There are, however, a few basic techniques in working with wire or grains (shot) that should be mentioned.

SOLDERING WIRE TO SHEET

The basic difference between soldering wire to sheet and other soldering lies in the position and the amount of solder. Since only a small portion of a section of wire contacts another surface, only a very small amount of solder is necessary for firm soldering. Too much solder, if all the pieces melt at all, causes a flooding of wire edges, which will give a blunt heaviness to a design.

Keeping in mind that solder is attracted to a join, always be sure to place the solder in contact with the wire more than with the sheet. (See Fig. 2–25.)

If you place the *paillon* against or on top of the wire, there will be greater contact with the wire and, when the correct temperature is reached, it will flow down the sides of the wire and for quite a distance along the join.

A flowing piece of solder may travel for an inch or more along an 18-gauge sterling silver wire. Consequently, it is best to use very little solder, and use it only where it will do the most good. (See Fig. 2–26.)

Note that the solder in Fig. 2–26B is placed at a junction of the wire and an edge. Should the solder flow onto the sheet rather than along the wire, the lump can

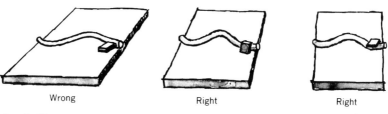

Wrong   Right   Right

fig. 2–25

47

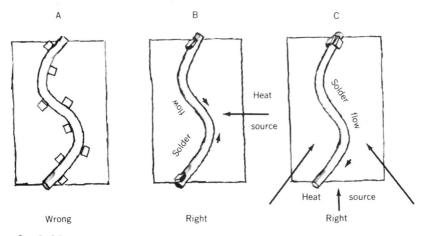

A   B   C

Heat source

Solder flow

Heat source

Wrong   Right   Right

fig. 2–26

easily be stoned away with a scotch stone. It would be more difficult to do so were the solder placed somewhere in the middle. The two pieces of solder in Fig. 2–26B are both on one side of the wire. By angling the flame from the opposite direction (arrows), the solder flows *to* the wire and the hottest area. This flame angle should only be reached just as solder begins to flow, otherwise the work may be unevenly heated. It is possible to "draw" flowing solder along a join with the torch by the same principle. (See Fig. 2–26C.)

Where a long length of wire is used, additional solder should be placed on outside curves—it is easier to remove mistakes—and on *top* of, or leaning against, the wire. (See Fig. 2–27.)

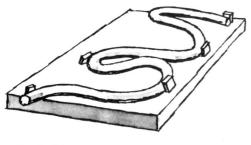

fig. 2–27

It is perhaps easier to solder thin wire to sheet than thick wire. This is because the heat flow between wire and sheet is almost immediate when the wire is small. With thicker wire, 14 gauge and up, heating should be as for overlay soldering. In all cases, if the wire is in close contact for its total length, there is no chance of melting the wire before the sheet itself becomes overheated. Any point where the wire *leaves* the sheet might be the point where the wire melts and breaks apart.

Where wire leaves the support and contact of sheet, as shown in Fig. 2–28, melting of wire is very possible. Adjust the flame size and the heating area accordingly and watch the color of the wire at all times. By alternately applying and removing the flame in an even manner, the total mass may be heated before projections become overheated. (See Fig. 2–28.)

An alternative is to place the wire on the charcoal, which would tend to distribute heat more equally. The difficulty with this approach lies in the placement of solder. It would have to be sandwiched between the wire and the sheet after having been applied to the wire first. (See Fig. 2–29.)

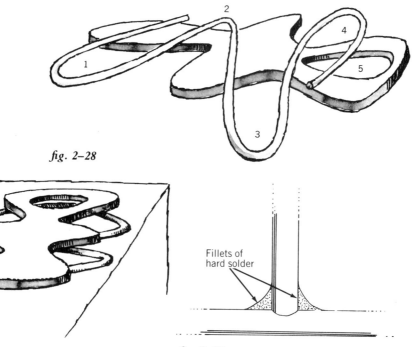

fig. 2–28

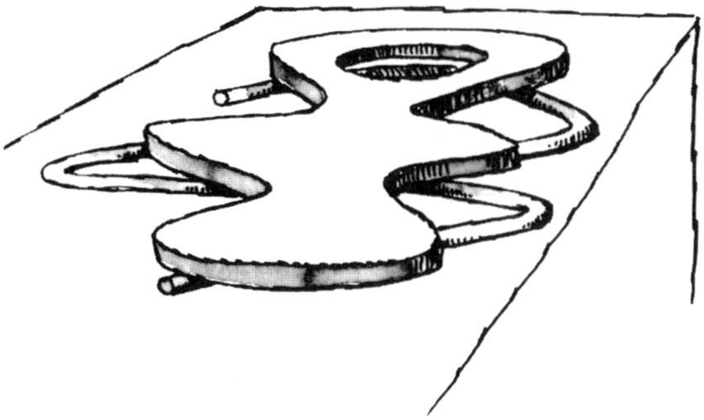

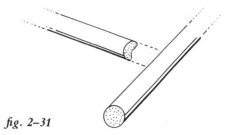

fig. 2–29

Fillets of
hard solder

fig. 2–30

SOLDERING WIRE TO WIRE

Soldering wire to wire is similar to soldering wire to sheet in that very little solder is used in order to prevent clumsiness and heaviness.

A smaller flame is necessary, since a large flame would tend to overheat areas of wire not under close observation. In most cases it is best to use a high-melting solder such as Handy and Harman "Hard," since this does not become quite so fluid as lower-melting solders. Because of this quality, it makes a stronger and better-looking butt or angle join by forming a fillet. (See Fig. 2–30.)

The best possible fitting of wires is important for strength and appearance. Merely nipping the wire with side or end cutters presents a crude ending that could destroy the linear continuity of wire. It also pre-

sents a poor surface for joining an end to another unit.

In Fig. 2–31, the end of one wire has been filed parallel to the join as well as concave to fit the curve of the other wire. This may be done with the round needle file. On an angled join, appearance is greatly improved by filing an angle to flow into that of the join. (See Fig. 2–32.)

Placement of solder for either of the

fig. 2–31

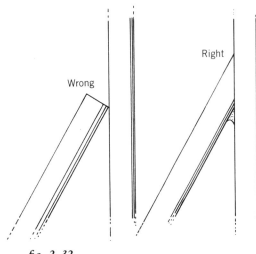

fig. 2–32

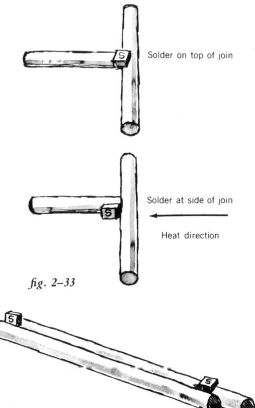

Solder on top of join

Solder at side of join

Heat direction

fig. 2–33

foregoing should be economical. One piece should do the job or the join will be bulky, leaving excess solder to be filed away.

Allow heat direction to pull the flowing solder to the join. If the join does not meet, the solder will jump to one or the other wire—whichever is the hotter. (See Fig. 2–33.)

In soldering wires parallel with each other, if possible always place the solder at the ends only in order to prevent "ghosts" along the length. (See Fig. 2–34.)

When soldering tight spirals of wire to a flat surface, it is best to premelt the solder where the spiral should go first, then pickle, reflux, add the spiral, and reheat. In this way the solder will already be in firm contact with the base, instead of melting into and around the spiral only.

Open spirals need solder placement similar to that for straight or curved wire.

fig. 2–34

SOLDERING SHOT OR GRAINS

If shot is to be soldered to a sheet surface, the solder may either be melted partially at the solder point, after which the fluxed shot is applied, or the solder may be applied with the shot as shown in Fig. 2–35.

If many shot are to be soldered in a row, it is best to engrave a guide line into which they can be placed. This should prevent the occasional moving of shot as the solder melts.

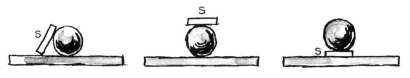

fig. 2–35

Where a cluster or textured surface of shot is needed, the area they are to occupy can first be coated with a film of melted solder. This should be done carefully, since overheating of melted solder causes the alloy to change. This usually prevents effective remelting. After the sheet (with the melted solder in position) has been pickled, rinsed, and refluxed, the fluxed shot can be put into position and soldering completed by placing the work on a nickel chromium screen on a tripod and heating from underneath. Since there is nothing to absorb and reflect heat in this instance, a somewhat larger flame should be used to prevent prolonged heating.

SOLDERING AT ANGLES

Perhaps the most difficult soldering operation—from the standpoint of easy solder flow—is to solder a vertical plane to a horizontal plane. The greatest difficulty lies in supporting the vertical well enough to withstand flame pressure and expansion. Here soft iron binding wire may be useful (be sure to remove it completely before pickling!) for holding parts in place, but usually a good job of edge filing allows a piece to stand unsupported.

If possible, solder may be placed on the edge and between the vertical and the horizontal plane. As the solder melts, the vertical drops into place and may fall over unless supported for a moment with tweezers or a pointer. (See Fig. 2–36.)

A safer technique (although it may cause a few "ghosts") is to place the *paillons* along one side of the vertical, edging against it but lying flat on the horizontal. Placed this way, there is less tendency for the solder to flow up the side of the vertical rather than along the join. Use long, thin *paillons* and avoid heating the vertical plane too soon. (See Fig. 2–37.)

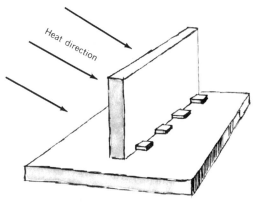

fig. 2–37

Similar principles govern soldering more acute angles, but they should be braced to prevent moving and falling during soldering. Pins of nichrome wire (used in heating elements) can be bent to shape and pressed into the soldering block for this purpose.

A very useful device for bracing vertical or diagonal pieces is a pair of cross-lock tweezers held in an articulated stand. (See Fig. 2–38.) This combination is capable of infinite settings and can act as a "third hand." Since the tweezers attract and absorb a good deal of the soldering heat, this system cannot be used for very small work, where heat transfer to the tweezers would be immediate.

A simple bracing method consists of using an old flat file, as illustrated in Fig. 2–

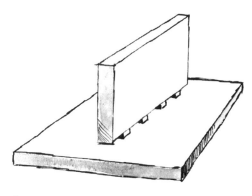

fig. 2–36

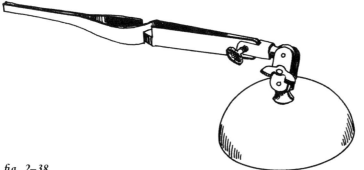

fig. 2–38

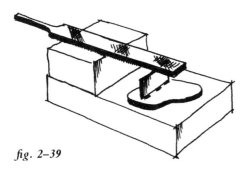

fig. 2–39

39. Be sure to use an old worn file; heating could ruin a good file.

When using liquid fluxes, always avoid an excess. Even after drying, an excess of flux could cause foaming, which could move delicate work. After an area has been thoroughly fluxed, the liquid excess may be drawn off with a blotter or cleansing tissue. Enough remains to do the job.

OVERHEATING STERLING SILVER

The possibility of overheating is always present during soldering. Often your attention is fixed so strongly at one point that accidental heat concentration at another point only a few millimeters away can cause the metal to melt unnoticed. This is especially true while soldering wire forms because of the small heat-dissipating area.

Silver that is being overheated goes through several stages and each one is serious:

1. The color changes from red to an incandescent red-orange.
2. The surface becomes shiny as it begins to melt.
3. The form begins to loose its solidity, often warping, sagging, and melting at the edges.
4. The edges draw in, and eventually the entire piece collapses into a large circular mass of molten metal. Wire might melt apart and draw away from the break.

Once silver has reached stage 2, it has changed its structure radically and may no longer be bent or formed, being much too brittle. In addition, the surface has become granular and roughened. This may sometimes be repaired by careful filing, sanding, and burnishing, but, due to excessive cupric oxide "fire" deep within, it will always look different from areas that haven't been overheated.

Overheating also causes weakened joins due to the burning out of zinc in the solder. Once gone, a porous metal composed mostly of silver and copper oxides remains.

It is more difficult to overheat bronze, brass, copper, or nickel silver, although damage to solder joints would be the same. Prolonged or high heating will also cause thick deposits of copper oxides on these metals. When these oxides are dissolved off in pickle, the metal surface often becomes scarred and uneven. Another over-heating danger occurs when brass (a copper-zinc alloy) and silver are heated together. These metals tend to collapse into each other at relatively low silver-soldering temperatures. Continued or repeated heating makes matters worse, since a new, lower-melting alloy is constantly being formed. Use only low-melting silver solders when combining these metals. Watch very carefully!

• soldering gold and karat gold

The same torches can be used for soldering gold as for fine and sterling silver. Since gold solders flow at a somewhat higher temperature than silver solders, a prepared flux should be used that functions well at such temperatures.

The principles of heating, solder size, placement, and pickling are also the same as for silver.

Only the gold solders and their actions introduce new factors. Solders for gold are, in most cases, karat golds of the same color as the basic metal but about 4 karats lower in purity. Thus, to solder 14K yellow gold, a 10K yellow gold solder of identical color is used.

Since gold solder never becomes quite so liquid as Easy silver solder, an even lower karat of gold must be used where a long flow is required, as for soldering wire to sheet.

One of the advantages of gold solder over other types is its slow-flowing tendencies. Occasional holes or gaps can be bridged by adding solder while heating. At the right moment, heat can be withdrawn, leaving the bulk of solder in place. This leads to the temptation to overload joins, however. As in silver soldering, the strongest and best-looking join uses only enough solder to join all necessary surfaces.

Gold may be pickled in a 10% sulfuric acid pickle or in a special gold pickle of eight parts water to one part nitric acid. This should be used in a Pyrex or porcelain bowl.

Color is *not* a good indicator of heat when soldering gold, for gold shows little color until its melting point is reached, and then it collapses quickly.

White, yellow, and green golds may be either air-cooled or quenched without affecting softness or hardness. Red golds tend to harden on slow cooling. They should be quenched while red hot. These factors are also important when *annealing* gold.

• soldering copper, brass, and bronze

In the soldering of copper, brass, and bronze, the rapid and heavy oxidation of copper presents considerable difficulty. If preheating is not done quickly and carefully, the fluxes will have exhausted their absorbing and protecting abilities and the solder will "freeze." As in silver and gold soldering, all surfaces must be free of oxides or the solder will not melt and flow. Because of heavy oxidation, flux should be applied as thickly as is practical.

Heat should be supplied rapidly to bring the temperature of the metal quickly up to the solder flow point.

Silver solders can be used for copper, brass, or bronze, but the difference in color may be disturbing. Solders somewhat closer in color are called *spelters,* and their use, *brazing.* Spelters are a copper-zinc alloy, 33% copper plus 66% zinc, for an easy-flowing but fairly strong join, but they cannot be overheated because the zinc tends to burn out, leaving roughness and pitting.

Aesthetically and practically, it is poor practice to use lead-based *soft* solders on jewelry. At times, however, it is necessary to do so to prevent problems. In attaching some of the findings and also sometimes

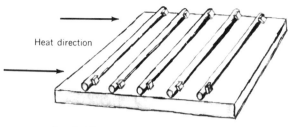

Heat direction

fig. 2-40

in combining brass with silver, soft solder is just about the only practical material to use.

● additional soldering information

1. When soldering near an already soldered vertical join, the join may be protected with a paste of water and yellow ocher, an iron oxide. Powdered rouge, whiting, and clay may be used for the same purpose. The paste on a join "dirties" it and prevents an easy solder flow. Do not depend on this too heavily! An overheated join will collapse *under* the yellow ocher coating at high temperatures.

   Always be very sure that flux and yellow ocher have not combined near the new join. One cancels out the other.

   Yellow ocher is removed when work is pickled, but it may be very stubborn if overheated.

2. Exact placement of shot can be achieved by using a small dapping punch to indent a shallow depression in which the shot can rest. Small shot moves about

easily as the solder melts, due to capillary action.

3. Straight parallels of wire also have the tendency to jump together as solder flows. A slightly curved wire is of course very stable, but if a straight section is needed in a design, four techniques may solve the problem of movement:

   a. Solder can be placed only on one side of each wire, the heat angled to draw the flowing solder only to its own wire. (See Fig. 2–40.)

   b. A clean shallow line can be incised with a burin or scorer and the wire placed into it. (See Fig. 2–41.)

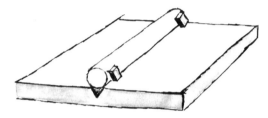

fig. 2-41

   c. On vertical or near-vertical surfaces a few *stitch* marks can be made to supply a brace for the wire. A stitch is a sharp-angled cut made with a burin, which leaves a prong or burr above the surface. These should be small so that they will not show after soldering. (See Fig. 2–42.)

   d. Since a previously melted join does not flow so readily the second time, each wire may be soldered on individually (with pickling and clean-

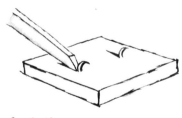

fig. 2-42

ing between each soldering) and thus reduce the chance of wires moving on subsequent solderings.

4. Cupric oxide (the deeply penetrating purple or black oxide in sterling silver or copper-gold alloys) can be prevented by: (a) Dipping the grease-free, warmed work into a saturated solution of boric acid and alcohol. The work is again heated. The heat ignites and burns off the alcohol, leaving the piece covered with a thin borax film. Handled carefully during fluxing and solder application, it may be soldered without the formation of cupric oxide. (b) Heating the work to a light brown color and dipping it into a solution of 6 tbsp. boric acid + 6 tbsp. potassium fluoride to 1 pint (pt.) of water. After removing and drying, the work can be prepared as usual for soldering. Do not inhale the fumes during soldering because potassium fluoride can cause nausea.

When cupric oxides occur, they can be removed in an acid bath. See "Removing Deep Cupric Oxides (Bright Dipping)."

5. Paste fluxes have qualities and disadvantages over liquid fluxes, and this should be taken into consideration. Paste fluxes prevent oxides better and longer during heating, but they tend to become so viscous that solder pieces and parts themselves may float about during heating. During preheating they foam enough to dislodge and displace parts, which may not be noticed until they have melted in the wrong position. After solder-melting heat has been reached, a *borax glass* is formed on the metal. This can be removed only in hot water or pickle.

Liquid fluxes, if used skillfully, work almost as well as paste fluxes, do not foam or bubble excessively, and are easily removed when work is dropped hot into the pickle bath. Their disadvantages, especially for the beginner,

lie in the short fluxing action at high heats. Liquid fluxes exhaust their protective films quickly, and prolonged heating may result in heavy oxidation of metal.

• soldering ferrous metals

Although not often used in handwrought jewelry, iron or the many forms of steel may sometimes need to be soldered.

The soft solders (lead base) can be used on almost all ferrous metals, but they do not make a very strong join. Silver solders, because of rather high flow points, might cause too much annealing of the ferrous metal parts.

Brass wire, usually quite pure, or a special spelter for iron or steel, can be used as a solder with a borax-base flux. Work cannot be pickled in nitric or sulfuric acid solutions because of the strong reaction on ferrous metals. Borax and other fluxing residue can be removed by hot water, and oxides can be removed by abrasion.

• pickling and cleaning

Several times during the soldering of a piece of jewelry, the excess oxides and old flux must be removed before soldering can proceed. Although this can be done by filing, sanding, or wheel bobbing, usually it is achieved by pickling.

PICKLING

The pickle for gold, silver, copper, brass, bronze, and other nonferrous metals is composed of one part sulfuric acid added to ten parts cold water. Remember to *add the acid to the water* while stirring with a glass rod, because water, when added to many acids, results in great chemical heat—even explosion.

Work can be dropped into pickle while

still hot after soldering, or it can be put into a solution while cold. When the pickle is then brought to boiling, the work will be clean of *cuprous oxide.* Cuprous oxide is the surface black or gray oxide, whereas *cupric oxide,* usually red or purple, penetrates deeper and is not removed by sulfuric pickles. See "Removing Deep Cupric Oxides (Bright Dipping)."

Cold work, if left in cold pickle long enough, eventually will be cleaned, but solder joints may also suffer when zinc in solders is dissolved.

Pickle can be stored in a Pyrex jar or in a covered stoneware crock. A sheet-lead vat, large enough for hollow-ware pickling and supplied with a steel plate beneath the bottom, may be mounted on a bench. A Bunsen burner beneath the steel plate supplies heat when hot pickle is needed. Small amounts of pickle are best heated in a copper pan with a handle. Continued use of sulfuric acid will eventually corrode a copper pan, so it is wise to rinse it in water after each use and also to dust it with sodium bicarbonate. It should be rinsed again before use, since the sodium bicarbonate will neutralize the pickle.

Steel or iron of any sort should *never* come in contact with the pickle. Once iron has touched the pickle, a galvanic process deposits copper on all work put into it. Use only copper, nickel, or brass tools to remove work from pickle. Work can be dropped in from a short distance when held in steel tweezers. Remember that pickles are very corrosive, so avoid splashing. Very hot pieces should not be dropped immediately into cold pickle, since the shock of rapid cooling may cause the metal to shatter. Let everything cool to a dull red before immersion.

RINSING

Rinsing must be done after each pickling to prevent corrosion of the metal when heat is again applied. If done carelessly, skin and clothing can be burned by acids. Flush all areas as well as possible. If the work includes pockets and hollows, these must be neutralized by boiling in a solution of one heaping tablespoon of sodium bicarbonate to one pint of water. If this step is neglected, the pickle could continue to corrode over a long period.

If an overlay of two sheets is incompletely soldered, all acid *must* be washed out between them before resoldering, since the acid salts formed during reheating would prevent solder flow.

Usually, after the first or second pickling, the surface of sterling silver work becomes frosty white. This surface is a very thin layer of pure silver left after copper oxides have been pickled away; it can be preserved as it is, or it can be carefully *burnished* to a high polish. Any abrasion or mechanical bobbing will of course quickly remove it.

Where a solid, dark patina of silver sulfide is desired (coloring), the pure silver deposit must be removed by scrubbing with a brush and fine activated pumice. This tends to cover the surface with many fine scratches, but if the pumice is fine enough this should not cause great polishing difficulties later. It is a waste of effort to polish work highly before soldering. If the surface is uniform and free of pits and scratches, polishing is simple after soldering and pickling have been completed.

A pickle for gold is made up of one part nitric acid to eight parts water, and it is used cold.

REMOVING DEEP CUPRIC OXIDES (BRIGHT DIPPING)

After *all* soldering has been completed, the cupric oxides, usually noticeable as a dull red to purple blush or spotting on sterling silver or 14K. golds, should be removed.

When done mechanically by wheel or hand abrasion, fine detail and crispness of design are often lost.

The oxides might be hidden by heating the metal to medium red and quenching in pickle repeatedly. This leaves a thin layer of pure metal on the surface. Great care must be exercised in buffing and polishing in order to avoid breaking through this layer to the oxides still remaining beneath.

A uniform and quite durable finish using the above technique may be developed this way.

1. Polish and clean the work after all soldering is done.
2. Polish with rouge once more to bring out the cupric oxide scale. Clean thoroughly.
3. To develop the cupric oxide scale uniformly throughout the work, heat it to about 1200° F (dull red), and allow it to cool slowly in the air.
4. When cool, pickle the work in hot sulfuric pickle for one minute.
5. The pickle dissolves the surface oxides, leaving a film of fine silver or fine gold.
6. Burnish the matte surface of the piece to a soft luster, using a fine brass brush revolving at 800 rpm with soapy water as a lubricant. (Some craftsmen use stale beer for this purpose.)
7. Repeat the entire process of heating, pickling, and burnishing at least three times to develop a durable surface of fine silver or fine gold.

The best technique for the average jewelry maker is to dip the work into a *bright dip* consisting of 50% nitric acid added to 50% water and used cold.

The work is carefully cleaned by pumice scrubbing and fastened to a length of stainless steel wire. (Copper wire, although used in normal pickling, would soon be dissolved.) The work is dipped into the bright dip for only one or two seconds if the solution is fresh, longer if the solution has been weakened by long use. Almost immediately all areas affected with cupric oxide turn black. Unaffected areas remain a cream to light gray color. If left in the solution too long, gas bubbles quickly form on the work, indicating that the acid is biting into the silver itself. If allowed to continue, the acid etches away solder, dissolves nickel-alloy findings, and leaves the work with a pitted surface that is difficult to remove.

After the cupric oxide has become black, thoroughly rinse the work in water, brush again with pumice until all the black is removed, and redip.

This may have to be repeated once or many times, depending on how often the work was heated and how high the temperatures were. When black cupric oxide no longer develops in the bright dip, and when all surfaces are a uniform light gray, the process is complete.

PICKLING NONSILVER ALLOYS

Alloys with high proportions of copper, such as bronze, brass, and nickel silver, oxidize easily and often heavily during soldering. The black surface oxide (cuprous oxide) readily dissolves in Sparex or in a 10% sulfuric acid solution. The deeper red to purple oxide (cupric oxide) requires stronger removal measures. This is especially critical on nickel silver. After each soldering the object should be pickled in the 50% nitric acid solution from five to fifteen seconds, depending on the age of the pickle. A fine mist of bubbles should rise. Rinse the object thoroughly in water, scrub with pumice and a bristle brush, rinse, and repeat as often as necessary until the metal is oxide-free.

Since the surface of bright-dipped metal is slightly roughened even after careful application, it should be lightly sanded once more before going on to the next step of patination (coloring).

SAFETY FACTORS INVOLVED IN PICKLING

Remember to stand well away from the pickle jar or vat when dropping in hot metal. A fine spray usually results, and this could affect clothing or skin long after the occurrence. Large work should be air-cooled first and then cleaned in hot pickle to avoid splashing.

Acid burns to skin or clothing should be immediately flushed with cold water and neutralized by a liberal dusting of sodium bicarbonate. If a skin burn is extensive, cover it with a thick paste of sodium bicarbonate and water to keep air from the burn. Cover the area lightly with a gauze bandage. Do not use greases or ointments on the burn.

● the application of findings

In most cases it is best to use sterling silver findings on sterling silver jewelry and the identical karat of gold finding for karat gold jewelry. Brass or nickel-alloy findings reduce the quality of the article and also cause soldering and pickling difficulties.

Many people prefer nickel-silver alloy joints and catches since they are stronger and resist heat better than sterling findings. If nickel-silver findings are used, remember to cover them with a small cap of wax when "bright dipping." A strong nitric acid solution quickly dissolves this alloy, so the finding could be ruined.

SOLDERING PIN ASSEMBLIES

The fluxing and heat applications in soldering pin assemblies are identical to ordinary hard soldering except that care should be exercised to prevent overheating of the projecting findings. This would cause the solder to run *into*, not around, the findings.

The safest method to avoid having findings immobilized by solder is to premelt solder in the desired location. In this way the most difficult fusion (melting solder to the piece of jewelry) takes place before the findings are placed in position. The solder should be about the size of the base of the finding. It is false economy to use too little solder since the findings are subjected to considerable strain when the jewelry is worn. (See Fig. 2–43.)

In Fig. 2–44A solder has been placed on the finding location. In Fig. 2–44B solder

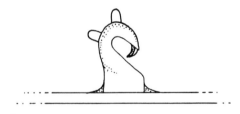

fig. 2–43

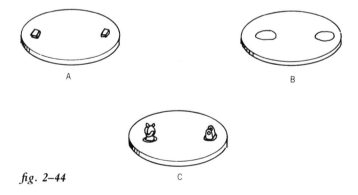

fig. 2–44

has been premelted onto the base piece. In Fig. 2–44C the joint and catch have been placed on the premelted solder. All units should of course be amply fluxed. Once the findings are in place, heating continues until the solder melts for the second time and fuses itself to the base of the findings as well as to the base piece.

To add spring to the pin, keeping it firmly in the catch slot even with the slide open, the joint should be slightly offset so that the pinstem extends behind the catch before it is inserted into the slot. (See Fig. 2–45.)

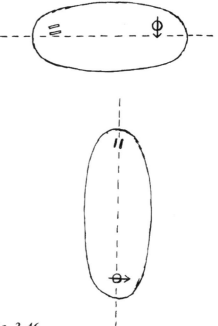

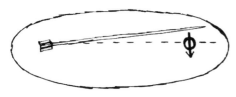

fig. 2–45

fig. 2–46

During the second heating you should see a shiny seam of molten solder around the base of each finding. Too often the flux alone adheres the findings, and during pickling everything falls apart! Be sure that you actually *see* the solder flow correctly.

Make sure that the slide in the pin catch is in the open position before heating. This reduces the chance of stray solder flowing up into the mechanism.

The process of premelting solder can be used for joints on some cuffbacks and on shot as well.

The proper position of the joint and the catch is important for balance and for appearance.

On a brooch worn with the long axis horizontal, the assembly should be placed above a median line so that the brooch will lie flat when worn. The catch should be to the right of the joint. The slot in the catch should face down so that if the slide opens by accident the weight of the brooch

on the pinstem will keep it in the catch. (See Fig. 2–46.)

When a brooch is to be worn vertically, the joint should be at the top, so if the pin disengages from the catch, the weight of the brooch will keep the pin in the cloth. The opening slot on the catch should face to the right.

Use an *easy* silver solder for ordinary work on silver and a *hard* solder on pieces to be enameled.

Soldering karat gold pin assemblies is done by the same method except that the appropriate karat gold solder is used.

Never solder with the pinstem in position. The high heat of soldering will anneal this nickel-copper alloy so much that it will become very soft and bend with the slightest pressure. Aligning the joint and the catch by eye works well. Have a tweezers or pointer in hand while soldering in order to reposition parts that move.

Pinstems are made with a fixed rivet in

place or with a hole through which a rivet is placed in attaching the pin to the joint. In both cases, pressure of some sort is used to spread the ends of the rivet to prevent it from falling out. Special rivet-setting pliers will prevent the possibility of damage caused by rivet setting with a hammer.

Check the length of the pinstem to be used in placing the joint and the catch in position. Do not allow the point of the pinstem to project past the edge of the brooch. This is unsightly and might cause scratches during wear. The point of the pinstem should project no more than ⅛″ past the catch.

Long pinstems can be shortened by clipping and refiling. If held in a ring clamp, the file marks can be removed easily and a sharp point formed by hard burnishing. All file marks must be removed or the point will not penetrate cloth easily.

SOLDERING EARRING BACKS

If hard solder were used in soldering earring backs, the delicate spring wires would become annealed and too soft for safe wear. Soft soldering is therefore necessary, and it is easy to do neatly if the solder is used economically.

Step 1. The spot to which the back is to be applied is touched with a bit of soft solder flux (glycerine and muriatic acid).

Step 2. Flux is also placed into the cup of the earring back.

Step 3. A small piece of soft solder (³⁄₁₆″ long for the average cup) is placed into the cup and melted to fill it by using a *small* soft flame.

Step 4. After allowing the solder to cool for a moment the finding is put in position.

Step 5. With the same small flame, the entire piece is heated only enough to allow the solder to show around the edge of the cup. Excess or prolonged heat will cause the soft solder to eat into the

silver. This will leave a rough depression that is impossible to remove.

Step 6. After the solder has melted, do not immediately cool the work. The solder remains fluid for some time. Cooling may be speeded by dropping water onto the join with your fingertip.

Step 7. After the solder has hardened, the piece can be cooled in water. It is useless to pickle soft soldered work, since the flux coats everything with an acid-proof film.

Step 8. The piece should be thoroughly scrubbed with soap and pumice to remove flux. Even better, it should be boiled out in a sodium bicarbonate solution. If some of the muriatic acid used in the soft solder flux remains around the finding, severe burning of the ear lobe could result.

Step 9. Any soft solder "ghosts" should be removed with a scraper and scotch stone.

Step 10. The work may now be given a patina and finished.

Remember! No hard soldering can be done *after* the work has been soft soldered.

SOLDERING TIE TACKS

The same techniques as for soldering earring backs apply for soldering the post of a tie tack to the back of the designed form. Here again, complete neutralization of acids is necessary to prevent damage to cloth and skin.

The tie tack can be held in position with locking tweezers or with iron binding wire. (See Fig. 2–47.)

FASTENING SPRING RINGS AND JUMP RINGS TO CHAIN

With commercial spring rings and jump rings no soldering is done because high heat would affect the strength of the parts.

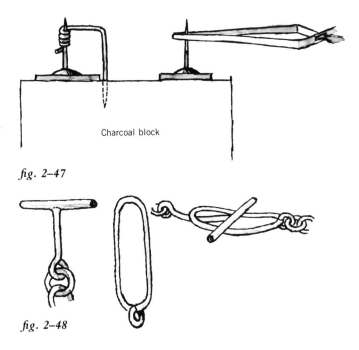

Charcoal block

fig. 2–47

fig. 2–48

On small chains the end links may be enlarged by inserting a pointed scribe into the last link and pushing it into a soft wood block. Using two chain pliers, the small ring on a spring ring is opened by a slight twist, the chain link inserted, and the ring again tightly closed.

Many craftsmen prefer to design their own findings for necklaces. In most cases these are better integrated with the chain design itself. A very basic form, the toggle, can be varied to adapt it to many types of chain. (See Fig. 2–48.)

Many people prefer to use a cord or leather thong in place of a chain for necklaces. Small caps or "cord ends" are commercially available. (See Fig. 2–49.) These are attached to cords or leather thongs of

appropriate thickness by gluing with a good epoxy cement.

Some craftsmen prefer to design and make their own cord endings. One method is to use silver, gold, copper or brass tubing with wire, which can be telescoped into it. (See Fig. 2–50.)

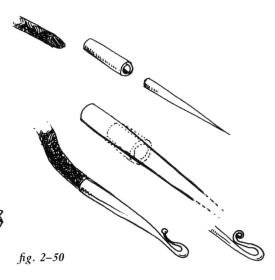

fig. 2–49

fig. 2–50

61

• coloring (oxidation)

The term "oxidation," although often used in describing the planned coloring of silver and other metals, is a misnomer. The metal does not oxidize but rather is affected by several sulfur compounds to form metal sulfides. The term "coloring," which pertains to the chemical color change of many metals in many ways, is more accurate.

The work can be colored only after all soldering, both hard or soft, has been completed and after the work has been thoroughly cleaned of fire oxides by pickling.

The chemicals used vary considerably, but the method of their application is often identical.

The work must be clean and free of oil or grease. With a brush and pumice remove all of the pure silver surface film left on the sterling after pickling. Also remove all copper oxides from other alloys by buffing or "bright dipping." Then immerse the work in the coloring solution until the desired strength of color is reached. By rubbing the surfaces that are easily reached with fine pumice, you can create highlights that will enrich both the form and the textural quality of the work.

It is best to remove the color only from easy-to-reach places, since protected areas free of color will tend to tarnish again quickly. On the other hand, it is not practical to allow color to remain where the friction of use will rub it off.

It is best to use the thumb and fingers for developing highlights. Brushes, emery paper, or steel wool tend to remove too much of the color, as well as scratch areas that are best left dark.

After pumice rubbing, flush out hidden grains of pumice with a sharp jet of water. If allowed to remain, they will contaminate the final polishing medium, causing scratches.

Coloring can be burnished to hold well even on exposed, convex surfaces by tumble-polishing, an industrial process that is used for finishing many pieces at the same time. Areas of the metal textured by sandblasting will also hold color well because the color remains in each small indentation.

COLORING TECHNIQUES FOR SILVER

DARK GRAY

Solution:

Potassium sulfide (liver of sulfur, K_2S)	½″ cube
Water	1 pint

The liver of sulfur dissolves quickly if heated almost to boiling temperature. The dry lump chemical as well as the solution must be kept in dark, airtight bottles to prevent deterioration.

1. Attach a length of silver wire to the cleaned silver piece and dip it completely into the heated—but not boiling—solution.
2. Remove the work quickly and check progress. If the solution is too hot, a heavy coating of silver sulfide is deposited that chips and flakes off when rubbed. The desired application creates a smooth transition from dark areas to light areas while rubbing. If the application is too heavy, it must all be removed by brushing or reheating and pickling. Then it again can be carefully dipped into the solution.
3. If the color is mottled with blues, purples, and greens, dip the work again and again until a uniform gray-black is obtained. Never leave the work in the solution while attending to something else!
4. Quickly rinse off all traces of the solution; otherwise it will continue to affect the metal.
5. Rub off excess sulfide with fine pumice. The pumice should be moist, not wet. Moisten the thumb or forefinger in water, then dip it into the dry pum-

ice before rubbing. If too wet, the pumice runs off the work without effective cutting. Rub in all directions to avoid parallel scratches.

6. Rinse the work thoroughly, dry it completely, and polish—preferably by hand since wheel polishing tends to remove much of the coloring from places where it should remain.
7. A light application of vegetable oil darkens the oxidation considerably. The work should be wiped dry afterward or the oil will catch and hold dust. A very thin film of beeswax dissolved in benzene works well and also protects the polished areas from tarnish for some time.

At times it may be desirable to preserve the beautiful blues, greens, golds, and purples that develop initially on silver, bronze, and copper after the first dipping in liver of sulfur solutions. Unfortunately, these films are thin and transitory. They can easily be worn away during handling, and they will become darker with time. If this colorful film rests in a protected area, the color can be maintained quite well with the application of a beeswax-benzene solution. Be careful to polish this film only with a very soft cloth.

Coloring chain with liver of sulfur or other chemicals is often necessary to reduce its often garish brightness as it comes from the manufacturer. A bright silver chain attached to a more subtly colored pendant calls too much attention to itself, where the pendant should be the focal point of interest.

To color chain, the whole length of chain is simply immersed in the warm coloring solution long enough for a solid color to develop. The spring ring—the small ring with an enclosed, spring-activated slide—is left off until the chain has been both colored and polished, for the pumice removal of excess color would clog the spring, thus ruining its action.

Excess color is removed by rubbing down the length of the chain with a pinch of moist pumice held between the thumb and the first two fingers. Rub down a number of times in both directions to remove an adequate amount of the color.

Do not pull on the chain too hard when removing excess color! Chain links made of thin wire can be pulled out of shape this way.

GOLD COLOR

Solution:

Ammonium sulfide (NH_4S)	1 G.
Water	7 oz.

1. Use the solution cold.
2. Dip the work and remove it when the desired shade is reached. A variety of shades from crimson to purple and brown can be achieved by repeated immersion or by heating the solution.
3. Remove color where desired as in the first formula.

LIGHT GRAY

Solution:

Platinum chloride ($PtCl_4$) in alcohol

1. Work can be dipped or the solution can be painted on.
2. A variety of gray to black values can be obtained by timing the dipping.
3. Finish as in the first formula.

BLUE COLOR

Place the work in a closed steel box with a little pure sulfur (S). Heat together until the silver turns blue. Do not allow the sulfur to touch the silver directly. For an even coloring place a little sulfur in each corner of the box.

DEAD BLACK

Solution:

A concentration of ammonium sulfide (NH_4S) in water used hot.

Use in the same way as the first formula but avoid overapplying.

FRENCH GRAY

Solution:

Platinum chloride
$(Pt + Cl_4)$ 1 G.
Distilled H_2O 500 Gs.

A hot solution brushed on or dipped will produce a different tone than a cold solution.

BLUE BLACK

Solution:

Water and liver of sulfur mixed with a small amount of ammonium chloride.

Dip work until the desired tone is achieved.

GREEN

Solution:

3 parts boiling H_2O + 1 part iodine, added to 3 parts hydrochloric acid.

Mix in a Pyrex or porcelain container. Apply by dipping.

COLORING TECHNIQUES FOR GOLD

BLACK ON 14K. ALLOYS CONTAINING COPPER

Solution:

Liver of sulfur as for silver, but used hot and with the gold heated before dipping.

PURE GOLD COLOR ON KARAT GOLDS

A pure gold surface on karat alloys can be achieved by combining the following in a heated crucible:

Potassium nitrate (KNO_3) 2 parts
Common salt   1 part
Alum   1 part

When heated, this combination becomes fluid. The work is first dipped into an acid solution of one part nitric acid to ten parts water, rinsed in boiling water, and agitated in the crucible solution for a few minutes. After rinsing the work each time in boiling water, it may be dipped again and again until the color of pure gold is obtained. This surface film is thin, so care must be exercised in polishing.

There are commercial gold coloring liquids available that turn the metal blue black. Be sure to read the use directions carefully, since these chemicals are very corrosive.

All the colors of gold (such as pink, antique, yellow, red, white, and green can be achieved by electroplating the entire work or separate areas that are not protected by a resistant film. Although plating is a widespread practice and has been used in one form or another for centuries, it is better to exploit the worked material to its best advantage rather than to disguise it with something else.

COLORING TECHNIQUES FOR COPPER AND BRASS

BROWN COLOR

Solution:

Copper sulfate   1 part
Water   2 parts

Dip work in a hot solution. Prolonged dipping forms a darker brown. For the most even coating it is best to brush the work thoroughly with pumice and water after the first brown coating. Reapplication of the solution develops a more uniform deposit.

BLACK COLOR

Solution:

Barium sulfide or ammonium sulfide used as a hot concentrated solution.
Dip carefully to avoid overapplication.

Copper and metals containing copper develop green and blue surface coatings when long exposed to air or earth containing certain chemicals. Most sculpture using copper, brass, or bronze is given this patina upon completion.

Japanese metal craftsmen have for centuries used patinas on a great variety of alloys and have developed this surface coloring to a rich and highly perfected art. (See Chapter 5.)

Perhaps the richest patina for copper-alloy metals is the green formed by copper nitrate. By changing the formula and the procedure, sage green, olive green, blue green, and a rich dark green can be obtained.

SAGE GREEN

Solution:

Copper nitrate	1½ G.
Water	6 oz.

Use the solution hot and paint it on the chemically clean metal. Several applications may be necessary.

OLIVE GREEN

Solution:

Iron perchloride or	
ammonium chloride	1 part
Water	2 parts

Apply as in the formula for sage green.

DARK GREEN

Solution: A paste is formed of

Copper sulfate	1 part
Zinc chloride	1 part
Water	1 part

Apply the paste to the metal, allowing it to dry completely. Wash off the paste and expose the work to sunlight.

ANTIQUE GREEN FOR BRONZE

Henry Wilson, in his book *Silverwork and Jewellry* (1902), gives this Japanese formula:

Solution:

Copper nitrate	48 grains
Sal-ammonia	
(ammonium chloride)	48 grains
Calcium chloride	20 grains
Copper sulfate	10 grains
Oxalic acid	10 grains
Water	4 fluid oz.

Additional ammonium chloride and copper sulfate create a darker color. A bright green patina results when the copper sulfate and the oxalic acid are omitted.

The clean metal is given a coating of this solution each day for several days. When the desired color is reached, the surface should be brushed with a dry brush. This can be done for several days, after which the color can be fixed by applying a thin, even coat of beeswax.

Beeswax can be brought to brushing consistency by heat or by dissolving it in benzol. The benzol evaporates, leaving a thin film of wax. Since this darkens the patina, an experiment should be made on a scrap of the same alloy before wax application.

Sometimes bronze develops a corrosive "disease" that continues to eat into the healthy metal until it has all disintegrated to a dry, white powder; the beeswax film helps to prevent this.

BLACK PATINA FOR BRONZE

Solution:

Ammonium sulfate	1 part
Water	2 parts

The solution is brushed onto the warmed, clean metal. Allow the surface to dry. Rinse the object in warm water and repeat the brushing with the solution until the desired color is obtained.

BLACK PATINA ON NUGOLD ALLOY

It is difficult to give NuGold a dark patina because it has been created to resist the effects of chemicals.

In order to use a liver of sulfur solution to darken NuGold, the metal must first be given a copper coating. This is done quite easily:

1. Wrap soft iron binding wire loosely around the NuGold object. If contact between object and wire can be achieved on the reverse side, so much the better.
2. The work must be immersed in a standard, *used* sulfuric-acid pickle solution. Dissolved copper oxides should have turned the solution green-blue in color. If a fresh solution is used, it is necessary to heat (red hot) and then quench a piece of copper in the pickle four or five times. Cupric carbonate can also be added to a fresh pickle solution until a blue-green hue develops.
3. In a short time a galvanic plating action deposits a thin film of copper on the NuGold.
4. After thorough rinsing, the work is immersed in a cold, diluted liver of sulfur solution.
5. Remove excess patina with fine pumice. This should expose the NuGold color again. If repeated coloring is required, clean the piece to uniform gold color and repeat the above process from the beginning.

Some bronze alloys and nickel silver are not easily colored with liver of sulfur solutions. However, there are excellent but rather expensive solutions available that work well on them. One solution, "Silvox," uses hydrochloric acid and tellurium dioxide, which reacts very quickly with the copper in the alloys. It takes some practice to learn how long work should be immersed. Quick rinsing is also important.

HEAT COLORING

A rich red-brown can be developed on copper and some bronzes simply by carefully heating the work until the color develops. This works best on highly polished surfaces that have not been washed after rouge polishing. Again, experience is required to know how long and how hot the work must be heated to develop the desired color. Remember, this can be done only after all silver soldering is complete. If the desired color is passed and the metal simply darkens to gray, it must be pickled and repolished before you can try it again.

On pieces such as earrings, which use some soft solder areas, this soldering must be done *after* the coloring!

• polishing by hand and machine

The final basic step in jewelry construction is the surface finishing. Some designs lend themselves best to a highly reflective finish, while others require a matte finish. Generally, forms that are contoured—positives or negatives—can best use the high polish. In forms with contour, the scratches of wear and the dulling through handling are kept to a minimum, since only small portions of the metal present a surface for contact. In addition, the play of reflected light and images over a polished, undulating surface is rich and varied. This quality increases the illusion of volume and lends a fluid softness to an otherwise rigid and resistant metal.

Flat planes form a surface that is easily affected over its entire area by a scratch or by fingerprints. A surface that is already textured by fine lines or fine scratches disguises many of these blemishes.

Jewelry, if worn often, acquires a surface quality of its own in time, which is characteristic and therefore appropriate.

The practice of applying a film of lacquer or plastic to metal is, in the author's estimation, unsound. Such a film protects a high polish only temporarily, and it soon becomes yellowed or spotty. To remove it and apply a new coat is not worth the time. A little rubbing with a rouge-impregnated flannel cloth restores the *metallic* quality much more easily.

Lacquered metal loses the feeling of metal, its temperature, its hardness, and its precision of edge and surface.

Lacquering would be justified only when the work must be displayed for lengths of time in exhibitions. Here it is preferable to having someone who is inexperienced in polishing do the occasional necessary cleaning.

HAND POLISHING

Polishing by hand has the advantage of safety and precision, unless one is experienced in using polishing motors.

If, throughout the construction processes, all scratches, dents, and warping are avoided or corrected, a final high polish is easy to apply by hand.

1. Remove all traces of coarser abrasives (such as fine pumice used in the coloring process). Flush the work under a hard jet of water and boil it in a solution of 1 tbsp. liquid detergent to 1 pt. water. Brush out the dissolved residue with a soft brush.
2. Dry the work thoroughly. Moisture in crevices and along wire appliqué will collect rouge dust that might be difficult to remove later. Blotting the work with cleansing tissue does this efficiently.
3. Examine the surface. If it seems quite dull, it should be buffed with a felt buffing stick to which Lea compound or tripoli has been applied. Boil out the work again as in Step 1 and dry it thoroughly.
4. When dry, the clean metal areas—not those left colored—are buffed with another felt-covered stick to which rouge has been applied. Rub rapidly, applying as much pressure as the work will allow. Constantly change the direction of rubbing to obtain a uniform polish.

5. It is usually at this point that the cupric oxide deposit begins to show itself if it has not already been completely removed by bright dipping. Since a high polish is impossible over such a deposit, it is necessary to go back to this step. Of course the metal must again be recolored, since coloring is also removed in bright dipping.
6. Once the polish is obtained, the work should again be boiled in a detergent and water solution.

A final light buffing with rouge (not enough to deposit dust again) spreads a protecting film of wax (used as a binder in stick rouge) on the metal.

Use a rouge-impregnated flannel cloth to brighten the highlights of a chain. Hold one end of the chain and rub down its length between two layers of cloth with the other hand. Reverse the direction a few times.

Trying to polish areas that are difficult to reach is wasted effort since they will tarnish quickly again in normal use.

Red rouge is used for silver and for red, green, or yellow golds.

White rouge is used for the platinum metals and for white gold.

Black and green rouge are used on all the above metals for a brighter polish.

Areas that are impossible to reach by hand buffing can be polished by burnishing. A straight or curved burnisher is used, applied with pressure and with a lubricant of a soda-free paste soap or light oil. Rouge or diamantine in cake form can be used as an additional fine abrasive while burnishing.

The burnisher should occasionally be polished on a piece of leather during the process. It should be coated with a film of beeswax and wrapped in chamois when not in use.

Small or delicate areas can be polished by trumming with a cord; cake or stick rouge is first rubbed into the cord.

MATTE FINISHES BY HAND

Matte finishes can be obtained without a motor in several ways:

FROSTING

The completed work, after having been pickled and bright dipped, is dropped hot into pickle, thus dissolving the copper oxides at the surface and leaving a light layer of the pure metal. A solution of one part sulfuric acid to eight parts water is used with sterling silver, while the same proportions of nitric acid and water can be used on karat golds containing copper. Several heatings and quenchings may be needed to achieve uniformity, and boiling the work in the pickle each time speeds the process. Of course coloring the metal and consequent highlighting are impossible because the fine film of pure metal would also be removed. A careful hand rubbing with whiting and water will add highlights here and there, but avoid using an abrasive which eventually must be cleaned by scrubbing.

SANDBLASTING

A frosted surface can be given to any metal by blowing at it fine, sharp grit with compressed air. The necessary equipment might be expensive, but a usable blower could be made of a large airbrush unit. Use more than one grit size to reduce clogging of feed pipes. The grit can be Carborundum, stone powder, sand, or quartz.

Areas that must be protected from the abrasive can be painted with hot wax or rubber cement. They can also be masked out with pieces of electrician's plastic tape cut to shape for very precise forms. The grit is either caught or deflected in this way.

By changing grits and air pressure, a considerable variety of surfaces can be obtained. It is important to remember, however, that each grain of sand hitting the metal surface acts like a small hammer

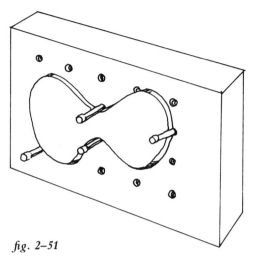

fig. 2–51

blow. Flat pieces especially can be badly warped out of shape unless they are firmly supported during sandblasting. (See Fig. 2–51.) A small flat piece of wood with a grid of nail-sized holes partially drilled through it makes a good holding and supporting device. Nails can be inserted temporarily to hold the work.

STEEL WOOL

The work can be rubbed, always *in one direction only,* with fine steel wool to obtain a bright matte finish. This works well on flat, exposed surfaces and allows partial highlighting of curves and edges. The steel wool should be folded into a compact ball and used with considerable pressure. Steel wool sizes from 1 down to 000 are recommended. If larger than 1, the scratches no longer appear as a fine surface texture; if finer than 000, the matte quality will not be obtained.

MACHINE POLISHING

Polishing to a high finish by machine is a time-saving process, but it requires greater skill and experience than polishing by hand. A motor with an rpm rating of at least 1,750 is necessary for efficient polishing.

The best quality, close-weave canton-flannel wheel should be used. With a 1,750 rpm motor, a wheel of at least 11″ is necessary to obtain the high speed in surface feet needed. If a smaller wheel is used, such as 6″ or 7″ diameter, an rpm of 3,000 is necessary.

The heat of friction, when the correct abrasive (rouge) and the correct speed are used, causes the surface of the work to flow. Minute scratches and pits left by previous operations are thus filled in and smoothed over. Consequently it is important to "cross polish." This means that the work is constantly being moved into a new polishing position during the operation.

In order to *charge* the wheel with rouge effectively, the rouge bar should first be dipped in kerosene. This allows the rouge to penetrate the wheel fibers, and less is blown away during the process.

When rouge cakes on the surface of the work during polishing, it means that too much rouge has been used or that the wheel speed is too slow.

Do not apply excessive pressure—this will not give a better polish but instead will "burn" the metal, causing roughness. A firm, even pressure throughout the operation is sufficient.

When wheel-polishing delicate sheet or wire forms, it is necessary to support the work firmly on a leather-covered board.

It is very dangerous to machine polish chain without safety precautions. The chain should be wrapped firmly around a board with rounded edges. The ends of the chain can be pinned down securely with tacks. On very delicate chain, apply a lighter than usual pressure to prevent stretching the links.

Hold all work with cleansing tissue. Fingerprints can also cause rouge dust to cake on the metal surface.

Hard felt or wood wheels are available in a variety of shapes and sizes for *lap polishing*. This technique is used where the sharpness of angles and edges must be preserved. An occasional reshaping of these wheels is quite simple, using the edge of a file or hacksaw blade while the wheel is in motion. Avoid cutting grooves into the wheel in this manner.

A nylon bristle wheel, using a paste of whiting and water, polishes delicate wire and filigree safely.

MATTE FINISHES BY MACHINE

PUMICE AND MUSLIN BUFF

Remove all blemishes with emery paper or by wheel cutting. Give the work a uniform satin finish using a 6″ muslin wheel revolving at 1,700 rpm and a paste made of pumice and water. Wash work thoroughly and color it. Polish again with the same materials to bring out highlights. Wash and dry the work with a clean, soft cloth.

WIRE BRUSHING

Use a wheel of nickel wire, fiber or nylon bristles, and a lubricating solution mixed with fine pumice. Wheel speeds for this purpose are much slower than for cutting or bright polishing. Speeds of 600 to 1,200 rpm are sufficient. Reversing the direction of a wire wheel now and then prevents bent tips, which will no longer scratch evenly. Use very light pressure, since bent tips flail the surface rather than evenly texturing it. The lubricating solution can be kerosene or soft soap and water, mixed to a milky consistency.

Commercial polishing techniques, such as electropolishing and drum tumbling, are usually not appropriate for use by the hand craftsman because they are designed for volume production.

ELECTROCHEMICAL POLISHING

There is a fairly simple electrochemical polishing system that can easily be set up in a work room.

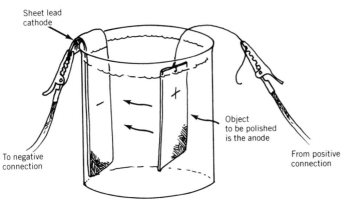

Sheet lead
cathode

To negative
connection

Object
to be polished
is the anode

From positive
connection

fig. 2–52

THE MATERIALS

Solution: 1 part "Electro-Glo 200"*
　　　　 3 parts (by volume) phosphoric
　　　　　　acid, 85% grade
Container: Pyrex beaker
Cathode: Sheet lead
Insulated copper wire, alligator clips
Power Unit:

1. Powerstat Variable Autotrans-
   former, Type 116B (In volts 120, out
   volts 0-140, Amps 30) Source: Superior Electric Company, Bristol,
   Conn.
2. Hoover Electroplater, Allcraft Tool

*Electro-Glo 200 can be purchased from the Electro-
Glo Company, 621 South Kolmar Avenue, Chicago,
Illinois 60624.

and Supply Co.; as well as other
dealers
3. D.C. Ammeter (0–1.5)
   Cat. No. 303 15PL
Sargent Welch Scientific Co., Skokie, Illinois

THE PROCESS

1. Use a current density of **5**–10 volts if
   the solution is agitated; or use 2 volts
   without agitation.
2. Use an amperage formula of ½ to 1
   ampere per square inch of surface on
   the object to be polished.
3. If the Hoover Electroplater is used, the
   negative pole and the 6-volt pole are to
   be used.
   Connect as shown in Fig. 2–52.

3   supplementary metal techniques

Although an imaginative designer can successfully limit himself to the basic construction techniques described in Chapter 2, there soon comes a time when the need for greater expressive latitude becomes felt.

More specialized processes such as forming, repoussé and chasing, and casting, introduce a new dimension to the jewelry form. So far we have found that the basic forms of metal sheets—rigid and usually quite thin—and metal wire lend themselves very well to a two-dimensional, almost graphic development. The translation of a visual idea to a sketch and further into a cutout metal shape is quite direct.

However, to exploit the full richness of metal, its reflective qualities and its malleability, a three-dimensional development may become necessary. This is achieved in two ways. Metal—in its sheet or wire basic form—can be bent or stretched to create a contour of positive or negative shape, or, having been heated to its melting point, it can be cast as a liquid into a designed form in a mold.

These and other techniques will be described in this chapter.

● forming

The same techniques and requirements are used in forming jewelry shapes as are employed in silversmithing, although on a much smaller scale.

By forming, giving contour to flat metal, a depth of dimension is created that results in a very different quality from work using only flat planes. The play of reflections and light over an undulating and highly polished surface lends a sculptural quality that often transcends the small size of the total form.

Although any practical gauge of metal can be formed, the structural strength achieved by forming allows the use of somewhat thinner gauges than necessary for flat designs.

The aesthetic danger in thin gauges lies in the appearance of edges. Thin gauges give a feeling of flimsy lightness, which detracts from the basic solidity of the work. A thickened or reinforced edge has been used by silversmiths for centuries to correct this disadvantage.

In most cases, a really extreme stretching of metal in forming is not necessary

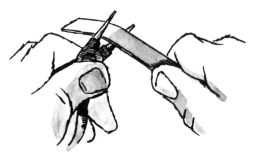

fig. 3–1

in jewelry making, so metal of 18 or 20 gauge, B and S, is sufficient. Forming techniques are basically of two types: bending and depressing. In bending, the flat metal is left in its original thickness throughout by merely twisting or curving it with pliers or over mandrels. (See Fig. 3–1.) It can also be curved by forcing it into half cylindrical grooves or other shapes in wood or steel.

Pliers for bending should have absolutely smooth, polished jaws. Jaws with serrations cause dents and roughness that are difficult to remove.

Do not hold the metal in the jaws tightly. Use a round-nose pliers for curved shapes and a flat or chain pliers for angles. One

jaw is used as a fulcrum around which the metal is carefully bent. The little finger of the pliers-holding hand is used as a brace to maintain the correct opening. This technique prevents denting flat metal as well as wire.

Special bending pliers have one flat jaw and one round or curved jaw. When using such pliers, always keep the flat jaw on the *outside* of the curve, for the sharp edges would mar an inside curve. (See Fig. 3–2.)

Forming by depressing uses punches or hammers to force flat metal gradually into a positive or negative contour so that the total surface is affected. The most direct method, and one in which few hammer marks are left, is to use a preshaped depression in wood or lead into which the metal is hammered, preferably with a punch shaped to fit the depression.

If the depression is carved into a maple or birch block, and if hardwood punches are used, many shapes of the same dimension can be made from the same die. Lead, being softer, loses its shape, and a mold shape can be used only once.

Where greater flexibility is needed—i.e., where a shape becomes complex in contour—the metal is shaped on a lead block with light blows of a hammer. These are the basic steps:

1. Anneal the metal carefully. (See the section on annealing for directions.)
2. At times it is advisable to develop concave and convex forms while the desired final form remains within a larger piece of metal. (Fig. 3–3.) Doing this has the advantage of preventing the often severe edge distortion that can occur if the shape has already been cut out of the larger sheet. Small contoured shapes—too small to hold by hand while hammering—are best done in this manner. The shaped areas can be virtually complete before it becomes necessary to saw them free and

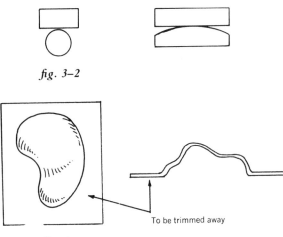
fig. 3–2

To be trimmed away

fig. 3–3

supplementary metal techniques

finish the edges. The final truing of edges and refinement of the surfaces must be done after forming is completed.

3. The sheet is placed on a smooth lead block or over a depression already hammered into the block. A lead block can be made by pouring molten lead into a small pan, such as those used in schools for tempera paint. Oil the inside of the pan lightly so that the lead will not stick. Be sure that there is no water in the pan or the hot lead will spatter. A block that has become too pitted or warped can easily be recast in the same way. Lead can be melted on a gas burner in any iron vessel. Brush the surface slag to one side with a stick of wood just before pouring.

4. The hammer should have a polished dome or sphere at one end and a polished broad surface at the other. A *French chasing hammer* is ideal for this purpose since it is small, light, and easily controlled.

5. Determine which area you want to depress the most. Start hammering with light, evenly weighted blows. Develop the shape slowly, working outward in a tight spiral from a central point. The weight of the hand and the hammer should supply enough downward force. Keep the blows so

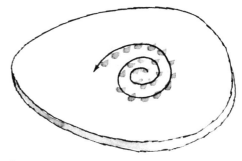

fig. 3–4

close together that one overlaps the other. In this way the growth of the contour will be even in shape and texture. (See Fig. 3–4.)

6. Hammer to within ⅛" of the edge, since this should remain at its original thickness.

7. After the first *course* of hammering, the piece may have become warped out of the desired shape. Before annealing, true the shape by hammering it on a wooden surface with a wood mallet. If edges are to remain on the same plane, they can be forced down by glancing blows of a wood or plastic mallet while the work is held at the edge of the bench. (See Fig. 3–5.)

8. The metal should be annealed after each course if it is to be deeply depressed. Important: When working on a lead block, all flakes and particles

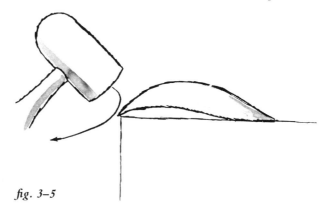

fig. 3–5

of lead *must* be removed before annealing. Even very small amounts of lead eat into and destroy the surface of precious metals when heated above 600° F. Lead can be removed by a thorough rubbing with steel wool or emery paper.

9. Start each new course from the same point and hammer uniformly over the entire depression to avoid hollows and dips. The piece can be angled to accommodate a new direction of hammering, and you will avoid much warping this way.

10. After each course—and before annealing—the edge should be thickened by hammering. (See Fig. 3–6.)

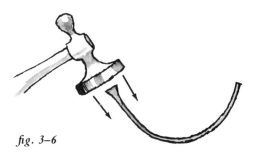

fig. 3–6

If cracks develop along the edge, clean and flux the work and solder the crack with *hard* solder. An untended crack will work deeper into the form with each course.

11. After the basic contour is achieved, the hammer marks must be removed. In most cases they are too raw and out of scale to be used as texture in jewelry. If the blows have been small and uniform, the refinement can be done with files and emery paper. A riffler file can be used on concave areas and a large, flat hand file for the convex surface and the edges. Sanding will remove file marks, or a scotch stone could be ground to shape for stoning concave areas. Finishing can then proceed as usual.

12. On simple forms the hammer blows can be removed by planishing. Use a polished steel form—a *stake*—which best follows the inner contour of the metal shape. Using the flat end of the planishing hammer, work again from the center toward the outside edges in an even, *growing* manner. Use lighter strokes than for forming. A slightly circular glancing blow helps fuse one plane into the other. (See Fig. 3–7.)

fig. 3–7

Overlap each blow and hit *only* where the metal is completely in contact with the stake. This contact can be felt by the solidity of the blow. A blow over air space feels very different.

Avoid thinning the metal more than necessary. Hammered over steel, the metal stretches horizontally and may warp badly if the blows are uneven or too heavy. Avoid planishing to the edge. This should be left as thick as possible.

If done correctly, planishing smoothes away dents on the inside at the same time the outside is refined. A little sanding or cutting on the wheel is all that is necessary to develop a smooth curve, free of facets and indentations.

If possible, the work should not be

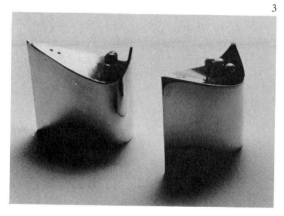

1 Container, Lane Coulter; silver, constructed with fused wire decoration

2 Container, Lane Coulter; silver, constructed with fused wire decoration

3 Salt and pepper shakers, Joe Zeller; silver with black and white pearls

4 Wall sculpture, Joan Slattery; wood, silver, bronze

annealed or soldered again. Planishing has work-hardened the metal to good advantage on thin forms. If soldering must be done, allow the work to air-cool completely and pickle it by boiling or soaking. Do not quench it hot!

13. Sharp angles or changes of direction are possible using the correct stakes. After the desired degrees of contour are formed, the metal can be bent over the slightly rounded edge of a polished, flat anvil stake. Once a bend is started, be sure to place the edge of the stake in the same crease each time. Serious scratches and dents can result if this is done carelessly. (See Fig. 3–8.)

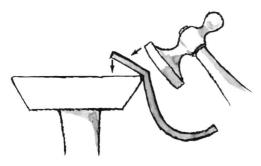

fig. 3–8

Do not try to form the angle with the first hammer blows. Let the new plane develop slowly with light, even, and *parallel* strokes. Edging the hammer forms dents that are almost impossible to remove completely.

• forging

Forging thicker gauges of metal—moving the metal through carefully placed hammer blows—enables the craftsman to design forms that express subtle relationships between thickness and thinness. Edges, especially, become vital elements in the feeling of a work. Narrow connections between one form element and another can be made both delicate and strong if they have been forged and compressed into shape.

Forging, as opposed to forming, compresses metal between a steel supporting surface—sometimes flat, more often convex or concave—and the blows of a steel hammer. Silversmithing *stakes* offer an almost infinite variety of forging supports. Silversmithing hammers, also in a great variety of shapes, are designed to push, compress, or smooth out softer metals.

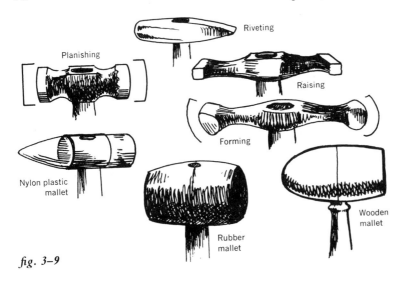

fig. 3–9

supplementary metal techniques

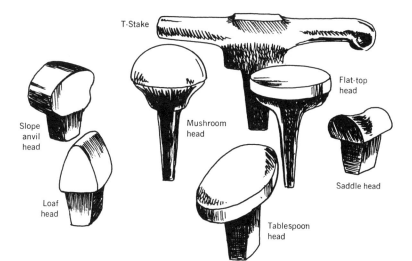

Slope
anvil
head

Loaf
head

T-Stake

Mushroom
head

Tablespoon
head

Flat-top
head

Saddle head

fig. 3–10

fig. 3–11

Keep all hammers, stakes, and anvils polished and free of rust. After use, a light film of oil should always be applied. This film must be wiped off to avoid contaminating the work before annealing.

Metal can be moved and shaped by carefully placed blows of a hammer of the correct shape. A piece of metal can be stretched by blows with a cross-pein hammer. (See Fig. 3–11 and Fig. 3–12.) A thick piece of round, square, or oblong stock can be tapered by rotating it while hammering. (See Fig. 3–13.)

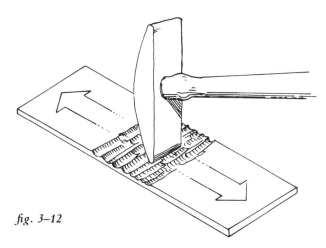

fig. 3–12

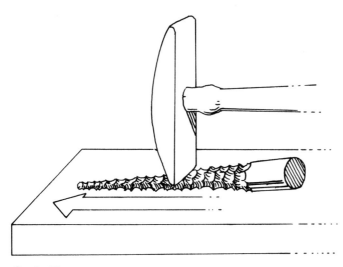

fig. 3–13

A narrow piece can be widened by hitting so that the indents run parallel with the length of the piece, as shown in Fig. 3–14. Often, when flattening round or square wire or rods, the piece bends off to the right or left. This is caused by excessive hammering on one side. To straighten the form out again, apply a similar force in hammering to the opposite edge. (See Fig. 3–15.)

A hammer that leaves no mark on the surface of the metal during planishing can be constructed. A strip of spring steel is formed, as shown in Fig. 3–16A. This is fastened to the hammer with heavy iron wire, first placing a cushion of fine-tex-

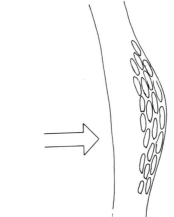

fig. 3–15

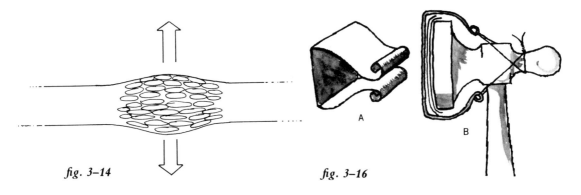

fig. 3–14

fig. 3–16

A

B

supplementary metal techniques

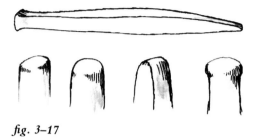

fig. 3–17

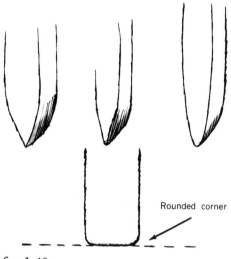

Rounded corner

fig. 3–18

tured cloth and paper over the hammer face. Fasten this buffer tightly enough so that it does not slip about in hammering (Fig. 3–16B).

● repoussé and chasing

Although there is a basic difference between repoussé and chasing, most work that uses repoussé must use chasing as well. Repoussé is simply the forming of a low or high relief by working sheet metal from the back. Chasing consists of defining, delineating, and texturing the surface of sheet metal after repoussé relief is complete, or on flat surfaces alone.

The tools and their uses are very similar. A chasing hammer is used for small work, and any larger hammer with a broad, flat face can be used for large work.

Various punches can be made or purchased. For repoussé, punches in a variety of shapes and diameters are used to force up the metal from behind. These are made of tool steel, are free of pits, and should be highly polished. Most repoussé tools are about 5″ long, are square or rectangular in section, and may be tapered at both ends to give a firmer gripping area in the middle. (See Fig. 3–17.)

Chasing punches are made in a much greater variety of shapes—as many as seventy are commonly used. They fall into several use categories:

Tracers—These are shaped basically like blunted chisels. They may have very thin edges or broad edges, depending on the quality of line they should form. They should be slightly rounded on the corners to prevent cutting the metal. (See Fig. 3–18.)

Curve punches—These are usually used with one blow of the hammer to incise the shape of the tool. They vary from flat semicircles to almost full round. Others form a variety of angular shapes. (See Fig. 3–19.)

fig. 3–19

1 "Bracelet-Form Sculpture,"
Christine K. Johnson; copper,
nickel silver, sterling silver,
Plexiglas, bone, hematite; 3½"
wide. *Photograph by the artist*

2 "Container with Removable
Lid," Christine K. Johnson;
NuGold, nickel silver, sterling,
Bruneau jasper; 4" high.
Photograph by the artist

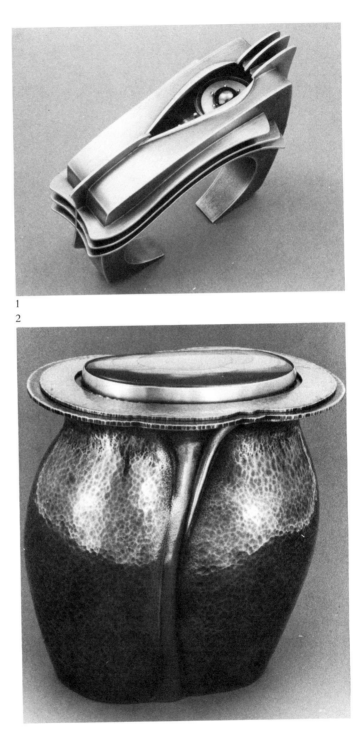

1

2

1

2

3

4

5

6

*All student work was done
by undergraduates at
the University of Illinois*

1 Pendant, Ilene Corman; copper repoussé
2 Pendant; bronze and copper repoussé
3 Pendant, Noreen Nepola; bronze repoussé
4 Pendant, Don Strandell; silver repoussé and wire
5 Pendant; silver, repoussèd and folded
6 Pendant; bronze, folded

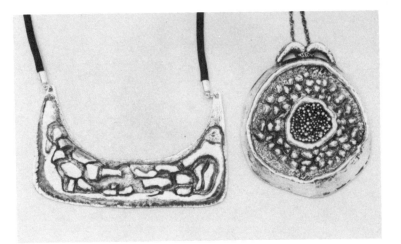

1

2

3

4

1 Pendant, Pat Monigold; silver, repousséd and folded

2 Pendants, Anita Fechter; silver repoussé

3 Pendant; silver, formed and folded

4 Pins, Brian Skelton; silver repoussé

5 Pendant; silver repoussé

6 Container, Barbara Minor; copper repoussé; 6" high

7 Pin; silver repoussé

supplementary metal techniques

5

*All student work was done
by undergraduates at
the University of Illinois*

6

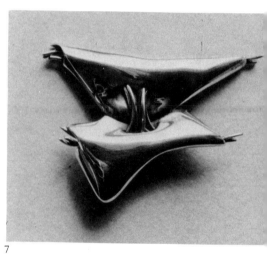

7

83

*All student work was done
by undergraduates at
the University of Illinois*

2

3

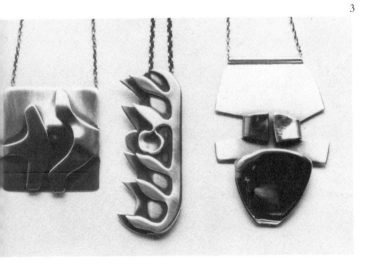

1 Pendant, Ellen Weinstein;
  bronze, repousséd and folded

2 Pendants; repousséd and folded

3 Pendants; silver, repousséd and
  folded

4 Neckpiece; formed silver with
  black pearls

5 Pendant, Sue Parker; brass,
  folded and pierced; 3″ wide

6 Buckle; brass, chased and
  sandblasted; 3¼″ wide

4

5

6

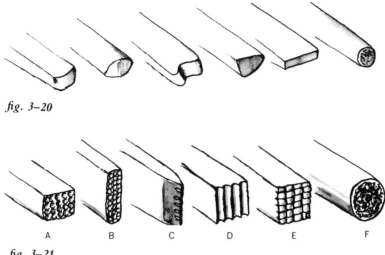

fig. 3-20

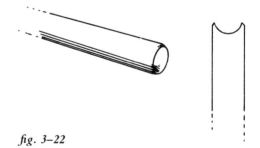

A　　　B　　　C　　　D　　　E　　　F

fig. 3-21

Modeling tools—Flat, convex or concave tipped tools for working the surface smooth or for punching down areas around raised relief. Be sure that the edges of the face are slightly rounded. (See Fig. 3-20.)

Matting and graining tools—These are used to texture a contour or to enrich the background around relief areas. They can have an infinite number of faces, each giving a specific texture indentation.

Fig. 3-21F can be made by filing a notch around a length of square or round tool steel, breaking it off, and using the rough end as the texture surface.

Ring tools—Made of round stock with a hemispherical depression in the tip, these tools must be well tempered and hardened since they may be easily dulled or have their edges broken. They are used to punch circular lines as texture or outline. They can be purchased in several diameters. (See Fig. 3-22.)

The craftsman is seldom able to purchase all of the repoussé and chasing tools he needs. Tools can be made by purchasing forged blanks that need only to have the ends shaped, or you can use square, flat, or round tool steel stock.

The stock should be no thicker than ¼"; stock that is any larger is difficult to hold and control. Taper the rod by forging or filing both ends. This makes it easier to observe the tool mark.

The working face can be filed to shape by using needle files—first a coarse file and then a smooth, worn file—polished with gradually finer degrees of emery cloth or paper. The corners of square or flat stock should be beveled to an octagon shape for easy holding, and the sides can be rough-

fig. 3-22

supplementary metal techniques

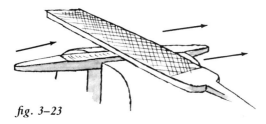

fig. 3–23

fig. 3–25

ened to prevent slipping by *drawing* the flat file along the length at right angles to the stock. (See Fig. 3–23.)

To harden the working face, the last ½" should be heated evenly to a bright red. Quench the tip very quickly in cold water, which should be in a container next to the heating area.

Polish the working face brightly once more and heat it again in a fairly soft flame at a point about 1" from the face. The heat will travel down toward the face, changing the color of the steel. The very moment that the face turns a dark yellow, it must again be quenched.

Many texture faces can be made in soft tool stock, which give a personal and very individual quality to one's work. (See Fig. 3–24.)

THE REPOUSSÉ TECHNIQUE

For repoussé, the work must be held on a surface that is both firm and resilient. A pitch mixture consisting of burgundy pitch, tallow, and plaster of paris with a little linseed oil added has been used for this purpose for centuries. Very good pitch

mixtures can be purchased ready mixed, but some craftsmen prefer to develop their own degrees of hardness or softness.

A basic formula for pitch is:

Burgundy or Swedish pitch	7 parts
Plaster of paris or powdered pumice	10 parts
Tallow or linseed oil	1 part

More linseed oil can be added in winter, when the pitch is cold, and less in summer, when more firmness is needed.

The prepared pitch is heated and poured into a form. The best form for small objects is a heavy, cast-iron hemisphere. This can be stabilized at virtually any angle when set into a holding ring. (See Fig. 3–25.)

For larger forms too wide or too long to fit into a bowl, the pitch can be poured into steel or aluminum pans. However, these are often too light and lack the firmness needed for accurate repoussé and chasing work. It helps to pour molten lead into the pan to the depth of half an inch or so before adding the pitch. The pitch should be poured so that it is higher in the center of the container than at the sides.

Melted pitch can also be poured into a hollow object that needs shaping. It may

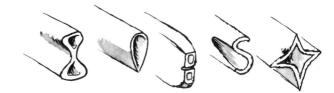

fig. 3–24

then be worked from the outside without danger of excessive denting.

The procedures in repoussé are:

1. Transfer the drawing in reverse to the cleaned reverse side of the metal with pencil or carbon paper. Lightly scratch the lines for permanence.
2. Heat the pitch so that a flat, smooth, bubble-free surface is formed. Do not allow the pitch to burn. The hard ashes of burned pitch give a rough, non-adhesive backing to an area, and this will cause difficulties. If a mound is needed to support a contoured piece, allow the pitch to cool a bit, wet the fingers, and model it to shape. The surface must again be heated to slight flowing before the work is applied.
3. Heat the work slightly and place it on the warmed pitch. Do not press it in too deeply or the pitch will flow over and hide the edges. Press down enough to form an even contact between the metal and the pitch.
4. When the pitch is quite firm, work a little over the edge of the piece to key it in. Allow it to cool completely. A piece can disappear very quickly when hammered into warm pitch!
5. Holding the tool as shown in Fig. 3–26, punch up the high relief gradually. Work from the lowest areas to the highest point, annealing as often as

fig. 3–26

necessary. As soon as the metal resists the blow of the punch, it should be annealed, since continued punching will only loosen the metal from the pitch, warp the entire shape, or even cause the overstretched metal to crack.
6. Removing the work from the pitch surface can be done in several ways: (a) The bottom of the pitch container can be given a sharp blow with a mallet, often dislodging small pieces of work that may already be loose. (b) A tracing tool worked between the metal and the pitch might pry it away with slight pressure. (c) The metal can be warmed by a small flame and lifted off. This is the safest method of removal. Be sure to use a small flame in order to focus heat only on the metal. This will heat the pitch below the piece, allowing the work to be pulled off with a minimum of pitch adhering to it.

When melted and soft, pitch can be wiped off of metal, especially if a cloth soaked in turpentine or benzol is used. It can also be burned off during the annealing process. Make sure that all traces of pitch have turned to white ash. A partially burned area of pitch, if dropped in pickle, will form a hard crust that will be difficult to remove.

7. After annealing and pickling, dry the work and again place it in the pitch, making sure that it is evenly supported over its entire surface.
8. Having observed areas that need greater contour, you can now work these to completion.
9. Remove the work, anneal, pickle, and dry it, and place it on the pitch with the top up for necessary forming or chasing on this surface. Avoid indenting the background more than necessary. Once the areas to remain flat are stretched, it is difficult or im-

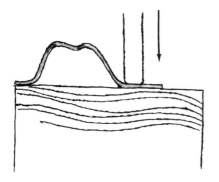

fig. 3–27

possible to flatten what is then excess metal.

10. To flatten or model the background, place the cleaned work on a block of close-grained wood. Use modeling tools to depress and flatten areas adjacent to the raised relief. (See Fig. 3–27.)

A set of *beading* tools, with its graduated series of circle-making punches, can be used to achieve a rich and controlled background texture. (Fig. 3–28.) Much historic Japanese metal work has this kind of background texture. (See Chapter 5.) The controlled, repeated series of indentations form an effective background for raised and polished shapes.

11. The proper action in repoussé is to move the tool slightly with each hammer blow so that one mark flows evenly into the next. Do not lift and replace the tool for each blow. The hammer blows should be light and made as rapidly as possible in order to move the tool evenly.

The modeling tool, as well as other chasing tools, should be held as illustrated in Fig. 3–26. The thumb and first and second fingers hold the tool, while the third and fourth fingers are braced on the working surface.

12. When textured tools are used, each position should be planned and the tool carefully placed in position before the hammer blow is struck. Indiscriminate hammering will result in a poorly defined surface.

13. Blunt relief forms can be sharpened and defined with flat modeling tools. It is necessary to melt pieces of pitch into the back of these areas first to support the metal. (See Fig. 3–29.)

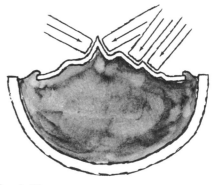

fig. 3–29

It is best to complete all repoussé work while the repousséd area is still within a larger square or rectangle of metal. Again, it is important to mallet down warped edges during the process so that you can tell formed rather than warped shaping. Do this with wood or plastic hammers on a wooden surface. After the repousséd form is completely defined and the surface well

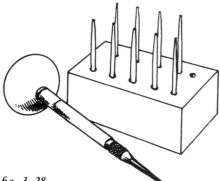
fig. 3–28

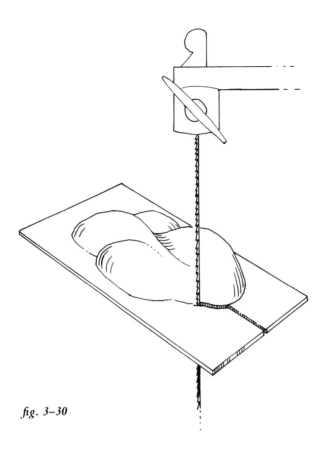

fig. 3–30

refined, the shape can be sawed away from the surrounding excess metal. (See Fig. 3–30.)

14. If done skillfully, the surface created by the tools needs no additional finishing. It is not always necessary or advantageous to remove all tool marks. Often a carefully worked surface texture, usually done with a small, round-ended repoussé tool and light, controlled hammer strokes, results in a nicer and varied surface that enhances the form. The piece by Ilene Corman on page 81 is a good example of such surface treatment. If scratches or dents must be removed, use a riffle file, a scotch stone and water, or a boxwood stick with pumice and oil. Try to an-

ticipate the effect of coloring the metal when determining the proportion of textured to smooth surfaces. Remember that rough or textured areas hold color better and remain darker than smooth areas. If highlights are needed, buff them with a hand buff and tripoli before coloring and polishing.

CHASING

The chasing process uses many of the previous tools and techniques, but instead of using a resilient surface, most chasing is done on a block of hardwood or steel. The work can be pegged down by careful placement of headless nails. For additional safety the nails could be covered with small

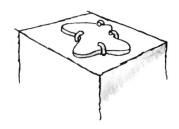

fig. 3–31

lengths of plastic tubing. Since the force of hammering moves both the chasing tool and the metal, these pegs should act as stops rather than as clamps. Often the same position of the pegs can be used for a great variety of shapes and sizes of metal. (See Fig. 3–31.) An alternative method is to use masking tape to hold the metal in position.

The technique of chasing a straight or curved line is as follows:

1. The design is *lightly* scratched onto the metal and the work is fixed to the wood or steel block.
2. Holding the tool as shown in Fig. 3–26, place it at the start of a line. Whereas in modeling or punching the tool is held perpendicular to the work surface, the tool is now angled slightly. You can see this in Fig. 3–32. The correct

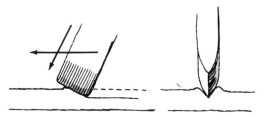

fig. 3–32

angle causes the tool to move toward the worker with each blow. In using the corner rather than the whole edge of a tracing tool, an even line is formed by continuous rapid blows of the chasing hammer. About 140 blows per minute is an average speed. If the total

edge is used, a series of short, jagged depressions results. This is very true when a curve is formed. If well done, no *stitches* should show on the edges or the bottom of the chased line.

The wood block should be heavy enough so that it does not move with each hammer blow. It can be clamped into a vise or to the bench with a C clamp, but this limits easy movement as curves are chased.

Other surfaces suitable for chasing are a steel block, pitch, leather with the rough side up and wetted, and a lead block. All but the first surface cause the chased line to show as an indentation on the back of the piece if it is 16 gauge B and S or thinner.

Chasing on a pitch bowl has the advantage of maintaining the best tool angle while hammering vertically. The bowl, in its ring, is tilted to the best plane. Even gravity seems to help in this. Dip the ends of chasing tools in a light oil for smoother working.

It is difficult to correct a slip with the chasing tool because the metal has been hardened around the line. Careful planishing or burnishing might help. Sometimes a slip can be remedied by engraving over the chased line, but this always leaves a very different effect.

• annealing

Metals can become hardened and brittle through heating, bending, forming, spinning, and hammering. When this occurs, work must stop until the metal has been made soft and malleable again. Every metal has several critical temperature and quenching schedules that result in annealing or softening work-hardened objects.

ANNEALING STERLING SILVER

Maximum annealing of sterling silver is achieved by heating it to 1400°F and quenching it instantly in cold water or pickle. This requires a furnace with a pyrometric control and a trapdoor above the cooling bath.

In the workshop it is more feasible to heat the sterling silver to 1100°F and then quench it as quickly as possible in water or pickle. Be sure to have the cooling liquid next to the annealing position so that no air-cooling occurs before quenching. The metal heated to 1100°F, when viewed in a darkened area, should show a dull red glow only!

Handy Paste Flux can be used as an accurate temperature indicator since it turns to a water-clear glaze at 1100°F. Handy Paste Flux and borax, the oldest known fluxing agent, afford a range of useful temperature indications:

	Handy Paste Flux	Borax
Solid	760°F	1125°F
Semisolid	860°F	1165°F
Viscous	1020°F	1330°F
Thin clear fluid	1100°F	1490°F

ANNEALING GOLDS

Yellow and green golds are heated to 1200°F, or dull red, and can be either air-cooled or quenched.

Red golds, also heated to 1200°F, must be quenched red hot to avoid rehardening. This is especially true of 18 K. red gold.

White golds are best heated to 1400°F, or cherry red, and can be either quenched or air-cooled.

ANNEALING OTHER NONFERROUS METALS

Copper, NuGold, and bronze can be heated to a bright red (about 1400°F) and quickly quenched. Brass, however, must *not* be quenched because it will harden drastically. Aluminum can be annealed at 650° and then quenched.

• heat-hardening precious metals

Sterling silver can be hardened by annealing it and then reheating it to approximately 600°F for fifteen minutes (a good heat-controlled electric furnace is needed for this!). Then it should be allowed to air-cool to room temperature. This will harden sterling silver to about the same degree as a 50% reduction by hammering or rolling. Simply heating sterling silver to 1250°F and allowing it to air-cool will result in a perceptible hardening.

Gold alloys can be hardened by heating the metal to 830°F, cooling it to 490°F for twelve to twenty minutes, and then quenching it quickly in pickle.

• casting

There are many methods for casting metals, and some of them are as primitive and limited today as they were thousands of years ago when they were first developed. The basic principle is the same: Molten metal is poured into a mold.

The earliest examples of molds are of baked clay or soft, porous stone. Even today the Indians of the Southwest use a form of *tufa,* a light volcanic stone, into which a design is carved. The clay mold, with varying details of construction, was developed independently in Africa, the Far East, India, and South and Central America.

In most cases the form to be cast was

supplementary metal techniques

first modeled in wax. The wax was carefully enclosed in clay, with an opening through which it could be melted out and into which the molten metal could be poured. This is the almost universal *cire-perdue* or *lost wax* process.

Around the beginning of this century a method was developed for forcing metal into a mold with great pressure by centrifugal action. This method had its first application in dentistry for the construction of false teeth, bridges, and crowns. Several decades later it was first used in making jewelry; it is now a basic process for the mass production of costume jewelry.

Other industrial applications have led to the development of centrifugal casting as a highly controlled, almost automated technique. Precise and accurate forms in many nonferrous metals and alloys are manufactured in this way for the electronic, aeronautical, automotive, and surgical tool industries. Even before the negligible machine-finishing of the cast objects is done, tolerances of 0.002″ to 0.005″ are possible.

The equipment for such controlled work is costly and extensive. Adequate centrifugal casting equipment for the personal shop, limited as it may be when compared to industrial possibilities, need not be overly expensive. However, it is true that consistent accuracy is sometimes impossible with limited equipment used under other than laboratory conditions.

Personal experience and the adaptation of much that has been learned about mass-production techniques can result in very fine creative forms, and this section is written to supply as much technical information as possible.

Designing an object in wax demands an entirely different concept than working the rigid metal forms of sheet and wire. Wax is a plastic material, easily molded to the changing wishes of the artist. It resists little, is receptive to every pressure or perforation, and can be used to form a replica of any solid form.

Here lies the danger. The temptation to make artificial flowers or insects, for example, exact in every detail, is so great that the majority of commercial jewelry designers fall victim to this ultimately boring ideal. Few artisans in history were able literally to mirror natural objects with tasteful results. Even then fantastic virtuosity of technique was necessary to compensate for the breaking of essential aesthetic laws against the slavish copying of nature.

To work in wax for jewelry one must, in a sense, adopt the sculptor's frame of reference. Since it is possible to alter mass, volume, and surface at will, these elements must be invested with the most sensitive and creative personality.

Although a nature form may be the point of departure, it should be only that and not the ultimate goal. The sophistication and the imaginative variety with which nature forms were interpreted in the lost-wax casting of pre-Columbian civilizations in the Western Hemisphere and on the West Coast of Africa are excellent examples of the design possibilities.

Working in a direction devoid of conscious natural references has equal dangers. The nonobjective form has, in the great majority of cases, the stamp of anonymity. It is much more difficult to infuse individual personality into a *free form* since so many combinations of tensions and planes already have become public domain. To repeat them with only minor changes is to perpetuate a cliché.

To work in the nonobjective idiom one must be well schooled in the perception of change and variety in natural forms. One must have the free will and the imagination to explore the unknown, backed by the knowledge of what has already been done.

1

2

3

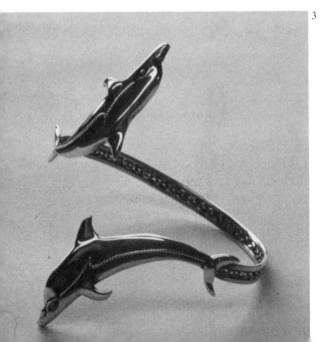

1 Pin and pendant; cast and patinated silver

2 Pin; cast silver and agate; 2″ wide

3 "Dolphins," Ric von Neumann; bracelet, cast and fabricated sterling silver; 2½″ wide

4 Pendant, Sandra Michelau; cast silver, wax poured into embossed plaster

5 Rings, Kay Gonzales; collection of cast silver

4

5

*All student work was done
by undergraduates at
the University of Illinois*

Taken as a whole, jewelry in the *round* rather than a flat plane concept is more effective in casting. The design is limited only by the size and the volume of the casting apparatus. The steps of construction are not too flexible, so they should be followed carefully.

MATERIALS AND EQUIPMENT
WAXES

Although an adequate model can be made of beeswax, wax products have been developed that have a much greater range of plasticity, strength, and stability. Casting waxes consist of combinations of mineral and organic waxes and various gums. These may be carnauba, candelilla, beeswax, and spermaceti (all organic waxes), and paraffin as a mineral wax. The gums are mastic, copal, damar, and resin. The combined ingredients *must* burn away without leaving a residue.

The prepared waxes come in blocks, sheets, rods, and wires of numerous shapes. They vary in hardness and in the temperature at which they become soft or melt. Colors are used as codes for the above properties by the manufacturers, but codes differ from one to another.

Some waxes are so sticky that they cannot be carved or smoothed. These are used for combining forms or, as wires, for spruing. Other waxes are so hard that they become adhesive only when heated to melting. These harder waxes can be softened to modeling temperature by a short immersion in water at 150°F. There are even harder waxes available that may only be carved, scraped, and sanded to shape, rather than being manipulated.

WAX-HANDLING TOOLS

Wax-handling tools can be simple and constructed for a specific purpose. Discarded dental spatulas and other shapes are excellent tools for this purpose. A 5″ length of 14-gauge copper wire, planished and polished to a spatulate tip, may be the only tool needed. A heavy sewing needle fixed into a section of doweling or into a mechanical pencil is ideal where a small local heat application is needed. A thin knife blade, or a set of blades to fix into a common handle, can be used for carving, cutting, and smoothing. Fresh, clean emery paper of No. 1 and No. 3/0 cut can be used for final smoothing. A small piece of well-used chamois leather is also good.

WAX MELTING

Most craftsmen use an alcohol lamp for wax melting, since this burns with a clean flame that is hot enough to heat a tool tip quickly.

Candles and various gas appliances are adequate, but they may incorporate so much carbon soot into the wax that the final cast metal surface will be rough or porous. Avoid a yellow reducing flame for wax working.

Large surfaces can be made smooth by brushing them with a very small flame held at the proper distance from the work. Direct contact often destroys detail, so heat by radiation is best.

A small flame can be formed by attaching the glass tip of a Pyrex eyedropper to a rubber gas hose. Packing the dropper loosely with cotton forms enough back pressure to make a very small flame. (See Fig. 3–33).

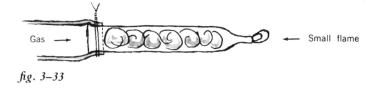

Gas →   ← Small flame

fig. 3–33

SPRUE EQUIPMENT

The completed model must be mounted on a sprue former or base that eventually forms the opening through which molten metal enters the model.

There are many designs of sprue bases available. Perhaps the best and easiest to use is a firm rubber form that allows the steel casting flask to fit into it tightly, eliminating the need to seal gaps and joinings with soft wax or clay. (See Fig. 3-34). If the casting flask (the steel cylinder) fits loosely enough to allow wet casting investment to leak out, some sealing may be needed.

The rubber sprue base comes in a variety of diameters to fit a variety of steel flasks. The flasks also come in a variety of heights—from 1¾″ in diameter and 2½″ high to industrial flasks 6″ to 8″ in diameter and 12″ in height. Keep in mind that a large flask, containing much wax and a great volume of investment, takes much longer to melt out the wax than a smaller flask. The meltout, or burnout, schedule must be adjusted accordingly.

If absolute accuracy is not important, and if expansion or contraction has little bearing on the final outcome, a casting flask can be made from an ordinary tin can. It can be used only once—prolonged heat will distort it too much—but work of an awkward size or shape can be accommodated where a rigid steel flask could not be used. If a tin can flask cannot be found of just the right height, a larger one can be cut down with light, curved metal shears. File or bend down dangerous burrs. It is also best to bind the can with heavy iron wire to prevent as much distortion as possible.

There are times when a model, by its shape and size, must be sprued up in such a way that a cylinder will not work. A thin tin can flask can be bent into a shape to fit it. Before investing the model in the flask, line the flask with sheet or strip asbestos. This takes up excesses of expansion and contraction that could cause fractures in the model area if neglected.

THE INVESTMENT

The investment is a form of plaster designed to set with a hard, very smooth contact with the model. It must be porous enough to allow gases to escape before the incoming molten metal. Above all, it must not break down under prolonged high temperatures or become soft enough to

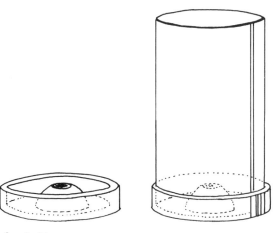

fig. 3–34

crack or crumble with the shock of molten metal forced in by centrifugal or vacuum action.

Plaster of paris alone will not withstand the heat requirements of an investment. The *cristobalite* investment most often used is made up of:

Plaster	Used as a binder
Silica (cristobalite)	High refractory properties
Boric acid	For uniform thermal change in melting out wax. The cooling investment should contract at the same rate as the cooling metal during casting.
Graphite	Used to prevent oxidation

The cristobalite investment has a crushing strength of 1500 lb. per sq. in., strong enough to withstand casting shock if it has been mixed properly and brought to the casting temperature correctly.

VACUUMS AND VIBRATORS

Completely eliminating bubbles from the investment is necessary to prevent having the bubbles cast as metal grains on the surface of the model. Large bubbles can distort or completely destroy delicate wax areas during the wax burnout.

Industrial equipment consists of a vacuum pump and a bell jar. Often the bell-jar bed is mounted on a vibrator, which dislodges bubbles from the model as the vacuum draws them to the surface of the casting investment. Combined investment vacuuming and vacuum-casting machines are available that are compact and uncomplicated and make an ideal small workshop casting unit. (See Fig. 3–35.)

If a special investment vibrator is unavailable, a constant tapping with a rubber mallet on the bench top helps to move

fig. 3–35
Courtesy of Swest, Inc.

stubborn bubbles to the surface. A small, vibrating sanding machine placed correctly will also work well.

THE CASTING MACHINE AND EQUIPMENT

It is best to purchase as large a casting machine as is practical. Although a design can be cast in sections—using a small dental machine, and then soldering the units together—it is far better to cast the total form in one operation.

Machines can be hand driven (as the earliest were), spring activated, or motored and controlled automatically by electricity. Of the three, the spring-activated machine is best for the jeweler, considering its efficiency and cost. (See Fig. 3–36.)

Machines can be designed for very small dental purposes or for larger general use. Often extensions for counterweights and larger crucibles are available.

The machine must be mounted carefully so that it will be perfectly level and free of vibration when in use. Bolting it to a heavy level bench at a 30″ height makes it easy to attend during casting. An unleveled machine loses much of its centrifugal force and the main bearings can be-

fig. 3–36
Courtesy of Swest, Inc.

come seriously damaged. Always oil the main shaft with a light machine oil before and after each casting.

Since most machines rotate on a horizontal axis, a sheet metal barrier should be constructed to prevent accidents due to excess hot metal spinning through the area. If an 8″ slot is left open at the front of the machine, the operator will have easy access to the spring release and, at the moment of release, can step to one side for protection. (See Fig. 3–37A.) A good transparent shield can be built using ¼″ Plexiglas, angle irons, and silicone ce-

ment. Many craftsmen mount the machine in an ash bucket or garbage can, bolted to a solid surface (Fig. 3-37B).

Some machines rotate on a vertical axis and need not be surrounded as carefully by a protective wall in case of spillage.

The casting machine uses counterweights to balance the weight of the metal-filled crucible and the casting flask. This balance must not be ignored, since uneven rotation could cause the molten metal to miss the sprue.

Crucibles of a refractory material are most often designed for use with specific machines. They are shaped to fit the crucible bed and retaining wall and, in most cases, cannot be used with other machines. When casting gold alloys, the crucibles must be kept clean by lining them with moistened strips of heat resistant material and relining them for each new melt. For casting silver it is best to use a heavily fluxed crucible without a heat resistant lining. Keep a separate crucible for gold, one for silver, and one for other metals. Do not allow them to become caked with heavily oxidized flux. Should this happen, the flux can be dissolved in boiling water and the crucibles slowly and completely dried before casting. An ideal melting crucible for use with a vacuum-casting unit is one with an attached heat-resistant handle. This crucible should also be glazed with borax before the first use.

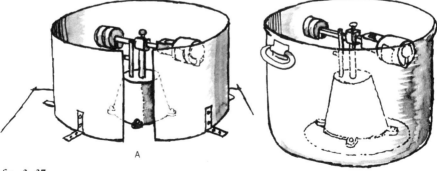

fig. 3–37

A

B

99

BURNOUT EQUIPMENT

Burnout equipment is rather critical, since an excessive reducing atmosphere (excess of combustion in the presence of oxygen) causes carbon and sulfur coatings on the inner mold surfaces. These result in porous, heavily oxidized castings.

The ideal melt-out furnace would be a gas-fired, vented muffle oven. Provision should be made for the gases that are released by burning wax. Wax should not come in contact with the heating elements if the oven is electric.

An accurate pyrometer for visual heat control is an absolute necessity.

A rheostat control or timer for maintaining the correct heat level at any point in the wax burnout is advantageous and time saving. Without it the operator must constantly supervise the schedule, which might take as long as eight hours.

Electric units such as enameling kilns are often used, but deposits on the heating elements caused by casting moisture and burning wax shorten the life of these elements as well as making the entire kiln interior unfit for fine enameling. If such a kiln is used, a *muffle*—a metal or fire-clay chamber—should be used. In addition, some means of venting gases should be arranged. Do not connect the hood di-

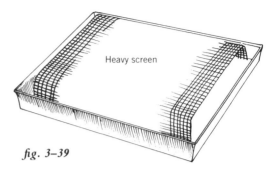

fig. 3–39

rectly to the kiln chimney, for this will draw out most of the heat. There should be at least 10″ of space between the chimney and the hood. (See Fig. 3–38.)

Kilns or ovens without muffles or venting devices can be used if the door is used for ventilation. There is, however, a greater possibility of oxidation of the investment with such equipment.

Trivets of refractory clay or stainless steel can be used to support the flasks above the kiln floor in the burnout. The ideal surface for flasks during the burnout is a heavy steel screen or grid with the edges bent to fit it into a low steel cake pan or cookie sheet. (See Fig. 3–39.) The use of this grid and pan will be explained in the section on "burning out."

A heat resistant glove and long-handled flask tongs are used to remove the hot

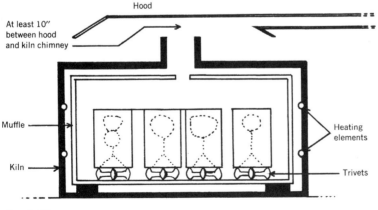

fig. 3–38

supplementary metal techniques

fig. 3–40

flasks. The tongs should be designed to hold the flask securely, since they must be used to place the flask into the cradle on the casting machine or over the vacuuming point during vacuum casting. (See Fig. 3–40.)

MELTING EQUIPMENT

Industry now uses high-frequency melting of metals for casting. The metal is in an enclosed atmosphere, is heated to flowing very rapidly, and remains completely free of oxides. This equipment is costly,

so most craftsmen use torch heating for this purpose.

Whatever the heat source may be—acetylene, oxygen-gas, or air-gas—the most important factor is to use a *reducing* flame in melting the metal. An oxidizing flame will so oxidize the metal that the casting becomes rough and porous.

When using oxygen and gas or gas with compressed air, turn on the gas first, then add enough air or oxygen until the yellow flame has just disappeared. (See Fig. 3–41.)

With acetylene torches, control of the air mixture is not always possible. Try for a flame that retains a tinge of yellow in the first half. An oxidizing flame is a clear blue throughout and is noisier than a reducing flame. A reducing flame may not melt metal so quickly, but it is much safer. Some craftsmen and manufacturers use oxygen/

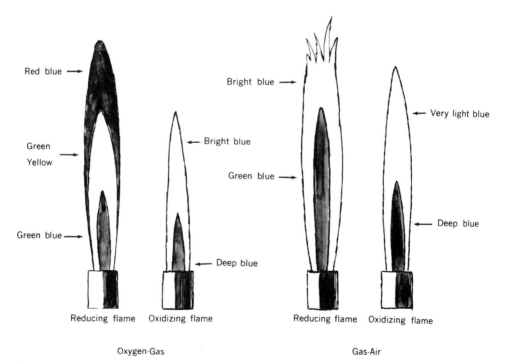

Red blue

Green Yellow

Green blue

Bright blue

Deep blue

Reducing flame Oxidizing flame

Oxygen-Gas

Bright blue

Green blue

Very light blue

Deep blue

Reducing flame Oxidizing flame

Gas-Air

fig. 3–41

101

acetylene torches, which are capable of intense heat. It is best to use a fairly neutral flame and heat the metal as quickly as possible in a preheated crucible—always a good idea anyway—to avoid oxidization as much as possible.

Some authorities recommend melting the metal in a crucible in a muffled melting furnace and transferring it to the heated casting crucible just before the cast is made. This technique has advantages where large amounts of metal are cast. Some machines will take up to 100 troy ounces of silver, which would be impossible to melt in the casting crucible with a torch.

For the jeweler-craftsman, melting the metal—one or two ounces at each casting—in the crucible attached to the machine is perhaps the best technique.

In addition to clean metal, various fluxes must be used. Special fluxes are designed for casting gold, silver, or other metals, and they should be used as directed in each case.

TECHNIQUE OF CENTRIFUGAL CASTING IN SEQUENCE

MAKING THE MODEL

Cold dental waxes can be carved or scraped, but when warmed by handling or hot water they may be modeled to form. Most casting waxes are not adhesive when cold, so the application of small pellets to build up a form is not possible. Special waxes used by sculptors are designed for adhesiveness and should be used with a built-up technique. Dental waxes can be built up in volume by applying drops of melted wax to a surface and allowing each drop to cool before applying the next. Small grains or spheres of wax can be applied to surfaces in this way, but if the drop cools too much before contact, it will break off. It is best to touch the junction of sphere and form with the hot tip of a needle to form a wax weld. Dental wax wires, when warmed slightly, can be curved or rolled to any

wire shape or lightly pressed to a warm surface. Again, a light touch with the needle tip ensures a good contact.

Even the most intricate and detailed textures and linear applications can be cast. The wax can be smoothed by brushing it with a small flame, by rubbing, or by light sanding. The surface of the cast object in metal will be identical to that of the wax, so it is important to finish this as perfectly as possible. Wax can be engraved or textured with engraving tools of various shapes. Repoussé matting tools can be pressed into warm wax for texture.

Extended shapes in wax sheet or wire will cast accurately if they are strong enough to withstand the investment process and if they are sprued carefully.

Carving waxes are very hard and can be drilled (at low speeds), sawed, filed, and sanded. Rubbing surfaces with a soft cloth or with your fingers imparts a smooth finish. Hard carving waxes are ideal for developing sculptural ring forms, which might have modeled areas of other waxes added as needed. The desired finger size can be drilled into a block of carving wax with a special bit called a *wood bit* (Fig. 3–42). These come in a variety of diameters

fig. 3–42

and some can be adjusted. Use as low a speed as the drill press can achieve in order to avoid excessive heating and melting of the wax form.

SPRUING THE MODEL

The sprue should always be attached to the heaviest part of the model. It should also be as short as possible and as thick or thicker than the *thickest* part of the model. It makes no sense to constrict the point of entry of the molten metal. (See Fig. 3–43.)

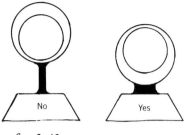

fig. 3–43

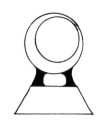

fig. 3–44

If a supplementary sprue is needed, it can be thinner than the main sprue. If one thick sprue is not possible, you will have to combine several. (See Fig. 3–44.) The total of these sprues should be at least as thick as is proper for a single sprue.

Placement of the sprue is mostly determined by the shape of the wax form. If the wax form has both thin and thick areas, supplementary spruing is necessary to avoid porosity. (See Fig. 3–45.) If part of a model is much *thicker* than the rest, extra spruing is also necessary. (See Fig. 3–46.)

SPRUING WAXES

Any wax will do in an emergency, but the

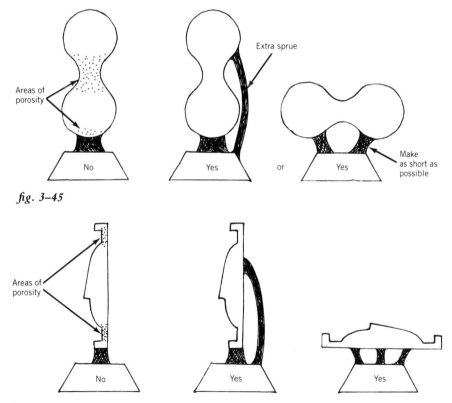

fig. 3–45

fig. 3–46

103

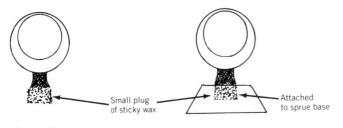

fig. 3–47

best is a special sprue wax, which will melt before most model waxes, clearing the sprue opening for rapid and efficient burn-out.

Use a "sticky" wax for attaching sprues to models and to the sprue base. These waxes are always somewhat flexible, and there is less chance (as with a hard wax) to have the model break away from the sprue former during investment and vacuuming. Professionals keep a small pot of melted sticky-wax on hand for dipping the sprue ends before attaching them to the model and sprue former.

As a general rule, small-diameter wax sprues are used only when mounting delicate filigree pieces.

WEIGHING THE MODEL

The model should be weighed before its final attachment to the sprue base. This should be done with the sprue and a small sticky-wax plug attached (which will be used to attach the sprue base after weighing). (See Fig. 3–47.) For casting silver, bronze, or brass, multiply the wax weight (including sprue and plug) by 9. For gold, multiply by 14.

The capacity of the casting crucible determines the ultimate mass of the wax model. Always plan to use more metal than necessary to fill the mold only, since a well-filled sprue opening assures a solid and complete casting.

It is possible to mount two or more models on one sprue or on several sprues coming from a common former. Again,

the capacity of the crucible is the determining factor.

If many reproductions of an original model are required, a vulcanized rubber or metal mold can be made into which the melted wax is injected. See page 120 for an explanation of this process.

DEBUBBLIZING

After being cleaned with a soft brush and cool water, the model must be coated with a solution to relieve the surface tension of the wax. The investment would not hold to the wax firmly if this were not done.

A mixture of green soap and hydrogen peroxide or one of the prepared *debubblizers* can be used for this purpose. Apply the solution carefully to avoid the formation of bubbles. Flowing it on from a soft brush is better than brushing it on with a scrubbing action.

The entire model can also be dipped several times into a container of debubblizing solution.

After application, gently shake or blow the wax completely dry. A very thin film of debubblizing solution remains over which the investment can be painted. Commercial solutions also control and limit excessive mold expansion during wax elimination.

Important! Do not use debubblizers or tincture of green soap on models to be *vacuumed* after investing. These solutions create *more* bubbles during vacuuming. Instead, special films for vacuum-bubble removal are applied by painting or spraying. Be sure to blow off excess solutions so that pools of liquid in recesses do not change the very critical investment-to-water proportions! Also be sure to reapply solutions after handling the model.

PAINTING THE MODEL

If no vacuum unit is used, the model must be painted carefully with investment to avoid air bubbles forming on the surface of the wax. It is very important to use exactly the same water-to-investment proportions and the same mixing procedure and time (nine minutes) in the preparation of prepainting investment as for final flask filling. If this is not done carefully, the investment next to the wax surface can break down during burnout or during casting.

Vibrate the air bubbles out and flow the investment onto the model, making sure that complex areas are filled and free of bubbles. Build up a layer ⅛" to ¼" thick all around, but do not allow the investment to set completely before filling the flask.

PREPARING THE CASTING FLASK

1. Line the interior of the casting flask with thin sheets or strips of heatproof asbestos substitute. If moist (not soaking), they will adhere to the flask tightly. Cut the strips to just overlap at the ends when in place. The lining should come to no more than ¼" to ⅛" from the top and the bottom of the flask. This offset allows the investment to key itself to the flask itself; otherwise the whole casting might slip out of the flask during the burnout process. The lining takes up expansion during the hardening and heating of the investment.
2. Dry the heatproof material as well as possible. A soaked lining will add too much water to the investment, causing it to crumble.

3. Place the flask over the model and seat it in the sprue base. Use plasticene or soft wax to seal the flask to the base if necessary.

MIXING AND POURING THE INVESTMENT

The cristobalite investments must be mixed according to rigid controls to conform to desired expansion and contraction tables. Exact weight, length of mixing, and vacuuming and setting times are all very important. (See Tables 3–1 and 3–2 for investment-to-water ratios by weight.) There will be 9 minutes of working time before the investment hardens. Always use a timer!

The procedure for mixing Kerr Satin Cast 20, for example:

To mix investment:

1. Place the correct weight of water (at room temperature) in a rubber mixing bowl. Sift in the correct weight of investment.
2. Stir thoroughly for three or four minutes. Use a spoon or a spatula. An electric beater will whip too much air into the mixture.
3. Vacuum air out of the slurry.
   a. Bubbles will rise to the surface.
   b. Mixture will rise up in a foam and then "break."
   c. After breaking, release the pressure slowly to prevent blowing the mixing bowl over with the force of incoming air.
4. Pour the slurry into the flask. Tip the flask if necessary so that the slurry covers the model from the bottom up. Pouring slurry over the top of the model often traps air in delicate passages. This causes casting blemishes. Slurry should come to within ½" of the top of the flask. Be sure that the top of the model is eventually covered by between ¼" and ½" of investment. Many craftsmen tape a stiff paper collar around the top of the flask to prevent splashing during the next vacuuming.

TABLE 3–1
DETERMINING INVESTMENT AND WATER REQUIREMENTS
FOR VARIOUS SIZE FLASKS TO BE USED WITH SATIN CAST 20 INVESTMENT

This chart provides a quick reference, showing at a glance the correct amounts of investment and water required for flasks of different dimensions. This chart was developed specifically for use with Kerr Satin Cast 20 investment.

TOP FIGURE: INVESTMENT
LOWER FIGURE: WATER

| | | Height of Flask | | | | | | | |
		2"	2½"	3"	3½"	4"	5"	6"	7"
Diameter of Flask	2"	5 oz. 57 cc	6 oz. 68 cc	7.5 oz. 85 cc	9 oz. 102 cc	10 oz. 114 cc			
	2½"	8 oz. 91 cc	10 oz. 114 cc	12 oz. 136 cc	14 oz. 160 cc	16 oz. 182 cc	20 oz. 228 cc		
	3"	12 oz. 136 cc	15 oz. 170 cc	18 oz. 205 cc	21 oz. 240 cc	1½ lb. 274 cc	30 oz. 340 cc	32 oz. 410 cc	2¾ lb. 500 cc
	3½"	1 lb. 182 cc	1¼ lb. 228 cc	1½ lb. 274 cc	1¾ lb. 320 cc	2 lb. 364 cc	2½ lb. 456 cc	3 lb. 548 cc	3½ lb. 640 cc
	4"	18 oz. 205 cc	23 oz. 262 cc	27 oz. 308 cc	2 lb. 364 cc	2¼ lb. 410 cc	3 lb. 546 cc	3½ lb. 637 cc	4 lb. 728 cc
	5"					3¾ lb. 682 cc	4¾ lb. 864 cc	5½ lb. 1000cc	6½ lb. 1182cc

Satin Cast 20 investment has a water/powder ratio of 40/100 and a working time of 9 minutes.

To determine the number of pounds of investment needed to fill any particular flask, divide the cubic inch content of the flask by 20.

To determine flask content in cu. ins.: For volume of round flask = 0.7854 × dia. × height;
For volume of square flask = width × length × height.

Source: Swest, Inc.

It is not necessary to fill the flask to the very top; fill it just so that the model has ¼" to ½" of investment covering it. Partial filling is sometimes the only way to accommodate the preferred short sprue in an available flask.

For vacuum-assisted casting there *must* be a ¹⁄₁₆" to ⅛" gap between the top of the investment and the top of the flask. (See Fig. 3-48.) Given a choice, it is probably better to use a shorter flask rather than partially filling a flask.

5. Five minutes will have passed by now. Don't forget to use a timer!
6. Carefully place the flask in the vacuuming area and vacuum again.
7. Use any leftover slurry to top up the flask, although this is not always necessary. Nine minutes should now have passed since mixing began.
8. Allow at least two hours for a complete setting time. If you must wait longer before starting the burnout, wrap the flask in a wet paper towel and place it in a sealed plastic bag. Before begin-

TABLE 3–2
RECOMMENDED PROPORTIONING FOR KERR INVESTMENT
SATIN CAST 20

Weight of Investment in Pounds	Heavy Casting 38/100		Regular Casting 40/100		Extra-Fine Casting 42/100	
	Ounces (cc.)	Yield Approx. (cu. in.)	Ounces (cc.)	Yield Approx. (cu. in.)	Ounces (cc.)	Yield Approx. (cu. in.)
1	6 (173)	21.3	6.4 (182)	21.9	6.72 (191)	22.5
5	30.4 (862)	106	32 (908)	110	33.6 (953)	112
10	60.8 (1725)	213	64 (1816)	219	67.2 (1907)	225
15	91.2 (2588)	320	96 (2724)	328	100.8 (2860)	338
20	121.6 (3450)	426	128 (3632)	438	134.4 (3814)	450
25	152 (4312)	532	160 (4540)	548	168 (4767)	562

NOTE: To determine flask content in cubic inches: volume of round flask = 0.7854 × dia.² × height; volume of square flask = width × length × height.

Source: Swest, Inc.

ning the burnout again, dip the flask in water for ten to fifteen seconds and then wait one or two hours before burning out.

A number of suggestions follow for setting up models and for increasing gas elimination from the flask during vacuum-assisted casting.

To help evacuate gases quickly during vacuum casting, it is a good idea to construct several side channels of wax or of lubricated ¼″ metal rod. (See Fig. 3–49). These channels allow gases to be vacuumed out ahead of the molten metal, not only through the investment at the down end of the flask, but through the sides as well. There are perforated casting flasks available that also perform this function. The perforations are taped closed before

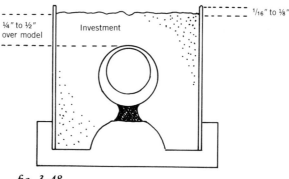

fig. 3–48

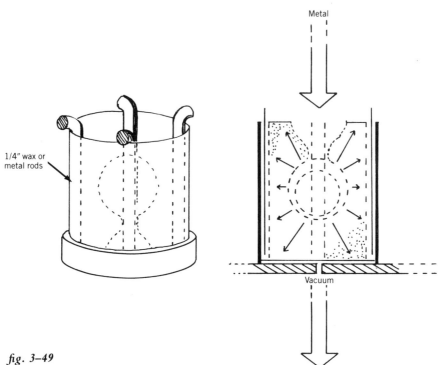

1/4" wax or
metal rods

Metal

Vacuum

fig. 3–49

pouring the investment and eliminating
bubbles. Another gas elimination technique which results in clean, smooth casting is illustrated in Fig. 3–50.

Building a ball or reservoir at the top
of a sprue "tree" helps collect much of the
flux and other debris that can occur in a
casting. (See Fig. 3–51.)

8 to 10-gauge
wax wire

Collection of
flux and oxides
after casting

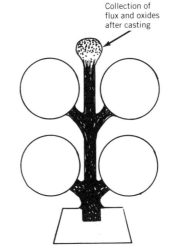

fig. 3–50

fig. 3–51

supplementary metal techniques

Heavy screen or grid

Metal tray

fig. 3–52

BURNOUT (WAX ELIMINATION)

The flask, or flasks, are placed sprue opening down into a preheated 300°F burnout kiln. By the time 350° has been reached, much of the wax will have melted out. This wax must be collected and removed before it bursts into flame. Smoke from burning wax can form deposits on electric heating elements that begin to arc and cause short circuits. Smoke also damages kiln linings in time.

A metal tray the size of the kiln bottom is covered with a sturdy steel or iron screen or grid. The flasks are placed on the screen, sprue opening down, to keep them above the tray. (See Fig. 3–52.)

Flasks should be stacked in such a way that melting wax drips between, not *into*, the flasks below. (See Fig. 3–53.)

Before the wax collected in the pan begins to smoke, remove the pan and replace the flasks with the sprue opening facing up. Be careful that no loose investment from the upper flasks falls into the sprue openings in the lower flask.

The burnout cycle in Table 3–3 deals with variety of flask sizes and wax model types.

It is necessary to run a check on the pyrometric dial of the kiln periodically. Don't trust the dial alone.

TIPS

Do not cast with the mold temperature too high for the type of metal being cast. (See Table 3–4 for melting temperatures.) Be sure that the *flask* is at the proper casting temperature, not just the kiln. The best way to assure this is to keep the kiln

fig. 3–53

109

TABLE 3–3
WAX ELIMINATION/SUGGESTED BURNOUT CYCLES

The following burnout cycles are recommended for furnaces equipped with the Swest Therminder or furnace to be controlled manually.

Select proper burnout cycle according to size of flasks.

5-Hour Cycle	8-Hour Cycle	12-Hour Cycle
For flasks up to 2½″ × 2½″ preheat furnace to 300°F.	For flasks up to 3½″ × 4″ preheat furnace to 300°F.	For flasks up to 4″ × 8″ preheat furnace to 300°F.
1 hour— 300°F.	2 hour— 300°F.	2 hour— 300°F.
1 hour— 700°F.	2 hour— 700°F.	2 hour— 600°F.
2 hour—1350°F.	3 hour—1350°F.	2 hour— 900°F.
1 hour—See note	1 hour—See note	4 hour—1350°F.
		2 hour—See note

NOTE: During last hour the temperature must be adjusted so that flasks are at correct temperature for casting.

EXAMPLE: Mold temperature for women's ring or items of lacey or intricate design should be 900°F. to 1000°F. Mold temperature for men's ring or items of relative heavier design should be 700°F. to 900°F.

Source: Swest, Inc.

TABLE 3–4
MELTING TEMPERATURES

Alloy	Melting Temperature (°F.)	Ratio of Metal to Wax	Flask Casting Temperature (°F.)
SILVER	1762	10–1	800
GOLD 10K Y	1665	14–1	950
GOLD 14K Y	1615	14–1	900
GOLD 10K W	1925	14–1	1000
GOLD 14K W	1825	14–1	950
B. COPPER	1800	10–1	800
PLATINUM	2900	21–1	1400
ALUMINUM	1280	2½–1	400
HERCULOY	1705	10–1	900
BRON-WHITE	1575	9–1	900
SILICON BRONZE	1778	10–1	900

NOTE: 1. Casting temperature should be approximately 100 to 150° above melting temperature. 2. Casting temperature will vary slightly depending upon particular alloy used. 3. Flask temperature will vary depending upon size of casting. 4. Pure silver melts at 1762° Fahrenheit. 5. Pure gold melts at 1945° Fahrenheit.

Source: Swest, Inc.

at the correct casting temperature for an hour or so before casting (refer to Table 3–3). Keep in mind that a large model requires a lower casting temperature than a model with a delicate, filigree-like pattern.

Generally it is not advisable to allow molds to cool to room temperature and then reheat them at another time. Expansion and contraction of the investment tends to break it down and fine detail and finish can be lost. It is best to cast as soon as possible after the correct flask temperature is reached.

If a casting turns out to be incomplete,

supplementary metal techniques

even though the metal was thoroughly heated and molten, the mold temperature was probably too low. The metal "froze" before it could reach all parts of the design.

If the casting was complete but roughened or porous, the mold temperature was probably too high, although other factors such as dirty metal might also cause this. If the metal remains liquid too long once it is in the mold, it damages surfaces and contracts too greatly upon cooling.

Before the model is invested, the correct amount of metal for the casting should have been determined. Remember! The weight of the wax model must include the sprue and the wax plug to which it is attached. Multiply the weight of the wax by 9 when casting sterling or fine silver, bronze, brass, and copper. Multiply by 14 when casting gold, whether fine gold or karat gold. This formula assures the necessary sprue button that supplies the reservoir of metal needed during the quick cooling of the casting.

The metal, usually scrap or in the form of casting pellets, must be as free of oxides and grease or oil as possible. Heating the metal to a red glow and then boiling it in pickle assures clean surfaces. Never use scrap containing solder of any sort. Sprue buttons from previous castings should be completely clean of old investment and also boiled in pickle. It is a good practice to "feed" used casting metal (silver or gold) by adding 50% fresh, uncast metal each time. Much pitting and deep cupric oxide staining can be prevented in this manner.

CASTING WITH A CENTRIFUGAL CASTING MACHINE

Before the burnout begins, the machine must be balanced with the casting flask in the machine cradle. Most machines have counterweights that can be locked into place after balancing.

If the machine is spring driven, it can be wound at this time. Manufacturers' directions vary, but generally most ma-

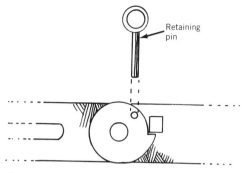

fig. 3–54

chines require four windings to ensure solid casts. The Kerr Centrifico machine directions recommend four windings for small to medium pieces and five windings for heavy flasks containing large pieces such as heavy buckles.

Some machines might require some modification to improve their effectiveness. It is easier to balance the machine with the flask in place if the arm holding the counterweight, the crucible and the cradle with flask, is in a straight line. Many machines are hinged to allow an extra swing at the moment of release. To ensure that all is in a straight line while balancing the arm, drill a hole through both parts of the hinge while all is aligned and a small removable pin can be dropped in to hold it while balancing. The pin, of course, is removed after balancing and before casting. (See Fig. 3–54.)

Some craftspeople feel that a totally free-swinging casting arm creates too much side force, which can splash molten metal out of the crucible while spinning. To correct this they suggest placing a "stop" at a point in the hinge so that the arm and the flask can form no *more* than a 45° angle. (See Fig. 3–55.)

After the required windings, a retaining pin is put into place to hold the spring-wound arm in tension until the proper moment, just as the metal reaches the fully molten state in the crucible.

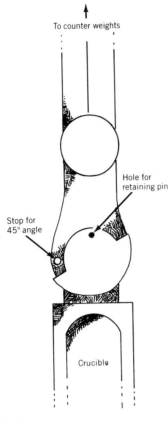

To counter weights

Hole for
retaining pin

Stop for
45° angle

Crucible

fig. 3–55

When the flask has reached the recommended *casting* temperature (not the height of the burnout temperature!), the crucible in the casting machine should be preheated. Sprinkle enough casting flux into the heated crucible to glaze the interior. The preheating should be done with a fairly neutral flame. If oxygen/acetylene is used, a #5 tip with 40 pounds oxygen pressure and 5 pounds acetylene pressure is recommended.

It is best to use separate crucibles for silver and gold. (Many casters line a gold crucible with thin, moistened sheets of heat resistant material before each casting. This heat resistant lining should also be pre-

glazed with flux). A third crucible is used for bronze, brass, or copper.

The crucible should be glowing red when the casting flask is removed from the burnout oven. Remove it quickly and carefully place it in the flask cradle of the casting machine. Make sure that the tip of the crucible fits into the sprue opening in the flask and that both are pushed together firmly. Adjustable cradles accommodate most flask shapes. This should be checked before the wax burnout begins.

With the flask in position, fill the heated crucible with the metal. Some craftsmen prefer to add the metal piece by piece as melting progresses because it takes less time. This would depend on the type of heat used.

The metal *must not be overheated!* It should be melted enough to move easily if the arm is shaken gently, but it should never *spin* or boil.

Keep the torch on the metal until after the release bar has dropped and the machine has started its spin. Never release the arm while the molten metal is moving. Allow any rocking to stop, and *then* let the casting arm flow from your hand in a follow-through motion. Make sure the retaining pin has been released! Allow the machine to stop its spin by itself. This ensures pressure long enough for the metal to cool in place.

Remove the flask and set it aside to cool before quenching.

Silver castings should cool in the flask for six minutes and most golds should cool for twelve minutes.

The hot flask can now be completely immersed in cold water. The reaction causes the plaster to disintegrate, allowing the casting to be removed easily. If the investment is bone white on the ends of the flask after the wax elimination but a dirty yellow-gray or black around the casting itself, it means that the wax was not completely burned out. This causes surface po-

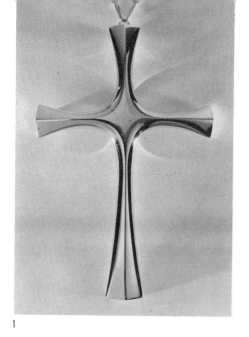

The jewelry of Ronald Hayes Pearson reflects two aspects of contemporary jewelry to perfection. First, he is a consummate craftsman. His forms, whether cast or constructed, are examples of complete control of the medium. Surface qualities enhance form, and details of function have been perfectly analyzed.

Secondly, his work reflects today's concern for form; not form as it translates a recognizable object, but form which has been invented by a mind aware of the effectiveness of contour, tension, and reflection. In each piece the innate quality of precious metal is exploited to its fullest and the result is jewelry of great personality and dignity. Photographs by Ronald Hayes Pearson

1 Pectoral cross and chain; 14K yellow gold; commissioned for Dr. Cadigan, Episcopal Bishop of Missouri; 1959

2 Silver bracelet; 1958

3 Silver necklace; 1954

rosity, and it could be so deep that removal is impossible.

The casting must be pickled in the standard 10% sulfuric acid solution, preferably by boiling. After rinsing and drying, the sprue or sprues can be nipped or sawed off. A successful cast will require little surface treatment before coloring and polishing.

These are sources of the common casting failures and their causes:

Rough surfaces and *fins:*
1. Too much water in the investment.
2. Dirt or drops of debubblizer or water on the wax.
3. Incompletely mixed investment.
4. Wax elimination too rapid. Steam causes investment to fracture and explode.
5. Casting metal too hot.
6. Flask heated too high.
7. Vibration for bubble removal too strong or too prolonged.
8. Incoming metal striking a flat surface.
9. Model too close to edges or top of flask.

Pitted castings:
1. Metal not completely melted.
2. Too much flux.
3. Dirty metal.
4. Sprues too large or too small or incorrectly placed for rapid entry of metal into the mold.
5. Broken fragments of investment formed during burnout or casting.
6. Heavily oxidized metal due to incorrect melting and fluxing.

Bubbles of metal on the casting:
1. Air in the investment.
2. Air trapped during the painting of the model.
3. Water or debubblizer drops on wax during painting.

Oxidized castings (if not excessive, slight oxidation is normal on all alloys):
1. Incomplete wax elimination.

2. Metal overheated in the casting crucible.

Incomplete castings:
1. Sprues too small.
2. Not enough sprues to extended areas.
3. Too much of the model below the line of contact of sprue with the model.
4. Too much investment above the top of the model.
5. Flask too cold during casting.
6. Metal not hot enough during casting.
7. Too little casting pressure.
8. Not enough metal.

Cracks in the casting:
1. Quenching while too hot (see cooling schedule).

VACUUM-ASSISTED CASTING

Vacuum-assisted casting uses a strong vacuum to pull molten metal into and throughout a mold. This is an unusually safe process because hot metal cannot be sprayed about through accident or clumsiness.

Vacuum-assisted casting units vary from one manufacturer to another, so it is important to follow each manufacturer's instructions carefully.

Following are additional tips to assist in this form of casting:

The bottom edge of the casting flask must be even so that it forms a good seal when vacuuming. This should be tested before burnout. It is best to have an 1/8" gap between the top of the investment and the rim of the flask. (See Fig. 3–56.)

Test the seal by placing the flask directly over the hole in the silicone rubber pad and turning on the pump. The pump gauge should quickly indicate 20 to 25 pounds of pressure. If pressure does not build up or is slow to build up, try to press down on the flask to improve the seal. If pressure still does not come up, the flask is defec-

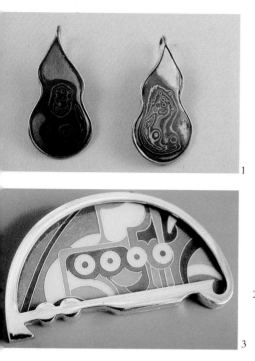

1 Earrings, Kim Kerbel;
mokume; 1¾″ long

2 Brooches and buckle, Robert
Schlie; two brooches of metal,
wood, gems; buckle, chased
and repoussé copper

3 Cloisonné pin, Alan T. Mette;
NuGold, silver, enamel; 2¾″ ×
1½″; 1980

4 Pendant, Greg Fensterman;
heat-colored copper, silver,
Plexiglas rod; 2¼″ high

5 Historic Japanese lamination
tests

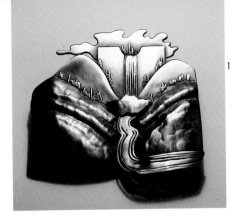

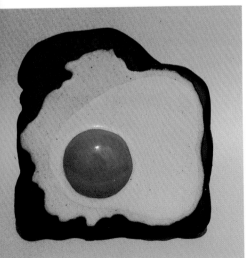

1 Buckle, Karen Cahill; mixed metal, 3″ wide

2 Buckle, Jon Wolfe; brass; 2½″ wide; 1978

3 Brooch, Ginger Nemecek; sandblasted bronze, copper, silver; 2¼″ high

4 Bracelets and brooch, student work; bronze, silver, Plexiglas

5 Sculpture, student work; sandblasted bronze and ebony; 2½″ wide

6 "Fried Egg on Toast," Hilary Packard; enamel on copper, electroformed Plexiglas; 4″ wide

1

2

3

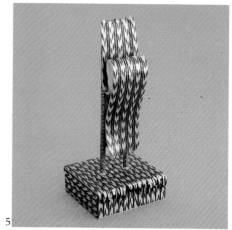

4

Eugene and Hiroko Sato Pijanowski are unique in this hemisphere in their efforts to restate, in contemporary terms, the best traditional Japanese metalwork. Both have studied and worked with honored traditional metalworkers in Japan and have, as a result, introduced to the non-Japanese world such processes as chiseling, traditional alloying, patination, inlay, overlay and methods of lamination (mokume-gane). Perhaps most important in this time of high precious metal prices, they have shown how the formation of new alloys and chemical patinas can greatly increase the expressive range of the decorative metalworker. In their own work, both artists use old processes and, to us, exotic materials to make strong, highly personal design statements that transcend the conventions of either the East or the West. Photographs courtesy of the artists.

1 Round pendant; mokume-gane, inlayed and chiseled metal

2 Six chiseled plaques; sterling silver

3 "Sato's Pendant"; sterling silver with gold inlay, mokume-gane, copper and kuromi-do

4 "Brooch 4-79"; mokume-gane, copper, and kuromi-do, 24K gold inlay, sterling silver

5 "Brooch with Stand, #2"; twisted and soldered fine silver, shakudo and copper wires

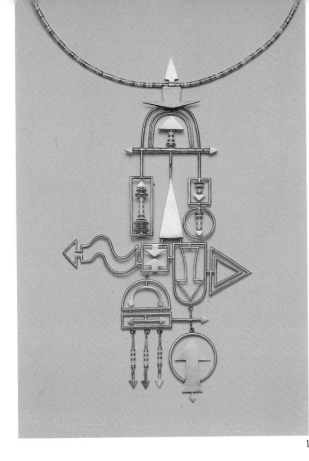

1

2

Wendy Ramshaw, an English artist/jeweler of
international reputation, works in a characteristically
formal, highly controlled mode. Interrelationships of
elements and exquisite technical mastery give her works
an almost austere beauty that is both highly
individualistic and functional to wear. Her work is very
much her own—though it has already influenced many
others throughout the world—but it never overwhelms
those who wear it: a quality too often ignored by those
who design and make objects to wear. Photographs by
Mike Hallson.

1 "Necklace without Direction"; 18K gold with white
  enamel; 1977. *Permanent collection of the National Gallery
  of Australia, Melbourne*

2 "Ring Set"; 18K yellow gold with red, orange and
  white enamel on a turned brass column, red acrylic
  inlay; 1978. *Permanent collection of the National Gallery of
  Australia, Canberra*

1

3

4

2

Barbara Minor obviously enjoys the sensuous quality of metal. Her work seems alive with a growth force, whether it be an abstract container or a rural landscape complete with farmyard animals. Metal is used as a responsive material that can be modified almost at will through repoussé, scoring, etching or chasing. In much of Minor's work, the mark of the tool, its signature, is left as a rich and intriguing surface texture to delight both eye and touch. This requires a delicate sense of scale and location—both quite evident in these pieces. All that Barbara Minor does is the result of profound philosophic dictates. Her work is often a tangible extension of her thoughts of environment and joy in it. Photographs courtesy of the artist.

1 "All-American Pig, Cow, Sheep"; Plexiglas, silver, brass, copper; 1976

2 Neckpiece; sterling silver and reticulated silver; 12″ × 8″; 1972

3 "Tony's Box"; bronze and sterling silver; 4″ × 6″; 1975

4 Box; repousséd, bronze; 5″ high; 1973

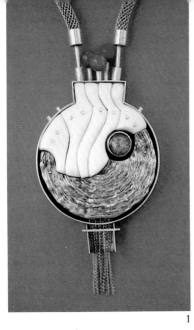

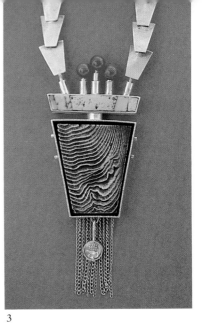

1   2   3

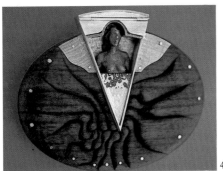

4

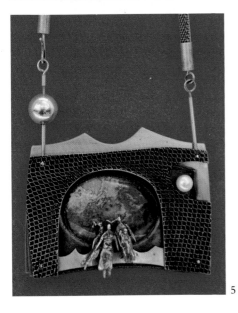

5

Francis Stephen could only be a jeweler/artist. In no other medium could he combine the great variety of rich materials with the delightful delicacy of forms and surfaces. His art requires smallness. It requires the exotic interplay of gold, silver, bronze, ivory, gemstones, patinas, rare techniques. Often a work will combine a dozen or more materials and processes—each in balance with the other. The art of "surprise" is obviously a pleasure to Francis Stephen. Hidden cavities, folding doors, buttons to push to reveal unsuspected riches, works as well developed front and back, all are characteristics of Stephen's pleasure as an artist/jeweler. The elements of a pendant are rationally related. . . pendant, hanger, chain, clasps, all are designed as part of the whole. This unity is the sign of the artist's intelligence and integrity. Photographs courtesy of the artist.

1 Pendant; carved ivory, silver, gold, carnelians; cast and fabricated

2 Pendant; silver, brass, bronze, baroque pearl and opal; reticulated, cast and fabricated

3 Pendant; silver, gold, carnelian, turquoise enpavé; fabricated, cast. *Owned by Anita Raney*

4 Buckle; carved teak, silver, brass and bronze; fabricated, cast and riveted. *Owned by William Lockhart*

5 "Maranatha"; silver, brass, agate, gold and pearl; fabricated, cast, electroformed and riveted

1

Eleanor Moty has explored new technology in the pursuit of new images and surfaces. Her pioneering in photoetching as a decorative metal process, often combined with electroforming and repoussé, has resulted in a very personal quality in jewelry and related objects. Her work has received national and international acclaim and illustrates dramatically how past and present need never be far apart. Photographs courtesy of the artist.

2

1 "Lightening Box"; marriage of metals, electroformed silver, agate; 1972

2 "Landscape" handbag; marriage of metals, electroformed silver, agate; 1973

3 Purse; silver, brass, moonstone, leather; 1978

4 Fan pin; photoetched silver, abalone, silk thread; 1981

5 "Crystal Pin III"; silver, brass, smoky quartz; 1980

3

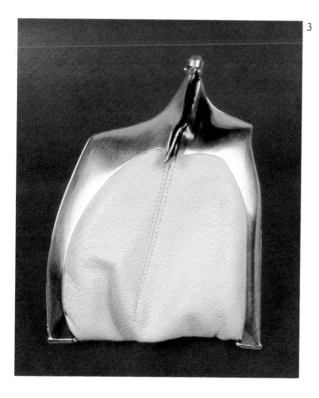

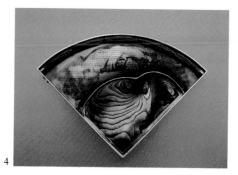

4

5

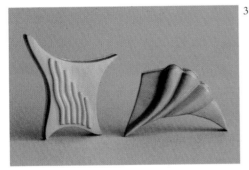

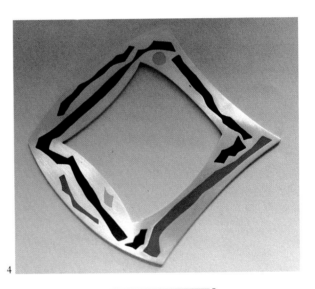

*Julia Manheim makes highly successful use of a
material that many still disdain to use as an
artistic medium: plastics. Since a material can be
what an artist makes of it—no more, no less—it
is fascinating to consider the very unique imagery
of those works in inlay and laminated plastics.
Julia Manheim, an English artist/jeweler, treats
this protean material with the delicacy and control
of a skilled graphic artist and it seems almost a
bonus that her work can be worn as well.*
Photographs courtesy of the artist.

1 Brooch; silver and resin; 1980

2 Brooches; silver and resin; 1980

3 Brooches; silver and boxwood; 1978

4 Bracelet; silver and resin; 1980

5 Bracelets; Perspex and inlaid resins; 1980

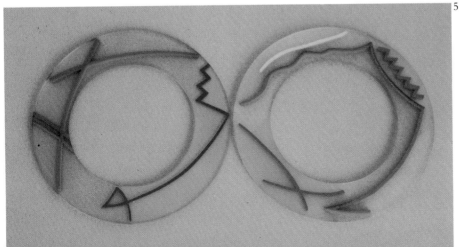

1

2

3

It takes humor, sophistication, and—above all—an unerring eye to combine pre-made elements into a fresh work of art. J. Frederick Woell uses the "found object" as if it were a raw material—to be used in total or dissected, if need be, to fill a communication niche in his delicate compositions. He combines the skills of a graphic designer, working with the abstract elements of line, surface and color, with superior facility as a metalworker. Photographs courtesy of the artist.

4

1 "The Winning"; pendant, cast brass and silver with found object; 3⅛" high

2 "One More for the Road"; pendant, cast brass; 4¼" high

3 "Flight from Egypt"; pendant, cast brass; 3½" wide; 1973

4 "Come Fly With Me"; pin, cast silver with turquoise; 2" wide

5 "Touchdown over Iwo Jima"; pin, cast silver; 2" wide

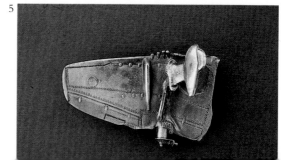

5

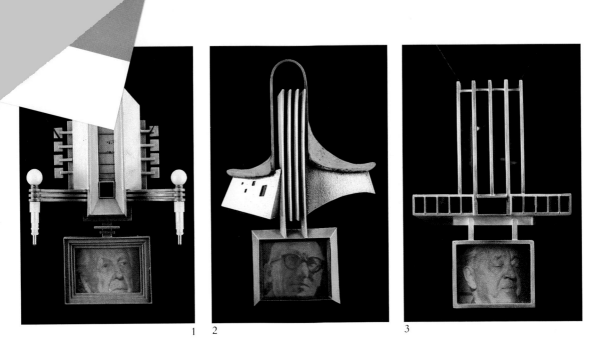

"Homage to the Master Builders" pendant series

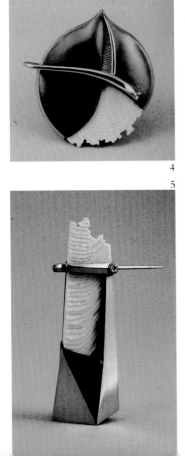

Dennis French is a superb craftsman who has developed the use of tool and material to that point where nothing stands in the way of developing the idea. Each work, though small in scale, is conceived as a three-dimensional entity—the perfect joining of sculpture and decoration. French combines materials for their aesthetic fitness, not to represent great value by obvious use of gold or precious gems. Porcelain, Plexiglas, brass, copper, 14K gold, diamonds. . . all are combined, how and when the artist dictates, to achieve a unity of form and idea. Each work stands as a total artistic expression. Photographs courtesy of the artist.

1 "Frank Lloyd Wright"; silver, bronze, pearls

2 "Le Corbusier"; silver, copper, glass, photoetching

3 "Mies Vander Rohe"; silver, acrylic mirror

4 Pin; gold plate on silver, porcelain, aquamarine

5 Pin; gold plate on silver, porcelain, cubic zirconia

Deborah Weintrob has successfully produced, in wearable form, an artistic expression that is difficult enough to master by two-dimensional, graphic means: the abstraction of landscape into its essential elements. Much of her life has been spent in the flatness of the central midwest. This sense of horizontal vastness under dramatic skies seems an unlikely motif for a piece of jewelry. Deborah Weintrob has succeeded in this because she uses metal as color and texture, and tonal value as a painter or printmaker would use line and pigment. Translating the grandeur of vast landscape to the small scale necessary for jewelry requires superior technical mastery, which is ever obvious in Weintrob's work. Photographs courtesy of the artist.

1 "Landscape"; reversible neckpiece with collar, sterling silver and ebony

2 "Landscape"; reversible neckpiece, sterling, shibuichi, brass and Plexiglas

3 Pin; sterling silver, copper, amaranth wood, fine silver; 1¾″ diameter

4 Pendant; sterling, reticulated silver and ebony

5 "Landscape"; bracelet, mixed metals, silver, copper, brass

1

2

3   4

5

1 2

1 Pala d'Oro detail, St. Mark's Basilica, Venice, c. 1100–1200 A.D.; gold, enamel, gems

2 "Warrior on Horseback," Italian pendant; gold, rubies, pearl, enamel; 9cm high. *Photograph © 1976, The Trustees of the British Museum*

3 Jade thumb ring, Mughal, 17th–18th century A.D.; India jade, rubies, emeralds, gold. *Photograph © 1976, The Trustees of the British Museum*

4 Sumerian jewelry, Ur, c. 2500 B.C.; gold, gems; woman's jewelry arranged as on body in tomb. *Photograph © 1976, The Trustees of the British Museum*

5 Etruscan fibula, Italy, c.650 B.C.; gold, granulation. *Photograph © 1976, The Trustees of the British Museum*

3

4

5

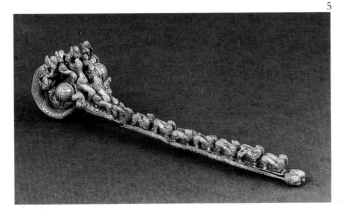

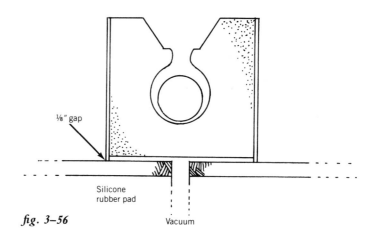

¹⁄₈″ gap

Silicone
rubber pad

fig. 3–56

Vacuum

tive. Perhaps a careful filing and sanding of the edge can correct the problem.

Once a good seal is assured, the burnout sequence should be started. When the flask has been cooled down again to between 550°F and 750°F casting can begin:

Step 1. Place the flask, opening up, on the silicone pad centered directly over the hole.

Step 2. Turn on the pump to achieve a vacuum of 20 to 25 pounds pressure.

Step 3. With the pump running, melt the correct amount of metal in a hand-held crucible. Prepare the crucible by lining it with a glaze of melted borax. This is done by dissolving powdered borax in alcohol, painting the interior of the ceramic crucible, and then allowing the alcohol to burn off. Use a separate crucible for silver, yellow gold, white gold, and any other metals. The crucible also should be preheated even before the flask is removed from the burnout oven. This speeds up metal melting and so reduces the buildup of oxides.

The metal should be melted with a fairly neutral flame. Heat only until the metal has completely melted. Test by gently shaking the crucible while continuing to heat. If no "peaks" of un-melted metal show, and the pool seems fluid, pour immediately. No additions of flux are necessary.

Step 4. Allow the flame of the torch to play over the "button"—the metal showing after the pour—for a few seconds. Turn off the pump.

Step 5. Allow the flask to cool for about two minutes before removing it from the silicone pad. It then can be quenched to break up the investment and to recover the model.

STEAM CASTING

The advantage of steam over centrifuge casting is the elimination of an expensive centrifuge. Once wax has been burned out of a mold, casting by steam pressure is very simple. When done correctly, steam castings can be as dense in structure and as delicate in surface as those cast by the centrifugal method.

The process follows:

1. Construct a *sprue former* of thin (22- or 24-gauge) copper. Form a hemisphere rather than the usual conical shape. See Fig. 3–57 for shape and size. A convenient form to use is the largest depression in a standard *dapping block*.

115

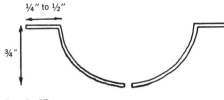

fig. 3–57

The bottom of the hemisphere should be truly rounded, since a flattened surface at that point will cause metal-flowing difficulties later.

2. Perforate a hole large enough for a piece of 14-gauge round wire to be used as a *sprue pin*. This diameter is very important. Metal will be melted directly in the hemispheric depression left after the mold investment has hardened and

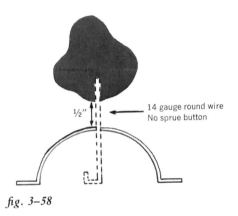

14 gauge round wire
No sprue button

½"

fig. 3–58

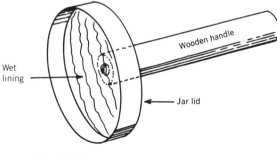

Wet lining

Wooden handle

Jar lid

fig. 3–59

after the metal *sprue former* has been removed. Too large a hole would allow early leakage of molten metal into the mold. It would solidify there, blocking further metal addition. A hole too small would make it difficult to inject enough metal to fill the mold. (See Fig. 3–58.)

3. Mount the wax model on the 14-gauge wire and with no more than ½" distance from the sprue former.

4. Invest as for centrifugal casting.

5. Have ready a plunger made in the following manner:
   a. Use a screw-top jar lid large enough to fit over the flask loosely.
   b. Screw on a section of ¾" wood dowel as a handle. (See Fig. 3–59.)
   c. Line the inside of the lid with 4–5 layers of very wet heat resistant material. Leave everything in a bowl of hot water until the last moment.

6. Once the wax has been eliminated from the mold and the temperature has reached 1200° F, casting should begin immediately.
   a. Place the casting flask, sprue opening facing up, on a heat proof soldering block or on a light, porous kiln brick. This base is necessary to allow gases to flow out and away as molten metal takes their place inside the mold.
   b. Immediately place the correct amount of metal (determined by weight) in the hemispheric sprue opening.
   c. Sprinkle the metal *lightly* with casting flux. Too much might cause blockage in the sprue hole.
   d. Melt the metal quickly and efficiently by torch. (See Fig. 3–60.)
   e. As soon as the metal is completely fluid, press the jar lid (filled with a heatproof lining) firmly over the end of the flask. (See Fig. 3–61.) Hold the lid in place for 15 to 20 seconds. It is possible to miss placing the jar lid squarely, thus tipping the flask.

116

supplementary metal techniques

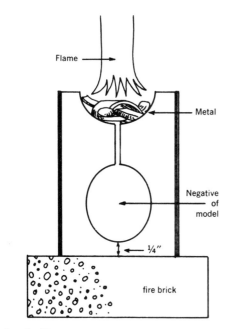

fig. 3–60

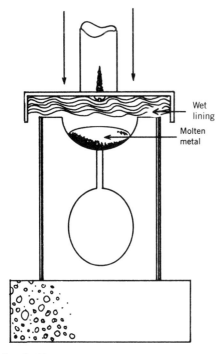

fig. 3–61

To avoid this disaster, have the jar lid ready above and slightly to the side of the flask. As one hand removes the torch, the other immediately presses the lid down. Under no circumstances should the molten metal be allowed to cool. Cooling is indicated by a dull film on the surface.

   f. Allow the flask to cool for a minute or two, then quench it in cold water as in centrifugal casting.

Objects such as rings cast very well in this manner, although pins and pendants of large or extended shape might cause problems. Steam pressure can push only so far!

CORE CASTING

Hollow forms can be constructed over a core made of casting investment that has been shaped by carving, filing, and sanding. Fig. 3–62 shows the shaped core with

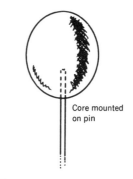

fig. 3–62

a piece of wire inserted into a hole drilled into the investment. The core is repeatedly dipped into melted wax. The wax should not be too hot in order to reduce the amount that runs off after dipping. Continue dipping until the core is covered with an even thickness of at least 1/32″. Very thin areas often collapse during casting, which results in incomplete walls.

A sprue of wax is attached at some point on the wax-covered core as a point of entry for molten metal.

Some means to hold the core in position once the wax has been melted out must be devised. This is done by carefully placing pegs of the same material to be cast—silver wire for a silver casting—through the wax coating and into drilled holes in the investment core. (See Fig. 3–63.) If a

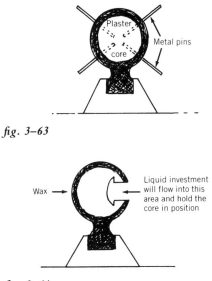

fig. 3–63

fig. 3–64

large opening will be left at some point in the hollow finished form, it is possible to key new investment into an aperture precarved into the core after it has been coated with wax. (See Fig. 3–64.) A great variety of interior textures can be achieved by drilling, grinding, and carving into the core surface. These negative indentations of course will be positive when cast.

After wax has been eliminated, the regular casting procedure can be followed to completion. Investment remaining in the interior is sometimes difficult to remove

after casting. Try picking it out with pointed tools. Avoid acid pickling work that has an investment core remaining. Acid is difficult to neutralize in the investment.

SUPPLEMENTARY CASTING INFORMATION

The craftsman can make his own alloys for casting. Pure copper is difficult to cast because it oxidizes so rapidly and heavily during melting. The addition of small amounts of silver lowers the high (1981°F) melting point and reduces oxidation somewhat without changing the color too much.

Mix the alloy before casting by melting the ingredients in a well-fluxed flat crucible. Stir the molten mass with a graphite rod and avoid overheating. Do not mix the metals in the casting crucible just prior to the casting itself.

To duplicate a simple form in wax (without undercuts), carve the form in intaglio on a smooth plaster of paris block. After it is well refined, soak the plaster thoroughly in water and pour melted wax into the carving.

Remove the wax as soon as it is completely cool by gently prying it out. Sprue mounting proceeds as for any wax model.

CASTING RINGS OF SOFT WAX

1. Use a dowel 4″ long that is the same diameter as the knuckle of the ring finger.
2. Wrap the dowel *smoothly* with *one* layer of thin aluminum foil. This will prevent the melted wax from sticking to the dowel. Tape or wire the foil at both ends to hold it on the dowel firmly.
3. Cut a strip of thin sheet wax as wide as the band of the ring and just long enough to join. Fuse the ends together carefully with a hot spatula.
4. Drip wax onto the wax band until enough bulk is formed for modeling or carving.

supplementary metal techniques

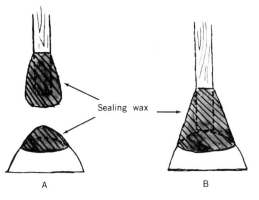

Sealing wax

A   B

fig. 3–65

5. Finish the model as completely as possible. Remember that the final wax model will be reproduced in metal exactly.

SETTING A STONE IN A WAX MODEL

1. Construct the bulk of the ring or other jewelry form.
2. Cut a flat bed for the stone. Leave a hole through the model if the stone is translucent or transparent.
3. Fix a small stick to the top of the stone with sealing wax or dopping cement. First heat the stone carefully, drop on a little cement, reheat, and apply the stick. Allow the cement to cool. (See Fig. 3–65.)

4. Place the stone with the attached stick in position in the bed of wax and build up the wax around it. Do not hide more of the stone than necessary, but allow enough wax around the base of the stone to key it in. (See Fig. 3–66.)
5. Remove the stone from the finished model by first softening the wax in *warm* water. Next, remove the stone carefully with a straight, parallel, upward pull.
6. Remove the ring from the dowel and finish the inside where necessary. Sprue it and cast.
7. With the holding stick still in position, replace the stone in the finished ring and planish the metal tightly around it with chasing tools. Stone or burnish the tool marks away. If the casting has contracted so that the stone no longer fits, use engraving tools or scrapers to enlarge the hole.

Some stones can be cast in position when incorporated in the wax model.

Soft stones, such as turquoise or malachite, and those with many fractures, such as opal or labradorite, are not suitable since they would change color or shatter.

Tough stones of the hardness of 8 or higher on the Mohs scale are suitable if handled carefully. The important factors are that the flask containing a stone should

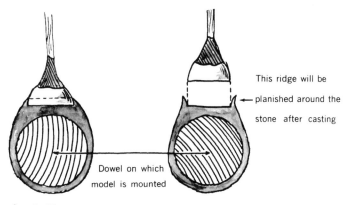

This ridge will be
← planished around the
stone after casting

Dowel on which
model is mounted

fig. 3–66

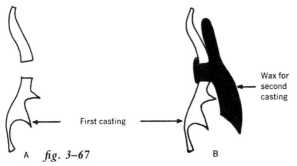

A   *fig. 3–67*   B

First casting

Wax for
second
casting

interlocking. A perforation or overlap area will be sufficient. (See Fig. 3–67A.)

2. Refine the first casting as completely as possible. It might be difficult to do so at a later stage.

3. Model the wax area for the contrasting metal directly onto, into, or around the casting, as shown in Fig. 3–67B.

4. Sprue the combined forms, connecting the sprue former to the wax area. Invest and cast.

A variant of this process consists of building wax directly onto a form (or forms) cut from sheet metal. Again, overlaps or perforations are necessary to key the two forms together. This latter process can result in an interesting combination of the hard, simple rigidity of sheet metal with the softer, organic, freely modeled wax area. (See Fig. 3–68.)

Adequate keying or overlapping is necessary since molten metal will (a) not fuse to solid metal during casting, and (b) the metal already solid and in the mold will probably have a thin coating of oxides on its surface. This "skin" may later dissolve away in pickling, leaving a loose joining of the two metals.

be heated as slowly as possible during wax elimination. At the risk of a rough casting, the metal should be cast while the flask temperature is high—at least 1000°F. The metal should be just hot enough to be fluid.

The cooling period is extremely important. The kiln or oven used in the burnout should be brought up to 1500°F in time to replace the metal-filled flask immediately after casting and then turned off. Allow the flask to return to room temperature in the closed kiln. Never quench the hot mold in water with the stone in place.

MULTIMETAL CASTING

Two or more metals of contrasting color can be combined by casting. Silver and copper, effective because of strong color contrast, can be combined in the following manner:

1. The first of the two or more metal areas is modeled in wax, invested, and cast in the usual manner. The only preparation required for the addition of another metal is some type of keying or

• rubber molds

Jewelry manufacturers have developed rubber moldmaking to a high degree for mass-production of delicate objects in a variety of metals. The artist-designer will find many instances when it would be useful to make several replicas of the same

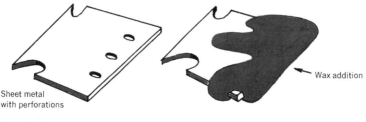

Sheet metal
with perforations

Wax addition

fig. 3–68

form to be included as elements in necklaces, bracelets, pendants, or earrings. Making limited editions of rings—perhaps with different gems in the same ring design—is easily done by using flexible rubber molds.

A rubber mold is built around a prototype of a piece of jewelry that has been made and completely finished in metal. The mold is carefully cut open, in two or more pieces, the model removed, the mold rejoined, and melted wax injected into the empty space as many times as desired. The resulting *wax* models are then set up individually or in clusters. A well-made rubber mold can be used to make hundreds of wax models.

The process of rubber mold-making requires some mastery, but the following tips gleaned from experienced commercial craftsmen should be useful.

Materials:

1. Aluminum mold frames of different sizes.
2. Wax injector.
3. Vulcanizer. (See Fig. 3–69.)
4. Mold rubber (Castaldo White Base).
5. Sprue formers and pins.
6. Parting knives. (Important! These should be the best quality available. B. P. or Rütgers brands are good.)
7. Parting powder or mold-release compound.
8. Two thick aluminum sheets (¼″ at least) ½″ wider in each dimension than the mold frames.
9. Two C-clamps.
10. Thermometer that goes to 350°F.
11. Solid aluminum block (same size and thickness as the mold frame).
12. Swest #5 gold wax (casts at 150°F).
13. Denatured alcohol.
14. Water.

MAKING THE MOLD

1. Trace and cut out nine rubber shapes from the inside of the mold frame.

fig. 3–69
Courtesy of Swest, Inc.

This should be enough to fill the space from top to bottom.

2. Remove the paper backing from all the sheets except the bottom one and rub them clean with alcohol. Keep cleaning with alcohol while handling all rubber. Remember, dirty rubber will not fuse into a solid block! When piling up the layers, clean one side, stick it onto another sheet, remove the backing, clean *that*, and so on.
3. Press in four or five of the layers.
4. Attach a ⅛″ bronze welding rod section to the model with silver solder. The rod should first be forged out on the end to flare it into a good fillet connection. This makes for easier wax injection. (See Fig. 3–70.) The length of the sprue pin is determined by the size and shape of the model.
5. Place the clean and polished model in the center of the frame. There should be ½″ to ⅜″ clearance both above and below the model. (See Fig. 3–71.)

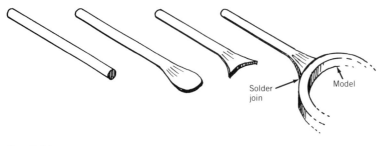

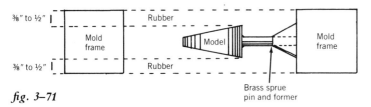

fig. 3–70

Solder join

Model

⅜" to ½"   Rubber

Mold frame

Model

Mold frame

⅜" to ½"   Rubber

Brass sprue pin and former

fig. 3–71

6. If casting a ring or any other form with a large, open interior area, the open area must be packed with rubber. (See Fig. 3–72.) With the model resting on half of the rubber sheets, pack the open area with strips of rubber (carefully cleaned with alcohol) in a coil. These strips should be slightly wider than the ring band. If there are undercuts and hollow areas in the design, fill them in with small, clean pieces of rubber as well.

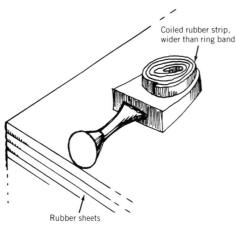

Coiled rubber strip, wider than ring band

Rubber sheets

fig. 3–72

If there are concave design areas on the front face of a ring, build up extra layers of rubber level with the ring thickness, as in Fig. 3–73. This extra rubber will spread and push *onto* the face of the ring during the vulcanizing process.

7. Cover the rest of the model with the remaining cleaned layers of rubber. Add on a small scrap piece of rubber about the size of the model directly above the model, as in Fig. 3–74. Some mold makers drill ⅛" holes through all four sides of the mold frame. This releases excess pressure and allows excess rubber to escape without affecting the model.

8. The rubber-packed frame is now *vulcanized*.

    a. Check the true temperature of the vulcanizer. The true temperature must be 300°F. To check this, some moldmakers use a solid block of aluminum just the size and shape of a mold frame. Drill a hole, from one end to the center, large enough to admit a good thermometer that registers as high as 350°F. When the correct temperature is reached,

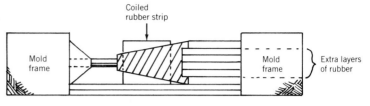

fig. 3–73

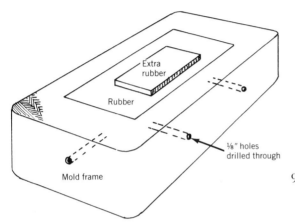

fig. 3–74

replace the block with the filled frame.

b. Lower the press gently. Do not press down on the mold until the frame is definitely hot to the touch. *Then* start a slow pressure. Use hand tightening only.

c. When firmly tightened down, leave the frame in place at 300°F for one hour. This vulcanizes the rubber.

d. Cool the mold in cold water for 10 minutes before pushing the rubber interior out of the frame.

9. The mold must now be cut open.

a. Construct a chain and clamp rig. This will reduce fatigue and many cut fingers! (See Fig. 3–75.)

b. Use at least *two* new blades for each mold cutting. Many molds are spoiled by a false economy with blades.

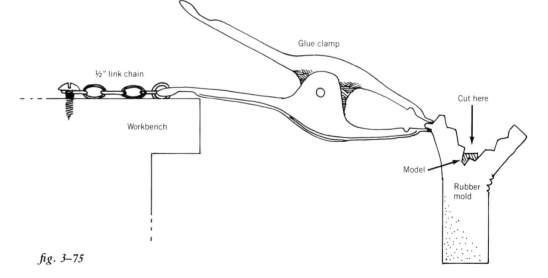

fig. 3–75

123

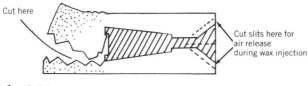

Cut here

Cut slits here for
air release
during wax injection

fig. 3–76

c. Cut along the edge of the model, not right at the middle. (See Fig. 3–76.) Also cut slits in the funnel formed by the sprue former for release of air during wax injection.

More cuts may have to be made leading away from the sides of the model if more air escape is needed during wax injection.

d. Cut a plug out of the ring center and continue to cut in different directions. Make these cuts irregular to form a "keying" surface (i.e., top and bottom will fit together in only one way and with no sideways shifting possible).

e. Make an ⅛" deep diagonal cut around the outside of the base of the model. This gives the mold more flexibility and allows the wax model to be removed easily after injection. Some mold makers also make a transverse cut shortly after the metal model is exposed during the first mold opening. This allows the rubber to be folded back easily for later wax removal.

10. Wax is now injected.

a. Hold the rubber mold firmly between two aluminum sheets. Use both hands or, better, a "C" clamp.

b. Brush the *side* of the mold across the injection nozzle of the wax in-

jector and then insert the nozzle into the sprue depression.

c. Inject the wax according to manufacturers' instructions.

d. Cool the mold in water for 10 minutes.

e. Open the mold carefully, remove the model, cut off the wax sprue, and mount for casting. Remember, the wax model will be only as good as the original. Sometimes parts of a model will be too thin to fill well during wax injection. This can be remedied by placing an index card with a window cut out of it on top of the rubber mold just before wax injection. (See Fig. 3–77.)

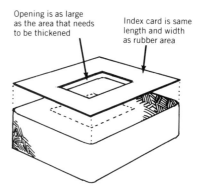

Opening is as large as the area that needs to be thickened

Index card is same length and width as rubber area

fig. 3–77

supplementary metal techniques

4　decorative surface techniques

Although form and shape alone can result in handsome jewelry, the artist may want to fulfill the decorative function of jewelry through surface enrichment. Often the innately precious quality of a jewel is best stated by the delicacy and variety of the surface treatment.

As in all other visual arts, the surface and the body of a jewel must relate to each other completely. A virtuoso treatment of the planes of an unimaginative basic form can result only in an unfortunate veneer—never in a total statement.

The great danger in surface decoration lies in overdoing it. Understatement is always more successful, since the viewer must then focus his own aesthetic awareness on the object to complete the total unity.

Perhaps the earliest forms of surface decoration consisted of embossing thinly hammered sheets of metal into figurative or geometric lines and shapes. Later, through the art of soldering, surfaces were covered by wire or metal fragments to create a rich play of light and dark over the jewelry. The casting techniques of the time translated the soldered wire into wax coils, which were handled in the same decorative manner.

When the addition of fused enamel became possible, even more surface enrichments were added, with texture as well as color playing a role.

Engraving, inlaying, lamination, granulation, and many combinations of techniques all combined in time to give the jeweler a great range of expressive possibilities. Many of these techniques were popular for relatively short periods in history, but as potential means for contemporary use all of them should be reexamined in the light of fresh attitudes toward decoration. Some of these techniques became so important to a culture that great skills in the handling of tools and materials resulted. Many volumes have been written, and long apprenticeships were often necessary for a jeweler to grasp the total possibilities. Other techniques have—in all but their museum identities—been lost to us. With the help of the historian, the chemist, and the metallurgist, much has been reconstructed, but even more must be relearned through individual experimentation.

Materials developed in our time, such as the many synthetic plastics, have seen only the beginnings of use as expressive media. Here, knowledge of past uses is nonexistent, and the artist-craftsman must use his own training in finding adaptations and new directions of expression.

In this chapter, then, are techniques described as they were once used and as they can still be used today.

● engraving

Engraving is a technique that can be considered an art of its own. To engrave skillfully one must spend considerable time in practice alone. The occasional use of engraving on a piece of jewelry cannot teach the craftsman more than the fumbling rudiments.

Excellent manuals are available that explain in detail how to engrave the most intricate lines and how to shape and maintain the cutting qualities of engraving tools. Only constant practice on a variety of metals and surfaces can translate the written explanation into a working knowledge of the art.

USING A GRAVER AND OTHER TOOLS

The tools of engraving are basically steel rods of various sections with wooden handles attached. They can be straight, for work on convex surfaces (Fig. 4–1), or angled for engraving flat or concave surfaces (Fig. 4–2). The wooden handles can be spherical or hemispherical in shape, depending on the intended use of the tool.

The cutting tool itself, called a graver or burin, can be filed, ground, and stoned

fig. 4–1

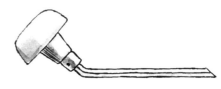

fig. 4–2

to a great variety of shapes. (See Figs. 4–3 and 4–4.)

The degree of angle on the cutting tip of the tool is very important. The best angle is 45°. Less than 45° causes a deep bite when cutting, but it preserves the point quite well. More than 45° makes a shallow and easier cut, but the point breaks often. (See Fig. 4–5.)

Most tools must be shaped and sharpened after purchase. If a tool must be bent—for engraving flat or concave surfaces—it can be heated to cherry red and bent against a heat-resistant pad while being heated. Avoid twisting the side or center lines; keep the sides completely parallel. Quench the graver completely under tap water. The face and the cutting angle can now be filed or ground by using an India stone and oil. Polish one-third of the graver from the cutting end with emery paper (from No. 1 down to No. 4/0). Heat this one-third with a blue, soot-free flame until a straw-yellow color develops on the metal and travels to the end. Quench the steel quickly in water.

The length of the graver might have to be shortened to allow for no more than ½″ to project past your fingers during use. The proper length can be broken off by placing the graver in a smooth-jawed vise, allowing the excess to project out to the side. A sharp tap on this projection will cleanly snap it off.

The tool can now be sharpened by careful rubbing on an oiled *Arkansas stone*, with an oil such as SAE 10. Use enough oil so that metal particles do not embed themselves in the stone. The final polish to the face and the cutting edge is given by a

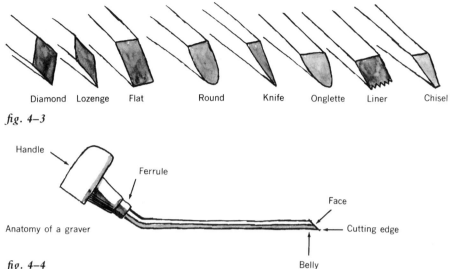

Diamond Lozenge Flat   Round   Knife   Onglette   Liner   Chisel

fig. 4–3

Handle

Ferrule

Face

Anatomy of a graver

Cutting edge

fig. 4–4

Belly

controlled rubbing on fine emery paper (4/0) placed on a sheet of glass.

Grinding devices are available, and some are calibrated to allow for the setting of desired angles. These can be used to hold the graver for all but the final emery polishing.

Gravers can be *heeled* so that they turn well to the right or to the left. Heeling is done by grinding and stoning an angle to the face top and the cutting edge so that the tool naturally makes a curve to the right or the left. The many heeling angles necessary to script-letter engraving can be studied in good engravers' manuals.

DESIGN TRANSFER

A scribe can be used to *lightly* incise guidelines that are freely drawn on the metal with ink or pencil.

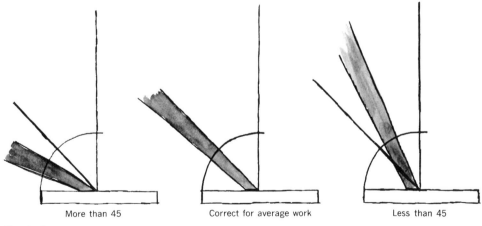

More than 45   Correct for average work   Less than 45

fig. 4–5

Chinese white or white tempera paint can be painted over the surface to take the marks of carbon paper. If tempera is used, a scribe should incise the lines since the pigment would chip off during engraving. Chinese white, rubbed onto the metal in paste form with the fingertip, can be engraved directly.

TOOL HANDLING

The object to be engraved should be firmly fixed to a surface that will allow the object to be turned easily. An engraver's ball or block set in a leather ring is ideal for small pieces, but it is expensive.

The object can be heated slightly and sealed to a wood block onto which a ¼″ thickness of sealing wax or stick shellac has been applied. The block is held firmly in a small vise, (Fig. 4–6). Once the sealing wax has cooled, the object can be engraved. To remove finished work, simply heat it with a small torch flame and pry it off. The small amount of wax adhering to the metal can be dissolved with benzene.

A pitch bowl or tray can also be used and the metal applied and removed as described in the section on repoussé techniques.

A cork- or lead-lined vise or a ring clamp can be used for objects in the round.

During engraving itself, one hand steadies and turns the working surface while

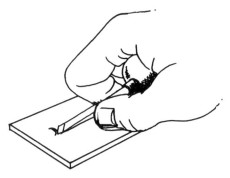

fig. 4–7

the other manipulates the graver. Many engravers hold the tool virtually in one place while moving the object into new positions. This is especially true for cutting curved lines.

The tool hand holds the graver so that the handle is comfortably cradled in the palm. The thumb acts as a brake, while the fingers control the angle and the position of the tool. (See Fig. 4–7.) Sometimes the thumb of the holding hand is pressed against the tool thumb as a pressure control, but a slip of the tool could cause a nasty gouge.

The entire action—the press forward, the downward pressure to bite the tool into the metal, and the turning action of the tool and the metal—should be done slowly and with complete control. Since a slip with a graver actually removes some of the metal, it is difficult to obliterate mistakes by burnishing.

Each cut should end with a slight release of forward pressure and a slight depression of the tool. In this way the tool rides up again and leaves no burr. If a burr remains, it can be cut off with a scraper held very flat to the metal to avoid shaving away the surface itself, or a graver cut from the opposite direction—and joining the first—can be used.

Lubricate the graver often by touching

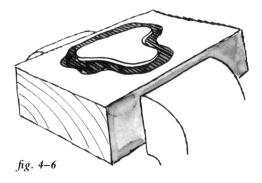

fig. 4–6

the tip to a cotton swab soaked with a light oil. Wintergreen oil has long been used by engravers for this purpose.

If a tool leaves a *heel mark*—a scratch behind the start of a cut—it is not heeled enough for the surface. This can be remedied by bending the entire tool at a point about 1″ from the ferrule on a 3½″ tool.

Prying up the point too quickly from a deep cut causes the point to break. The point will also break when the face angle is too flat, making the point long and narrow. Improperly tempered gravers, being too hard and brittle, also tend to lose the point easily.

A broken or dulled point must be sharpened with stones and emery paper again; make sure that the original angle (if correct in the first place) is maintained.

The sharpness of a point can be tested by pushing it into the surface of the thumbnail lightly at a flat angle. If it is deflected, it is not sharp enough for clean engraving.

OTHER USES OF THE GRAVER

Aside from the commonplace inscription engraving on jewelry, the graver is useful in a number of ways:

To create a line in surface design.
To develop a surface texture by cross-hatching or other repeated cuts.
To cut depressions and lines for inlaying niello, enamel, or other metals.
For removing solder from between fine wire areas.
For pushing up burrs in *bead* settings of small stones and for *bright cutting* planes around faceted stones.
For leveling top edges of bezels after they have been burnished around stones.
For enlarging bearings (depressions) into which stones will be set, as in cast jewelry.

● etching

When man first noticed the action of acids on metal is not known, but it is known that pre-Columbian Indians used oxalic acid obtained from plants to dissolve copper on the surfaces of copper-gold-silver alloys to achieve a pure gold surface.

In more recent times, the technology of chemical manufacture has resulted in the development of many new acids that can be used on metals.

The process is simple. The metal to be etched is thoroughly cleaned of all grease and oxides. The areas to remain as raised surfaces are covered with an acid-resistant substance. The entire piece is immersed in an appropriate acid solution (depending on the metal) and allowed to remain for as long as necessary until the acid dissolves the exposed metal to the desired depth. The result should be—after the resist is removed—a surface composed of raised and lowered areas which carry out the meaning of the design.

ACID SOLUTIONS

The acid solutions, called *mordants*, used for ferrous and nonferrous metals are:

For gold of low karat (18 K or lower):

Hydrochloric acid	8 parts
Nitric acid	4 parts
Iron perchloride	1 part
Water	40 to 50 parts

For silver:

Nitric acid	100 cc.
Water	300 to
	400 cc.
or	
Nitric acid	1¼ pts.
Water	1 pt.
Isopropyl alcohol	¼ pt.

Agitate the work constantly. The temperature should be over 75°F.

For copper:

Nitric acid	1 part
Water	1 part
or	
Potassium chloride	2 parts
Hydrochloric acid	10 parts
Water	90 parts

This forms a slow, even etch that does not underbite as readily.

For brass:

Nitric acid	1 part
Water	1 part
or	
Sulfuric acid	10 oz.
Nitric acid	2 oz.
Hydrochloric acid	2–3 drops
Sodium dichromate	⅛ to ¼ tsp.
Water	1 gal.

For aluminum:

Ammonia	¾ oz.
Copper sulfate	2½ gm.
75% Phosphoric acid	1–2 drops
Sodium hydroxide	7 oz.
Water	1 gal.

Etch for three minutes at 145°F. Rinse the object well and immerse immediately in a 40% nitric acid pickle (40 parts acid + 60 parts water). Rinse again and dry.

For steel or iron:

Hydrochloric acid	2 parts
Water	1 part
or	
Nitric acid	1 part
Water	10 parts
75% Phosphoric acid	1–2 drops per gal. of the above mixture

or	
Nitric acid (commercial)	50 oz.
Isopropyl alcohol	8 oz.
Water	1 gal.

Use at room temperature if over 70°F.

RESISTS

The resists are generally composed of wax, vegetable gums, asphaltum, lacquers, or plastics. Some formulas are:

1. *Beeswax.* Immerse the entire object, once it is chemically clean, into molten wax. Warm the metal before immersion to avoid heavy deposits of wax. After etching, beeswax can be removed by heating the object to remelt the wax and then wiping it off. It can also be dissolved with benzene.

2. *Wax pencils* can be used for laying out any delicate lines that are to remain unetched.

3. *Thin shellac* can be painted or dipped on.

4. *Sealing wax* (basically shellac) can be dissolved in alcohol by saturating 1 oz. of alcohol with shavings of sealing wax. Stir this thick liquid thoroughly and brush it on. Add alcohol if it becomes too thick. Use alcohol as a solvent after etching. This is a good resist for the edges and the bottom of an object, but it tends to chip when it is scratched in designing.

5. *Gum guaiacum* dissolved in alcohol in the same manner described in formula 4 makes a good flexible resist. Use a strong solution of sodium hydroxide as a solvent.

6. Make a varnish from:

Liquid asphaltum	16 oz.
Benzene	3 oz.
Turpentine	4 oz.

This has strong acid-resistant qualities, but it should be dried thoroughly with

1

3

1 Construction, Susan Clausen; mixed
media with etching; 2″ high

2 Buckle, Melinda Duncan; copper,
electroformed and etched

3 Pendant, Hilary Packard; sterling silver,
etching and repoussé; 3½″ wide

a little warmth before immersion in the acid bath. If it is still wet, it lifts from the metal, causing *underbiting*. Remove this resist by boiling the object in a strong lye solution, or dissolve it in benzene.

7. A *ball ground* resist, often used by copperplate etchers, is composed of:

Beeswax	2 parts
Asphaltum	2 parts
Burgundy pitch	1 part

The ingredients are melted together and, when cool enough, rolled into balls about 2″ in diameter. They are then enclosed in a bag made of a square of finely woven cloth. The ends are brought up and tied or wired together tightly to make a short handle. While the ball ground is still soft, it should be pressed on a flat, heated surface so that the ground penetrates the cloth. (See Fig. 4–8.)

The well-cleaned and polished metal is then heated to a temperature that will melt the ground but not cause it to burn. The ball is rubbed over this heated surface to deposit a fairly even layer of ground. Additional heat should spread the ground on the metal in an even, translucent layer, or it can be rolled smooth with a soft brayer (roller).

After cooling, the back and edges of the

fig. 4–8

object should be painted with a liquid resist. The ground can be darkened by carefully smoking it over a small turpentine flame. Be careful not to scorch the ground! Smoking makes the line scratched by a needle or knife down to the bare metal more visible.

Some etchers build a small wall of wax around the area to be etched. This contains the acid so that edges and other areas need not be protected.

The process of etching varies with the mordant and with the metal. In general, the object is left in the bath until a line has been etched deeply enough to be felt with a steel point. Remove the object from the acid before testing.

Bubbles are formed by the action of the mordant and should be brushed off as they form. If they are allowed to remain, they will cause uneven biting. A feather can be used to brush these bubbles away.

Watch constantly for particles of ground that may have broken away. If this occurs, remove the work and the ground and reapply it more carefully. Sometimes a violent biting, indicated by excessive foaming, causes the ground to break away. Dilute the formula a little at a time and try etching again until bubbles form slowly and evenly.

A Pyrex baking dish makes an ideal etching bath. Work can be lowered into it on a cradle made of a loop of cotton string. Do not use wool or synthetics, since many of these fibers dissolve in nitric or other acids. (See Fig. 4–9.)

If you have access to a rectifier or a plating machine (such as a Hoover Electroplater), you can *electroetch* with great clarity and precision.

The process can be used on copper, bronze, brass, and silver, although a separate solution should be used for silver only.

1. Make a solution of 10% to 25% nitric acid. It should be at room temperature.

decorative surface techniques

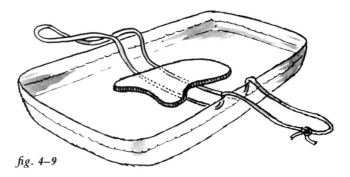

fig. 4–9

2. Place the solution in a 500 cc. beaker and attach as in Fig. 4–10.
3. The stainless steel cathode should have about twice the surface as the work to be etched.
4. Current Density (CD) depends upon visible reaction. If bubbles form violently, reduce the CD until a slow etching takes place.
5. Disconnect and remove the work, rinse, and then test for etching depth with a needle.

JEWELRY USES OF ETCHING

1. As a decorative surface defining line and form.
2. To create depressions into which enamel niello, or other metals can be inlaid.
3. To texture large areas of metal. A long etch in a fairly strong mordant results in a finely pocked surface, which holds coloring solutions well.
4. To texture or model the metal surface for *basse-taille* enameling techniques.

• filigree

The filigree process has had almost worldwide application. The Near East has for centuries been the focus of skilled workmanship in this delicate art. Filigree may consist of wire soldered to wire with no background support, or it may be wire soldered to a larger metal surface. Traditionally, flat wire has been used more often than round or square wire. Since it is flat, it can be bent to shape easily with fingers and tweezers. The wire is usually very delicate, perhaps 22 gauge by 28 gauge. When

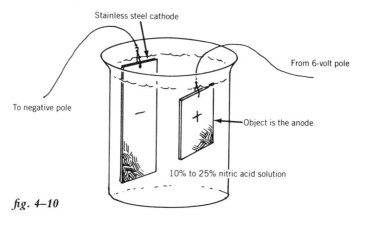

Stainless steel cathode

From 6-volt pole

To negative pole

Object is the anode

10% to 25% nitric acid solution

fig. 4–10

fine wire is to be applied to a contoured surface, a round wire of the desired gauge is easier to use because it bends to the surface more readily in all directions.

Fine silver and high-karat golds are most often used for filigree because of their malleability. Sterling silver or low-karat golds must be annealed thoroughly if they are to be flexible enough.

Well-annealed wire of virtually any gauge is available from the refinery, but often you may need a specific gauge. Rather than waiting for a special order, draw the wire to the desired gauge through a drawplate. The tools needed for wire drawing are:

1. *A drawplate.* This is usually a bar of hardened steel about ¼" thick which has been perforated with tapered holes that increase in size from one gauge to the next. The holes can be round, square, oblong, triangular, half-round, or elliptical. Some drawplates have a good range of holes of several shapes.

    The drawplates used to manufacture wire have the holes drilled through a hard mineral such as corundum (ruby and sapphire).

2. *Draw tongs.* These are specially designed pliers that have an easily gripped handle and serrated jaws for secure holding of the wire as it is pulled through the dies in the drawplate. Most draw tongs have a blunt, squared-off nose to enable the wire drawer to grip a maximum amount of the wire projecting through the die.

3. *Beeswax.* This is rubbed into the holes of the plate or onto the wire to lubricate the wire as it is pulled through the die. The heat of friction and compression melts the wax into a covering film. To draw wire without a lubricant is difficult, and it can damage the drawplate.

PREPARING AND DRAWING THE WIRE

The wire must be pointed by grinding or filing so that enough projects through the die for the tongs to grasp firmly. The taper of the point should start 1" back from the wire end.

The drawplate should be placed horizontally into a smooth-jawed vise. If inserted vertically, a hard pull on the wire could cause an expensive drawplate to break in half. The vise should be attached to a heavy bench, since a great deal of strength is sometimes necessary to draw heavy wire.

Place the pointed and lubricated wire end through the first hole into which it does not fit easily. Grasping it firmly with the tongs, draw it through with a steady pull, keeping the wire perpendicular to the drawplate at all times. (See Fig. 4–11.)

Move to the next hole in line. Do not skip a hole since this will cause the wire to break, if it can be pulled at all!

Since the wire is compressed and thus elongated, it soon becomes brittle.

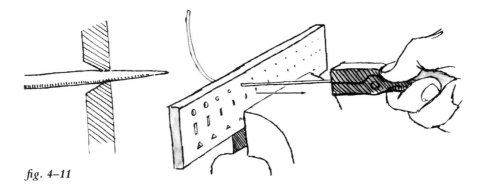

fig. 4–11

decorative surface techniques

To soften wire by annealing, wind it compactly into a coil. A length of silver wire is wrapped around the coil to prevent expansion and to keep the wire solidly tight. Loose loops are easily overheated during annealing. If iron binding wire is used, it must be removed before pickling, so a length of sterling wire, which may be used again and again, saves time. (See Fig. 4–12.)

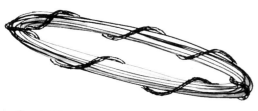

fig. 4–12

The coil can be painted with a temperature-indicating flux, which becomes water-clear at 1100°F. Placing the coil on a thin nickel-chromium sheet or wire grid allows the torch to heat all sections of the coil evenly.

If a kiln with an accurate pyrometer is available, the coil can be placed on a trivet and brought safely up to annealing temperature. This has the advantage of heating even the interior of the coil thoroughly and with a minimum of oxidation.

As soon as the correct temperature has been reached, the coil must be quickly quenched in cold water or pickle.

After rinsing the coil, dry it thoroughly to prevent rust in the drawplate dies if you are going to do additional drawing.

The wire is gently unwound and straightened and drawn through the dies until it again becomes too stiff and springy.

Two annealings usually suffice when drawing wire from gauge 10 to gauge 28 B and S. The first annealing takes place when the wire has become tough and the second when the drawing is complete. Unannealed wire is almost impossible to bend accurately.

SOLDERING FILIGREE

Small pieces of solder and a small accurate flame are necessary when soldering together the delicate wire forms of filigree. Cut sheet solder, usually *Easy*, into tiny *paillons*. Pieces 1/64″ square are not too small. Be sure that the thickness of the sheet solder is less than that of the wire. Solder can be rolled thin through a rolling mill or planished with a smooth-faced hammer on a steel block. The solder should be clean to reduce oxidation.

There are many ways in which filigree designs can be set up for soldering. Most craftsmen lay out the pieces on a smooth charcoal surface and heat from the top. Others glue the pieces to a thin sheet of annealed steel or nickel-chromium with a paste made of a little gum tragacanth and flux (liquid flux, since it does not foam as readily, is better than paste flux for this purpose). The sheet is placed on a tripod and the work is heated from below. The advantage here is that small pieces are not easily blown out of place by the flame.

A third, more complicated technique consists of:

1. Pressing the wire shapes about one-fourth of their diameter into a thin, flat sheet of beeswax.
2. A box wall is built around the impressed forms with thin cardboard and the enclosure is filled with a heat-resistant plaster such as that used in casting.
3. When the plaster is hard, the wax sheet is pulled away cleanly, exposing the wire again. After the plaster is completely dry—*important!*—the joins are cleaned with a thin knife blade and soldered as usual.

The plaster will dissolve in cold water if quenched immediately after soldering is completed, or it can be soaked away in a very dilute sulfuric acid pickle. A light brushing will remove plaster from hard-

Cut number 1

Cut number 2

fig. 4–13

to-reach places. The work can be cleaned by boiling it in pickle.

Remember that solder will flow to the hottest point, especially when wire is being joined. Heat the *entire* piece equally. A small-pointed steel scribe can be used occasionally to move solder into a join just as it flows.

Previously soldered areas can be protected by a thin paste of yellow ocher when additional soldering is necessary. See "Additional Soldering Information" in Chapter 2.

• inlaying

The contrast of color or texture plays an important design role in a piece of jewelry. Dark metals can be combined with light-colored metals with dramatic results. Wood and plastics can create not only a color contrast but also a surface change when inlaid in metal or into each other.

For Japanese inlay techniques and tools, see Chapter 5.

INLAYING METALS

Soft metals have been inlaid into depressions in bronze, iron, and steel for centuries in many parts of Europe and Asia. Much of the impressive armor of the Middle Ages and the Renaissance was decorated in this way. Brass and copper inlay work is still practiced in the Moslem countries and in India in much the same manner as it has been for thousands of years.

There are many ways of laying one metal into another. New variations are developed occasionally with advances in metallurgy. Perhaps the earliest technique consisted of carving or engraving lines and depressions into which another metal was hammered. This method is still worthy of attention today.

For inlaying wires into flat or curved surfaces, engrave a line with two cuts of the graver. If a burr results, so much the better. The cuts should be narrower at the surface than at the bottom. (See Fig. 4–13.)

With a narrow-pointed chisel or graver, the bottom of the engraved line should be *plinked* with small pointed projections every ½″ or less. The softer metal of the wire will be pierced by these sharp points, keying it in place. (See Fig. 4–14.) Fine silver, gold, or other soft annealed wires are then hammered into the groove with a small smooth-faced hammer. The hammer face should be slightly convex so that a tilted blow does not mar the metal. Punches of the right shape can also be used for this. The wire should be a little thicker than the depth of the groove so that it will move into the undercuts. (See Fig. 4–15.)

Large, flat inlays are set in a similar manner. The depression can be etched to the desired depth or carved out with a chisel or graver. The sides should be un-

fig. 4–14

decorative surface techniques

fig. 4–15

dercut with a graver in any case. The small points, as shown in Fig. 4–14, should be raised about ¼″ apart and pointing in many directions.

By laying a small polished steel block over the entire inlay, it can be planished down evenly without the danger of hammer marks.

A simpler technique is to make the base form of two sheets, one solid as a backing, and one with the depressions cut out with a saw. Solder the two sheets together carefully; make certain that the solder runs to all edges. Plink the bottom with a graver and hammer in the inlay.

Shot can be used as the inlay material by drilling and filing a hole into which it fits tightly. A few taps of the hammer spread the shot into the undercuts of the hole. (See Fig. 4–16.)

A variation consists of filing the inlay piece so accurately that it can be soldered into place without hammering.

When inlays are to be hammered, they should fit perfectly but should be one or two gauges *thicker* than the depth of the depression. This allows the metal to spread into undercuts. If differences in surface remain after hammering, they can be filed and stoned away. If it is impractical to use a metal of thicker gauge for the inlay, the

inlay should be domed slightly and filed to fit exactly before hammering.

Another technique, as venerable as it is dangerous, combines finely powdered gold or silver with an equal amount of mercury. The ingredients are worked in a mortar with a pestle until they are of a heavy pastelike consistency. This amalgam is burnished into the prepared depressions and kept at a temperature of about 150°F for two or three days. This must be done with great care and with good ventilation because mercury vapor is highly poisonous. After a few days most of the mercury has evaporated, but the entire piece should be heated to 1100° to 1200°F to remove the last traces. The inlay metal now can be burnished again and the whole form polished.

Dental silver amalgams for filling cavities can be used for this purpose, but this metal is never so white as sterling or fine silver.

A simply inlaying technique uses solder as the inlay. The foundation metal must have a high enough melting point so that the solder can become completely fluid before the foundation metal nears to overheating. Use a liquid or powdered flux mixed with filed solder, and use a larger amount than the depression will hold to compensate for the decrease in volume when the solder melts.

Inlaying copper into photoetched depressions can be done by electroforming the copper into another, contrasting metal, as shown in #4, page 230.

The granular copper can be left above the surface, or it can be filed flush with

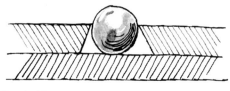

fig. 4–16

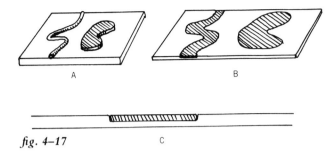

fig. 4–17   C

the surrounding metal. This is one of the best ways to inlay on contoured surfaces.

One metal can be *embossed* into another most efficiently by rolling through a rolling mill. This is a form of inlaying. Both metals to be used must be well annealed. Typically, a small piece of sheet or a length of wire is soldered onto a background piece of metal. Because embossing distorts both the overlay and underlay, precise designing is not possible. (See Fig. 4–17.)

Resulting edge distortions must be filed away. In addition, the *inlaid* effect is never as good as in a true inlay because a slight gap always shows between the two metals. However, highly interesting if somewhat unpredictable results are possible.

INLAYING NONMETALLIC MATERIALS

Wood, mother-of-pearl, and other organic materials can be inlaid effectively in metal.

The inlay procedure using two sheets as the base is most effective for this purpose. Pieces of fairly soft materials, such as wood, can be forced into the inlay depressions with light blows of the hammer or punch. A good mastic cement, as used in fastening Formica to wood, is necessary for inlaying fragile shell and thin sections of stones or gems. For stones or gems, the material should be cut and filed to fit perfectly. If this can't be done, the depression can be made to accommodate the material. Solid plastics can be used as wood is used, and liquid plastics, colored or clear, can be poured into lines and depressions. The champlevé enameling technique is also an inlay process.

A method of inlaying fragments of broken gemstones of certain types in metal depressions recently has become widely used in Mexican jewelry, although it has been an important technique in North Africa and India for centuries. A depression is created by soldering a perforated, thick gauge of metal to a backing sheet or by constructing an enclosure of flat wire. (See Fig. 4–18.)

Lumps of raw gem material, such as turquoise, malachite, or coral, are broken into small fragments $1/8''$ diameter or less. These are packed into the depression in such a way that a large number of flat surfaces face upward. Sealing wax—which comes in several colors such as red-orange, black, and green—is crushed to small grains and sifted into and over the imbedded gem material. (Be sure to use enough sealing wax to allow for shrinkage of volume when the wax melts.)

The work is gently heated from below until the wax melts, thus cementing the gem particles securely. Filing, stoning, and

fig. 4–18

138

decorative surface techniques

polishing develop a handsome, level surface of contrasting texture and color. Liquid thermosetting plastics can be used instead of sealing wax in this process.

• married metals

Married metals, most highly perfected by jewelers and metal smiths of Mexico in recent decades, combines contrasting colors of metal *edge to edge* so that they are all on one plane.

There are three difficult aspects to this handsome process:

1. Sawing and filing edges so that they meet perfectly everywhere.
2. Applying the right amount of solder and avoiding warping and moving during soldering.
3. Removal of excess solder on completion.

By following these steps, you will be able to control the process better.

1. Metals such as copper, bronze, brass, nickel, and silver should be of at least 16 gauge; even 14 gauge is not too thick. A great deal of surface filing will take place later in the process. All pieces should be well annealed and pickled clean.
2. Color contrast can be too subtle, so aim toward strong light-dark interplay.
3. Saw out and refine a first piece, making sure that the edge to be joined to the next piece is precise and *vertical*, not beveled.
4. Lay the finished first piece on a larger blank of the second piece. (See Fig. 4–19.) Using a sturdy needle, carefully trace around the joining edge of the first piece.
5. Saw on the *waste* side of the needle-scored line on the second piece and file up to the line. Make sure that you keep the edge vertical. Test for

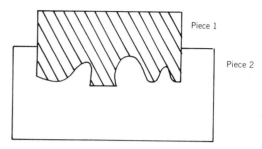

fig. 4–19

matching fit. This cannot be ignored because hard solder will not fill in gaps between edges.

6. Repeat for the third and subsequent shapes. When all are sawed and filed, test for flatness on a smooth steel block. Warps should be flattened by *very light* taps with a wood or plastic hammer while the work is on the steel block.
7. Select a smooth, clean asbestos sheet and place the joined design in position. Paint the seams with flux and distribute snippets of "medium" or "hard" silver solder edge to edge along all joinings. (See Fig. 4–20.) Be prepared to use an excess of solder. It is much more difficult to add solder to fill gaps during a second soldering. Have extra fluxed solder pieces handy to add if necessary while soldering the first time.
8. Heat slowly at first to dry the flux and to settle foaming. Recheck the place-

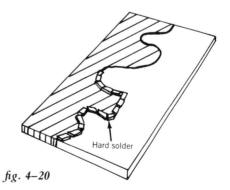

Hard solder

fig. 4–20

139

1

2

3

4

1 Buckle, Anita Sison; marriage of metals; 3″ wide

2 Pin; marriage of metals, copper and nickel silver; the copper is patinated black with liver of sulphur

3 Pendant; silver, copper, bronze, brass; chased and repousséd; 2½″ wide

4 Pendant, Susan Clausen; marriage of metals; 2⅛″ wide

5 Sample of marriage of metals, copper and bronze; the copper is patinated black

6 Pendant; silver, brass washers, mohair yarn; 4″ long

7 Pin, Judy Hugentobler; ebony, copper with embossed silver wire; 2½″ high

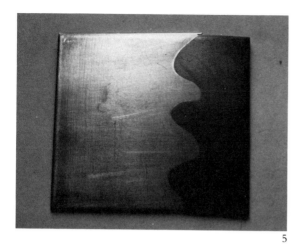

5

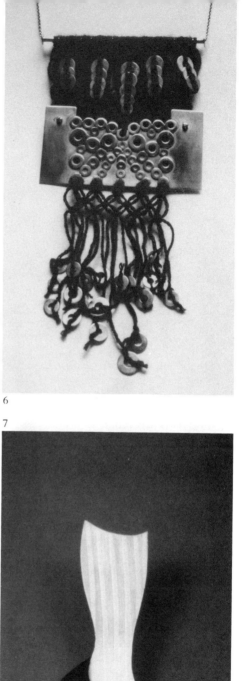

6

7

All student work was done
by undergraduates at
the University of Illinois

ment of the solder. Use a steel pointer to push strayed solder back in line. Heat directly and uniformly over the entire metal surface. Ideally all solder melts at the same time, but some drifting apart can occur. Use the pointer to push edges together again, all the while keeping the torch on the metal. It is often possible to push molten solder into a join it may have avoided with the pointer. Remember, as soon as the flame is removed the solder "freezes!"

9. After pickling, file and scotch-stone excess solder away from the surface. It is possible to do some forming or repoussé at this point, but, since the different metals have different degrees of malleability, this should not be excessive.

10. A high polish is not recommended since reflections hide color contrasts. A wire-brushed, steel-wooled, or sandblasted surface and coloring to contrast even more is much more effective.

11. It is a simple matter to combine drilled holes with wire of the same diameters to form contrasting dots of color. Small sections of wire ($\frac{1}{8}''$) are forced into the holes, soldered in place, and filed and stoned flush with the surrounding surface. Copper wire inlaid in a lighter metal is most effective as it darkens in time.

● enameling

Much has been written in recent years about the art of fusing a colored, glasslike substance to metal under high heat. Contemporary uses of this ancient form of decoration are constantly being devised, and new means of fusing enamels to new alloys have been developed that give enamels far greater range than in earlier times. In this section, only the techniques applicable to the enrichment of jewelry will be described, since a comprehensive discussion of the medium would make a book in itself.

Enamel consists of proportions of flint, lead oxide, soda, and potassium hydroxide. This forms the *frit*, or enamel flux—a clear, colorless glass form. With different proportions of lead oxide and potassium hydroxide, this frit may fuse at higher or lower temperatures.

Metallic oxides are added to the frit to produce the many colors available in enamels. The addition of tin oxide makes the colored enamel opaque or translucent, depending on the proportion. In general, opaque colors fuse at a somewhat higher temperature than do the transparents.

Enamels can be fused to many metals, some of which must first be plated or treated in a way to ensure a good bond of enamel and metal. The techniques of application and fusion of the metal are similar for all of the ways in which enamel may be used.

THE ENAMELS

The basic consistency of enamels is in sheet or lump form. This may be ground to a fine granular texture with an agate or mullite mortar and pestle.

The ground enamel must be thoroughly washed to remove impurities. At the outset of washing, the water is milky, but when this milkiness disappears the enamel is clean enough for fusing. It can be dried on a thin sheet of metal and stored in tightly stoppered jars, or it can be used immediately in its wet, pastelike consistency. A few drops of a gum solution, such as tragacanth or one of the proprietary solutions, enables the moist enamel to adhere to metal surfaces until fusion takes place.

Enamels can be purchased already ground and in a variety of grit sizes. When ground, they tend to decompose much more rapidly than do lumps, so it is best to grind the small amounts used in jewelry when needed.

Decomposition shows as white flakes and milky patches in colored, transparent enamels after fusion.

THE METALS

The most appropriate metals for enameled jewelry are gold (a special enameling gold is available), fine silver, and copper. Sterling silver, though much more durable than fine silver, tends to discolor transparent enamels and, when soldering is necessary, it is affected by the high-melting solders necessary in enameling.

Because fine silver, even after being enclosed in the hard, glasslike enamel, is very soft and easily bent, it must often be set in sterling silver for strength. The enameled portions may be set in the manner of gemstones in bezels or in other holding devices.

All of the metals must be annealed and completely free of oxides and dirt to ensure complete fusion of the enamel. If the object is pickled after annealing and kept under water until ready for the application of enamels, it remains clean.

In some cases, a highly polished surface on the metal is necessary to the enameling technique. After the annealing and pickling process, the surface is burnished with a highly polished agate or steel burnisher without any polishing compound.

A grease- and oil-free surface may be enameled, even if it is heavily oxidized, with rich and interesting results. A clear enamel flux combines with the metal oxides to form a range of browns, reds, and greens.

APPLICATION

The enamel can be applied to the surface in a number of ways. Alternative methods used on small surfaces are:

1. Dry the wet enamel to a paste consistency by holding the edge of a blotter or cleansing tissue to it to absorb excess moisture. With a small polished spatula—made from a 5″ length of 12-gauge copper or silver wire—inlay or spread a small amount of the paste over the metal surface. Use the spatula to spread the layer evenly.

2. Apply the enamel paste to an area that has been moistened with a dilute gum and water solution. Prepare the solution by dissolving a small amount of powdered gum arabic or tragacanth in wood alcohol and add enough distilled water to make a thin solution. A mixture that is too thick can cause discoloration of the enamel after firing. Several prepared adhesive solutions on the market are clean, easy to use, and leave no residue in firing.

3. Sift dry enamel through a fine mesh screen onto a surface coated with the gum solution. The solution should not be too dry before the sifting or the enamel will fall off. After one layer of enamel has been fired, subsequent layers may be applied onto masked portions of the object. The portions to be kept free of enamel will have been covered with paper or masking-tape stencils. When the enamel-gum solution is dry, carefully lift off the masks.

If enamels must fill depressions in the metal, they should be loaded into the depression until the enamel rises above the surrounding surface. After fusing, enamels have about half the volume of dry enamels. Often two or more applications are necessary to fill a depression up to the surface. (See Fig. 4–21.)

When metal of 18 gauge or thinner is used, it is best to "counterenamel." This consists of the application of a layer of enamel to the back of the object for every layer on the front. It prevents warpage of the cooling metal after firing, which causes the enamel to crack. Doming the object slightly also helps.

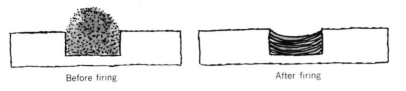

Before firing   After firing

fig. 4–21

FIRING

Enamels can be fired (fused) in an electric kiln or with a torch. The use of a kiln assures a more evenly distributed heat and, with a pyrometer, a firing schedule can be developed that takes much of the guesswork out of this process.

A torch can be used for small pieces especially. It has the advantage of allowing complete observation of the firing process. Direct contact of torch flame and enamel should be avoided if colors are to remain clear. If the work is placed on a tripod covered with a square of nickel-chromium mesh screen, it can easily be heated from below.

A pulsing heat, caused by a rhythmic touch and withdrawal of the flame, seems to fuse the enamel easily without too much danger of overheating the metal.

Before setting prepared work in the kiln or applying the torch, evaporate all moisture from the enamel. This can be done by absorbing most of it with the corner of a blotter, then completing the process by a gentle preheating at the mouth of the kiln.

If too much moisture remains, steam causes the enamel to lift away from the metal and to scatter particles. If this occurs, remove the work and start over again after completely washing off the enamel.

Fire the work long enough so that the enamel becomes viscous. Often it will draw away from edges slightly, but with continued heat it will flatten out again. Overheating will again cause the enamel to crawl away from edges, as will an unclean surface.

At times, small gas bubbles work their way to the surface, and, if firing is stopped, they cause small pits. These often work out with subsequent firings and should not be filled with grains of fresh enamel. New applications of enamel seldom have the same color or clarity as the original.

After firing, allow the object to cool slowly. Never quench it in water or pickle because the enamel will crack.

FINISHING

The most common finish is the freshly fired enamel itself. This has a reflective and lustrous smoothness that tends to confuse the eye. Sometimes a stoned finish brings out color relationships better, and a slight polishing with a rouge buff restores enough of the luster without the garish reflections.

Opaque enamels are often left matte after stoning by many Oriental enamelers to define color separations and changes further.

A short dip in hydrofluoric acid etches the enamel enough to give it a translucent, frosted appearance. Hydrofluoric acid is extremely dangerous to use, so observe the proper safety precautions. The rules are:

1. Work with rubber gloves in a well-ventilated room.
2. Do not inhale the acid fumes.
3. Have a paste of bicarbonate of soda and water ready in case acid touches the skin. Rub on the paste gently and rinse off in cold water.
4. Keep the acid in its wax, plastic, or lead container. Never pour it into a glass jar or tray.
5. Apply the acid with a cotton swab on

decorative surface techniques

a stick. Continuous rubbing for about a minute etches the enamel well.

6. Pick up the object with wooden tongs and rinse it in cold water until free of acid (test with soda paste), or rinse the entire surface on which the object was placed under a gentle stream of water. The work can be placed on a thin board for this purpose.

If some enamel areas are to be left glossy, they can be painted with melted beeswax to protect them during etching. Remove the beeswax with hot water and a rag or with benzene.

CLEANING AND SOLDERING ENAMELED WORK

The metal areas can be pickled cold in a 10% sulfuric acid bath to remove the oxides of firing. Then they can be finished as usual.

Findings should have been soldered on with *hard* or high-melting silver solder before the first enamel firing. Enamels are fired in preheated kilns at about 1500°F, and many solders begin to break down at this temperature. The findings can be protected by a coating of yellow ocher paste to prevent this.

Delicate findings such as earring screws or clips must be applied with soft solder (lead base) after all firing has been completed. Otherwise prolonged high temperatures would soften them too much. If counterenamel has been used, keep a small patch of metal bare of enamel where findings must be applied in the above manner.

One of the best ways to attach enameled units to other metal forms is with rivets. The least stressful riveting can be done by using metal tubing for the rivet. This must also be soldered with *hard* solder before enameling.

The process is illustrated in Fig. 4–22. It can be used to rivet together units of metal in other processes as well.

A. Solder a length of tubing securely in place with a high-melting-point solder. The tubing should be long enough to project $\frac{1}{32}''$ to $\frac{1}{16}''$ past the edge of the rivet hole.
B. Complete enameling.
C. Drill a hole just the size of the tubing and modify it as in Fig. 4–22C. File or scrape a bevel in the top edge of the hole to accommodate the fillet of solder around the base of the tubing. Otherwise, the pieces would not come together well, and force could crack the enamel if this step is avoided!) Another, broader bevel should be made at the *bottom* of the hole to allow for flaring of the tubing when the rivet is set. This assures that only a minimum amount of tubing projects from the hole.
D. Use a conical pointed tool to flare the tubing outward.

DECORATIVE PROCESSES

Most of the enameling forms have been in use for more than two thousand years. The first enamels were inlaid in pockets or cells in metal and used much as precious stones in the decoration of jewelry. The earliest examples of enamel work are from

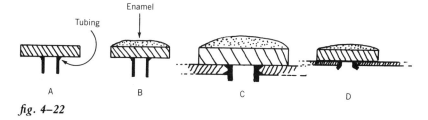

fig. 4–22

Cyprus, Egypt, and other areas of the Middle East. At a later date the knowledge spread to the north and east, where refinements and variations eventually developed.

In the Orient, the Chinese, and later the Japanese, developed the techniques of *cloisonné* and *plique-à-jour* to the highest degree, whereas the Western enamelers of France and the Byzantine Empire developed the *limoges*, *grisaille*, *basse-taille*, and *champlevé* processes to high perfection.

During the Renaissance the enamelers of the French city of Limoges developed a reputation for excellence that remains unmatched today. At that time enamels were often used almost as a painting medium in the *grisaille* or *limoges* technique or as integral elements in the highly complex and sculptural jewelry of the time. A fine example of sculptural enameling can be studied in the Francis I saltcellar of Benvenuto Cellini.

Most enameling on jewelry was done on gold or gold-gilded bronze, silver, or copper during this time. The transparent colors allowed the often richly carved and textured metal to shine through in the *basse-taille* technique.

The contemporary adaptations of some of the major processes follow:

LIMOGES OR PAINTED ENAMEL

1. The cleaned metal is first covered with a fused surface of enamel flux or an opaque color.
2. Other colors are added, either moist and pushed into place with a small brush or sifted on over stencils or masks.
3. Each layer is fired separately, but it may consist of as many colors as desired applied side by side. Since the granules of enamel do not fuse with each other but remain as separate spots of color, finely ground colors must be used to form subtle transitions.
4. As many as twenty or more layers of thin color may be applied before completion, so it is important that a comparable thickness of enamel be applied to the back of the piece as the work proceeds to avoid warping in the metal.

Since *limoges* is a painting process, the success of the piece is in proportion to the craftsman's pictorial design sense. Much mediocre work has been done recently in *limoges* enamel, since the rich color alone may be exciting, but it takes more than a permissive smattering and scattering to come up with a work that is both imaginative and of good craftsmanship. It is too easy to allow this benevolent material to dictate the final result!

GRISAILLE OR CHIAROSCURO ENAMEL

The chiaroscuro effect of strong lights and darks is the basic *grisaille* quality. The forms are developed in white—with occasional touches of other colors—onto a black or dark blue background.

1. The metal is covered with a fused layer of opaque black or a dark blue transparent enamel. This is best sifted onto a gum-moistened surface for even distribution.
2. Opaque white enamel is ground very fine—almost to an impalpable dust if possible. This should be mixed, after thorough washing, with a thin oil or gum solution. Oil of lavendar is usually used for this purpose and may be purchased from enameling suppliers.
3. The white is applied in a fairly thin layer where the form should develop. As they are fired, the white particles sink into the dark background and become gray.
4. Subsequent layers of white over all or parts of the original area become more and more opaque and white as thickness builds up. In this way very subtle modeling can be developed. It can also be enhanced by the slightly raised white highlights.

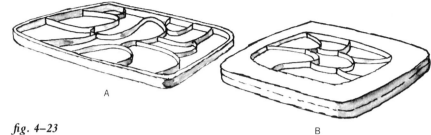

fig. 4–23

A

B

Both the *limoges* and the *grisaille* enamels are best set in a framework of unenameled metal, both as a protection and as a textural and color contrast.

Since enamels do not readily flow when molten, they can be applied to contoured or sculptural surfaces with no danger of distortion. Both of these techniques lend themselves well to this treatment.

CLOISONNÉ OR CELLED ENAMEL

The ancient process of cloisonné can be carried out in a number of ways. The enamel is basically placed in *cloisons*, or walled enclosures, formed by thin, flat wire.

1. The wires, usually of fine gold or silver for flexibility, are either spot-soldered to the basic metal or bent to shape and placed on a surface of enamel. This can be done in two ways: The enamel, usually a thin layer of clear flux, can be fired and cooled. The wire is then put into position and held in place with a thin gum solution. A good solution consists of 1 teaspoon powdered gum tragacanth to 1 quart of water. The gum is first dissolved in a small amount of wood alcohol to which water is then added with some force. The object is refired, causing the *cloisonné* wire to embed itself in the soft enamel. It is important that the cloisons do not sink through the enamel to the metal below. Such contact transmits heat to the cloisons and they often melt along with the enamel! It is also important that the

first layer of enamel be thin so that the *cloisons* are not immediately filled. Overfiring may also cause the fine silver wires to collapse.

The outer edges of a *cloisonné* panel should be reinforced with a heavier wire (Fig. 4–23A), or the enamel area can be cut out of a sheet and soldered to a backing, as shown in Fig. 4–23B. *Hard* solder must be used in all soldering.

The wires must touch each other to form solid cells. If gaps are left, one color might flow into another. This can be done intentionally at times when the wire is used only as a linear device. In this case the color may even be the same in every cell.

A variation of the wire technique consists of cutting out the *cloisons* of thin sheet, perhaps 18 to 20 gauge, and soldering them to the surface of the base. (See Fig. 4–24.)

If the design is to be left in the interior of a form, the *cloisonné* wire should be at least twice as thick as usual. During the stoning process, one of the finishing procedures, enough vibration is developed to crack or bend fine narrow wires if they are not otherwise supported.

fig. 4–24

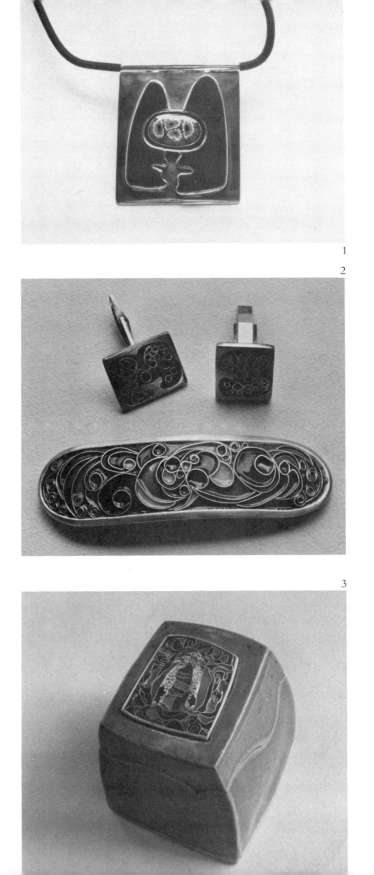

1

2

3

1 Pendant; silver, ebony and millefiori

2 Cufflinks, Barbara Goodman; champlèvé, cloisonné and silver. Barrette, Beverly Fagan; cloisonné and silver

3 Box, Joyce Moty; porcelain celadon. Inset, Eleanor Moty; cloisonné enamel

4 "Go West Young Man, Go West," Alan T. Mette; copper, cloisonné enamel; 2⅛" diameter; 1980. *Photograph courtesy of the artist*

5 "Open Wide, Baby," Alan T. Mette; silver, copper inlay, plique a jour; 7¼" × 6"; 1978. *Photograph courtesy of the artist*

4

5

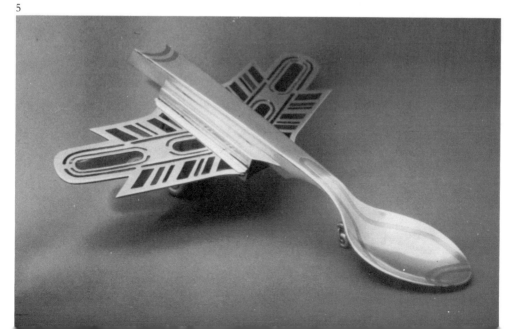

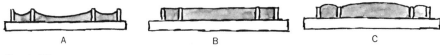

fig. 4–25

2. The colors can now be placed into the cells in paste form and fired. The enamel surface can be left slightly concave (Fig. 4–25A) or flush with the top of the wire (Fig. 4–25B), or even slightly convex (Fig. 4–25C). When this is done, the last layer of enamel is fused after all stoning is completed.

To stone the enamel or the tops of the *cloisons*—as shown in Fig. 4–25A and B—the work is placed on a chamois-covered board and rubbed firmly with a scotch stone until the wire and enamel surfaces are both clean and level. This should be done under running water so that metal and abrasive particles float off. In the case of Fig. 4–25B, the enamel may be left matte from stoning or refired to a gloss. In this case it is best to etch the enamel lightly with hydrofluoric acid to remove all stoning debris. This would cause clouding and spotting if allowed to remain. After the etching, the enamel is refired in a hot kiln—about 1600°F—for a short time (just long enough to cause surface fusion).

PLIQUE-À-JOUR OR WINDOWED ENAMEL

Plique-à-jour is a variation of the *cloisonné* process where there is no background behind wire and enamel. The effect is similar to that of a stained-glass window, and, as with stained glass, it must have a source of light shining through to be effective.

Plique-à-jour is most striking when applied to pendant earrings, which allow light to come from behind.

There are basically three methods for handling this rather difficult technique.

1. Perhaps the oldest technique consists of applying the cloisonné wire to a sheet of thick mica. The wire is spot soldered only where absolutely needed, since the fused enamel will eventually hold it all together. A heavier wire or enclosure of sheet metal should surround the cells because the unit will be quite delicate.

With the mica as a background, the cells are charged with transparent enamels. For the greatest clarity of color, the enamel should be ground only to about 80 mesh. The larger the particles are—within reason—the brighter and clearer the color will be.

The enamel is fused and reapplied until the cells are filled to the tops of the *cloisons*.

Using the chamois-covered board, scotch stone, and water, grind both front and back so that wire and enamel are even.

Since transparency is important, it is best to etch the enamel clean with hydrofluoric acid and then to refire it quickly.

2. The second method uses a sheet of copper foil, 30 to 32 gauge, as a backing. The wires are glued to the backing with a somewhat thicker gum solution than usual. The copper foil should be chemically clean to prevent discoloration of the transparent enamel.

After the enamel has been fired enough to fill the cells, the frontal surface is painted with hot beeswax. Make sure that all edges and sides of the wire are completely covered.

The entire piece is suspended in a solution of nitric acid consisting of 1 part acid to 2 parts water. This solution will quickly eat away the copper foil backing. Be careful that the etch does not attack the wires!

The work can be stoned, cleaned,

and refired on a mica sheet as in cloisonné.

The best method for supporting the work for the final firing is to set it on edge on a nichrome or stainless steel trivet. The danger lies in overheating to the point where gravity will cause the enamel to sag or even open up in the cells. A quick, high heat with constant observation is required! (See Fig. 4–26.)

It is best to avoid enamel areas larger than ¼″ squares that are not intersected with a cloisonné wire.

To key the enamel even more thoroughly, early craftsmen ran the flat wire through the round-hole drawplate just enough to give it a slightly curved section. The concave side was exposed as much as possible to the larger enamel areas.

3. The simplest technique consists of piercing and drilling through sheet metal to form the cells. These may be as close together as desired, or they can be separated by considerable metal surfaces.

The perforations, if no wider than ⅛″, can be as long as needed, but since the enamel charging technique utilizes capillary adhesion, wider areas would collapse during firing.

fig. 4–26

The inner edges of the perforations can be left rough after filing to act as a key for the enamel.

The enamel is mixed with a thicker than usual gum-water solution and floated into the cells with a fine brush.

When completely dry, the work can be supported as shown in Fig. 4–26, or it can rest horizontally on a standard enameling or ceramic tripod. When fired in the latter manner, it is a good idea to reverse the sides for each new firing in order to compensate for the slight sagging of the viscous enamel.

If holes appear through the enamel as a result of insufficient charging or excessive heat, they can often be refilled and refired.

Since some enamel usually runs over onto the flat surrounding metal, it is necessary to stone, etch, and refire the piece to complete it.

Although the contrast of a large metal surface enclosing the enameled windows is very effective, the entire surface can be enameled with clear colors or flux, allowing the perforations to stand out as darker areas.

CHAMPLEVÉ OR INLAID ENAMEL

The Byzantine enamelers brought this technique to its most effective peak with a subtle use of rich enamel colors surrounded by gold or gilded metal surfaces.

The effect of *champlevé* is similar to that of inlaid metal in that both the metal and the enamel may have a common upper surface.

The oldest practitioners used very thin metal that was punched down or stamped to form the cells to be inlaid. Often these thin, weak units were set in bezels or prongs or were tacked to larger surfaces with gilded nails. *Cloisonné* wire was often used within the *champlevé* cells to carry out the design, forming a combination of the two techniques.

Another method of forming the depressions consisted of carving them into a thick sheet with chisels and gravers. This often left an irregular texture showing through clear enamel, although opaque enamels were most often used.

Of the many possible *champlevé* processes, two are most often used today. The first is really an etching process used on copper or silver. The cells are left unpainted with etching ground and the rest, back and edges, thoroughly covered. The piece is then etched as described in the etching section of this chapter, but somewhat deeper than usual. A depth of between $1/32''$ and $1/16''$ is usually sufficient.

If the edges of the cell are irregular as a result of prolonged underbiting, they may be redefined by engraving.

After the ground is removed, the piece should be annealed and pickled to clean it. Enamel is placed wet into the cells and fired. It often helps to place a drop of water into the cell before adding the enamel. This causes the granules to float into all corners and pockets. Excess water can be removed as described earlier.

The enamel can be left slightly concave or filled to the metal surface after the final firing. It can then be stoned and finished as usual.

The second technique uses two sheets of metal. One has the cells sawed out of it and the other serves as the backing. The top piece can be as thin as 22 gauge, but the back should be thicker for strength. (See Fig. 4–27.)

Since in most cases the enamel will cover only a small part of the total surface, counterenameling is usually unnecessary.

BASSE-TAILLE OR SCULPTURED ENAMEL

In *basse-taille*, a variation of *champlevé*, the bottom and sides of the cell are chased, carved, or ground to create textures or intaglio forms. The transparent enamel, being darker in deeper sections, carries out the modeling of high and low relief.

The enamel may cover an entire textured surface, forming the entire jewelry unit, or it may fill a central cell carved into thick metal. The most complex sculptural forms were created in this manner in the Renaissance with great skill in arranging the light or dark areas.

With a flexible shaft grinder, using a variety of stones and drills, it is possible to achieve somewhat the same effect today.

Small cut shapes or granules can be fused or soldered into the bottom of a cell and covered with enamel with interesting textural effect. (See Fig. 4–28.)

The textural possibilities in the use of chasing tools, punches, gravers, grinders, drills, etching, and fusing are unlimited.

It is possible to combine many of the techniques described in one piece, but it is also possible to overdo what should be done with sensitivity and discrimination

fig. 4–28

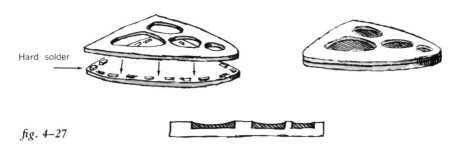

Hard solder

fig. 4–27

decorative surface techniques

from the start. Because of its luster and brilliance of color, enamel is a very dominating medium and must be controlled to avoid a garish or trite result.

ADDITIONAL ENAMELING INFORMATION

FIRING

Enameled metal pieces can rest on ceramic trivets or tripods, or special holding devices can be constructed of nickel-chromium screen or stainless steel sheet metal. Some of the shapes into which metal sheet can be bent to assure adequate heating from all points are illustrated in Fig. 4–29. It is important to avoid spilling granular enamel on holding devices since it will fuse there to contaminate future work. If spilling does occur, file or grind all surfaces that may touch the enameled work before each firing.

It is very important that the unfired enamel be absolutely dry before applying heat in fusing. This will avoid small steam explosions that scatter the enamel. Adequate dryness can be determined in two ways. Ground enamel, because of the rough surfaces of each particle, is lighter in color when dry than when wet or fired. When the applied enamel is again the color of its dry original form before application, it is usually dry enough for firing. Many enamelers preheat the work at the mouth of the kiln or with a torch. If the enameled work is placed before a dark background, small tendrils of steam can be seen so long as moisture exists. When these disappear, firing can proceed, although it is always best to check for displaced enamel grains before finally firing the work. It is much

more difficult to remove these mistakes by scraping and stoning *after* firing.

The length of the firing period is difficult to define since many types of heat are used for this purpose. Also each brand of enamel—and sometimes each color—has its own fusion point.

Close observation is best. The enamel will go through several easily noticed stages during firing:

1. It becomes quite dark—although still retaining its particle shape.
2. The particles become less sharp and defined and the metal begins to turn dull red.
3. The particles fuse to each other and the total mass sinks as the enamel becomes fluid. The surface is still uneven as bumps without ridges. The enamel and the metal may now glow with the same red color.
4. If edges of the metal or walls of *cloisons* or *champlevé* depressions were not clean enough, the molten enamel may crawl away from these areas.
5. Unless the above areas were extremely dirty, the enamel, now thoroughly fired, will spread to its confining areas. The surface will be quite smooth and flat and highly reflective. At this point the work should be removed from the kiln or torch and examined. If small gas bubbles have formed near the surface, they may be pricked with a needle and the enamel reheated for a short period to fuse these depressions together.

The work should now be cooled as evenly and slowly as possible to avoid excessive contraction of the metal.

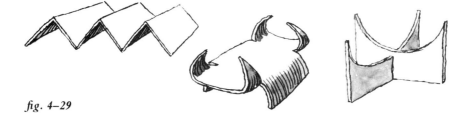

fig. 4–29

Cracks develop when the relatively inert cooling enamel cannot keep up with the more rapid contraction of the cooling metal to which it is fused.

When using copper especially, be sure that oxide flakes have not been deposited on enamel surfaces before any refiring. They would discolor both clear and opaque enamels with dark flecks. Examine the surface with a magnifying glass or eye loupe.

To do highly professional work, it is important that your workshop be dirt- and dust-free. Ground and lump enamels should be kept in tightly stoppered glass vials until used. The cardboard cartons and envelopes in which many enamels are shipped are not good for storage because particles of paper eventually contaminate the enamel and discolor it in firing.

Mortars and pestles should be kept scrupulously clean and used only for grinding enamel. Use only mortars and pestles that are hard enough to withstand lengthy grinding without wear. Agate is the traditional material, but a newer ceramic material, *mullite*, works very well, although it is not much less expensive than agate.

Enamels during use can be kept in small, individual, shallow pans or in depressions in a ceramic paint tray, such as those used for tempera painting. Enamels should be returned—if unmixed—to their separate containers after use.

If work must be interrupted while a piece is being charged with enamel, cover the piece with a small bell jar or its equivalent to protect it from dust.

As mentioned before, enamel does disintegrate in time—especially on constant exposure to air. The opaque enamels do not suffer as much as the transparents, since the effect is one of cloudiness and lack of clarity in color. Consequently, it is always best to regrind and wash at least the transparent enamels just before use.

The decomposed enamel floats off in rinsing, leaving only clear, evenly colored particles in the mortar.

● combining metals with other materials

Metals, especially the precious metals, have a beauty of their own and do not need the enrichment of other materials unless a more meaningful design statement can be made by such a combination. The jewelry designer must always make the correct decision: to allow the metal to dominate the total concept, or to place it in a position of backing or surrounding another material.

It is interesting that in the past complex, highly sophisticated civilizations tended to use metal only as a vehicle behind or around gems or enamel, while simpler cultures used the colors of gems and enamel only as accents in a larger metal treatment. Perhaps both directions are valid, but since metal has been the basis of most jewelry throughout history, it would seem logical that hiding it completely behind incrustations of diamonds and layers of enamel diminishes its value as a material of great beauty and personality.

The balance between materials must be decided in each case—it cannot be covered by a formula. As in all expressive endeavors, restraint and understatement are better than flamboyant exhibitions.

The following sections describe how nonmetallic materials can be used either by themselves or in combination with metal.

WOOD

Exotic or domestic hardwoods such as ebony, rosewood, amaranth, cocobolo, walnut, maple, and many others are all usable because of their dense texture and grain beauty. Being hard, they can be sawed into thin sheets or carved in the round

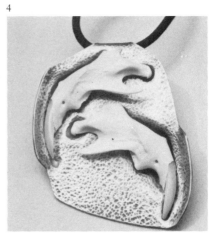

*All student work was done
by undergraduates at
the University of Illinois*

1 Lisa Francona; silver, bronze, mokume, ebony inlay with
fine silver sheet

2 Comb; sterling silver, rosewood; 2″ high

3 Pendant; sandblasted bronze, walnut; 2½″ high

4 Pendant; sterling silver, teeth; 2½″ high

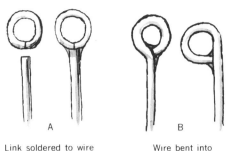
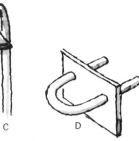

A	B	C	D
Link soldered to wire	Wire bent into circle and soldered	Wire thinned, bent and soldered	U-shape soldered into holes in thin metal plate

fig. 4–30

with little danger of splitting or chipping. Many of these woods can be worked almost like metal. The jeweler's saw, files, emery paper, and various polishing media can be used to give them shape and finish.

Since large pieces are not necessary to the jeweler, it is often possible to purchase scrap wood from lumber companies that supply the furniture industry.

Wood can be used in jewelry in a number of ways:

Small sculptured forms with only metal in the findings.
Set in a bezel as a gemlike unit.
Inlaid into the surface of a metal form.
Alternating with metal or other materials in necklaces, bracelets, and earrings.
Metal inlaid into wood, the wood forming the major part of the design.

A few points are worth mentioning regarding the uses of wood.

Where an independent form of wood is used, the findings must be applied so that they function well and will not be too noticeable. For pendants, a hole can be drilled at the top or just behind the top of the form. The hole should be about one and one-half times the diameter of the wire used to make the pendant loop, and it should be as deep as possible.

The wire loop can be made in several ways, as shown in Fig. 4–30.

The wire stem should be bent into a wiggle shape to fit the hole tightly. It can be cemented into place with one of the

excellent epoxy cements. If a large hole is impossible, the wire stem can be roughened by striking it with the edge of a rough file to achieve the same effect. (See Fig. 4–31.)

Dense woods such as ebony can have the drill hole threaded and a threaded wire stem screwed into place with a little cement in addition.

For heavy hanging objects, the hole can be drilled at an angle and the wire stem bent to a hooked shape. (See Fig. 4–32.)

Pin assemblies and cuff link or earring findings can be attached by soldering them

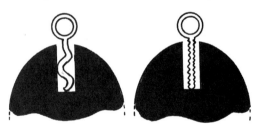

fig. 4–31

fig. 4–32

decorative surface techniques

to a small 20- or 22-gauge sheet of appropriate shape. The sheet is fastened to the wood with pegs and a good epoxy cement. The wire for the pegs should be of the same size as the hole; 18-gauge wire fits the hole drilled by a No. 60 drill bit very well and is strong enough for most pegging needs. It is best to score the back of the metal plate and to remove all grease, wax, or oil from the wood at the point of contact. This assures a good bond of metal and wood with the adhesive.

In most cases two or more pegs are better than only one. With one peg the units may twist eventually and break the adhesive bond. It is simple to solder on two pegs at the same time without the danger of having one fall over while the second is being soldered:

1. Bend the wire into a "U" shape, placing the vertical ends as far apart as needed. Make sure these ends are parallel (even if they are to be soldered to an irregular surface) and that the ends are filed flat. (See Fig. 4–33A.)
2. Premelt a small piece of solder at each point to be touched by the wire end.
3. Hold the fluxed "U" shape with cross-lock tweezers and put it on the premelted solder patches. Rest the hand holding the tweezers on the soldering table to keep everything steady, or use a "third hand" soldering stand. Heat to remelt the solder around the base of the pegs. (See Fig. 4–33B.)
4. Cut off surplus wire to the desired peg length. File ends flat. (See Fig. 4–33C.)

Be sure to remove a little of the shoulder of the hole into which a peg will go. Otherwise the fillet of solder at the base of the wire will prevent a close fit.

Lining up the wire pegs with the drilled holes is simple with the following technique:

1. After soldering, file the ends of the pegs even and level with each other.
2. Carefully perforate a piece of tracing paper with the pegs, making the holes as small and perfect as possible.
3. Use the paper as a template to indicate where the holes should be marked on the wood for drilling.

Or use this technique:

1. Rubber cement the plate to the wood in its correct position.
2. Drill through the plate and into the wood as far as necessary. Use a guide on the drill bits to control the drilling depth.
3. Remove the plate. Rub off the rubber cement. Solder the pegs into the holes of the plate. After soldering, the pegs will line up perfectly with the holes in the wood.

Remember that all soldering, both hard and soft, must be completed before the wood and metal are combined. If metal must be colored, do this before combining, since the coloring chemicals may discolor the wood.

When set in a bezel, the edges of the wood must be chamfered or beveled to a cabochon shape. A little epoxy cement, not enough to show after setting, can also be used. (See Fig. 4–34.)

Wood can be inlaid into metal by preparing a depression of the exact shape as the wood, but with inward-sloping edges. If the wood is slightly too large for the hole, so much the better. A few taps with a hammer on a small steel block will set

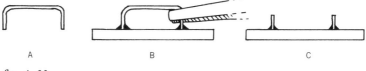

A B C

fig. 4–33

157

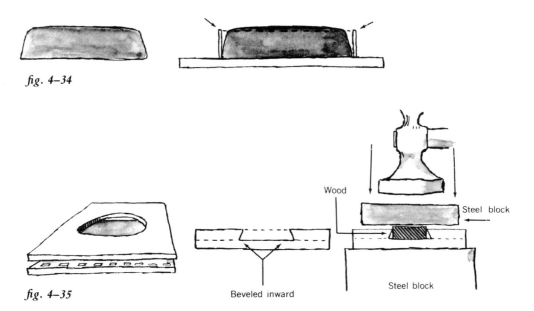

fig. 4–34

fig. 4–35

Wood

Steel block

Steel block

Beveled inward

the wood into the hole tightly. A spot of epoxy cement also helps.

It is best to cut the hole to hold the wood first and to use it as a template for the wood form. By careful sawing and filing you can achieve a very good fit.

Since some forcing of the wood may be necessary, an end grain shape is better to use than one with the grain running horizontally. (See Fig. 4–35.)

Both metal and wood are filed and sanded together to a level surface.

A reversal of the above process consists of inlaying the metal into the wood.

Unless one is skilled with a knife or engraving tools, cutting a bed into wood for a flat metal shape is quite difficult. The edges must be precise and vertical so that no gaps show between the two materials. A thin piece of wood can be pierced and set in a bezel with a metal form of the same thickness used as an inlay, but it will have little strength unless fully supported at the edges and back.

Routing out depressions as deep as the thickness of metal to be inlaid can be done if a good drill press is available. The drill press should be able to lock a *router* bit or a dental *drum* bit at a specific point. This allows the piece of wood to be moved around under the high-speed bit to form a vertical sided depression of even depth. (See Fig. 4–36.)

The metal should be fitted to the depression in the wood. This can also be done in Plexiglas, nylon, or Delrin plastics, since filing the metal to fit is often easier than routing a precise-edged depression. If the router bit cuts too far, the resulting gap, if not too large, often can be filled with a paste made of epoxy and the sawdust of the wood being used. Eventually this can be filed and sanded flush with the metal and surrounding wood. It is a good idea to score the underside of the metal inlay deeply so that the epoxy cement adheres well when the wood and metal are finally combined. A peg can of course be soldered to the underside of the metal, but this is seldom necessary.

Thin lines of metal can be inlaid in wood by inserting thin sheets of metal into lines sawed into the wood with fine jeweler's saw blades. Complex angles and curves

decorative surface techniques

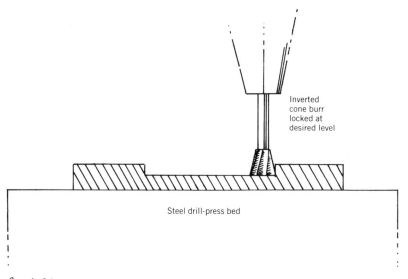

Inverted
cone burr
locked at
desired level

Steel drill-press bed

fig. 4–36

must be avoided because the wood can break easily when fibers are short. The metal must be rolled to the same thickness as the width of the saw cut. (See Fig. 4–37.)

The thin sheets are carefully bent to shape and lightly tapped into the cut. They should be wide enough to go completely through the metal. Both wood and metal are filed and sanded level.

Circles of metal can be inlaid by drilling holes into or through the wood and in-serting wire of the same size as the drill bit. Both wire and sheet should be of fine, unalloyed metal, if possible, in order to allow for burnishing to fill in any gaps that occur. But with careful fitting, any metal can be used.

When wood forms are used to alternate with metal shapes in necklaces, for example, they can be backed with thin metal to which the connecting links are soldered, or, where thickness permits, they can be drilled to allow passage of a chain or thong.

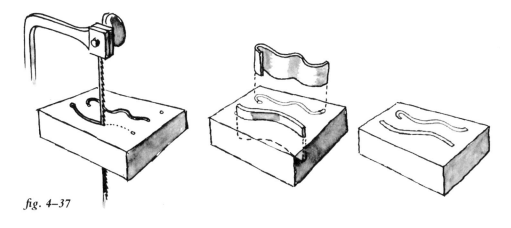

fig. 4–37

159

1 Pendant, Hilary Packard; Plexiglas, electroforming, and gems; 4″ wide

2 Pendant, Laurel Hoyt; sterling silver, shells, Plexiglas; 3¼″ wide

3 Rings, Dan Lewis; cast sterling silver and Plexiglas

4 "Storm" pin, Robert von Neumann; white and clear Plexiglas, gold; 1½″ wide

5 Neckpiece, David W. Keens; sterling silver, 14K gold, agate, polyesters

6 Pendant, Greg Fensterman; sterling silver, Plexiglas formed by heat bending, sandblasting, pearls; 3″ high

1

2   3

160
decorative surface techniques

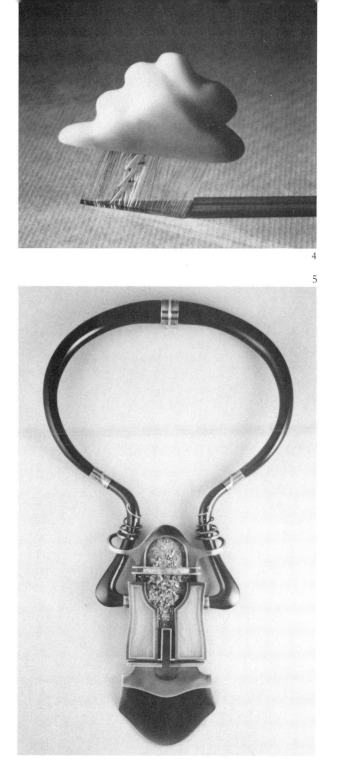

4

5

6

In time, such a hole will wear considerably, so it is best to insert a section of thin metal tubing as protection.

Hardwoods can be finished by soaking them in a container of melted beeswax for half an hour. They can be buffed to a soft luster by hand with a soft, lint-free cloth.

BONE

Bone can be used in the same ways as wood, but has the advantage of greater strength in working. Both hardwoods and bone can be polished to a high luster with emery paper and white rouge. With colored abrasives there is danger of staining the material by forcing the abrasive into the grain. Should this occur, brush the object lightly with a soft brush and a detergent solution. This raises the grain in the wood, so it must be resanded when completely dry.

PLASTICS

The many types of plastics developed in recent years have been misused so often that many artists feel they have little inherent potential as a creative medium. This cannot be true, since a material is never good or bad in itself. It can only be the intelligence behind the working of a material that may be lacking in imagination or sensitivity.

Plastics have such a variety of characteristics that some types can always be found that are suitable for serious decorative art forms. Using only two of the several basic qualities—the hardness and the rigidity of Plexiglas and nylon and the liquid-forming potential of the polyesters and epoxys—an imaginative craftsman may find an infinity of worthwhile jewelry applications.

Perhaps one of the reasons that plastics have a bad reputation is that they have often been used to simulate other materials, such as marble, glass, wood, and metal.

Taken as pure basic materials, the colored or clear plastics are no more obtrusive than any other substance, and they can be used as decorative media in their own right.

As rich as the solid plastics may be as decorative materials, the liquid-forming plastics have even greater potential. They can be cast into forms, and other materials can be imbedded in them while liquid. After hardening, they appear as floating images in a clear, transparent substance.

Some of the countless materials that could be imbedded in plastic for jewelry are delicate wire and sheet forms, too fragile to stand normal wear; plant forms such as leaves, grasses, bark, and other fibers; fabric; wire mesh; insects; rough and polished stones; and complete constructions of precious metal, which are enhanced by enclosure within transparent plastic.

By laying in a layer at a time, a unique sense of dimension can be developed. Solid forms can overlap or curve around each other. Translucent forms can reveal others far beneath them in the plastic.

USING POLYESTERS

The steps to follow in using polyester plastics are similar for plastics of all types. Each manufacturer supplies information regarding proportions of resin to catalyst, setting temperatures, setting times, and so forth. Some additional information for specific uses follows:

MOLD CONSTRUCTION

1. Construct a form into which the plastic will be poured. The mold can be made of thin metal, such as shim brass, heavy paper or cardboard having a glossy surface, or plaster of paris. Small glass bowls or trays can also be used if coated with a separating film for eventual removal of the hardened plastic.

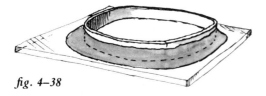

fig. 4–38

Porous materials should be sealed with a thoroughly dried coating of shellac and also coated with a separating film.

Thin metal forms can be built on a sheet of glass and held in position with an outside fillet of plasticene. (See Fig. 4–38.)

2. The polyester is prepared by measuring very specific amounts of resin and adding measured amounts of hardener. At this time a number of special dyes for liquid plastic can be added. Small amounts of transparent dye create faint color tones or opaque dyes may be used for deep, rich color.

A sheet of colored plastic, transparent or opaque, can be cast, hardened, and sawed into small units. The units are then inlaid in clear or colored plastic in a mold.

Shaping can be done by sawing, filing, and sanding, using metalworking materials in each case.

Cutting or buffing can be done with tripoli compound on a fairly slow wheel. Do not apply too much pressure or buff too long between cooling dips in water, since the plastic surface may soften and absorb the cutting compound.

Final polishing can be done in the same manner by using white rouge as the polishing medium. The plastic surface can be protected somewhat by waxing and polishing. If it becomes badly scratched during use, it can be repolished and waxed to maintain its transparent clarity.

USING ACRYLICS

Most of the acrylics are shaped and finished in the same way as polyesters. They can be sawed by machine or with hand saws. Since considerable heat is developed in sawing, it is possible to weld plastic chips to the saw blade. To prevent this, use long strokes to clear the chips, use no excessive pressure, and pause occasionally to let the plastic cool. Filing and buffing with tripoli compound refines these plastic forms very well. White rouge on a soft, unstiched-flannel polishing wheel brings up a fine lustrous polish. Remember to cool the plastic frequently while buffing and polishing. Excessive heat of friction melts the surface and fuses buffing and polishing debris into the plastic. If this happens, file or sand away the debris and rebuff.

Twist drills used for soft metals work well in drilling acrylics. They cut cleaner, more transparent holes if they are lubricated with beeswax. Drilling pressure should be light, steady, and slow—about 2½″ per minute.

Acrylics, such as the several forms of Plexiglas, can be formed by heating. Hot water does not produce high enough temperatures for forming, so an electric oven heated from 250°F. to 300°F. must be used. Infrared lamps can be used, but they will easily overheat the surface of a sheet before the interior is soft enough for forming.

Two methods of achieving a desired form are practical for the craftsman.

1. The Plexiglas is heated to about 275° F, quickly removed and bent to shape by hand, and immediately covered with a soft insulating blanket to slow down the cooling time. If cooled too quickly, the piece may assume its original shape. Use insulated gloves or holding clamps to bend the sheet to prevent burning the fingers!

2. A mold can be constructed of wood—suitably protected with a coat of synthetic rosin varnish—or made of cristobalite casting plaster. The sheet is

placed over this mold and the two are placed in the oven together. As the plastic softens, it sags into or over the mold, following simple contours quite accurately.

Again, the plastic must be cooled slowly by turning off the oven with the piece left inside or by insulating it properly if removed.

There are several cements to be used on one or more of the plastics. The polyesters are best cemented with small amounts of the same material, while the acrylics usually require a solvent that causes a welding action. For Plexiglas either ethylene dichloride or methylene chloride can be used as a cementing solvent.

A number of books and manufacturers' pamphlets describe in detail the many variations and complexities of the plastics. These are listed in the Bibliography.

• gemstones and lapidary work

There are hundreds of minerals that possess the beauty and durability necessary to a gemstone. At various times in history a mineral, because of its color or rarity, became precious to the jeweler. At a later time fashion may have relegated this mineral to obscurity, putting another into its place.

Stones considered precious today usually possess a combination of richness in color and real or artificial rarity. The diamond is by no means a rare stone—its high cost is carefully maintained by mining and diamond-cutting syndicates.

Most of the *precious* stones are clear or translucent and are cut into facets to exploit their refractive and reflective qualities. Diamond, emerald, sapphire, ruby, and some opals are considered by most gemologists to be *precious,* while all other stones are considered *semiprecious.*

The semiprecious stones are too numerous to list, since their value varies from one jeweler to the next. If a stone has a color or texture that is pleasing, it can be used in jewelry even though it is very common.

The following list contains many of the better-known gems, both precious and semiprecious. The listing is divided by colors, although a mineral often has several color phases. These will be mentioned after the stone's listing in each case.

The symbol O means opaque, T means transparent, and TL means translucent.

Some gems are hard and tough, and resist wear well, while others are soft and easily shattered. One measurement of hardness for minerals is called the Mohs Scale of Hardness. This scale ranges from 1, the softest mineral, to 10, the hardest mineral. The list of gemstones also contains the numbers of this scale. (Table 4-1).

Stones of a hardness of 6 or less should be set so that they will be protected from abrasion and shock.

Stones are cut into two basic shapes. The oldest form—little changed for several thousand years—is the *cabochon* cut. This refers to any stone that has not been cut into facets to reflect or refract light. Usually these stones have an evenly rounded top, but this may vary considerably.

The second basic cut is that of the *faceted* stone. These stones have mathematically precise planes ground into the surface, which reflect light as well as breaking it into spectrum colors. Diamonds, if cut as cabochons, are uninteresting, colorless, and glasslike. However, cut with facets, they assume sparkle and brightness.

Recently raw gem materials have been used in jewelry with dynamic effect. Often these fragments—or *roughs*—are refined by tumbling them for many hours in abrasive-filled rotating containers. The effect is that of a highly polished water-worn pebble, which still maintains its original fragment shape even though smooth and flawless on the surface.

TABLE 4–1
HARDNESS AND QUALITY OF GEMSTONES

Color	Mineral	Hard-ness	Quality	Color	Mineral	Hard-ness	Quality
Black					Alexandrite (under incandescent light)	8½	T
	Agate(all ranges from white to brown to black)	7	O; TL		Carnelian	7	TL
	Hematite	6½	O		Coral	3½	O
	Obsidian	5	O; TL		Garnet	6½–7½	T
	Onyx	7	O; TL		Jasper	7	O
Purple					Ruby	9	T; TL
	Amethyst	7	T; TL		Spinel (also pink, blue, green)	8	T
Blue				*Pink*			
	Aquamarine	7½	T		Rhodochrosite	6½	O
	Azurite	4–6	O		Rhodonite	6½	O
	Lapis lazuli	6	O		Rose quartz	7	O; TL
	Sapphire	9	T; TL		Tourmaline	7–7½	T
	Sodalite	6	O	*Brown*			
	Turquoise	4–6	O		Agate	7	O; TL
Green					Amber	2–2½	O; TL
	Agate (moss agate)	7	O; TL		Cairngorm	7	TL
	Alexandrite (in daylight)	8½	T		Smoky quartz	7	T
	Amazonite	6	O		Tiger eye (often dyed red, blue, and green)	7	O
	Aventurine	7	O	*Opaque White*			
	Bloodstone	7	O		Pearl (with green, red, pink, brown, blue, and gray tints)	3–4	O
	Chrysocolla	4–5	O; TL				
	Chrysoprase	7	TL		Quartz	7	O
	Emerald	8	T	*Clear or Translucent White*			
	Jade(also white, gray, brown, black)	6½–7	O; TL		Agate	7	TL
	Malachite	4–5	O		Diamond	10	T
	Olivine	6½	T		Moonstone	6	TL
	Peridot	6½–7	T		Quartz (rock crystal)	7	T
	Tourmaline(also pink)	7–7½	T		Spinel	8	T
Yellow					Zircon	7½	T
	Agate	7	O; TL	*Opalescents*			
	Topaz (corundum)	8–9	T		Labradorite	6–7	
	Topaz quartz	7	T		Opal	6	
Red							
	Agate	7	O; TL				

Some of the more common cabochon shapes are shown in Fig. 4–39.

STONE SETTING

THE BASIC BEZEL

In general, the faceted stones are cut with many flat planes to reflect light. They are set with prongs or in crowns to allow light to penetrate the stone easily. Cabochon stones, rounded or flat in section, are most often set with bezels or inlaid into metal.

Of the many stone-setting processes, the bezel is effective and the least complicated. The bezel material is usually a thin strip of fine silver or gold shaped to fit the stone closely. This collar is soldered to the ob-

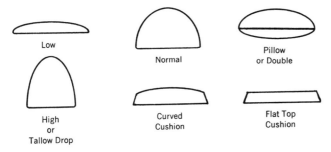

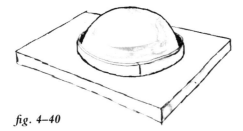

fig. 4–39

fig. 4–40

ject and, after the soldering, coloring, and polishing have been completed, it is pushed against the side of the stone to hold the stone firmly. (See Fig. 4–40.)

Bezels made of thin strips of well-annealed copper or bronze can also be used if color match is important, but they are never as malleable and easily formed around the stone as fine silver or gold.

Following are the steps in constructing a simple bezel:

1. Determine the width of the bezel strip. The strip must be wide enough to go over the inward curve of the stone to just the right height. In Fig. 4–41A the bezel is too high. When burnished around and over the stone, it hides much of the stone, and the excess metal wrinkles and folds.

In Fig. 4–41B the bezel is too low. Not enough metal could be burnished over the curve of the stone to secure it well.

In Fig. 4–41C the bezel is of the correct height. It is low enough so that a minimum of metal will be seen from the sides and the top. The bezel metal itself is 26- or 28-gauge in thickness.

2. After a strip of bezel metal of the correct width has been cut, it is carefully bent around the stone at the base. A mark is made where the ends overlap. The strip should fit around the stone tightly and be without kinks. (See Fig. 4–42.)

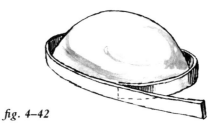

fig. 4–42

A   B   C

fig. 4–41

decorative surface techniques

3. Cut the strip a bit smaller than the mark would indicate. This takes up the slight slack caused by overlapping the ends. It is better to have the strip too short than too long.

4. The two ends of the strip must be filed to fit perfectly. If the cutting shears have twisted the metal, a firm pressure with flat-nose pliers will align the ends.

5. Fit the ends tightly together by press fitting. This is done by moving one end over the other several times so that tension will hold the edges together.

6. Use a small flame to melt one small piece of *hard* solder into the join. Place the solder on the outside of the bezel. Since the bezel is of malleable metal, it need not be formed perfectly before soldering. It may be shaped to a flat oval for stability during soldering and later brought to the shape of the stone. (See Fig. 4–43.)

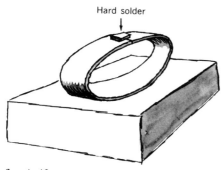

fig. 4–43

Apply the small flame from the top. If the solder seems to flow to one side of the join only, quickly focus the flame on the opposite side. This often draws the solder into the join. Tweezers or a steel pointer can be used to push the melted solder into the join while heat is being applied.

7. Pickle the bezel and remove all flux in hot water.

8. Fit the bezel around the base of the stone. It should be just tight enough to allow the stone to drop through without tilting. If the bezel is too tight, it must be stretched. This can be done by inserting a smooth rod of steel of the right diameter and rolling the bezel back and forth on a hardwood block. Apply pressure to stretch the metal. Check the fit often to avoid stretching the bezel too far. (See Fig. 4–44.)

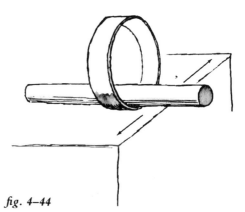

fig. 4–44

If the bezel is too large, it must be cut open to remove a section and soldered again. Make two cuts, one on each side of the old join.

9. The bottom and the top edges of the bezel should be parallel. They can be filed true with a fine flat file—number 0 cut—or rubbed flat on emery paper. Remove all burrs of metal on the edges. Burrs remaining on the top edge cause a frayed surface after the stone is set, and burrs on the bottom edge might cause difficulty in soldering.

10. A hole the shape of the stone and about three-fourths of its diameter is cut into the backing metal if the stone is transparent or translucent. It is best to drill

a small hole through the backing even for opaque stones. This makes it easy to remove the stone if it becomes necessary.

11. The finished bezel is placed around the hole and soldered to the backing. *Easy* solder is used in most cases and is placed on the inside of the bezel in a symmetrical pattern. It is not necessary to wire the bezel into position because gravity will hold it in place. Use as small a flame as is practical. Concentrate it around the outside of the bezel in such a way that all the solder will flow at the same instant. Correct heat should draw it to the inner bottom edge. Do not lean the solder pieces against the bezel. Check constantly that the solder has not moved during heating. (See Fig. 4–45.)

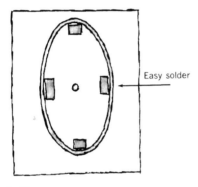

Easy solder

fig. 4–45

If the solder has run up onto the inside wall of the bezel, and not along the bottom edge, it means that the bezel area was heated too soon. Pickle all work, rinse, reapply flux and one or two *small* pieces of *Easy* solder to the inside (as in Fig. 4–45), and reheat, making sure that the base under the bezel is at least as hot as the bezel before concentrating the heat at that point. The first solder should now run down to join the new solder as it flows around the bottom edge. Be sure that you can see molten solder all around the base of the bezel before removing the heat. If the solder refuses to flow all around, stop heating, pickle the work, and find out why. Perhaps bezel and base are not in contact. A gentle downward push on the edge of the bezel often establishes contact. *Important!* Be sure to check the fit of the stone at this point. If the stone fits easily, reflux and reheat until the solder flows all around.

If the stone has a convex bottom half, the bezel must have an inner shelf or *bearing* to keep the stone off the backing metal. A stone of this shape is impossible to set firmly otherwise.

If the curve is slight, a small inner ring of wire may give the desired height. With deeper curves it is necessary to solder in an inner bezel. Some craftsmen prefer to use a manufactured bearing bezel, available in a variety of shapes.

An inner bearing is necessary even for flat-bottomed stones if the backing metal is curved, as in a ring or bracelet. In this case, the bezel should be wide enough to allow the filing of a compensating curve. The inner bearing should be soldered in place before the bezel is filed to fit the curve of the backing surface. (See Fig. 4–46.)

Never solder the bezel into a position where it becomes impossible to burnish the edge around the stone. Do not allow the side of the bezel to be soldered to another element in the design. This would make it impossible to burnish the top edge evenly.

A bezel can be asymmetrical in shape to fit an unusual surface or stone shape, but only enough bezel metal should be used to hold the stone securely. Excess bezel material wrinkles easily in burnishing.

12. The stone is usually set after the whole work has been colored and polished. The burnishing can be done with a small curved burnisher or with a stone

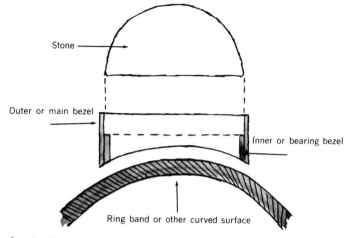

fig. 4–46

pusher. In both cases the bezel is pushed against the stone at opposing points in at least eight places before a final, even pressure is applied all around the stone. Fig. 4–47 diagrams the beginning pressure points. The pressure points are opposed in sequence to keep the stone centered. After the bezel is crimped inward at eight points, the stone pusher is moved slowly around the circumference with short, even, overlapping pressure.

After the bezel lies smoothly around the stone, the burnisher can be used to remove any tool marks. Have com-

plete control of the burnisher at all times, since a slip here can cause considerable damage.

The top edge can be made smooth and the stone tightly set by running the pusher around the edge once or twice. (See Fig. 4–48.)

THE REVERSE BEZEL

Cabochon stones can be set *into* the backing metal in a number of ways.

In one technique the hole through which the stone penetrates is cut and filed to the

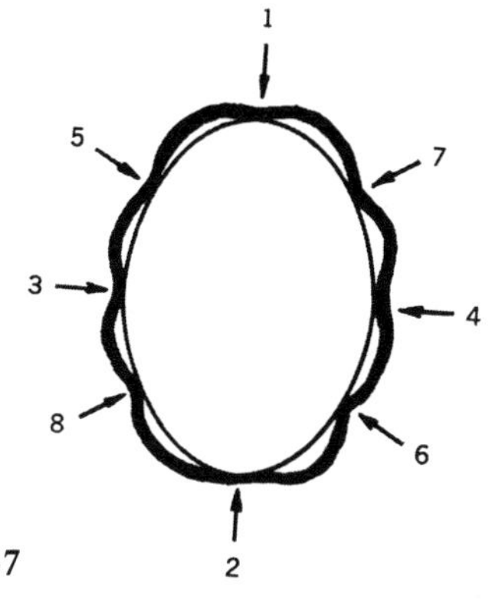

fig. 4–47

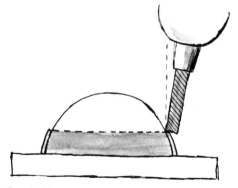

fig. 4–48

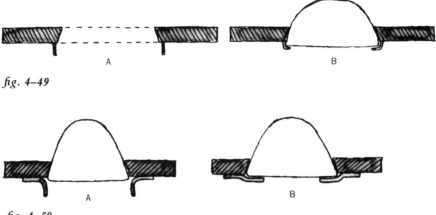

fig. 4–49

fig. 4–50

right size and angle to fit the stone securely. (See Fig. 4–49.)

If the stone is transparent or translucent, a narrow bezel is soldered on the reverse of the backing metal, as in Fig. 4–49B. This is burnished over sharply to press the stone firmly into the hole cut for it. Do not use more bezel width than necessary.

If the stone is opaque, three or four tabs of fine silver, 22 gauge, can be used to clamp the stone into place. Note that in Fig. 4–50A the tabs are soldered only to a

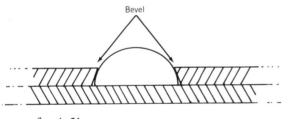

fig. 4–51

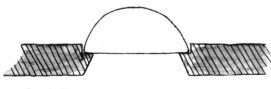

fig. 4–52

point *near* the edge of the hole. If soldered to the edge, the tabs could not be bent back to admit the stone.

A flat-based stone with chamfered edges can also be inlaid into other materials such as wood, plastics, or bone. The hole for the stone is carefully prepared as for a reverse bezel. The wood or other material is cemented and pegged or riveted together as in Fig. 4–51. Since the top edge of the hole is smaller than the maximum diameter of the stone, the stone is held securely.

THE GYPSY SETTING

The gypsy setting, although more complicated, uses no bezels or tabs on the reverse, which might be unsightly in a design.

For this setting various drills and burrs are necessary. The first step consists of drilling a hole through the point under the center of the stone with a No. 65 twist drill bit.

A drill just the diameter of the stone and with a flat end is used to cut a bearing for the stone. This cut should be only about /32″ deep.

A tapered burr drill is used to cut a tapered hole from the reverse to give a section, as in Fig. 4–52. The small hole first

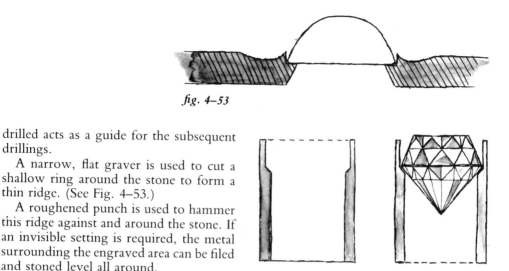

fig. 4–53

drilled acts as a guide for the subsequent drillings.

A narrow, flat graver is used to cut a shallow ring around the stone to form a thin ridge. (See Fig. 4–53.)

A roughened punch is used to hammer this ridge against and around the stone. If an invisible setting is required, the metal surrounding the engraved area can be filed and stoned level all around.

FACETED-STONE SETTING

Faceted stones can be set in any of the above ways, but they are shown to best advantage by prong or crown settings. When light is allowed to reach the stone from all sides, as well as from the top, reflections from the insides of the facets give the stone greater brightness and color.

There are a number of techniques for making a prong or crown setting for faceted stones. Perhaps the most basic method consists of making a short tube, or *collet,* of 16- to 18-gauge sterling silver (a lighter gauge in gold). This tube should be of the same outside diameter as the stone and as high as the setting is to be. Tubing of the desired wall thickness can be purchased for this purpose in square or round section.

If the tube is to be constructed of sheet, it should be made in such a way that the join meets perfectly for its entire length. This can be done by overlapping the ends while wrapping the sheet around a mandrel of the correct size and making the join with a cut of the saw. The ends are carefully brought together and soldered with *hard* solder. True the tube on a mandrel if necessary. True the top and bottom edges with a flat file.

fig. 4–54

Next, fasten the tube to a pointed stick of the right size with melted sealing wax. The stick can be held in a ring clamp for convenience.

A bearing about $\frac{1}{16}''$ deep must be cut into the inner top edge of the collet to form a seat for the stone. (See Fig. 4–54.) This can be done with a narrow, flat graver, with a drum burr in a flexible shaft tool, or with a narrow scraper. Do not make the bearing too thin, since this will weaken the prongs when the stone is set. At this point the collet is too small to allow the stone to fit into the bearing. After the prongs are cut they are bent out enough to slip the stone into position.

The prongs are cut by angling the saw— with a 0 blade— in such a way that one prong at a time is formed. The collet can be held on a small dowel with sealing wax. (See Fig. 4–55.)

The other prongs, usually of an even number, can be cut in the same way.

The result at this point looks quite heavy and detracts from the light, airy setting the stone requires. Much of the bulkiness can be avoided by beveling the edges, as well as the curve, at the base of each prong.

fig. 4–55

fig. 4–56

If the collet is to be high, the base should also be notched symmetrically to increase lightness. (See Fig. 4–56.)

The file and saw marks can be removed with folded bits of emery paper or with a trumming string and tripoli.

After it is polished, the collet is soldered to the backing metal with small pieces of solder at appropriate points. Use enough solder to ensure a strong join.

After the entire work is finished and polished the stone can be set. The prongs are slightly bent outward by pressing down between them with a round dapping punch somewhat larger than the stone.

The stone is set in place and, while it is held securely with the index finger of one hand, the points of the prongs are pressed over the edge or *girdle* of the stone. Press at opposing points at all times. Use a stone pusher whose surface is slightly roughened to prevent slipping.

Most craftsmen use a graver to cut the sides and the top of the prong to a point. A polished, curved burnisher is used to give the final downward pressure to the points so that they cannot catch on clothing. (See Fig. 4–57.)

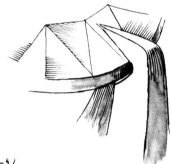

fig. 4–57

For small stones, 5 mm. or less in diameter, simple bearing settings can be made of thin-walled silver or gold tubing with an inside diameter slightly smaller than the girdle diameter of the stone. A bearing is ground or drilled a short distance down from the upper edge of the tubing, similar to that in Fig. 4–54. The stone is dropped onto this bearing, and the edge is burnished around the stone as in a bezel setting.

Crowns and other types of facet settings can be purchased ready-made with collets to fit virtually all stone shapes and sizes, but for work that is integrated throughout all of its parts, a manufactured fitting of this sort is seldom harmonious.

THE PAVED SETTING

Another basic setting is the *paved* setting for both cabochon and faceted stones.

A hole is drilled as a guide for larger drills to follow. Then with a flat drill a hole is drilled deep enough to seat the stone securely, but not so deep that much of the stone is hidden. A hole 1/32″ deep is sufficient for most stones.

Another hole, somewhat smaller than the diameter of stone at its base, is drilled through from the reverse side. If the stone has a curved or pointed bottom, a tapered burr drill must be used for the last hole. (See Fig. 4–58.)

fig. 4–58

Next, the piece is completely finished, after which the stone is temporarily fixed into the bearing with a drop of melted sealing wax. This can be removed later by a soaking in benzene.

A lining graver is used to make a series of four to six cuts 1/16″ long aimed toward the edge of the stone. These cuts should angle quite steeply into the metal and stop just short of the stone. An upward tilt of the graver lifts up a small prong of metal at the end of each cut. (See Fig. 4–59A.)

This prong is pressed down and next to the stone with a beading tool of the right size. This tool, usually purchased as a set of twelve points, consists of a round wooden handle and ferrule into which small steel rods are fixed. The rods taper at the

tip and end in concave depressions of various diameters. By rocking and turning the tool gently but firmly, the prong of metal is worked into a small spherical *grain,* which clamps the edge of the stone into place (Fig. 4–59B).

Many stones can be set side by side into the surface of a piece by this technique. This gives it the name of *en pavé,* or paved setting.

SETTINGS FOR UNUSUAL STONE SHAPES

There are times when a stone must be set away from a backing material. In these cases structural strength of the setting is all-important, since otherwise the stone might easily be lost.

Many of the finest stones seen today are cut asymmetrically or are left in a polished but irregular form, as in tumbled stones. In most cases they have no bottom plane, nor do they have an even girdle around the circumference. To set these stones well tests design and construction ingenuity, since the setting should, in most cases, be unobtrusive.

The now too-familiar wire wrapping of tumbled or rough stones is one simple method, but the technique always looks the same. Certainly this is a criticism.

There are other "cage" settings that can be related better to the total design of a work.

For rounded or plane-cut stones that are to stand free, the sketches shown in Fig. 4–60 may suggest additional directions.

The electroforming process, described

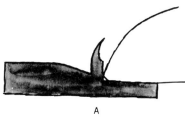

A

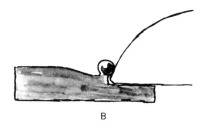

B

fig. 4–59

fig. 4–60

in Chapter 6, suggests a great range of stone-holding possibilities.

PEARL SETTING

The most secure way to set a pearl, or any other partially drilled semiprecious stone, is also the most difficult. It is worth mentioning because it shows the pains to which earlier jewelers went to achieve a craftsmanlike piece of work, and there might be times when maximum security is necessary.

The pearl must be half drilled. If it cannot be purchased this way, you may have to do this yourself.

A drilling jig is simple to construct. Take a strip of 14-gauge aluminum sheet, 10″ × 2″, and bend it in half lengthwise. Next, drill a series of holes ½″ from the open end and through both halves of the clamp. Make these holes 1/32″, 1/16″, 1/8″, and 1/4″ in diameter. Using appropriate round dapping punches, make a series of smooth hemispheric depressions on the inside edges of each hole; sand and polish them so that the pearl will not be damaged during drilling.

Make a sliding sleeve of a strip of aluminum or other metal and, after forming it around the clamp (as in Fig. 4–61), crimp the ends together. This sleeve, when pushed up toward the pearl, will press the clamp jaws tightly onto the pearl. (Fig. 4-62).

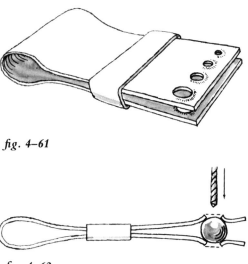

fig. 4–61

fig. 4–62

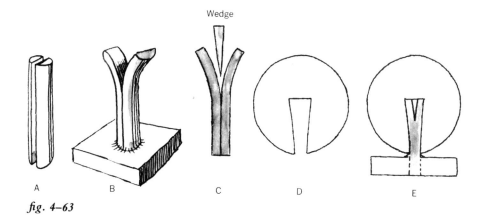

Wedge

A   B   C   D   E

fig. 4–63

Although there are special drill bits and bow drills made for pearl drilling, a sharp twist drill bit in an electric drill press or flexible shaft tool will do as well. Use a low speed and add water occasionally for cooling. It is easy to drill too far through cultured pearls, since the hard nacreous coating thinly covers a softer interior. Use a bit of tape on the drill bit as a depth indicator, or set the bit into the chuck at the right depth.

The peg is constructed by using two pieces of 18-gauge round silver or gold wire and drawing them through the drawplate together. In time the wires become half round in section and can be drawn to the same diameter as the hole in the pearl. The two half-round sections of wire are soldered partially with hard solder. It is necessary to bend the ends apart slightly so that solder does not flow along the entire length. The peg is now soldered into place. Next, construct a small wedge of

metal to spread the two wires apart when the pearl is lightly forced onto the peg. (See Fig. 4–63C.)

The hole in the pearl must be enlarged at its interior end. This is done with a very small dental burr that is rotated around the inside but not the outside opening of the pearl. (See Fig. 4–63D.)

A small drop of pearl cement is placed in the hole on the end of a piece of wire and the pearl pressed onto the peg with the wedge lightly in place. (See Fig. 4–63E.)

If this is done accurately, the pearl cannot fall off.

Another technique uses a cup of thin metal into which a solid peg is soldered. The cup can be punched out on a lead block with a dapping punch the size of the pearl. The cup should not come up to more than the quarter of the height of the pearl. (See Fig. 4–64.) A small hole is drilled into the center of the cup and a wire peg—just

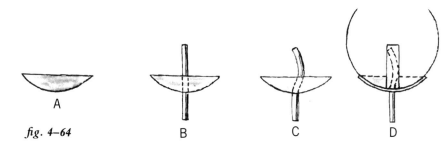

fig. 4–64   A   B   C   D

175

a little thinner than the diameter of the hole in the pearl—is soldered into it. (See Fig. 4–64B.) Place the solder on the convex surface of the cup. If necessary, the projection of wire can be nipped and filed off, or it can be fitted and soldered into a hole in the piece of jewelry. (See Fig. 4–64C.)

After the work is polished, a drop of pearl cement is placed in the pearl hole and into the cup. The interior of the cup should be roughened with a scriber and the wire peg should be bent slightly. When the cement hardens, the bend in the peg acts as a clamp. (See Fig. 4–64D.)

Pearls can also be set in cups with prongs. These can be constructed or purchased in a range of sizes. Pronged cups are usually used with undrilled pearls.

Pearls that are drilled through completely can be set in several ways.

1. A peg of fine silver wire is soldered to the backing metal. The diameter must be just that of the drilled hole in the pearl. Allow 1/32″ of wire to project past the top of the pearl when it is in position. A beading tool of the right size is used to compress and round off the projecting end. This acts as a rivet. Do not use too much pressure because pearls chip and scratch easily. (See Fig. 4–65A.)
2. A peg made of two wires, as in Fig. 4–65B, is soldered into place. The peg should fit the hole tightly. The ends should project at least 1/16″ past the top

of the pearl. Then they are bent down over the pearl to hold it.

3. A peg of fine silver with a small sphere of gold or silver soldered to one end is placed through the pearl and through a hole drilled in the backing metal. The peg should fit this hole tightly. The projecting end is burnished or spread over with a burnisher or a pointed punch to rivet the peg into place. (See Fig. 4–65C.)

Baroque or irregular pearl shapes can be set in beds of thin fine silver or 24K. gold sheet. These must be formed to fit the contour by repoussé techniques. The addition of a peg and cement is advisable.

Sometimes baroque pearls have a flat base, in which case a bezel construction would work well.

There are several kinds of pearl cement available, but the liquid types, usually a resin and a catalyst, are the easiest to use. Most cements dry slowly, so it is best to clamp the pearl in position with a padded spring clothespin for at least twenty-four hours.

BASIC LAPIDARY TECHNIQUES

The variety and the complexity of lapidary tools and equipment have greatly increased in recent years. Thousands of people find satisfaction in the act of creating striking gems from often uninspiring rough mineral materials.

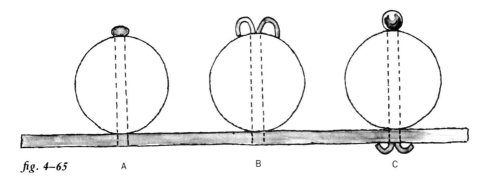

fig. 4–65   A   B   C

decorative surface techniques

The activity has become so important that many companies now produce cutting saws, grinding wheels, and polishing units. Other companies collect and sell rough gem materials from all over the world.

It is not within the scope of this book to go into great detail about a craft that has its own history and complexities. It should suffice to state generally the basic steps of lapidary work and to describe the most necessary equipment.

Since there are several excellent dealers in cut and polished gems—most of whom are willing to send the craftsman a good variety of stones on consignment—most jewelry makers are able to satisfy their needs directly.

There will be times, however, when a stone of certain size, shape, and color must be designed for a specific piece of jewelry. Here an elementary knowledge of lapidary work becomes necessary.

Although much cutting and polishing, especially of such soft stones as turquoise and obsidian, can be done by hand with the proper abrasives, the range of possibilities is limited by both time and gem characteristics.

Lapidary units can be purchased in sep-arate parts or constructed from the most basic fittings. However, it is convenient to use a combined unit, which includes a slab and trim saw, grinding wheels, both rough and fine, and interchangeable sanding and polishing discs or drums. (See Fig. 4–66.)

The steps in forming a simple cabochon stone follow:

SAWING

The rough gem material is first sawed into usable slabs. This can be done by feeding the slab into the revolving saw by hand or by clamping it into a cradle that will move it forward automatically. The saw for this purpose is a thin disc of bronze, copper, or steel. Diamond chips or dust are embedded in slits on the edge of the saw or fused to the edge by sintering. For most stones, a speed of 2,000 to 3,000 surface feet per minute is adequate. This means that if a 10″ saw is used it will require an electric motor running at 1,725 rpm with a motor pulley 2½″ in diameter and an arbor pulley (to which the blade is attached) of 4″ diameter.

The saw must run through a lubricating and cooling bath. Cooling is necessary to

fig. 4–66
Courtesy, Highland Park Mfg. Co.

1

2

3

4

5

6

1 Pendant, Vivian Faulkner-King; silver, copper, jasper set from behind; 2⅛" high. *Photograph by the artist*

2 Pendant, Don Strandell; silver and rosewood

3 Pendant; bronze, walnut, agate set into wood from behind; 2⅛" high

4 Pendant; ebony, silver tubing and wire

5 Pin; sandblasted bronze and pearl

6 Pendants; silver, copper, ebony, ivory, and moonstone

7 Pins and pendants; silver and ebony

8 Pin, pendant and cufflinks; silver, ebony, ivory, and jade

7

8

All student work was done by undergraduates at the University of Illinois

1

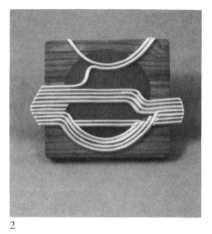

2

3

4

1 Macramé necklace, Eleanor Moty; copper wire and handmade porcelain beads

2 Buckle, Kim Kerbel; silver and bronze wire, ebony and cocobolo wood; 2″ wide

3 Pendant; Ric von Neumann: sterling silver, bezel-set opal; 2″ wide

4 Pendant, Louis Marek; silver and ebony

5 Buckle; copper, silver, brass; 3″ wide

6 Macramé necklace, Eleanor Moty; brass wire with crystal beads

7 Leopard pin, Jean L. Ascoli; copper, silver, bronze, polyester resin, turquoise; 2″ × 4″; 1978. *Photograph courtesy of the artist*

8 Pendants, Sandy Klynstra; bronze and brass with ebony and leather

5

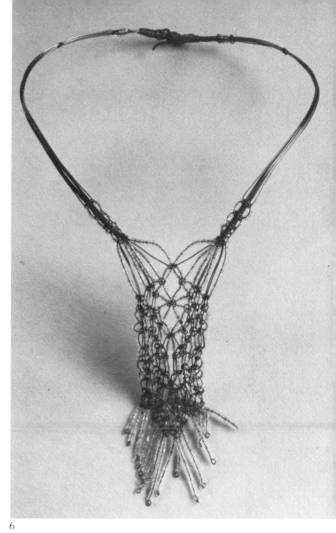

6

8

7

181

prevent cracking the stone, and lubrication reduces wear on the saw edge. Although water can be used, a commercial miscible (water-soluble) oil designed for slab sawing is far superior. The sludge and debris collected after considerable sawing should be removed regularly to reduce wear on the blade.

While cutting, enough of the lubricant should be picked up by the saw so that the cut never runs dry.

Hold the work firmly so that the saw is not bent during cutting. A steady, even pressure, just hard enough to continue the cut, is best. Never cut completely through a slab. Join a long cut with a short one from the opposite direction.

After the slab has been cut, it can be trimmed to a usable shape in the same way.

GRINDING

The blank is ground to its contour shape on a rough grinding wheel (100 grit). For most stones a surface speed of 4,000 to 6,000 feet per minute is best. Pulleys may have to be changed as the diameter of the wheel decreases with wear. A slow wheel is not only inefficient but also quickly forms grooves and pits that may break the gemstone.

Water should drop onto the forward surface of the wheel during grinding. If ground dry, the wheel's frictional heat can crack or permanently discolor a gemstone.

Unless the blank is very small, it is simpler to hold the stone by hand rather than mounting it on a dop stick. Rough-grinding the stone to a symmetrical shape and to a specified outline takes considerable practice. Remember that the revolving wheel can be dangerous. It can easily cut into a finger almost before you notice it.

When grinding edges, avoid chipping by first grinding a slight bevel on both top and bottom edges. This bevel of course must be renewed as the edge is ground away to the desired circumference.

Flat surfaces can be ground on the side of the wheel. It is often difficult to cool this surface with water, so the stone temperature should be checked often.

After the basic form has been ground on the rough wheel, it can be refined to remove flats and irregularities on the smooth grinding wheel (220 grit) running at the same speed.

DOPPING

Before going to the next step, sanding, the stones must be mounted on dop sticks. These can be made of 5″ lengths of hardwood doweling. A range of diameters from ⅛″ to ¾″ will handle many stone sizes. The stone is attached to the dop stick with a dopping cement made of sealing wax, stick shellac, and beeswax. This combination can be purchased ready to use from lapidary supply houses. Sealing wax alone is an adequate cement, but it tends to be brittle.

The cement is heated just to melting in a small container and the sticks are dipped to a ¼″ to ½″ depth. After allowing the cement to bond to the wood for a moment, remove the sticks and set them, cement end down, on a smooth metal surface. On cooling they should have a small, flat platform of wax to which the stone may be fused.

The stone must be heated properly to assure a strong bond. A small oven can be constructed, using a tin can into which a small alcohol burner is placed. (See Fig. 4–67.)

Since the bottom plane of the stone is sanded and polished first, the stone is placed flat side down on the oven top and is heated, using a very small flame to reduce heat shock. The correct stone temperature can be determined by placing a small drop of liquid shellac on the stone. When this bubbles, the stone is hot enough. On sensitive stones, such as opal and obsidian, less heat should be used. The stone should be just hot to the touch.

fig. 4–67

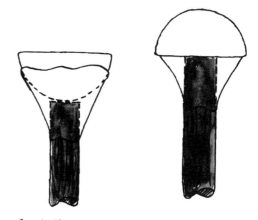

fig. 4–68

When the stone is warm enough, the prepared dop stick is heated and placed into position, and the stone lifted to a metal sheet. As the cement cools, the stick should be centered and checked for the correct angle. It should be at right angles to the flat plane of the stone. The warm cement can be modeled around the base of the stone with the fingers. Dip your fingers into cold water before touching the cement or it may burn. Never allow cement to form over the edge of a stone, since it will pack into sanding surfaces and greatly reduce the cutting action. Allow the cement to cool completely before going to the next step.

A well-dopped stone should look like the sketch in Fig. 4–68.

SANDING

Sanding can be done in a variety of ways: on circulating belts of abrasive cloth, on discs of cloth or paper cemented to wheels, or with loose abrasives on wood or metal horizontal laps.

The method used with the machine illustrated in Fig. 4–66 is the second technique. Discs of abrasive paper in three grit sizes—220, 400, and 800—are cemented to a vertical wheel with a special rubber cement. The wheel is padded with sponge rubber under a tight cloth cover. This resilience is necessary when sanding curved surfaces. The abrasive paper should be the wet-or-dry type and be water-cooled to avoid overheating the stone or causing the dopping cement to soften.

The sanding wheel should revolve at about 4,000 feet per minute. Keep in mind that only the outside portion of the wheel diameter achieves this speed. Speed is reduced quickly toward the center of the wheel.

In sanding, the dop stick is held with the tips of all four fingers on one side of the stick and the thumb on the other. The stick forms a line with the wrist and lower arm. By rotating the hand at the wrist, you achieve a circular or oscillating motion so that the stone never rests long in one place. The pressure on the stone against the wheel varies with the hardness of the stone, but it should be uniform at all times. Sanding *with* the saw or grinding marks removes scratches faster than sanding *across* them.

The marks of the previous operation

should be removed before going to the finer abrasive, and all abrasive debris must be carefully washed off between steps. When the 220-grit sanding is finished, the stone should be symmetrical and the subsequent abrasives used only to make it smoother.

POLISHING

After sanding, the stones and dop sticks must be carefully washed to avoid contamination of the polishing materials.

The polishing buffs can be of wood, leather, felt, or foam rubber covered with chamois.

The polishing media for soft to medium-hard stones are: cerium oxide, tin oxide, levigated alumina, rouge, tripoli, zirconium oxide, and Linde A ruby powder.

The polishing media for hard stones are chromium oxide and diamond powder.

The polishing buff is wetted thoroughly with water and a little detergent. The abrasive powder is brushed on after being mixed to a heavy cream consistency with water.

A low speed of 450 to 800 rpm is used in polishing, along with considerable pressure. Since pressure is necessary, the back of the stone should be supported with the thumb and forefinger. Use the same oscillating action of the wrist as in sanding. Check the stone surface frequently after wiping with a paper tissue. If the stone has been carefully ground and sanded and the correct polishing powder used, the polishing step should be completed quickly.

The stone can be removed from the dop stick to expose new surfaces for sanding and polishing by heating and removing it with a quick twist. What cement remains can be dissolved off with alcohol or benzene.

After polishing, the stone should be cleaned by brushing it with warm, soapy water and a soft brush.

DRILLING

Drilling holes through gemstones is simple, but it takes time. There are special drills made for this purpose, both electric and hand operated. An ordinary electric drill press, however, can be adapted for drilling.

The materials for drilling are:

1. Several 2″ to 3″ lengths of thin-walled sterling silver, stainless steel, or bronze seamless tubing. Outside diameters can range from 1/16″ to 3/4″ or larger.
2. A small, 3″ × 3″ open box of wood or metal.
3. Plaster of paris.
4. No. 10 motor oil.
5. Fine (400 grit) carborundum or fine diamond powder (100 to 200 grit).

The box is half filled with a thick mixture of plaster of paris. The gem material is imbedded into the soft plaster so that the top of the stone is just level with the plaster.

After the plaster is hard and completely dry, it is sealed with a soaking coat of shellac or lacquer. This prevents it from absorbing the lubricating oil during drilling.

The abrasive powder is mixed to a creamy consistency with the oil and poured into the box to the depth of at least 1/8″.

The box must be clamped securely into position on the drill press table so that the drill will constantly touch down at the same point.

The drill is prepared by lightly scoring the edge of the end with a thin-bladed knife and a light hammer. These scorings will grip the abrasive enough to cut the stone. (See Fig. 4–69.)

The tubing is accurately centered in the chuck of the drill press. Any wobble will cause inefficient drilling and may jam the drill itself. Make sure that the tube will come down at the right point on the stone.

Perhaps the most important action in

decorative surface techniques

fig. 4-69

drilling is to use a light up and down pressure of the drill. Just touch the drill to the stone and lift it again. This allows lubricant and abrasive to flood the bore after each stroke. The up and down strokes are repeated with even pressure until the drill has cut almost through the gem. At this point even lighter strokes are used until the drill goes through.

The stone is now reversed and drilled through from the other side to make the hole sides parallel.

The plaster is carefully chipped or broken away from the stone, and the stone washed with warm water and detergent to dissolve any oil absorbed by the surface.

Construct a small shield of heavy paper and masking tape at a point where the tubing enters the jaws of the drill-press chuck. This prevents abrasive particles from working up into the drill shaft, where considerable damage could result.

FACET CUTTING

Many of the stones cut cabochon are also cut with facets to reflect light.

The equipment for facet cutting can be extremely simple, but is may require years of practice to achieve the skill needed for accurate and rapid faceting.

Today several mechanical devices are available that take out the guesswork and intuition of older techniques. The equipment consists of a horizontal lap or wheel. This may be made of hard metal such as steel, iron, or copper and a soft metal such as lead, tin, or zinc. In addition, wood, plastics such as Lucite or Plexiglas, and wax-impregnated cloth cemented to aluminum are used.

The abrasives for cutting are silicon carbide or diamond powder. Cerium oxide is often used for polishing.

The most important, and rather costly, item of equipment is the faceting head. This machine allows the lapidary to set the dop-stick-mounted stone at any angle desired. With the gauges available, he can plot the precise angles of planes used in any of the many faceted cuts. (See Fig. 4–70.)

Faceting, even more than cabochon cutting, is a precise and complex craft in itself.

Although the secrets of lapidary techniques in the past were jealously guarded, there are many excellent and readable texts

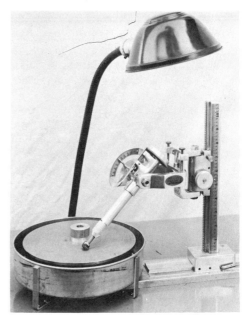

fig. 4–70
Courtesy, M.D.R. Mfg. Co., Inc.

185

now available on the subject. These are listed in the Bibliography.

• glass in jewelry

STAINED GLASS

Fragments of stained glass, available from manufacturers of stained glass and stained-glass window studios, can be sawed, ground, and polished with the same techniques and materials that are used in working the softer gem materials.

The undulating surface, irregular bubble formation within the glass, and of course the rich color possibilities make this an intriguing material when used as a focal point in a design.

Fragments of stained glass can be set in bezels or other gem settings, or they can be suspended after holes have been drilled at strategic points. Stained glass is quite soft and easily shattered, so holes for direct suspension must be located far enough from the edge of a form.

Small chips of stained glass can be melted into spheres and globules with a clean reducing flame or in a kiln. If fused in a kiln, the fragments should be placed on sheet mica so that no serious adhesion takes place during melting.

With care, shapes created in this manner can be attached, while still molten, to gold and silver wires leading to a number of decorative uses in a delicate design.

Since glass and metal have different rates of expansion and contraction, it is important to cool the combined units as slowly as possible.

GOLD GLASS

The art of combining metallic sheets of gold with glass has a long history. About three thousand years ago the Egyptians began to develop a technology of fusing gold foil or leaf between layers of glass, but the skill did not reach its peak until a few centuries before the birth of Christ. From that point on, Egyptian, Greek, and Roman work developed considerably until the fifth century A.D. Since then, the art has been in decline, and today only a few individuals, after painstaking research and effort, have again been able to use this very intriguing decoration.

As in all combinations of metal and glass, the problems of variable expansion and contraction rates must be solved.

It is possible, through experiment, to find or develop the correct glass mixture, heating and cooling schedule, and mold material for constructing gold glass for jewelry uses.

Historically, gold glass has been used in the construction of mosaic tesserae, pendant forms for jewelry and beads, but perhaps its greatest use was in the medallions inlaid into the bottoms of drinking glasses and cups.

This is another of the old decorative methods—in great part still a mystery—that has the combined attraction of rewarding research and extreme potential in jewelry design.

• surface treatments

CHASING

Chasing, as described in Chapter 3, is used in combination with repoussé to delineate and clarify a design. It can also be used in limitless ways to cover the surface of metal with an imaginative texture of indentations.

Since chasing tools come in such a variety of shapes and sizes, the creative combination of several at a time can form a unique surface. Using alternately heavy and light strokes of the hammer, you can achieve different effects with the same tool. (See Fig. 4–71.)

Simple chasing or indenting tools of limited life can easily be made of nails and spikes by filing the points flat and then

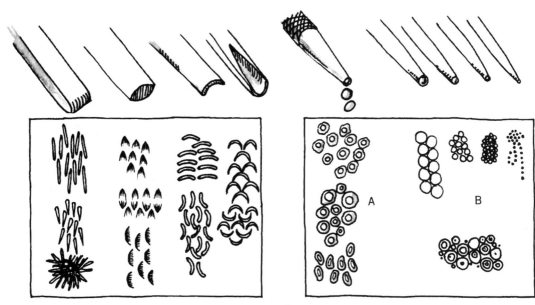

fig. 4–71

fig. 4–73

filing the design imprint into the flat surface. It is best to file the surface into thin ridges rather than to leave large flat areas. Flat areas do not imprint into metal very easily, and they tend to bounce with the hammer blow, blurring the edges of the

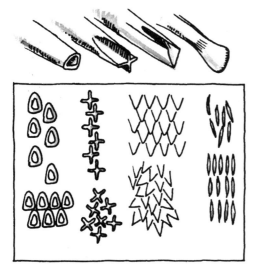

fig. 4–72

indentation. Fig. 4–72 shows effective nail indenting tools and their marks.

Nail sets bought in the hardware store are never perfectly round. This slight irregularity adds a quality to a surface that more precise punches may lack. (See Fig. 4–73A.) For small circular indentations, a set of beading tools can be used. (See Fig. 4–73B.)

Matting tools used in repoussé work are designed to create an even but varied surface that is often rich in its profusion of raised and lowered texture. (See Fig. 4–74.)

PLANISHING

The surface treatment of planishing has been misused so often that many craftsmen avoid it altogether.

If used with discipline and moderation—with attention to the relationships between the sizes of the marks and the object—there is nothing inherently bad about this surface treatment.

Planishing consists of covering a convex

187

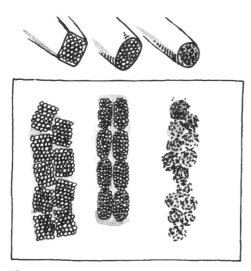

fig. 4–74

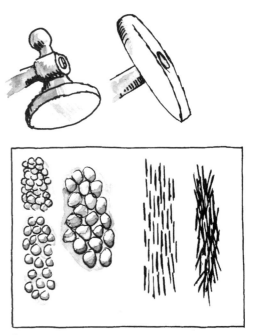

fig. 4–75

surface with a uniform and overlapping series of flat planes or facets.

The size and weight of the planishing hammer, the flatness or curve of its polished surface, and the force of the blow all determine the shape and extent of the facet. A controlled, spaced overlapping of small-sized planes or depressions is more effective and less garish than the effect resulting from the irregular hope-for-the-best banging that is so often seen. (See Fig. 4–75.) For a fine example of planishing, see #2, page 80.

DRILLING

Precise depressions or perforations can be achieved by using drill bits of the same or varied sizes. Cone and bud drills give a shape to each depression that cannot be achieved in any other way. (See Fig. 4–76.)

On fairly thin metals a combination of drilling and indenting can be used to form craterlike projections or depressions. Metal of 20-gauge B and S or thinner is best for this. The hole is drilled first and then a tapered punch of the right shape is used to drive a small crater up or down.

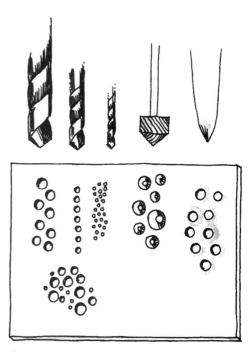

fig. 4–76

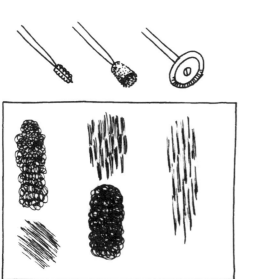

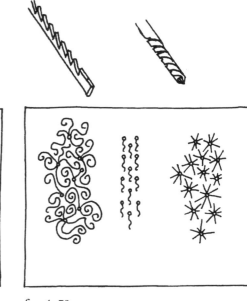

fig. 4–77

fig. 4–78

GRINDING

Delicate surfaces can be cut and ground into the metal surface by use of a flexible shaft tool and a variety of small abrasive heads and dental drills. Each angle and pressure of the tool forms an effect of its own. (See Fig. 4–77.)

PERFORATION

With a fine-bladed jeweler's saw and a small drill, a linear perforation is possible which, with oxidation, can form a strong surface quality. If the perforated section is to be backed by a solid sheet of metal, only a minimum of solder should be used in combining the two sheets. Excess solder will flow into the sawed lines and greatly reduce the effectiveness of the texture. (See Fig. 4–78.)

FUSING

When done with sensitivity and discrimination, a technique of combining sheet or wire forms by heat without soldering can result in controlled forms that turn an accident to a purpose.

If scraps of sheet metal or wire are combined in a purely emotional manner, letting them fall where they may, the result might be intriguing, but it is seldom a serious statement of the artist's intent. In this way the forms are limited to the occasionally exciting accidents of natural objects, and as such they become anonymous.

With a concept in mind the craftsman can start with a shape or a combination of shapes, perhaps sawed out quite carefully, which establish a framework within which the technique is contained.

With careful heat control it is possible to fuse two surfaces by causing a surface metal flow that bonds the forms. The surface, upon cooling, has the characteristic *orange peel* roughness of overheated metal, but it can be filed, stoned, and buffed where highlights are needed. (See Fig. 4–79.)

The surface of a sheet form can also be heated until it is semifluid, at which point wire, also heated almost to melting, can be added. The wire, when hot enough,

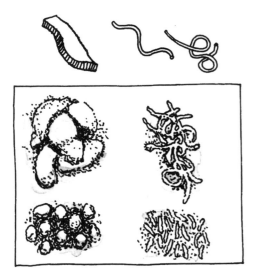

fig. 4-79

becomes very flexible and may be built up on itself to form high areas.

Where a design requires controlled placement of wire, pieces can be precut and formed and then fused into place in the same way that sheets of metal are combined. Balls of shot, perhaps of different metals, can also be attached in this manner. Silver filings can be placed or sifted onto sheet at the right moment, and when fused, they form a surface texture contrasting with the roughened flat areas. Filings of metals with a higher melting point than the base form can also be incorporated.

MELTING

Another accidental technique consists of dropping fully molten metal into water of various temperatures and depths. The height from which the metal is dropped also controls the forms to a degree.

A depression carved into a charcoal block, with a pouring groove to the edge added, makes an adequate melting crucible.

Again, the successful use of these accidentals depends on the selectivity of the artist. It is often too easy to be satisfied with superficial results in the name of "happy accident" or "freely evolved form."

traditional techniques

• several traditional japanese processes

No other people have used metal as expressively as the Japanese. During the 450 years of relative isolation before the mid-nineteenth century, Japan was able to support many metal craftsmen. Some three thousand workers of note are recorded for this period, each belonging to one of more than sixty distinct schools that developed unique design and technical qualities. Most were specialists in one or another aspect of sword decoration. The warrior, or *Samurai*, class made the sword a revered object upon which great sums were spent (Fig. 5–1). Japan's leading painters often worked with famous metalworkers in designing and fabricating such objects as *tsuba*—sword guards (Fig. 5–2), *fuchi-ka-*

shira—ferrules and caps on the sword handle (Fig. 5–3), or *menuki* (Fig. 5–4).

Metal was used as a color medium, and many subtle combinations of alloys were developed to extend the palette of the

fig. 5–2   Tsuba

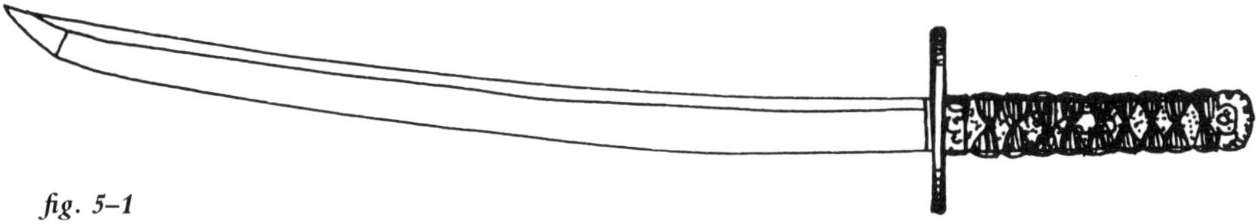

fig. 5–1

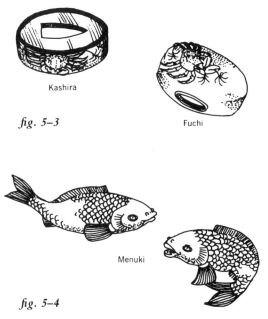

Kashira

Fuchi

fig. 5–3

Menuki

fig. 5–4

metalworker to a degree unknown in the West. Patinas added even greater coloristic range to the basic metal colors.

Great technical skills in repoussé, chiseling, inlay, damascene, overlay, and lamination were developed, often in very small scale. The *menuki*—a small, high-relief element placed under the lacing of the sword hilt to improve the hand grip—illustrated in Fig. 5–5 are only 1¼ inches long.

The placement of *tsuba*, *fuchi-kashira*, and *menuki* varied little over the centuries. Fig. 5–6 illustrates these elements.

While one artist might design and produce the *tsuba*, another would produce the *fuchi-kashira–menuki* combination. The latter were related in design, but the *tsuba* stood by itself.

A dagger, the *Kogatana* (Fig. 5–7), and a skewer, the *Kogai*, were sometimes worn on the outside of the scabbard and held in place by being passed through holes made for them in the *tsuba*. (See Fig. 5–2.) The dagger handle, the *Kodzuka*, was often decorated with the same materials and design elements as the *fuchi-kashira* and *menuki*.

The sword blade, the handle with its silk wrapping over a ray-skin cover, and the scabbard were each made by specialists in these forms. In fact, one sword may have been produced by ten or more artisans.

Techniques developed in the production of sword decoration were:

Uchidashi = Repoussé. (Fig. 5–8.)
Kebori = Chiseling. (Fig. 5–9.)
Ukibori = Chasing
Ishime = "Stone" surface. Overall texture technique that includes:

fig. 5–5A
A pair of Japanese menuki in gold, silver and alloys. *Reproduced with permission of Cooper-Hewitt Museum, The Smithsonian Institution's National Museum of Design.*

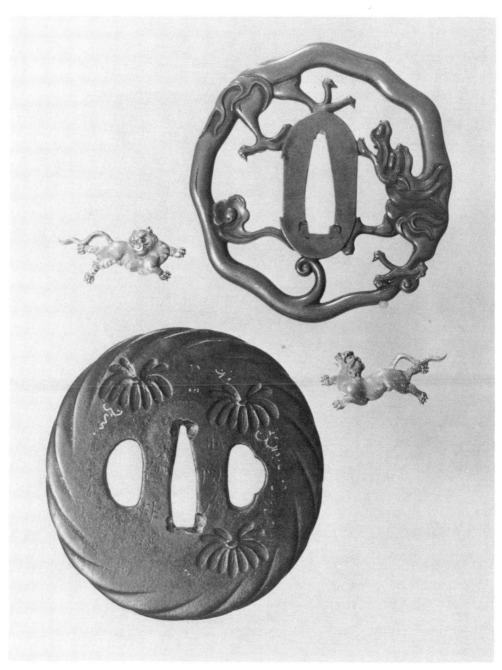

fig. 5–5B
Two Tsuba (sword guards) and a pair of menuki in iron and gold. *Reproduced with the permission of Cooper-Hewitt Museum, The Smithsonian Institution's National Museum of Design.*

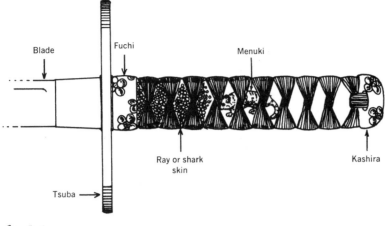

Blade

Fuchi

Menuki

Ray or shark skin

Kashira

Tsuba →

fig. 5–6

Kodzuka ↓

Kogatana

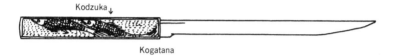

Kogai

fig. 5–7

fig. 5–8

fig. 5–9

Nanako = "fish-roe" pattern, leather grain, pearskin, silk, tree bark. (Fig. 5–16.)

Nunome zōgan (Cloth inlay) = Damascene. (Fig. 5–10.)

Zōgan or *Honzōgan* = True inlay. (Fig. 5–11.)

Hira zōgan = Flat inlay.

Taka zōgan = Raised inlay.

Gomoku zōgan = "Dirt inlay." Scraps of brass wire applied at random.

Iroe = Thin cappings soldered onto repoussé forms. (Fig. 5–12.)

traditional techniques

fig. 5–10

fig. 5–11

fig. 5–12

Mokume or *Yosefuki* = Lamination of metals of different colors. (Fig. 5–31.)
Yosemono = Filigree.
Shippo = Enameling.
Keshi = Gilding with mercury amalgam.

Before describing some of these techniques and the tools used in their development, mention should be made of the fascinating range of alloys used by traditional metalworkers and in some cases the patinas used to achieve additional color.

A basic alloy, most often patinated black, was *Shakudo*, which consisted of from 2 to 8% gold plus 92 to 98% copper. A variant called "blue gold" consisted of ten parts gold plus ninety parts copper. Although a Japanese technique for coloring *Shakuda* black consists of boiling the work for fifteen to thirty minutes in a solution of one part copper aceto-arsenite ($Cu(C_2H_3O_2)_2 \cdot 3CuAf_2O_9$), plus one part copper sulfate ($CuSO_4 \cdot 5H_2O$), plus twenty parts of water, the author has found a simpler and effective solution that seems to work as well:

2 heaping teaspoons ammonium chloride (NH_4Cl)
3 heaping teaspoons cupric sulfate ($CuSO_4 \cdot 5H_2O$)

Dissolve in 200 cc. of boiling water. Boil the work in this solution for fifteen to twenty minutes. Work must be polished—the alloy itself must be exposed—and absolutely free of grease or oil. To darken the effect even more, a light vegetable oil finish works well. Hot beeswax also works well, but the work must be carefully wiped while still hot to avoid rubbing to remove excess wax. Rubbing could affect the uniformity of the black patina.

Another popular alloy was *Shibuichi*. Translated, this word means "three-quarters" and refers to the basic mixture, which consists of seventy-five parts copper plus twenty-five parts silver.

Other silver-copper alloys ranged from the so-called gray silver, a 50% copper plus 50% silver mixture, to more complex alloys of 50 to 67% copper plus 30 to 50% silver with traces of gold and iron added.

A characteristic "pearskin" grain in *Shibuichi* is produced by first melting the copper in a crucible, adding the silver and heating only until all is melted together, then stirring with a thin hardwood stick. Once mixed it is poured into a well-oiled iron pot (a vegetable oil is mentioned), although an oiled ingot mold will do as well. The mold should be hot to enable a good full flow of metal. To color *Shibuichi* a handsome violet to plum color (depending upon alloy proportions), dip it in a boiling solution of:

1 heaping teaspoon salt
2 heaping teaspoons cupric sulfate $(CuSO_4 \cdot 5H_2O)$
200 cc. water

Dip *Shibuichi* only long enough to bring up the desired color. The addition of a heaping teaspoon of cupric nitrate $(Cu(NO_3)_2 \cdot 3H_2O)$ to this solution will develop a beautiful, deep purple-black on *Shibuichi*. Do not dip the object in the boiling solution for too long. This solution gives a light lavendar patina to sterling silver.

Sentoku—a brasslike alloy—consisted of eighty parts copper, fifteen parts zinc, and five parts tin. Treated chemically, this alloy was colored brown to warm chrome yellow.

Pure gold, silver, and copper were sometimes used as a basis metal upon which others were added by soldering or inlay, but usually they were used in small amounts as accents on darker colors. The ability of pure gold and silver to resist chemical corrosion made these metals especially useful when large areas were to be patinated, leaving small areas bright and untouched.

● uchidashi (repoussé)

Uchidashi, or repoussé, was well developed in the production of *fuchi-kashira* and *menuki*. Metal was annealed to maximum softness and then shaped with punches, often made of bamboo. Such punches, although quite hard, did little to blemish metal surfaces. The metal was mounted on a pitch bowl or block as in the West, although the pitch mixture was somewhat different:

Rosin	1 part
Powdered clay	1 part
Vegetable oil	½ to 1 teaspoon

Fig. 5–13 shows a sampler made in the nineteenth century to illustrate steps in making *menuki* of copper by repoussé.

● kebori (chiseling)

Chiseling often took the place of Western engraving with burins. A great variety of chisels were used, as were hammers of many shapes and weights. The chisels and hammers were used in much the same way that chasing and repoussé tools are held, except that greater tool angles were used to give brushstroke-like incisions in the metal. (See Figs. 5–14 and 5–15.)

● ukibori (chasing)

Chasing was used not only to refine repoussé forms but often to create a background relief texture called *Ishime*, which included textures with names such as "Fish-

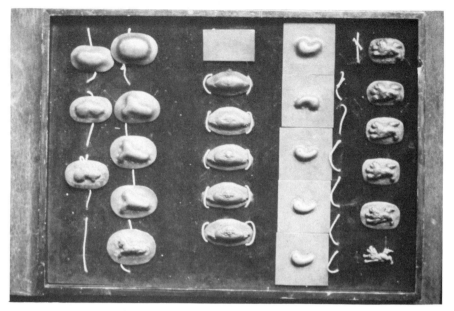

fig. 5–13

fig. 5–14

fig. 5–15

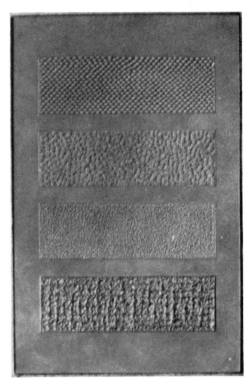

fig 5–16

fig. 5–17

most popular, and it was often executed by specialists who formed regular, uniform rows of perfect little hemispheric indents using a cup-headed punch. Fig. 5–17 shows a section of a *Kogatana* with a *nanako*-patterned background.

● nunome zōgan (cloth inlay/damascene)

Nunome zōgan, still practiced today in commercial jewelry making in Japan, consists of embedding pure gold or silver foil in roughened areas of another metal. Although most effective in mild steel, it can also be done in work-hardened copper and other harder metals.

The inlay area is first roughened with a special chisel (Fig. 5–18). Note that regular crisscross scoring takes place over the entire area. Fig. 5–19 shows a workman

roe," "Leather grain," "Pearskin," "Stone surface," and "Silk." Fig. 5–16 shows a sampler of repeated chasing marks. Work was chased in pitch or on a steel block. *Nanako*, or the fish-roe pattern, was the

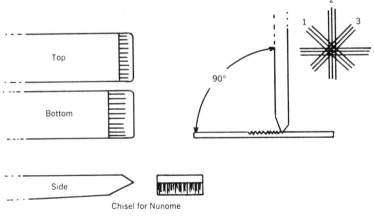

fig. 5–18

fig. 5–19

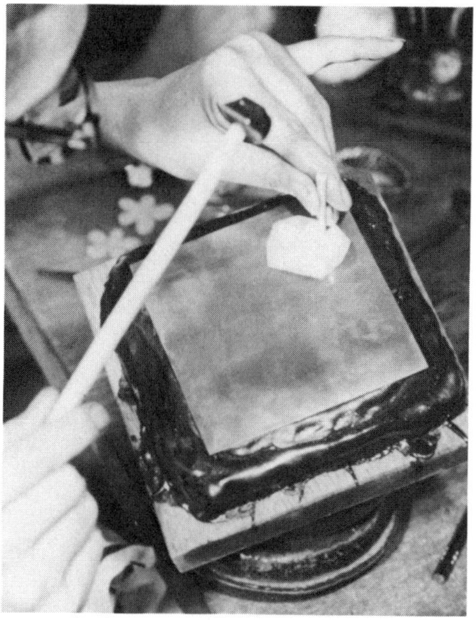

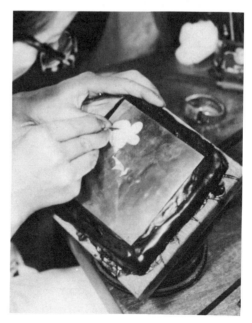

fig. 5–20

scoring a flower form in copper. Fig. 5–20 shows how the foil— in this case silver of 34 to 36 gauge—is hammered into the scored area with a small, light hammer and a bamboo punch.

A sharp-edged chisel or knife is used to trim excess foil away (Fig. 5–21). The attached foil is now burnished to make it smooth (Fig. 5–22). If the foil was too thin, as sometimes happened when inexpensive sword decoration was offered, the scoring quickly wore through the foil and it fell away. Fig. 5–23 shows a section of *nunome zōgan* on an iron *tsuba* where little gold remains in the roughened areas.

After foils were affixed and burnished, the surrounding surfaces were etched away with nitric acid. The action of the acid was neutralized by boiling the work in green tea. Today bicarbonate of soda would work as well.

The entire surface of the work was then

fig. 5–21

199

1

2

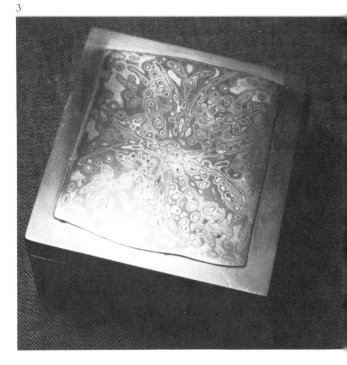

3

1 Test showing marks made by a variety of chasing tools; 2″ wide

2 Pendant, Jody Nathanson; mokume; 4″ long

3 Box lid; mokume; 3″ square

4 Buckle; mokume; 2¼″ diameter

5 Pin; mokume; 2½″ wide

6 Pendant, Allene Kaplan; mokume; 2″ long

7 Pin; mokume; 2″ long

8 Brooch, Carol Luhman; mokume; 2½″ long

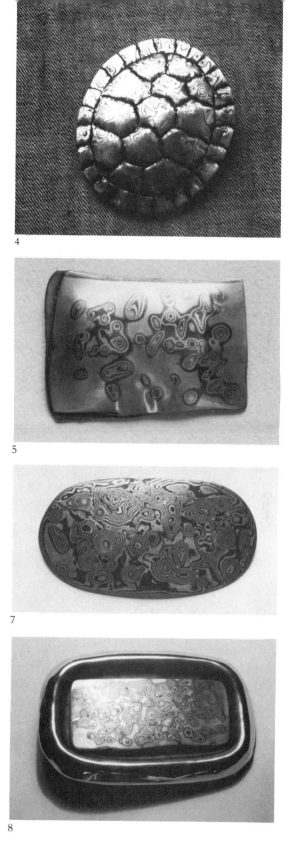

4

5

6

7

8

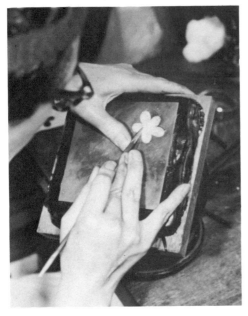

fig. 5–22

fig. 5–23

either patinated black or it was given many layers of true lacquer, which was then baked on to the point where it carbonized black. In both techniques the gold or silver areas were then polished out by careful rubbing with water and a charcoal block. Fig. 5–10 is an excellent example of *nunome zōgan* in a variety of metals.

• honzōgan (true inlay)

HIRA ZŌGAN OR FLAT INLAY

In Japanese inlay small chisels were used to cut a bed into a basis metal into which another, often softer, metal was hammered or soldered. Sometimes an aperture was sawed out of the basis metal, into which a carefully fitted second metal was soldered. Figs. 5–24 through 5–28 illustrate this process.

TAKA ZŌGAN OR RAISED INLAY

In *Taka zōgan* the inlaid metal projected above the basis metal and was often carved or otherwise modeled in relief (Fig. 5–29).

GOMOKU ZŌGAN OR "RUBBISH" INCRUSTATION

Scraps of wire, often brass or copper, were fused in random patterns into the surfaces of other metals. These were either allowed to remain on the surface or were hammered flat.

IROE OR "COLORED" INCRUSTATION

Often cappings of thin sheets of gold, silver, or other metals were shaped around and soldered to the repoussé relief of another metal (Fig. 5–30).

Gilding with a mercury-gold amalgam (*Keshi*) was also used to introduce color in certain, usually raised areas. There is great danger in breathing toxic mercury fumes in this process, so great care must be exercised to ensure strong ventilation.

Gold or silver electroplating, after areas not to be plated are first masked out, can achieve much the same effect as gilding, and with greater safety.

MOKUME, YOSEFUKI OR LAMINATION

Fig. 5–31 illustrates the fascinating variety of patterns created by Japanese metal-

Hira zōgan

Step 1. The inlaid piece of metal must have a slightly beveled edge and must be carefully finished. The inlay is used to trace an outline accurately on the basis metal.

fig. 5–24

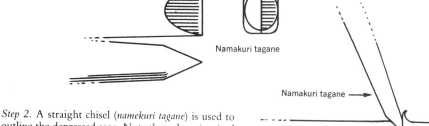

Namakuri tagane

Step 2. A straight chisel (*namekuri tagane*) is used to outline the depressed area. Note that a burr is raised at this time.

Namakuri tagane →

fig. 5–25

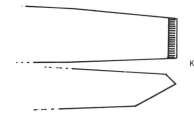

Kiri tagane

Step 3. A cutting chisel (*kiri tagane*)—note its special shape—is used to cut the depression smoothly.

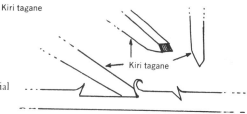

← Kiri tagane

fig. 5–26

Step 4. If care was taken in marking and carving out the depression, the inlay should just fit in.

fig. 5–27

Step 5. A matting tool (*narashi tagane*), made by filing a rounded, flat end onto a piece of tool steel and then striking several light blows with the flat side of a hand file before tempering it, is used to hammer the burr onto and over the bevel of the inlay. Riffle files, and eventually a scotch stone, are used to smooth out all surfaces.

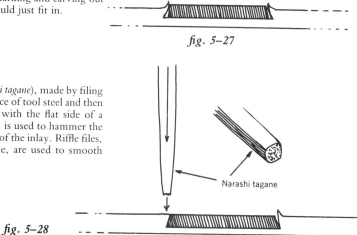

Narashi tagane

fig. 5–28

Taka-zōgan

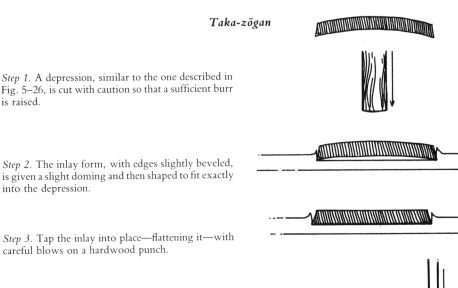

Step 1. A depression, similar to the one described in Fig. 5–26, is cut with caution so that a sufficient burr is raised.

Step 2. The inlay form, with edges slightly beveled, is given a slight doming and then shaped to fit exactly into the depression.

Step 3. Tap the inlay into place—flattening it—with careful blows on a hardwood punch.

Step 4. The matting tool is used to beat the burr down around the inlay. Files and scotch stones remove marks of the matting tool, or a surface texture (graining) can be brought right up to it.

fig. 5–29

Iroe

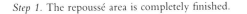

Step 1. The repoussé area is completely finished.

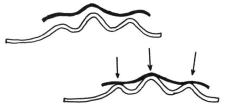

Step 2. Fine gold or silver of 28-gauge thickness is roughly shaped to fit the repoussé contours. It is then soldered into place.

Step 3. With bamboo, hardwood, or steel chasing and modeling tools, the "capping" is made to follow the contours of the repoussé. A second heating often helps solder to flow even further at this point to affix the capping firmly.

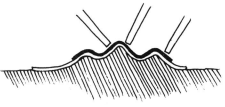

fig. 5–30

204
traditional techniques

fig. 5–31

workers in this process. There are several methods by which such results can be achieved.

● thin-gauge lamination

One of the traditional decorative metal processes used by Japanese artists prior to mid-nineteenth century consisted of alternating light and dark metals in layers that often contained sixteen or more laminates. By forming raised areas in such sheets, filing these bumps level, then stoning them smooth, a rich variety of designs and visual textures were achieved that could not have been created in any other way. (See Fig. 5–31.)

The traditional process seemed to consist of fusing the layers of metal together by heat and hammering. This requires considerable skill and experience, and the effect can more easily be achieved by soldering, although even then it requires careful attention to detail!

For jewelry purposes, experience has shown that it is best to start out with 18- or 20-gauge metal no more than 2″ × 2″ square. A rectangle of 1″ × 2″ will work even better.

A number of metals can be used, although a simple and effective combination (and perhaps also the most dramatic) is copper and fine silver.

MATERIALS:

1. A rolling mill or, if unavailable, a well-finished forging or planishing hammer and a smooth anvil or steel slab. (See Fig. 5–32.)

2. A clean, flat asbestos pad or other smooth, heat-reflective surface.

3. Fifty or more pieces of Easy silver solder cut into pieces ⅟₁₆″ square.

fig. 5–32
Courtesy of Swest, Inc.

to measure thickness of sheet during rolling or hammering.

9. Bench shear if possible. Otherwise, a jeweler's saw and blades.

10. Chasing punches, repoussé tools, and chasing hammer.

11. Lead block (at least ½" thick).

12. Plastic or hardwood mallet with a smooth, flawless face.

13. ½" or ¼" scotch stone and a good, sharp #2 cut hand or bastard file, 8" length.

14. Potassium sulfide (liver of sulfur) or Silvox for coloring final *mokume*.

15. Fine pumice.

THE PROCESS:

1. A piece of 18-gauge copper, 1" × 2" or 2" × 2" (approximately) and a piece of fine silver of the same size (sterling can be used, but it is somewhat less effective in the final coloring) are carefully flattened by light tapping with the plastic or wood hammer if necessary. Sheet metal cut on a bench shear is *pinched* off, leaving a burr. This must be removed by careful malleting or filing. (See Fig. 5–34.) Check for flatness at eye level along the surface of the steel block.

2. Both pieces of metal should be thoroughly degreased. They can be heated to cherry red (beginning to glow) and then boiled in hot pickle, or they can be scrubbed thoroughly with *cold* water

4. Fresh silver solder flux—a paste flux works better on copper than a liquid flux.

5. Pickle—Sparex or a 10% sulfuric acid/water pickle.

6. One pint of water in which a heaping tablespoon of bicarbonate of soda has been dissolved. Use a Pyrex or aluminum pan so that the solution can be boiled.

7. A small spatula (See Fig. 5–33) made by heating a ¼" mild steel rod to bright red and then forging it flat on the end while hot. File it clean before each use.

8. B & S (American Standard) gauge plate

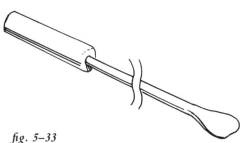

fig. 5–33

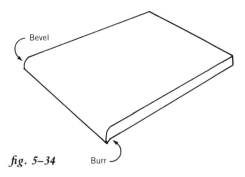

fig. 5–34

Bevel

Burr

and Comet scouring powder. A film of water should remain on the surface of the metal and not draw up into droplets. From now on work should be held by the edges or with clean tweezers only.

3. All joining surfaces should be covered with a thin layer of a good paste flux. If too much flux is used, unmelted solder drifts out of position and some melted flux might even remain between the sheets, causing pits, bubbles, and tearing later in the process. Too little flux is also bad because the copper, or copper alloys such as bronze or nickel silver, tends to overload a thin layer of flux with oxides, thus inhibiting the complete flow of solder.

There are special high-melting-point fluxes, such as Nicrobraz for stainless steel (see Sources of Supply), that are good for the high temperatures and prolonged heating needed when soldering copper to nickel silver in thin-gauge *mokume*. Since these fluxes protect against excessive oxidation, they increase the likelihood that solder will flow completely between layers.

4. Solder pieces are placed in orderly ¼" squares to assure that the entire inner surface between layers is well covered with solder. (See Fig. 5–35.) Be careful to place solder all around right up to the edges. Solder tends to flow away from edges and the edges must be thoroughly soldered for good *mok-ume*.

5. The prepared sheets of metal can now be heated, either on a heat-retentive surface, such as a charcoal block, or from underneath on a nichrome mesh screen on a tripod. (Remember that a larger flame must be used when heating from below since no heat is reflected back onto the work.) Use a large flame and try to heat the entire piece uniformly and all at once. Watch at eye level for signs of solder melting. Solder, as always, will melt first onto the hottest of the two sheets, i.e., the sheet closest to the flame. Do not be fooled by the first "drop" of one sheet onto the other. Continue heating until flux begins to come out to the edges all around and, soon thereafter, a shining seam of molten solder. If warping occurred and some sections of the sheets are not soldered together, use the clean, bare-metal tip of the flattened ¼" rod to press the top sheet down while maintaining soldering heat all the while.

When soldering seems complete—a seam of solder showing around all four edges—cool the work for a moment and then pickle it in hot pickle. Be sure to remove all copper oxides and borax glass (from the flux) in this step.

Rinse the work and inspect the edges carefully. If gaps still show, reflux, blow flux into the cracks, and heat again until the solder melts. Press down gaps where necessary.

6. Repickle, rinse, and neutralize any pickle that still remains in cracks or gaps. If this is not done, the faces of the rolling mill rollers or the face of the polished planishing hammer will be etched and damaged when the slab of soldered metal is thinned out. A bicarbonate of soda and water solu-

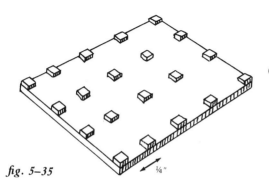

fig. 5–35

¼"

tion brought to a boil will neutralize any acid remaining on or in the work. Boiling for a minute or two should be sufficient. Remove the work, rinse in water, and dry thoroughly.

7. The soldered sheet must now be thinned to 18 gauge by rolling it in a rolling mill or by careful and accurate hammering with a flat planishing hammer on a flat steel bench anvil. Using a rolling mill is by far the easier method since the sheet ends up uniformly thick. Since no two kinds of metal have the same degree of malleability, the soldered slab will begin to curl, especially in the beginning stages. It is best to reduce the space between rollers by small amounts. Usually it is not necessary to anneal the laminate during each rolling or hammering sequence. By the time the sheet has reached 18-gauge thickness, it will be somewhat curved by the rolling. This distortion can be flattened by the following methods:

   a. Rolling the sheet through at right angles to the last thinning rolling. Do not reduce roller space while doing this. That would simply curl the laminate in a new direction.

   b. It is sometimes easier to cut the laminate exactly in half and then follow Step a. with each piece.

   c. Use a flat plastic or hardwood hammer and a smooth-faced flat anvil to hammer the sheet flat. Remember that excessive force in hammering compresses the metal even more, and this could increase the curling.

   After the two halves are flat with very little gap between them, repeat the process of soldering and rolling from Steps 2 through 7. Each soldering doubles the layers. This could go on endlessly, to the point where the *mokume* texture is so del-

icate as to be invisible to the naked eye! Experience has shown that *four* solderings—for a total of sixteen layers—results in rich and dramatic textures and tonal contrasts.

As mentioned, metals such as bronze, brass, and nickel silver can be used as well as fine silver and copper. Avoid combining brass with fine or sterling silver, however. Those metals collapse into each other at the slightest overheating. Nickel silver has the tendency, especially during the third or fourth soldering, of collapsing into the alternating metal. Apply heat with great care and heat only enough to melt the solder. *Easy* solder is recommended to increase the temperature range between melting points of solder and metals. Subsequent soldering of *mokume* with other metal forms must be done with a low-melting solder, such as Silflo silver-brazing solder.

8. After the desired number of layers have been reduced to 18-gauge thickness, the sheet is textured in the following steps:

   a. The area to be textured is "bumped" up from the reverse side with an assortment of repoussé and chasing tools. The work is placed on a smooth lead block for this step because it is necessary to "bump" up metal sharply, leaving the surrounding sheet as flat as possible. If this were done on the softer pitch, the entire sheet would soon warp.

   b. The depth of the above indentations is critical. The bottom of the indent should not go very far past the middle of the thickness of the metal. (See Fig. 5–36.) If the indent is too deep, a hole can be filed completely through in Step 9.

   In Fig. 5–37, the chasing shapes

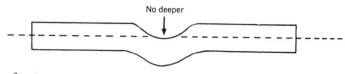

fig. 5–36

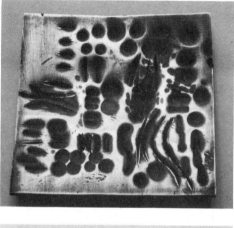

fig. 5–37

and patterns relate directly to the surface; note the distortion between a mark and its result.

c. If forming or repoussé is to be used in *mokume*, it must be done before bumping up. If more than slight bending is attempted after bump-ing and filing, the piece will either bend in the wrong places or break. This is caused by the eventual thick-thin/thick-thin dimension of the metal.

9. After bumping is completed, mallet the sheet as flat as possible. A slightly *convex* surface makes filing and fin-ishing even easier. Of course, re-poussé areas should also be checked again for contour.

File the bumps off with firm strokes of the flat hand file. (You can also use a belt sander with a medium-grit sandpaper, although it could easily re-move too much metal.) File until all bumps are level with the unbumped metal—no depressions should re-main—and remove file marks with the flat side of a scotch stone, using plenty of water in the process. If thin sheets of metal peel and tear away during this step, it means that at some point the solder did not completely flow be-tween the layers or a small patch of flux remained between the sheets. This tearing can often be repaired by a care-ful soldering with a low-temperature silver brazing solder.

Before soldering, be sure that the surface is completely clean. If you buffed or polished before this step, it is unlikely that the solder will flow freely. Be careful not to overheat dur-ing this step because the solder be-tween layers, once fluid again, would change and obscure the texture de-sired.

10. The back of the laminate is now rough and unsightly. Often this is hidden

209

when a *mokume* element is joined to other elements in a design. Otherwise it might be necessary to solder on a thin covering sheet of metal, especially if the rough surface will come into contact with bare skin.

Most often the *mokume* is formed in a sheet from which sections are cut to be used elsewhere. Again, these pieces must be soldered in place carefully with a low-fusing solder.

11. After soldering, pickling, and neutralizing, the *mokume* area at least should be colored to bring out the texture fully. This can best be done—if the laminate consists of copper and fine silver—by quick dippings into a cold, dilute solution of liver of sulfur. The copper should be darkened while the silver remains light. When other metals are used, stronger, perhaps warmed solutions might be necessary.

If the first attempt darkened the design too much, you can remove the patina with fine pumice and hand rubbing. Sometimes the slight waxy film left after rouge polishing keeps the silver from darkening during the redipping.

After the final dipping has formed the expected light-dark contrast, the work should be carefully dried and then left matte. A high polish makes color and tonal differences difficult to see.

In time the copper layers become darker and darker, which further enhances the richness of *mokume*.

VARIATIONS IN LAMINATION

A Japanese process called *Guribori* consisted of ending the laminating process with a thick piece of metal (14 gauge, 12 gauge, or even thicker). This slab was then chiseled into, ground into, or filed to expose the laminates. (See Fig. 5–38.)

Linear laminates of alternating light and dark squares can be created by soldering together four or five sheets of 16-gauge— or even thicker—metal of alternating colors. Four sheets can be used to ensure that a light sheet remains on one side and a dark sheet on the other. If possible, a high-melting solder should be used for this so that no remelting takes place at a later stage. Saw off strips from the end of the slab. (See Fig. 5–39.) These strips can be soldered edge to edge to create a sheet. Some filing and stoning may be necessary to flatten everything out, although interesting contours can be formed by sawing curved shapes. (See Fig. 5–40.)

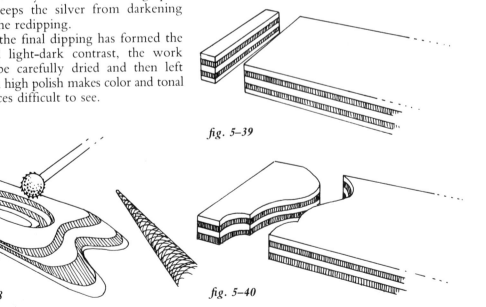

fig. 5–39

fig. 5–38

fig. 5–40

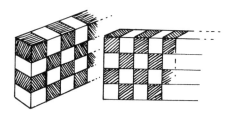

fig. 5–41

The same slab might be sawed in two directions to form a linear strip of alternating light and dark squares or rectangles. (See Fig. 5–41.) These can be soldered into long strips or edge to edge in a checkered pattern. The even geometry can be modified by hammering or rolling the sheet.

Japanese lamination combined many metals and alloys to create subtle patterns. This can be duplicated if the craftsman is sure that any alloy to be used will not suddenly melt during the many solderings. The commercial bronze alloy called NuGold has the disturbing habit of collapsing into silver when both are heated to approximately 1500°F.

Tactile as well as color surfaces can be formed by dipping a completed laminate in a 40% nitric acid solution. If work is left in this etching solution too long, all exposed copper will dissolve. Although this results in a rich tactile surface, the color contrasts of copper and silver will no longer be possible.

● niello

Niello is a mixture of various nonferrous metals and sulfur that can be inlaid by fusion into grooves or depressions in a metal base. It is an ancient technique, much used in the Middle East. Although it was often used in the decoration of armor and other metal work during the Renaissance, it has been used rarely in recent times. Today the center of this work is Thailand, which produces large amounts of niello jewelry for export.

Because of its strong black or blue-black color, niello is an effective contrast medium with light-colored metals, and it can be used over large surfaces where a patina or chemical coloring would not wear well during use.

Several formulas have been handed down by such medieval chroniclers as Theophilus and Pliny, as well as by the Renaissance artist, Benvenuto Cellini. These formulas, along with more contemporary ones, give the jeweler a wide range of possibilities, and since each craftsman must prepare his own niello, variations as to melting point are always possible.

PREPARATION OF THE BASE

Although many metals can be inlaid with niello, it is most often used on sterling silver, karat gold, copper, and brass. On alloys that in themselves fuse at a low temperature, a low-melting niello is of great importance.

The most delicate lines or networks of crosshatching can be engraved or etched into sheet or cast metal. The depth is important, since a thin layer of niello is apt to be more free of gas bubbles and porosity. On the other hand, if the engraved areas are too shallow, they can be filed away accidentally when the excess niello is removed. A depth of $1/64''$ to $1/32''$ is adequate.

Larger cells can be engraved, chiseled out, or pierced out of 22- to 24-gauge metal backed with 18-gauge, or heavier, metal, as described for *champlevé* enameling in Chapter 4.

It is not necessary to angle the edges of the depressions or to *plink* the bottom surface, since the niello will fuse itself thoroughly to the base metal. Smaller pieces of metal can be soldered into the interior of a cell; these should have a surface that is level with the surrounding metal. In early

1

2

Philip Fike, American goldsmith, has for several years concentrated on reconstructing the technique of niello. He has had notable success in mastering a process difficult to carry out with perfection, and about which little is known today.

Though once a popular form of metal decoration, especially in the Middle East and Renaissance Europe, its use today as a living art form is virtually limited to Thailand, which has developed a considerable export industry around this technique. Mr. Fike has experimented with many formulas for combining the elements of silver, copper, lead, and sulfur which constitute niello. In addition, he has devised new methods of application and fusion which give him greater control of the rich black amalgam.

The illustrations of both contemporary and historic niello work show it in its most effective balance; that of the soft, lustrous black of niello and the reflective lighter color of gold, silver, or other metals. It is said that niello developed as an offshoot of copper engraving as a graphic art. It is certainly true that it is a most effective means for creating a two-dimensional contrast on metal and can thus be used as a linear surface texture or form delineator.

1 Ring, Philip Fike; gold and niello

2 Pair of shears inlaid with silver and niello; Egyptian, 3rd century B.C. *The Metropolitan Museum of Art, Rogers Fund, 1939*

3 Hilt of Viking sword, iron, copper, and niello; Norse, 10th century. *The Metropolitan Museum of Art, Rogers Fund, 1955*

4 Pair of wedding bands; Philip Fike; silver and niello

5 Caucasian firearm, inlaid with silver, niello, ivory, and damascence. Daghestan, ca. 1825. *The Metropolitan Museum of Art, Rogers Fund, 1931*

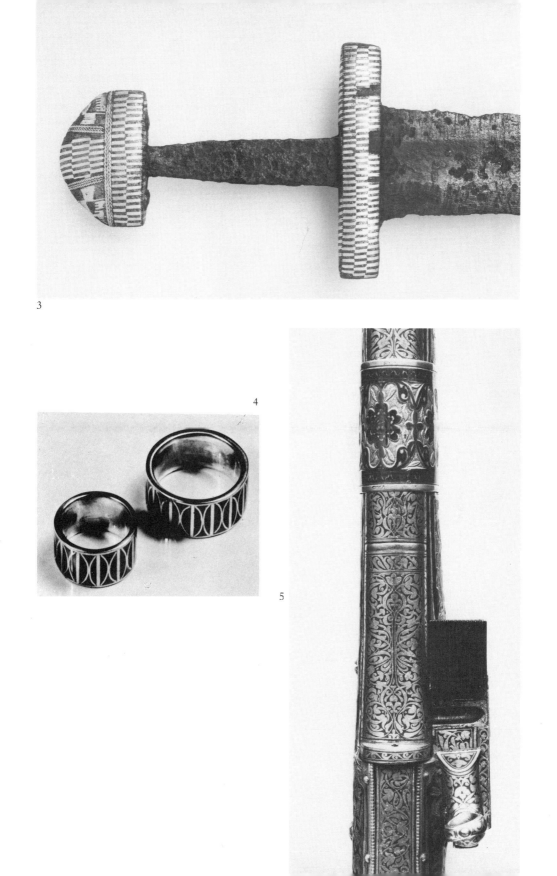

3

4

5

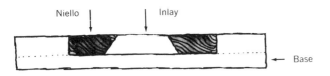

fig. 5–42

Cypriot work small metal pieces were inlaid in such a way that the fused niello held them firmly without the use of solder. In this case the metal inlay should have edges angled to a broader base. (See Fig. 5–42.)

After engraving and chiseling are completed, the work should be heated and pickled to remove any oxides and grease film. Keeping it in distilled water until it is charged with granulated niello will prevent further oxidation. In etched areas all oxide residues should be cleaned out with a fine steel-bristled brush.

PREPARATION OF THE NIELLO

With minor variations, the ingredients of niello are mixed in the following manner:

1. The metallic elements of copper, silver, lead, and antimony (when used) are melted together in a crucible, preferably in a muffle furnace. The silver is melted first, then the copper is added, next the lead, and finally the antimony. When all parts are completely melted, the mass should be stirred well with a strong stick of charcoal or a length of porcelain or graphite rod. Any slag forming on the surface should be removed with an iron spoon. The mixture is kept just molten until the next step.

2. In another crucible—a deep narrow shape is best—the powdered sulfur is melted. This process requires a powerful ventilating fan and hood. The sulfur fumes are profuse and acrid.

3. When the sulfur is completely melted, the molten metals are poured into the sulfur-containing crucible. The entire crucible is shaken to mix the elements and, after additional sulfur is added, the now solidified amalgam is remelted. When molten, it is stirred again.

4. The amalgam can be poured into an ingot and then broken up with a mortar and pestle, or it can be poured onto a lightly oiled steel slab and broken up with a hammer. When poured into water, it breaks up into many small fragments, but it tends to explode if the container is not deep and large.

The fragments are ground to about 80 mesh in a mortar and placed in stoppered containers. It is a good idea to screen the niello to avoid large pieces later. Some authorities claim that a powder-fine niello is more free of porosity, while others insist that larger granules fuse better.

APPLICATION AND FIRING

The clean metal surface is lightly fluxed with a dilute ammonium chloride solution; be sure that small depressions do not become filled with the liquid. An older fluxing technique consisted of painting the metal with a barely milky borax solution made by grinding a borax cone on a slate with an excess of water.

Next, the depressions are completely filled with granulated niello. On areas too narrow to be inlaid, the entire surface should be covered with niello. Since niello loses about half of its volume when melted, it should be applied thickly enough so that additional niello will not be necessary. It is always best to fuse the niello only once.

Preheat the work gently so that the water in the borax or ammonium chloride solution evaporates without disturbing the niello.

The object can be placed in a kiln at about 1000°F to fuse the niello, or it can be placed on a thin iron or steel sheet and heated from beneath with a torch. Do not touch the niello with an open flame; this will burn it, causing roughness and pits. When overheated, because of its lead content niello will quickly eat into silver, causing blemishes that may not be removable. Apply the heat only long enough to cause the granules to melt and spread slightly over the surface of the object. A temperature of around 700°F fuses most niello. A small polished spatula, lightly oiled, can be used to smooth the niello into all of the depressions. Do this as quickly as possible, since prolonged heat, even if not too high, can cause the lead sulfide to fuse into the basic metal.

With some of the low-fusing formulas it is possible to add additional niello while the work is still hot. It can then be burnished into place with a warmed spatula.

FINISHING

After the work has been air-cooled—*not* quenched!—it can be filed or scraped to expose the raised areas. The niello should remain in the depressions.

It is best to file with a worn medium-coarse file until almost through to the basic metal, and then to finish the work by stoning with a scotch stone under water. Do not use mechanical cutting or buffing, since the softer niello will wear away faster than the surrounding metal, losing the effect of a continuous surface.

After the stoning, the surface can be sanded with fine emery paper wrapped around a flat stick and polished with a felt hand buff and rouge.

VARIATIONS

Interesting variations of the basic niello process consist of mixing gold, copper, or fine silver filings or scrapings with the granulated niello before fusion. These are filed, stoned, and polished at the same time as the niello, causing an interesting color and texture. The tendrils of metal formed in drilling through silver, gold, or copper can be aligned in parallel rows in a niello-filled depression. After stoning, they present a repeat pattern of shapes.

When niello is applied to more than one plane of an object, it can be mixed with a small amount of a gum solution to hold it in place. The work must be heated in a hot kiln so that no direct flame touches the niello. The work, held in locking tweezers, must be rotated rapidly enough to prevent having the molten niello flow out of the depressions. It is best to use a somewhat greater amount of niello for this process so that enough will always remain in the depressions, even if some sagging takes place. This process is generally difficult to perfect, since molten niello has little capillary adhesiveness.

FORMULAS

All metals used must be free of oxides and grease and, when silver is used, it should be fine silver rather than sterling.

1. Pliny

Silver	3 parts
Copper	1 part
Sulfur	2 parts

2. Cellini

Silver	1 part or 1 oz.
Copper	2 parts or 2 oz.
Lead	3 parts or 3 oz.
Sulfur	Half a handful

3. Augsberg No. 1

Silver	1 part
Copper	1 part
Lead	2 parts

   Presumably added to about ½ cup sulfur

4. Augsberg No. 2

Lead	1 part
Mercury	1 part
Sulfur	1 part

5. Rucklin No. 1

Silver	3 parts
Copper	5 parts
Lead	7 parts
Sulfur	6 parts
Ammonium chloride	2 parts
Borax	24 parts

6. Rucklin No. 2

Silver	1 part
Copper	2 parts
Lead	4 parts
Sulfur	5 parts

7. Persian Niello

Silver	15.30 gm.
Copper	76.00 gm.
Lead	106.00 gm.
Flowers of sulfur	367.00 gm.
Ammonium chloride	76.00 gm.

8. Modern French

Silver	30 parts
Copper	72 parts
Lead	50 parts
Sulfur	384 parts
Borax	36 parts

9. Recipe described by H. Wilson in "Silverwork and Jewellry"

Fine silver	6 pennyweights (dwts.)	.300
Fine copper	2 dwts.	.100
Fine lead	1 dwt.	.050
Fine flowers of sulfur	½ oz.	.500

10. Theophilus

Silver	2 parts

Copper	1 part
Lead	½ part
Sulfur	Some (an excess?)

11. Karmasch (Russian—18th century)

Silver	15 gm.
Copper	90 gm.
Lead	150 gm.
Sulfur	750 gm.

12. Contemporary Russian

Silver	1½ oz.
Copper	2½ oz.
Lead	3½ oz.
Sulfur	12 oz.

13. Bolas No. 1

Native antimony sulfide, finely ground	2 parts
Native lead sulfide, finely ground	1 part
Powdered sulfur	8 parts

14. Bolas No. 2

Silver	2 parts
Copper	4 parts
Antimony	1 part
Lead	1 part
Sulfur	1 part

15. Spon

First Crucible:

Flowers of sulfur	27 oz.
Ammonium chloride	2¾ oz.

Second Crucible (Poured into first after fusion):

Silver	½ oz.
Copper	1½ oz.

| Lead | 2¾ oz. |
| Ammonium chloride | Trace |

16. Heinrich

Silver (either sterling or fine)	1 oz.
Copper	2 oz.
Lead	3 oz.
Sulfur	6 oz.

Mr. Leonard Heinrich, Armorer for the Metropolitan Museum of Art, has repaired many valuable historical works with formula No. 16, using the following technique:

a. Melt the silver and the copper in a crucible.

b. Add the lead and stir with a charcoal stick.

c. Pour this mixture into a larger crucible containing the sulfur. Stir and cover. Let cool.

d. Melt again.

e. Pour into a bowl of water, preferably through a screen, which breaks the niello into small grains.

f. Wash in cold water until the water remains clear.

g. Grind in an agate mortar until as fine as possible.

h. Place in a fine linen cloth bag and shake so that only the finest grains come through. Take the coarser grains left in the bag and regrind. Repeat until all is fine. Finely ground niello melts more rapidly and uniformly, leaving fewer pits.

i. Wet the work with Handy Flux (a paste flux) thinned to the consistency of milk. Make a paste of the niello with a saturated ammonium chloride-water solution. Apply the paste to the parts to be covered as you would enamel.

j. Place the work on an iron plate or sheet and heat from below with a torch. About 700°F is sufficient to fuse the niello. Do not bring the metal to a glow and don't fire it more than twice or the niello will pit the work.

k. When the work is cool, scrape off the surplus niello and polish with water of Ayr stone and a burnisher. If using a motor-driven buff, use a large-surfaced felt wheel.

17. Student experiment:

Silver	90%
Copper	10%
Antimony	1%
Sulfur	In excess

a. Melt silver and copper together.

b. Add molten mass to sulfur already melted in a larger crucible.

c. Add antimony and additional sulfur wrapped in a twist of tissue while above mixture is still molten.

d. Stir with a charcoal stick and let cool.

e. Remelt and apply as in other formulas. A niello with a higher melting point as well as a harder texture may have 1% to 2% nickel added to the above formula.

A successful niello formula uses the following equipment:

2 crucibles (100 dwt. BURNO with covers)
Surface plate
Ingot mold for casting wire
Iron mortar and pestle
Hardwood dowels

The alloy consists of:

Sterling silver	6 pennyweights (dwt.)
Copper	2 pennyweights (dwt.)
Lead	2 pennyweights (dwt.)
Sulfur, powdered	1 lb.

The procedure is as follows:

1. Melt borax into both crucibles. Roll the molten borax glass around the interior to line the walls. Pour out the excess.
2. Melt the copper in one of the crucibles and reduce the heat slightly.
3. Add the silver; mix both well when molten with a thin, hardwood dowel.
4. Add the lead; stir again with the dowel.
5. Reduce the heat.
6. Ladle in a generous amount of sulfur (fill the crucible) and stir again. Make certain that there is strong venting at this point. Breathing burning sulfur fumes is very painful!
7. Repeat Step 6 twice.
8. Grasp the crucible with crucible tongs and shake it to mix the ingredients further. Allow the excess sulfur to burn off, but avoid overheating the niello unnecessarily.
9. Pour the molten mixture onto the surface plate, leaving a button of flux residue in the crucible.
10. Add new borax to the crucible, melt it, and pour out as much residue as possible.
11. Add and melt a spoonful of borax in the second crucible.
12. Drop in the niello that has been cooled on the surface plate. Melt it carefully, noting just when it becomes molten.
13. Shake and agitate the crucible.
14. The final pour can be made into the ingot wire mold in order to form rods of niello, or it can again be cooled on a surface plate. Pour just before solidification starts.
15. As in Step 9, allow residue to remain in the crucible. Heat again and pour residue away.

16. Niello poured onto the surface plate can now be ground to about number 80 mesh in the iron mortar and pestle and fused.

An alternative formula that yields a good blue-black niello consists of the following:

Fine silver	9 parts by weight
Copper	1 part by weight
Lead	1 part by weight
Bismuth	1 part by weight

Melt the above ingredients, as in the previous directions, and saturate with sulfur.

• granulation

Perhaps the most difficult jewelry technique to master today, granulation reached its highest level of excellence in the ancient world. As early as the sixth century B.C., the Etruscans were able to construct jewels of almost unbelievable delicacy and precision.

The process consists of fusing—without the use of solder—small grains (shot) to a solid surface in such a way that they are attached only at the point of contact. (See Fig. 5–43.)

The Etruscans, and later the Greeks, were able to cover considerable surface areas, as well as to align these grains to form geometric and figurative designs, using gold grains as small as $\frac{1}{160}''$ in diameter. The effect of a surface evenly covered with grains of equal size is that of a frosted shimmer of great individuality.

Since these early craftsmen had no optical aids, such as magnifying glasses, they

This   not   This

fig. 5–43

employed children for this work, and it is said that their eyesight was usually permanently damaged by the age of ten or twelve.

The art of granulation fell into disuse in early Christian times, and only at a few points in later history were attempts made to reconstruct the process.

Old records of the technique are vague and often contradictory. Often the chemicals referred to had ambiguous names virtually invented by the chronicler, who, in most cases, had only hearsay knowledge of the technique. From the writings of the twelfth-century monk Theophilus come the most accurate accounts of granulation, and it is from these that modern goldsmiths evolved new approaches to the process.

The construction of the grains is not difficult. Although gold has most often been used, silver, platinum, and alloys of these metals have also been treated in this manner. If the grains are to be fairly large, $1/64''$ or more, they can be prepared by cutting fine wire into measured lengths. Smaller grains can be made by filing a sheet of metal with coarse or fine files and melting the filings into shot.

In order to melt the metal efficiently, a high, rather narrow crucible must be used. Powdered charcoal is first placed in the bottom of the crucible to the depth of at least $1/2''$. Over this is placed a loosely sifted layer of filings or wire snippets. Another layer of charcoal is followed by more metal particles, and so on, until the crucible is filled.

The filled crucible is placed in a muffle furnace and heated to at least 1900°F. The crucible is allowed to cool and the contents then poured into a pan of water to which a little detergent has been added. The perfectly spherical grains fall to the bottom of the pan and the charcoal can be carefully rinsed away.

The grains are free of oxidation because of the reducing atmosphere of the surrounding charcoal. They can be graded to size through fine mesh screen, as used in glaze preparation in ceramics.

The fusion of the grains to each other and to more solid surfaces evidently is the result of a molecular exchange. Basically, the process consists of using a form of copper salt mixed with some sort of organic glue or adhesive. This solution is used to cement the small grains or, if desired, other small shapes, into position. The entire work is heated with a reducing flame until the copper compound forms an oxide while the glue carbonizes. The carbon of the glue combines with the oxide of copper and passes off as carbon dioxide, leaving a thin molecular layer of pure copper. This film combines with molecules of gold from both the grains and the base surface to form a strong, delicate bond.

Pliny, in the first century A.D., recorded that the copper salt was derived from finely powdered chrysocolla, a semiprecious stone rich in copper silicate, and an animal hide glue was used as the carbonizing adhesive. Other historians mention the use of the gemstone malachite, which contains copper carbonate.

Another method consists of collecting scales of cuprous oxide by alternately heating and quenching a sheet of copper. These flakes of cuprous *firescale* are then finely ground with a glue solution. The solution is then used to adhere the grains in position. Although this method does result in a strong bond, the scale particles must be finely ground and carefully applied in solution, since the slightest overheating causes them to pit both grains and surface material.

The problem of proper heat control is difficult to master. Long experience evidently taught the ancient craftsmen how to determine the correct heat when using a bed of glowing charcoal as the heat source.

One researcher explains the process in the following terms:

No craftsmen in metal have ever developed the delicacy of design in gold work to quite the degree achieved by the Etruscans and Greeks of the 4th to 7th centuries B.C. Although tools and methods of working were primitive compared to those of today, they were handled with such complete knowledge and authority that it is difficult to believe that work was done without magnification or other aids.

In more recent times, from the 16th century to the present, many artist-craftsmen have tried to emulate these early masters. Some have succeeded in close approximations; most, only in clumsy efforts little related to the exquisite precision and delicacy of Greek and Etruscan work. No records exist which give an accurate account of materials and processes used in adhering the minute, perfect spheres of gold to a surface or to each other; this has made it necessary for each later craftsman to virtually reinvent the process for himself. That two renowned artist-craftsmen have succeeded in this task can be seen in the work of Professor Elisabeth Treskow of Germany and John Paul Miller of the United States. Both of these excellent goldsmiths have not only developed the techniques but also captured the aesthetic spirit of the past in order to develop a highly personal and contemporary expression of the art of granulation.

1

2

1 Etruscan gold fibula (cloak pin), Rusellae, Italy, 7th century B.C. *The Metropolitan Museum of Art, Purchased by Subscription, 1895*

2 Etruscan gold fibula, 7th century B.C. *The Metropolitan Museum of Art, Fletcher Fund, 1931*

3 Gold earrings, Madytos, Greece, 4th century B.C. *The Metropolitan Museum of Art, Rogers Fund, 1908*

4 Etruscan gold earrings or buttons, 6th century B.C. *The Metropolitan Museum of Art, Rogers Fund, 1913*

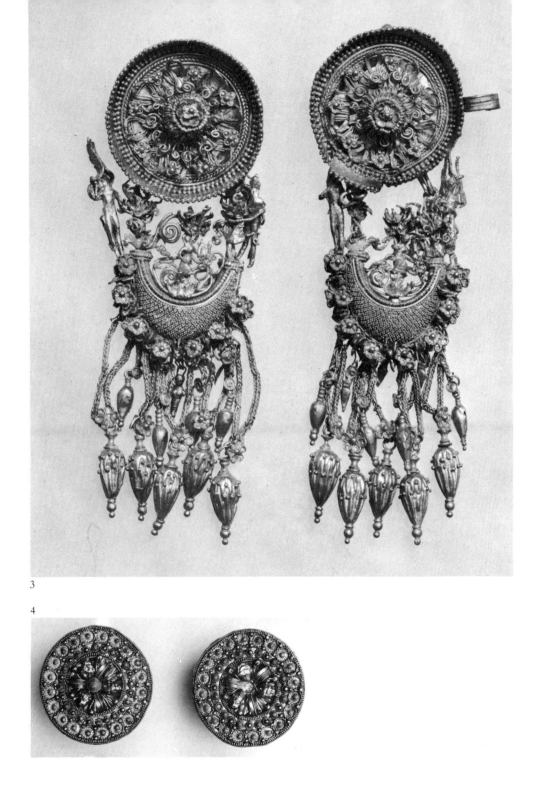

3

4

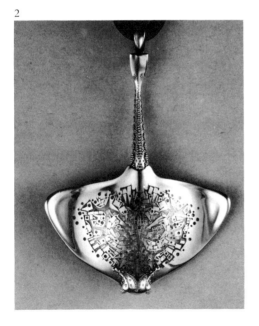

1

John Paul Miller, an American goldsmith, has developed the ancient art of granulation to a degree seldom seen since the Etruscan gold jewelry of the 7th to 4th centuries B.C. By combining the textural richness of granulated gold with the brilliance of enamel, Miller has given his jewelry a timeless excellence which satisfies today as it would have in ancient times. The infinite variety of shape and surface design found in sea life has been a successful source of stimulation for this master craftsman's interpretation.

2

1 "Cuttlefish"; gold and enamel
2 "Skate" pendant; gold and enamel
3 Marine motif necklace; gold
4 "Snail" pendant; gold and enamel
5 "Caddis Worm" pendant; gold and enamel

3

4

5

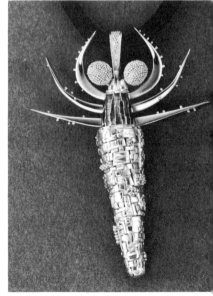

223

6

7

6 "Crab" pendant; gold and enamel

7 "Squid" pendant; gold

8 Brooch; gold

9 "Fiddler Crab" pendant; gold and enamel.
   Photo by Frasher

10 "Briars" brooch; gold

11 "Argonaut" pendant; gold and enamel

8

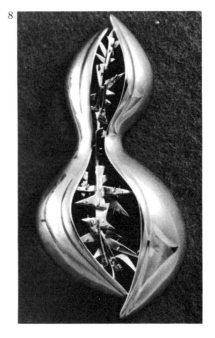

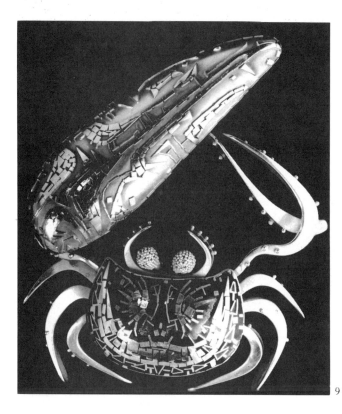

9

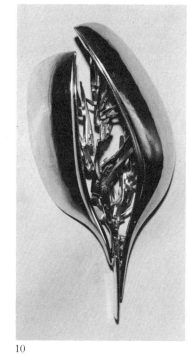

10

11

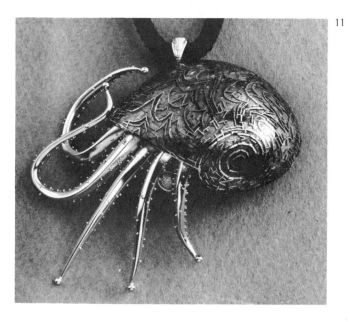

For many years, Professor Elisabeth Treskow of Cologne, Germany, has been acknowledged as one of the few master goldsmiths this century has produced. In both design and technique, her work has been in the vanguard of that of a group of superior craftsmen produced by Europe in the traditions of the finest guild systems of the Renaissance.

One of the first in modern times to master the difficult process of granulation, Professor Treskow has used it successfully in the surface enrichment of her extremely personal and technically perfect jewelry. Photographs by the artist

1

2

1 Pendant; gold granulation and precious gems

2 Brooch; gold granulation, pearls, and precious gems

3 Necklace; gold granulation

4 "The Three Kings," detail of the chain of office of the Mayor of Cologne; gold granulation, enamel, chased gold, and gems

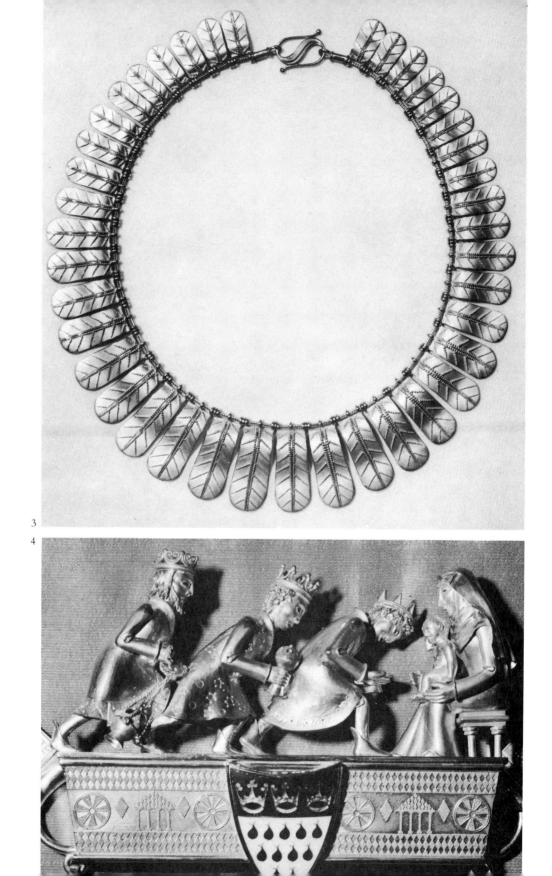

3

4

1. Mix a cupric hydrate with a glue such as seccotone.
2. Place the grains into position with this mixture.
3. Heat the unit slowly in a reducing atmosphere.
4. At 100°C the water has evaporated from the glue and the cupric hydrate converts to cupric oxide.
5. At a higher temperature the glue carbonizes and the cupric oxide is reduced to metallic copper, which forms a fine coating in the joints between the grains and the base surface.
6. At about 900°C this copper begins to alloy itself, partly with the underlying gold, partly with the gold from the grains, and this alloy fuses the grains to the base surface.
7. At a somewhat higher temperature the copper from the melted alloy diffuses gradually into the gold where, to all purposes, it disappears because the amount of the gold is about 1,000 times greater than that of the copper in the alloy.

A simple granulation technique, which might leave a slightly roughened surface however, is done in the following manner:

1. The metal (fine silver, sterling, high-karat gold) is heated to dull red, pickled, and dried. Avoid touching any surfaces with your fingers.
2. The grains or other small units, along with the unit to which they will be fused, are all given a coating of copper by immersing them in a steel or iron cup containing a 10% sulfuric acid and water solution and a tablespoon of copper carbonate. Rinse and carefully dry all parts.
3. Adhere the small units to the large with a droplet of gum tragacanth solution (mixed to a thick consistency). Allow the gum to dry thoroughly.
4. Place the work on a charcoal block and heat it with a soft reducing flame until a faint surface shine develops on all units. This indicates that fusion, as described above, has taken place.
5. Work can now be pickled and cleaned as after soldering.

Another method of achieving delicate solderless fusion is currently being investigated. This process seeks to exploit the phenomenon of *diffusion*, the process of molecular interchange by contact. If given enough time, two pieces of like metal will eventually exchange molecules at a point of contact even at room temperature. If this process is accelerated by controlled heat in the correct atmosphere for a controlled period of time, a strong and precise fusion will take place.

SHOT MAKING

For general decorative purposes, shot can easily be made by melting small scraps of metal (or measured lengths of wire if all are to have equal diameter) with a gas-air torch flame on charcoal. Since fragments of metal to be melted are usually small, it is easy to blow them away with the torch flame. Scoring shallow depressions into the charcoal will hold the metal during heating.

A small amount of metal results in fairly spherical shot. Larger shot often becomes more oval in cross section as the weight of the molten metal forces itself outward.

Once the metal has drawn up into a sphere, the air should slowly be turned off, allowing only a gas flame to bathe the shot. Done this way, the shot will cool oxide-free and with a smooth surface.

6   some contemporary techniques

• electroforming

The fascinating technique of electroforming is an artistic development of the conventional electroplating process, long used to deposit one metal upon another. In addition to metal, any other organic or inorganic material can be electroformed to strengthen it and give it permanence.

The process, in brief, consists of passing a direct electric current through a solution supercharged with a metal ion. This changes the metal ion from a positive ionic state to a neutral state and deposits it on a receptive base of solid metal or on a metal-painted material, called a *cathode*. So that the metallic ions in solution are not depleted too quickly, and in order to complete the circuit of the current, an *anode* of the same metal as that in solution is also placed in the solution. The anode metal is also ionized and goes into the solution.

It is simple to electroform (electrodeposition is another term for the process) on a conductive metal surface such as copper, silver, or gold. Other materials—as well as less conductive metals—may be prepared for the depositing process by being coated with an electroconductive paint.

Most often this is a very finely powdered pure silver—the best conductor—mixed with a quick-drying clear lacquer. A spray bronze paint is also available, which is both cheaper and easier to find. Sources of electroforming supplies are listed under "Supply Sources for Tools and Materials."

Such fragile substances as wax, thin plastic, styrofoam, paper, metal foil, bone, grass or wood fiber, and insects are first carefully degreased—electroformed surfaces will not adhere to greasy or oily surfaces—thoroughly dried, and given a good coating of varnish or plastic lacquer. This is to prevent later absorption of acid solutions that may be difficult to neutralize. When the protective coating is thoroughly dry, the object can be sprayed or painted with the conductive paint. Prior to this, a copper or silver conductive wire should be firmly affixed to the model. The wire can be as fine as 20 to 22 gauge. It may be necessary to solder the conductive wire temporarily onto the metal form to be electroformed in order to make a secure join. This should also be painted with conductive paint, at least around the area where it connects to the form (Fig. 6–1 illustrates a form made of thin paper and modeled

1 Pendant, Hilary Packard; crab shell, copper, mother-of-pearl, electroformed; 3½" wide

2 Pendant, back view

3 Bracelet, Carol Anne Fooks; copper electroforming over reticulated silver

4 Demonstration pin, Robert von Neumann; photoetching on bronze with an inlay of electroformed copper; 2½" wide

5 Pendants, Karen Krett; electroformed celadon porcelain, shells, etc.; 2" to 2½" wide

6 Cup; copper, electroforming over wax wire around gemstones; 6" high

7 Pins and pendants, Melinda Duncan; bronze, silver, copper electroforming

1

2

3

4

All student work was done by undergraduates at the University of Illinois

230
some contemporary techniques

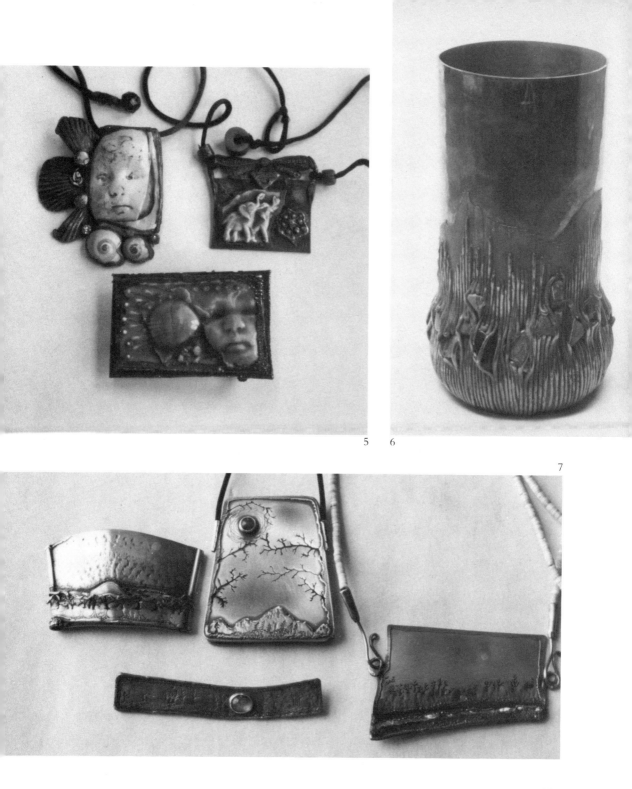

5 6

7

231

fig. 6–1

wax to which an 18-gauge wire has been attached). The paper can be cemented together with any strong, waterproof cement before being varnished.

The following step-by-step explanation deals first with the electrodeposition of copper on a wax form, and then discusses how silver is electrodeposited.

COPPER ELECTROFORMING

1. Finish the model completely in order to minimize buffing or filing on what may end up as delicate surfaces. If you use a liquid-absorptive material (paper, cardboard, wood, fiber), make sure that it is thoroughly coated with wax or waterproof varnish.
2. Affix a 20- or 22-gauge copper or silver wire to the model with wax or epoxy cement, as in Fig. 6–1.
3. Remove grease or oil with liquid detergent, water, and a soft brush.
4. Paint all surfaces to be electroformed with an electro-conductive paint, including the first inch of the attached wire. There will be times when areas are not to be electroformed at all, or that will be formed later with a different current density for a different effect. These areas must be "stopped

off" with a good opaque varnish (for visibility) or a thin coating of wax. They will of course *not* be painted with the conductive paint (Fig. 6–2 shows a form of metal and wax that has some areas stopped off).

5. Prepare a solution for electrodeposition of copper. Here are three choices:

SOLUTION A:

Copper sulfate	1 pound
Sulfuric acid (H₂SO₄)	100 cubic centimeters
Distilled water	½ gallon

(To be used with 6 volts, ½ amp. at 72°F)

SOLUTION B:

Copper sulfate	32 ounces
Sulfuric acid	10 ounces
Distilled water	1 gallon

(2 volts, ½ amp. at 80°F with moderate agitation and full filtration)

SOLUTION C:

| Copper fluoroborate | 60 ounces |
| Distilled water | 1 gallon |

A pH (colorimetric) of 0.3
(4 volts at 100°F with constant agitation and filtration)

SOLUTION D:

Cupric sulfate	20 ounces
Sulfuric acid	3–5 ounces
Distilled water	1 gallon

(½ to 4 volts, 1 to 100 amps., 80 to 100°F)

These solutions should be kept in large 1000 cc. Pyrex glass jars and fixed with tight-fitting lids to reduce evaporation when not in use. They should also be filtered through chemical filtration paper after each use.

6. Prepare an appropriate copper anode. It can consist of a sheet of 20- or 18-gauge copper that is formed into an incomplete cylinder surrounding the

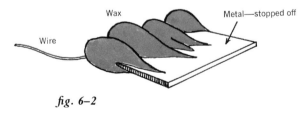

fig. 6–2

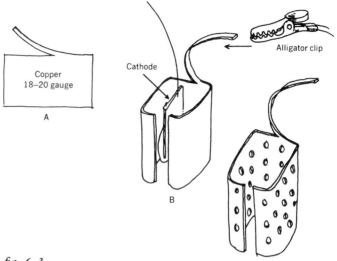

fig. 6–3

object to be electroformed (the cathode). To provide an attachment point to which a wire might be affixed to the current source, a strip can be cut and bent as in Fig. 6–3A. In Fig. 6–3B the anode has been bent to conform as much as possible to the shape of the cathode. The anode should not be closer than ¼″ to ½″ at any point from the cathode. The ends of the anode should not touch each other. To allow for better circulation of the solution, drill holes into the anode at various points. (See Fig. 6–3C.) Plan the anode so that the point of connection and the top of the anode remain above the solution to decrease corrosion of the connection.

Another anode plan consists of making one or more copper buss bars to cross the top of a plastic or glass container. These bars are attached to the positive (+) connection for the anodes; another buss bar is attached to the negative (−) connection for the work to be electroformed (cathode). (See Fig. 6–4.)

The anode for each piece to be elec-troformed should have about the same surface area as the piece of jewelry. If two anodes are used as in Fig. 6–4, each should be one-half the surface of the jewelry. The anodes should be chemically clean before use. Heat them to annealing temperature, pickle them in a 50% nitric acid solution for 4 to 5 seconds, rinse, and use. Examine them periodically because they are eaten away quickly.

7. Current sources. The least expensive—and somewhat primitive—electrical source is a used 6-volt automobile battery. This might require half an hour of recharging with an inexpensive battery charger. An *ammeter* must be used to indicate the amount of current moving through the system. A 22-ohm *variable rheostat* must be used to deliver a current flow of ½ to 1½ amperes. (Fig. 6–5 shows how this system is connected.)

A more complex and controllable current source consists of a type of transformer called an electroplating *rectifier.* This unit regulates direction and flow of both voltage and amper-

233

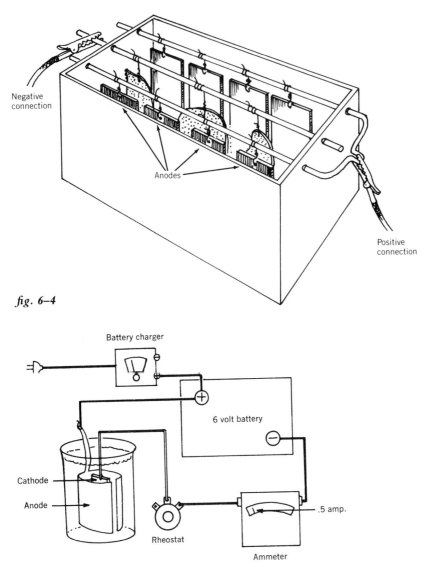

Negative
connection

Anodes

Positive
connection

fig. 6–4

Battery charger

6 volt battery

Cathode

Anode

Rheostat

.5 amp.

Ammeter

fig. 6–5

age and makes the ammeter and rheostat unnecessary.

8. Suspend the prepared cathode in the
plating solution. The current source
should not be connected at this stage.
A frame can be built over the jar from
which one or more objects (cathodes)
can be hung.

9. Connect the current source. There are
a number of variables that will determine the quality of the final surface.
Whether it will be smooth and follow
the cathode contours closely, or
whether it will consist of granular or
even dendritic surface growths, depends upon such factors as:

some contemporary techniques

a. Changing voltage and amperage.
b. Changing solution strength, or allowing debris to collect in the solution.
c. Changing the plating solution temperature.
d. Changing the degree or direction of circulation of the solution.
e. Changing anode shape, size, or distance from the cathode.
f. Varying the length of time the cathode remains in the solution.
g. Selective "stopping off" of certain areas at stages in the process.

10. After a deposit of copper that has enough thickness to withstand handling has been applied, wax can be melted out by immersing the formed object in boiling water. It can then be returned to the plating bath for additional deposition if needed. It is imperative, of course, to remove all wax from the metal surface by washing the object with a solvent such as benzene.

The metal deposited can be polished or given a patina, or it can be plated with silver or gold by conventional electroplating.

11. Findings can be soldered in place, or they could be affixed before electroforming and integrated into the cathode. Conductive paint should have been brushed around the base of pin findings, but the mechanism of catches should have been "stopped off" to prevent solidifying them in the plating process.

SILVER ELECTROFORMING

Electroforming in a silver solution requires that the metallic object be covered in an electrocleaning bath for up to thirty seconds. It should then be rinsed and given a silver *strike* in a *strike* solution for an additional thirty seconds in order to create a good adherent base for further deposition.

If nonmetallic materials painted with silver conductive paint are being used, they must first be given a light plating of copper. This will prevent the silver paint from being eaten away or affected by heat in later plating.

The following are solutions for silver electroforming:

SOLUTION A:

Alkaline electrocleaning bath

Commercial Alkaline Electrocleaning Solution
Stainless steel anode
(8-volt current for 30 seconds at 180°F)

SOLUTION B:

Silver strike for nonferrous metals

Silver cyanide	½ ounce
Potassium cyanide	12 ounces
Distilled water	1 gallon
Stainless steel anode	

(6-volt current for 30 seconds at 80°F)

SOLUTION C:

Silver cyanide forming bath

Silver cyanide	15 ounces
Potassium cyanide	18 ounces
Potassium carbonate	2 ounces
Potassium hydroxide	1 ounce
Distilled water	1 gallon

Pure silver anode, annealed
(2-volt current at 115°F for as long as desired. Rapid agitation and constant filtration are necessary)

When silver-cyanide and gold-cyanide-plating solutions (for the electrodeposition of silver or gold) are used, a controlled temperature is important and can be managed by use of an aquarium heater in the solution. Circulation and filtration are also important and can be achieved using

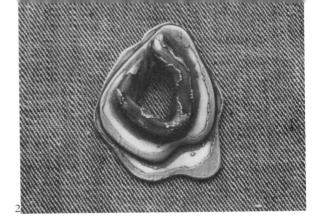

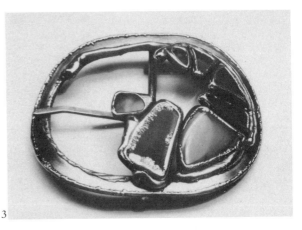

*All student work was done
by undergraduates at
the University of Illinois*

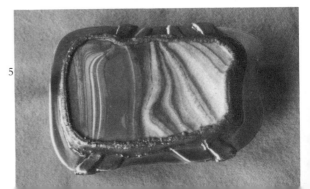

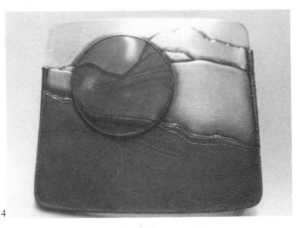

1 Bracelet; bronze, abalone, copper
electroforming

2 Pendant; bronze, agate, copper
electroforming

3 Buckle, Christine Bartling; silver, copper,
electroforming, tumbled stones; 2½" wide

4 Buckle; silver, brass, copper, picture agate

5 Buckle; silver, agate, copper electroforming

4

5

aquarium filters and pumps. If greater agitation is needed, stirring devices are available that keep liquids moving without forming air bubbles, which might affect the plating process. *Warning!* Cyanide solutions are deadly! Work only in a well-ventilated area, and avoid direct internal or external contact! (Eli Lilly Co. offers a cyanide antidote kit, Stock No. M76.)

If the electroforming tank is to be kept in use for long periods of time, some means must be found to reduce evaporation of the solution. Covering the surface, edge to edge with Styrofoam or expanded polyurethane packaging particles effectively covers the liquid.

There are unlimited aspects of design involvement in the electroforming process. Gemstones, especially delicate mineral specimens, can be set in hard-to-reach areas by simply growing metal around them. Fig. 6–6A shows how silver conductive paint can be painted around the base of a stone that has been cemented in place. Metal will grow on the painted area, holding the stone firmly. Irregular stones can be held in a lattice of painted lines, which will also hold after forming (Fig. 6–6B). Pearls, mother of pearl, abalone, some turquoise, and other porous gem materials should not be electroformed in place because acid solutions can mar and even dissolve them.

Findings should have been soldered or formed into place before any gemstone is

added. Heat could dam
soldering.

If you want to form a
that could be very attract
lowing:

1. Prepare a 15% to 25%
   lution.
2. Dissolve a good amount o ⌐ean copper scrap in the solution.
3. Prepare an electroforming bath unit with copper anodes at least twice the surface volume of the work to be electroformed.
4. Plate at about 1. to 1.5 amps. per square inch of the object until the granular surface is formed.
5. Continue plating in the usual copper sulfate solution at a low-current density (70 milliamps per square inch or less) to "cement" the granular particles together firmly.

Electroformed surfaces, whether copper, silver or gold, are quite dense and pure, and vitreous enamels adhere to them well.

● photoetching on metal

Photographic and other images can be etched into the surface of a variety of metals by using special resists—acid-resistant chemical films—that are also light-sensitive. The process has been highly developed in the electronic industry, which

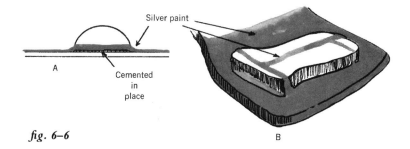

Silver paint

A   Cemented
                    in
                  place

fig. 6–6   B

1 Pin, Rosalee Spiegel; photoetching

2 Pins, Eleanor Moty; photoetching; 2″ high

3 "Prairie House," Eleanor Moty; photoetched bronze, silver, and copper

4 Portrait pins, Eleanor Moty; photoetched silver and copper

5 "Fish House," Eleanor Moty; photoetched copper, silver, and bronze

1

2 3

4 5

produces complex printed circuits in this way. The equipment must be simplified somewhat for the studio workshop, but even then, the process is still complex and requires attention to detail and procedure.

Simply defined, the process consists of preparing a sheet of metal with a photo-sensitive emulsion. Either a photographic negative in halftone dots or an india ink drawing on acetate sheet (all contrasts must be black and white—no half-tones) are exposed onto the photosensitive emulsion by timed ultraviolet light. The exposed film on the metal is then developed and fixed, and the clear areas are washed away to clean metal. These clean areas are then etched in a variety of ways. The following is one successful method.

CLEANING THE METAL

MATERIALS

1. Clean bristle brush.
2. Drill bit for drilling wire holes.
3. Wire hook.
4. Lonco Copperbrite (London Chemical Co.; see Supply Sources).
5. Comet cleansing powder.

METHOD

1. Drill a hole for wire suspension in one or more corners of the metal.
2. Scrub metal thoroughly with a brush and Comet cleansing powder. Use *cold* water. Warm or hot water tends to spread any grease or oil film even thinner.
3. Dip the metal into the Lonco solution for 10 seconds with agitation.
4. Scrub the surface again, making sure that the surface to be etched is not touched by hand. A film of cold water should remain, unbroken, for at least 20 seconds.
5. Wipe the metal dry with lint-free paper and immediately coat it with the resist. Do not use compressed air to dry the metal unless a good oil filter is being used. Canned compressed air is safe.

APPLICATION OF THE RESIST

MATERIALS

1. Pyrex or stainless steel tank or tray, deep, narrow shape is best.
2. An appropriate photochemical resist. Kodak produces a variety of resists for a variety of materials. KPR (Kodak Photo Resist) works well on silver, copper, bronze, brass, nickel silver, and steel. If other resists are used, follow manufacturer's directions carefully.
3. A "dark box." (See Fig. 6–7.)

METHOD

1. Dip the clean, dry metal into the resist and let it drip dry. Be sure to stir the resist thoroughly—without bubbles!—before each dipping.
2. Air-dry the coated metal in the "dark box" for at least one hour.
3. Bake (called the "prebake") metal for 15 minutes at 110°C. If a special heat-control oven is not available, use a darkened kitchen oven set between 225°F and 250°F. Be sure the oven has reached this temperature before introducing the metal.
4. The work can be dried in the light-proof box for at least 24 hours if no oven is available.
5. Remove, cool, and keep darkened until exposure.

IMAGE EXPOSURE

MATERIALS

1. Negative.
2. Exposure box. (See Figs. 6–8 and 6–9.)
3. Timer.

METHOD

1. Place the negative, emulsion side down, on the resist-coated metal.
2. Make sure that all the metal pieces to be exposed at the same time are of the same gauge. Different thicknesses might

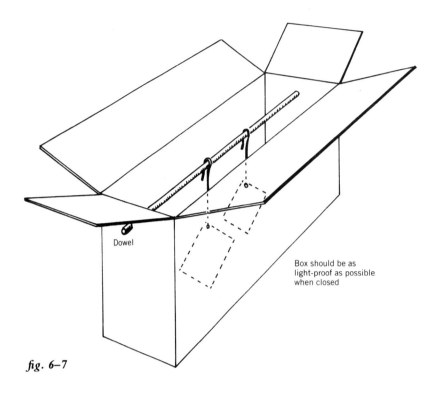

Dowel

Box should be as
light-proof as possible
when closed

fig. 6–7

prevent good negative-to-metal contact. Thin plastic tape can be used to
attach the negative carefully to the metal
so that it does not move when the glass
sheet is placed on it.

3. Cover the negative/metal with a thick
   sheet of glass (¼″ plate glass or automobile glass works well) while the metal
   rests flat on a fairly firm foam-rubber
   bed.

4. Place the ultraviolet light source over
   the glass (3″ to 6″ depending on exposure times required). With the U/V
   light suspended 3″ above the object, an
   exposure time of about ten minutes
   works well. For a distance of 5″ to 6″,
   a period of 15 minutes is approximately
   correct. It is a good idea to run tests
   on distance/exposure time ratios, since
   U/V tubes vary and also change with
   age. One type of tube used successfully
   is the G.E. 15-watt G15T8 germicidal

tube. This is a clear glass, unfiltered
unit that is dangerous to the eyes. Use
it with extreme caution! Be sure to expose *both* sides of the piece of metal to
assure complete acid resistance in later
steps. An inexpensive on-off timer can
give accurate time intervals.

5. After exposure, go immediately to the
   developer.

DEVELOPING THE IMAGE

MATERIALS

1. Glass tray.
2. KOR Developer (Kodak Ortho Resist
   Developer).
3. Small airbrush unit. This is very useful,
   since developer *sprayed* onto the exposed metal areas scavenges the dissolving resist from delicate areas more
   effectively than dipping.

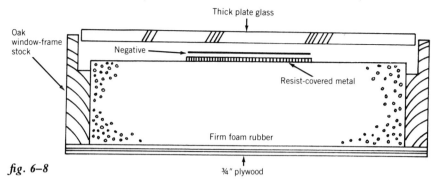

Thick plate glass

Oak window-frame stock

Negative

Resist-covered metal

Firm foam rubber

¾" plywood

fig. 6–8

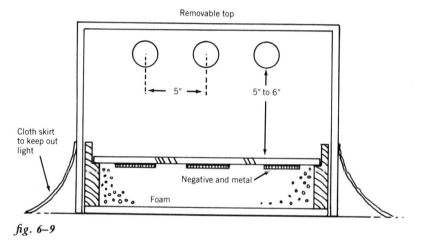

Removable top

5"

5" to 6"

Cloth skirt to keep out light

Negative and metal

Foam

fig. 6–9

METHOD

1. Remove unexposed areas of metal by dissolving them with the KOR. During this exposure period, the dark areas of the negative over the resist-coated metal obviously prevented U/V light penetration. Those unexposed areas are dissolvable with the KOR. These, then, are to be etched. Where the resist *was* exposed to U/V light, the resist polymerized into an acid-resistant coating.
2. Rinse in clean, cold water. Dry carefully with paper tissue.
3. Postbake for 15 minutes at 110°C. (See Step 3.) Allow to cool. If the resist peels

off during the developing process, it may have been overexposed, the metal may have been dirty, the objects may have been overbaked, or the chemicals may be too old.

The object may now be treated in a variety of ways. The exposed metal sections can be electroplated with a contrasting metal. They can be electroformed, with copper or other metal encrustation contrasting with the smooth surface of the resist-protected areas. The work can also be etched through a variety of techniques to bring out the texture or figurative de-

241

sign of the original photograph or drawing.

An interesting process consists of photochemically etching a light-colored metal, such as sterling silver, nickel silver, or brass, and then electroforming in the etched depressions with copper. The electroformed areas are built up to slightly above the protected areas, then filed and stoned flush. Complex inlays can be created in this way. (see #4, page 230.)

If you want to electroform on the unetched metal (i.e., bare metal exposed after the developing process in Step D), a special step is useful to prevent the electroformed areas from peeling off later. This step is also useful in general electroforming where the metal cannot grow around or into contours that would mechanically lock it in place.

Step 1. Electroplate the metal for 20 to 30 minutes with a current density that is just below the point where "burning" of the surface starts.

Step 2. Reduce the current density to normal plating amperage for 5 to 10 minutes with a little agitation.

Step 3. Increase the current density again and repeat the process 5 to 6 times before resuming normal electrodeposition.

ETCHING THE IMAGE

Many etchant solutions can be used, but the ferric chloride solution used in industry works with greatest precision. Industrial heat-controlled and timed etching units are expensive, but it's possible to build an inexpensive home workshop unit.

MATERIALS

1. Etching Bath Unit. (See Fig. 6–10.)
2. Aquarium pump and ⅛" plastic tubing.
3. Etchant solution: a. 42 Baumé ferric chloride, Photoengraver's grade.
   b. Hydrochloric acid.

METHOD

1. Prepare the solution by mixing the liquid ferric chloride with 5% hydrochloric acid by volume (9.5 cc. ferric chloride plus .5 cc. hydrochloric acid). This

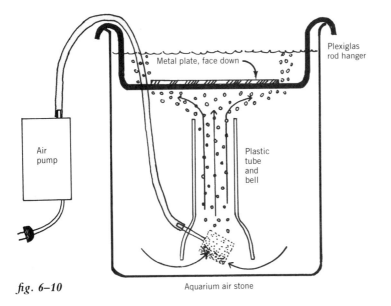

fig. 6–10

Metal plate, face down

Plexiglas rod hanger

Air pump

Plastic tube and bell

Aquarium air stone

some contemporary techniques

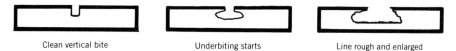

Clean vertical bite　　　　Underbiting starts　　　　Line rough and enlarged

fig. 6–11

solution etches copper, brass, bronze, nickel silver, sterling silver (should be about 80°F), and stainless steel. Etching time will vary with each metal.

2. Spray the etchant from below with a steady force. In Fig. 6–10 this upflowing of etchant is achieved by directing a flow of air bubbles and etchant against the inverted object. The length of time depends on the desired etching depth, but it is important to remember that underbiting eventually causes rough line edges and pitting. (See Fig. 6–11.)

Ferric chloride is not corrosive on organic materials (although it can discolor skin and clothing), so tape the work to a sheet of Plexiglas to keep it inverted in this process.

If you plan subsequent plating or electroforming, clean the etched areas of residue left after etching. This can be done by immersing the work in a 10% ammonium persulphate solution for about a minute. This solution etches down to bare metal, and a gentle brushing under cold water should leave a clean surface to be plated.

The electroetching process described in Chapter 4 can also be used to good effect.

When etching and/or electroforming are completed, a Kodak solvent or burning off will remove the resist.

● reticulation

Reticulation is a decorative metal process wherein an alloy of silver and copper is treated to create a distinctive corrugated, or "reticulated," surface. This process was developed in the workshops of Peter Carl Fabergé, Jeweler to the Imperial Court of Russia, in the late nineteenth and early twentieth century.

The following description of the process will result in a corrugated blank of reticulated metal from which forms may be cut out to use as elements in jewelry and other objects. Although some control is possible, you must be prepared to take advantage of random textural results. (See Fig. 6-16.)

THE ALLOY

830 parts fine silver (sterling will also work) 170 parts copper. By contrast, *sterling* silver is 925 parts fine silver + 75 parts copper. A usable measurable quantity is: Silver 41.5 dwts + copper 8.5 dwts. This amount results in a piece approximately 2″ × 4″ × 20 gauge.

MATERIALS

1. Heat resistant pad or charcoal block (6″ × 6″ × ½″ works well)
2. Ceramic or graphite crucible. The type used in casting, consisting of a small, shallow ceramic dish with an 18″ handle, is good.
3. Ingot mold, adjustable (for sheet)
4. Acetylene torch. Prest-o-Lite works well.
5. One-quart Pyrex beaker or bowl.
6. Hotplate or stove for boiling pickle (use a heating pad under the Pyrex to prevent cracking the glass).
7. Copper tongs for removing the sheet from the pickle.
8. Borax flux.
9. Rolling mill, or 2½-pound forging hammer and a steel slab if a rolling mill is unavailable.
10. Gas/compressed air torch, if avail-

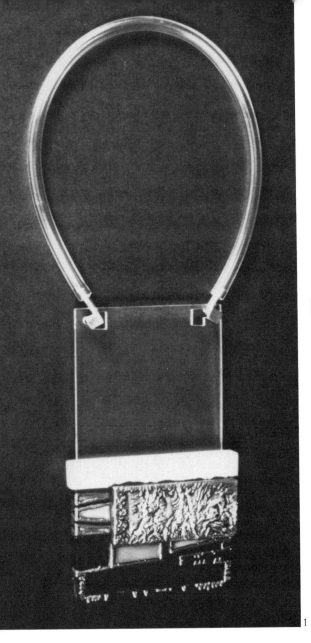

1

1 Pendant, Hilary Packard; copper, silver, Plexiglas, reticulated metal; 3½" high

2 Detail of pendant

3 Pendant, Hilary Packard, silver and reticulation; 3¼" long

4 Cookie cutters, Laurel Hoyt; silver, copper, reticulation, mokume, electroforming; 3¼" to 3½" diameter

5 Box, Hilary Packard; sterling silver, reticulation; 5" long

6 Box; bronze, reticulation; 3½" long

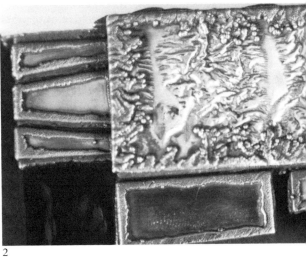

2

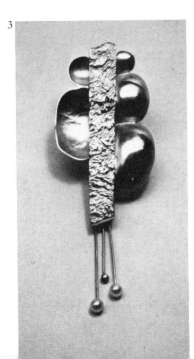

3

All student work was done by undergraduates at the University of Illinois

244
some contemporary techniques

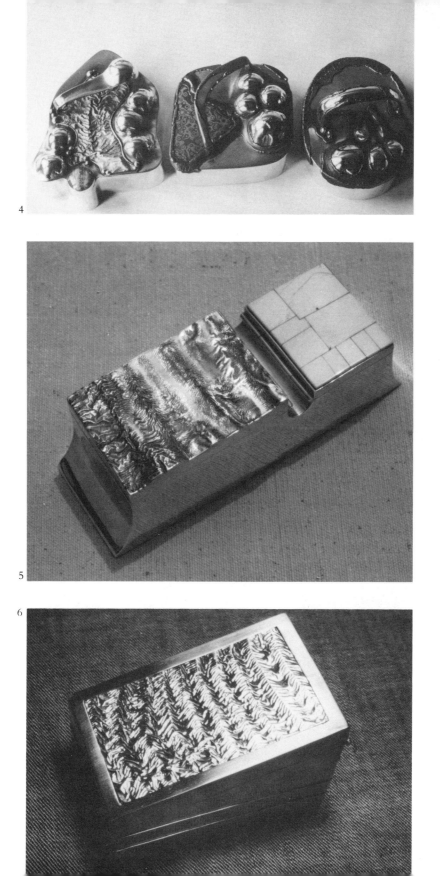

4

5

6

245

able. Good for forming a variety of flames.
11. Brass brush.
12. Liquid detergent.
13. Pointed tweezers.

METHOD

1. The ingot mold should be prepared by "smoking" the interior with carbon. This can be done easily with an acetylene torch by closing your hand over the air intake in the torch handle. The resulting sooty flame quickly coats the ingot surfaces.

   Adjust the ingot mold to 1" to 1½" width to accommodate the 41.5 dwt. silver + 8.5 dwt. copper amount. Use larger or smaller widths for larger or smaller volumes of the alloyed metal.

2. Preheat a ceramic or graphite crucible, lightly coated with borax flux, to a red glow.

3. Both silver and copper should be free of oxides, oil, or grease film. This is best done by heating to dull red and boiling in an 8% sulfuric acid solution (1 part H_2SO_4 + 8 parts H_2O). Add the acid to the water!

4. Add the copper to the heated crucible, sprinkle with a very small amount of borax flux, and heat until molten. If the copper is slow to melt, add a small amount of the silver to start an alloy-ing action that will result in a lower melting temperature. An acetylene flame is more effective than a natural gas-air or propane torch for efficient heating.

5. Add the silver and heat until molten. A gentle shaking of the crucible hastens complete melting. The molten mass should be completely smooth, with no peaks or projections sticking up. The mass should be fluid when shaken. Stir several times with a ¼" hardwood dowel to assure that the two metals are completely mixed.

6. While keeping the torch on the metal in the crucible, carefully but quickly pour the metal into the ingot mold. Open the mold and cool the ingot in water.

7. The ingot will be ⅛" thick and about 1½" × 3" (or 1" × 4") long. It must be thinned by hammering before it can be rolled to *20-gauge* thickness in a rolling mill. The most effective hammer for this is a 2½-pound forging hammer with a narrow, 1⅝" wide wedge.

   Strike firm, overlapping blows at right angles to the long axis of the ingot and then parallel to the long axis. (See Fig. 6–12.)

8. After hammering, anneal the blank to sterling annealing temperature. This

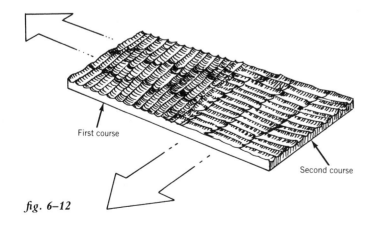

First course

Second course

fig. 6–12

can best be determined by using Handy Flux, which, when painted on the surface of the metal, becomes water-clear and free of bubbles and discoloration at about 1150°F. At that point, *quickly* quench the blank in cold water.

9. Repeat hammering as in Step 8 and anneal again.

10. Roll in a rolling mill or hammer out with a smooth forging hammer and smooth anvil surface (annealing as needed) until the sheet is 20 gauge thick and *as flat as possible*. This is important!

11. Prepare a new heat resistant block by heating it to a red glow, driving off moisture, and burning off the bonding material.

12. On the hot heat resistant material begin to heat the metal uniformly using an oxidizing flame (a flame that has more *air* in the mix than would be used for soldering). Do *not* use flux! Use a large enough torch flame so that the sheet can be heated efficiently. Heat until the copper in the copper-silver alloy oxidizes on the surface. A gray-black fire scale should result. Do *not* heat until the metal begins to glow.

   Turn the piece over and heat the back in the same manner. Wait 10 to 15 seconds before quenching the sheet in water. Quenching the thin sheet while too hot will cause warping.

13. Prepare a special pickle of 8% sulfuric acid and water (1 part sulfuric acid plus 8 parts water). *Always* add the acid to the water to prevent a possibly dangerous boiling reaction! The solution should be placed in a Pyrex beaker or pot and brought to a low boil. Drop in the sheet of metal and boil for 3 to 5 minutes. (Be sure to have adequate ventilation to remove hot acid vapors. Also, add water carefully to replace the amount boiled away during this process.) Rinse the sheet in clean water.

14. Both surfaces must now be burnished to smooth out the remaining particles of pure silver after the oxidized copper has been dissolved off in Step 14. This is done by brushing the surface firmly with a *brass* wire brush and using undiluted washing detergent as a lubricant. Rinse in clean water and dry.

15. Again heat the heat-resistant sheet, and heat the metal to bring up more copper oxide. Be sure to avoid developing red heat in the metal. Repeat Steps 12, 13, and 14 *six* or *seven* times. With each heating, less copper oxide will show, making it increasingly difficult to judge how long the heating should be. Just avoid letting the metal glow.

   After six or seven heatings, picklings, and burnishings, the sheet of metal will have an exterior of pure silver (melting point 1761°F) over an interior of the 830% silver/copper alloy (melting point well below 1600°F). (See Fig. 6–13.)

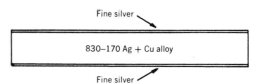

Fine silver

830–170 Ag + Cu alloy

Fine silver

fig. 6–13

DEVELOPING THE RETICULATION

1. Prepare the heat resistant sheet as in Step 12 (perhaps the reverse side of the same sheet) and place the metal sheet on the hot heat resistant material.

2. Develop a short, narrow oxidizing flame with the torch, 3½″ to 4″ long by ½″ wide.

3. Heat the entire sheet of metal until a faint glow develops as seen in a darkened area of the soldering bench.

4. Concentrate the flame on one corner of the metal sheet until wrinkling develops. Do *not* pause, but continue to

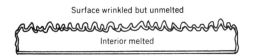

Surface wrinkled but unmelted

Interior melted

fig. 6–14

move the torch along the metal at a rate that allows the metal to continue wrinkling. (See Fig. 6–14.) Do not allow a bright red glow to develop. This usually means that the pure silver coating has been burned through and the area will not reticulate.

What happens in this step is that the interior of the sheet of metal begins to melt. The exterior, a fairly thick layer of pure silver, resists melting because it has a much higher melting point. It is a characteristic of melting metal to shrink inward, to turn into a pool of molten metal. The silver exterior does not shrink but wrinkles up like a thin deflating rubber balloon. Ridges and depressions result.

5. Patterns of ridges can be developed by angling and moving the flame in various ways. A herringbone pattern can be achieved by moving the angled flame across the sheet and reversing the angle at the next crossing. (See Fig. 6–15.)

This piece of textured metal can be burnished again (the surface is still pure silver and will maintain brightness for a long time), or it can be oxidized. In addition, it can be rolled gently through the rolling mill for a different effect. An excellent example of silver reticulation is shown in Fig. 6–16.

Remember, when soldering a reticulated portion to other metal forms, use a low-melting solder since the melting point of the 860 alloy is quite low in itself.

GOLD RETICULATION

14K. yellow or red golds are already alloys consisting of ten parts (out of twenty-four) of metal(s) other than gold. Yellow gold of this karat is generally a copper-silver-gold mixture with a melting point of as low as 1565°F, compared to the melting point of 24K. (or pure) gold at 1945°F. 14K. red gold melts at 1670°F.

Gold is prepared for reticulating in much the same manner as silver. After a uniform yellow surface is developed, anneal it again with an oxidizing flame until a black surface layer has formed.

Begin to heat for reticulation. A wash of yellow ocher mixed with water can be used instead of the black oxidized surface coating. The selective placement of yellow ochre can result in interesting contrasts of surface.

fig. 6–15

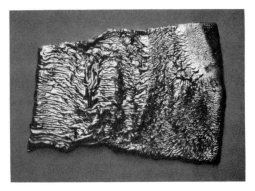

fig. 6–16

some contemporary techniques

7 possibilities in jewelry design

Jewelry has many shapes, many uses. It may vary in size from a tiny accent pin to a spectacular necklace. The only real limitations to shape and size are those that the wearer or prevailing styles might impose. Because jewelry contains a personality within itself, it can ally itself with the personality of the wearer.

Many jewelry designer-craftsmen work directly with the client in order to evolve a design most admirably suited to the client's vision.

Another designer-craftsman may prefer to design to satisfy his own personal vision, without any specific wearer in mind. In this case, there might be a somewhat greater regard for the absolute limits of size and weight of the object. Since these limitations have been well established through centuries of use, common sense and a little insight are really all that is necessary.

Each century, and almost every society within that century, has had a fashionable jewelry form. To the Egyptians, the large, pendant collar necklace was important. During the Renaissance, a rich, linked chain and several ornate finger rings on each hand were the mark of the well-dressed aris-

tocrat. The style of dress in many parts of India and Southeast Asia requires that a jewel be worn in the side of the nose and that rings be worn on toes as well as fingers.

Only within recent times in the West have jewelry uses been limited virtually to rings, cuff links, and tie ornaments for men, and to earrings, necklaces, pins, and rings for women. Fortunately, within these rather arbitrary restrictions, there is a wealth of variety, a limitless world of ideas available to the designer-craftsman.

The design and construction details of a number of basic jewelry forms will be described in this chapter. The list may be incomplete, however, because new approaches to the use of jewelry are being found every day. The information is fundamental, and the designer-craftsman interested in creating jewelry will quickly develop his own variations and refinements.

● pins and brooches

The size of a pin would not be important except that weight becomes a serious fac-

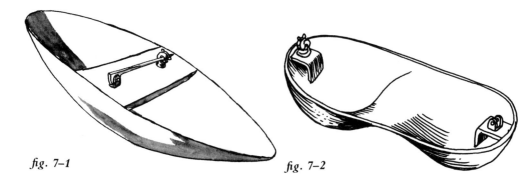

fig. 7–1

fig. 7–2

tor as the size increases. Although a pin may be designed specifically to be worn only on heavy suit or coat fabric, most pins must be light enough so that they do not stretch light dress materials.

As a general rule, sharp points should be avoided. The pin is fixed to the cloth and will not give way when accidentally brushed by a hand or arm.

Pins are usually flat rather than three-dimensional because the weight distribution in the round could cause the pin to hang forward from the dress rather than resting against the surface. A slight contour usually works well if the pin assembly is fastened so that the piece is easily pinned to the dress.

Most contoured pins have either a flat back or a bar of flat metal to which the pin may be attached. (See Fig. 7–1.) A

complexly contoured pin might also have the catch and joint attached to small steps soldered to the curve of a contour. Solder the step in place first, premelt solder onto its top surface, then add the finding. (See Fig. 7–2.) Many jewelers prefer to make the findings of a piece themselves rather than use manufactured ones so that the complete work has been dictated by the craftsman. Factors such as the flexibility of a pin stem or its delicacy must be considered when making a joint or a catch. Two of several simple, handmade pin assemblies are shown in Figs. 7-3 and 7-4.

In Fig. 7–3 the pinstem—best made of nickel-silver wire—is soldered to a three-part hinge with a vertical bar next to the hinge, creating the downward tension necessary for a tight fit in the catch.

In Fig. 7–4 the pin and the catch are all

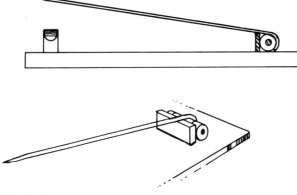

fig. 7–3

possibilities in jewelry design

fig. 7–4

part of the piece itself. The pin stem is sawed out of the same piece as the object, and when all soldering or other heating is complete, it is compressed by careful planishing to make it properly springy.

Many small pins are now fastened by clutchbacks as for tiebacks. In this way, two or more small pieces of jewelry can be worn in an arrangement decided by the wearer. The so-called Kewpie catch (See Fig. 7–5) can be used in a similar manner.

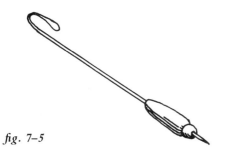

fig. 7–5

Applying pin assemblies is described in Chapter 2.

The back of a piece of jewelry should be treated with the same concern for excellent craftsmanship as the front. The bottom edges should be beveled, even though on the top edges the design might require a precise angular treatment.

Remove all traces of oxidation from the back. This would rub off on clothing.

• pendants

A pendant can be no more than a simply set stone on a chain, or it can be a richly interpreted form in the center of related shapes that form the chain. Size and shape restrictions are limited to the potential wearer. The pendant can be quite delicate in construction, since it is mobile enough to move with a touch. Sharp projections should be avoided; they would catch in the dress material.

Most pendants are suspended from one point. Since they may turn during wear, it is especially important that the reverse surface be well constructed and finished. Many designer-craftsmen take advantage of this mobility by making the back as interesting as the front. Often both designs are quite different from each other, giving the pendant a double value as a decoration.

The loop through which the chain is run can be incorporated into the design of the back or the top so that its function does not distract the eye.

Simply drilling a hole at the top of the pendant through which a link is placed is too raw and insensitive for well-designed objects. The intrusion of the hole and link breaks the unity of the design.

Fig. 7–6 illustrates a number of pendant loop possibilities.

Since hanging or falling natural objects are usually larger below a horizontal median (as in water drops), the eye finds it more esthetic when a pendant is smaller at the top than at the bottom. Pendants of this shape give a sense of stability. This principle could also be applied to pendants of a basic linear form, such as those made of wire or sheet-metal strips on edge.

The chains of pendants and necklaces in

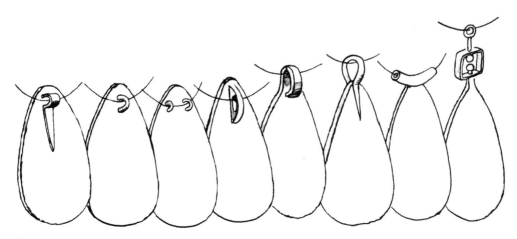

fig. 7-6

general average 18″ to 24″ in length for most purposes.

● necklaces

Necklaces can be of several basic types. They can consist of identical or alternating links of wire or be made up of articulated units of sheet metal. They can be collars—solid in form but flexible enough to slip around the neck.

Necklaces can combine units of wood or plastic with alternating metal forms for variety in color and surface.

LINK NECKLACES

Links have been made for at least three thousand years—and the method is still as simple today. For round links of the same size, a rod of wood or metal just the size of the inside diameter of the desired link is wrapped with one or two turns of wax paper. This allows easy removal of links later.

Wire of the desired gauge and shape is first annealed and pickled and then wrapped in a tight spiral around the rod.

A simple way to do this is to clamp one end of the wire into a vise and alongside one end of the rod. (See Fig. 7-7.)

The wire is wound around the rod as tightly and as evenly as possible. Each complete turn will make one link, so it is possible to predict the number as you work. (See Fig. 7-8.)

fig. 7-7

fig. 7-8

possibilities in jewelry design

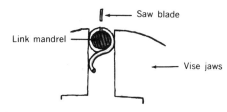

fig. 7–9

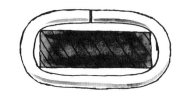

fig. 7–10

The coiled wire on the rod is next placed into the jaws of the vise and all the links cut through at once with a fine jeweler's saw blade. (See Fig. 7–9.)

Each link will now slide off as a separate but incomplete circle. Often a fine barrette file must be used to remove a burr left by sawing, since the link ends must meet perfectly for strong, efficient soldering.

The links may need to be flattened in addition. This can be done by bending and counterbending the ends together with two chain pliers. Avoid marring the links by using controlled pressures and by avoiding pliers with rough edges and surfaces. (They have no place on a jeweler's bench anyway!)

Oval links of round or square wire can be made in the same way by using a rod with a rectangular section. The mass of the wire will cause a rounded rather than an angled corner as the wire is wound around the rod. When heavy wire is used, it is best to round the edges of a metal rod

slightly to prevent cutting into the wire during the winding.

Square or oblong links can be made by hammering the wire around a rod of the correct shape in order to form the angled corners. They can also be made individually by scoring the inside edge of the wire in four places. This can be done with a triangular needle file on heavy wire or by tapping a knife edge lightly into the wire if it is of a small gauge. These miters will allow the bending of sharp corners, but they may be weak. On large links or boxes made of sheet, it is best to run a small seam of *hard* solder into each bend before soldering the ends together with *easy* solder. Note that the notch in Fig. 7–11A is cut a little past the median line of the wire thickness. This is necessary for sharp, clean angles.

Links are combined to make the necklace by soldering units of two together, joining two such units with a single link to make a chain of five, and so forth.

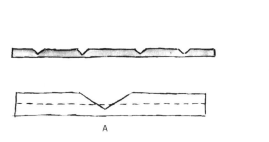

A

B

fig. 7–11

253

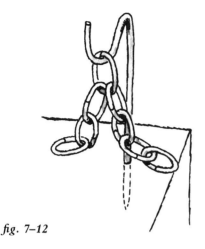

fig. 7–12

Applying the solder is simple. Have each link join clean and fluxed. Melt very small *paillons* of solder into shot on a charcoal block. Using a small soft flame to heat the link to the soldering temperature, pick up a solder grain with a flux-moistened steel pointer and place the grain on the join at the right moment. With a little practice this can be done with great speed. Use just enough solder to fill the join; an excess causes a lump on the join that may be impossible to remove and may cause links to fuse together completely.

Solder each join as far from the next join as possible, and use a thin dab of yellow ocher to prevent remelting of joins once they are fused.

Be sure to examine each join carefully, since an unsoldered link will eventually cause the chain to break.

A simple stand can be constructed to facilitate soldering of links. It is made of heavy-gauge iron wire that is annealed and oxidized to prevent solder adherence. (See Fig. 7–12.)

There are countless link combinations that can be used to make up chains of either massive or delicate quality. See the Bibliography for a list of books showing diagrams and formulas for a number of interesting link chains.

Links can be made of twisted wire, which allows a greater use of oxidation to contrast highly polished areas. Two or more strands of round, square, oblong, half-round, or triangular wire can be twisted together to make the wire from which the links are formed. Using wire of different gauges and different metals often results in interesting link forms.

Wire can be twisted in several ways as in Fig. 7–13. A single strand of square or oblong wire can be twisted in the same way. Wire should be well annealed before twisting, since it quickly becomes brittle.

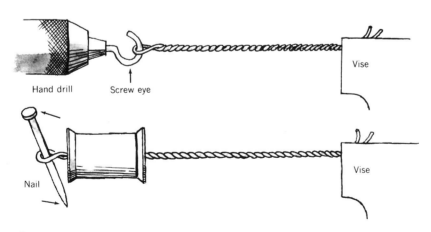

Hand drill   Screw eye   Vise

Nail   Vise

fig. 7–13

possibilities in jewelry design

UNIT NECKLACES

Unit necklaces are made up of individual shapes of metal or other materials and joined together by some sort of linkage for flexibility. The linkage can form an important aspect of the total design, or it can be kept hidden and minimized. Units can be strung together on a small but sturdy machine-made chain if the contrast is not too distracting.

This is a good time to remind the beginner that it is extremely dangerous to machine-polish linked chain. Either hand-polish chain, which is better for delicate links anyway, or wrap the *entire* chain around a board and thumbtack the ends down so that nothing loose touches the wheel!

The following are some unit linkage possibilities. Fig. 7–14A uses half-links soldered to the back of each unit. A fine chain joins the units, and hollow spheres are used to maintain the spacing. Without spacers of some sort, the weight of the units will cause them to slide together during wear.

Fig. 7–14B uses sections of U-shaped

wire through drilled holes in each unit and headed with a grain of shot.

Fig. 7–14C uses horizontal half-links to connect a long oval link between each unit.

Fig. 7–14D uses sections of seamless tubing through which a fine chain is run. The tubing could be placed below the top of the unit as well.

Fig. 7–14E uses a tongue projecting from the edge of each unit, which is bent through and around a hole or slot in the next unit.

Fig. 7–14F uses loose sections of tubing as spacers for edged strips of metal, wood, etc., and also to hide the machine-made chain.

Thongs and cords of leather and cloth fiber are often used as chains or suspensions, but these wear out and easily become soiled. When using such materials, design for occasional and easy replacement.

Necklace clasps can be machine made or, better, designed as a part of the necklace itself.

Fig. 7–15 illustrates several basic fastenings. Variations and new forms are constantly being developed by imaginative jewelry designers. Fig. 2–50 in Chapter 2

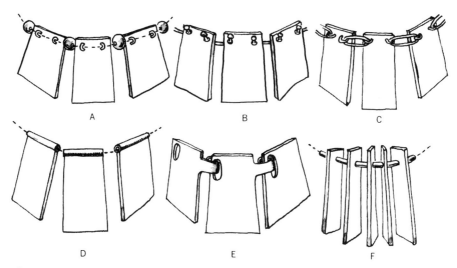

A   B   C

D   E   F

fig. 7–14

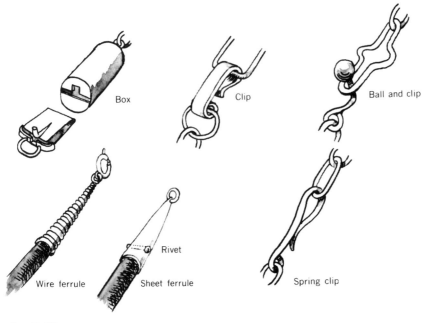

Box

Clip

Ball and clip

Wire ferrule

Rivet

Sheet ferrule

Spring clip

fig. 7–15

shows a clasp made of tapered wire and tubing, which integrates well with the materials and design of many pendants.

● earrings

Basically of two types—button and pendant—earrings offer an excellent opportunity for light and delicate handling of precious materials. They must be light in weight to be comfortable, and since they are worn in a safe zone, thin wire and thin sheets of metal may be used with greater assurance than in other jewelry forms.

Although it is possible to construct the earring backs yourself, it is often better to use manufactured findings, which are both sturdy and pleasing in design. Above all, they work efficiently. Earring findings are of four types: screw and patch, clips, pierced-ear wires, and pierced-ear screws. The directions for applying earring findings are given in Chapter 2.

Again, the size of an earring can be a personal choice. On the average, an overall diameter of 1″ for button-type earrings—those worn at the earlobe—is customary. For pendant earrings—those that are mobile and hang below the earlobe—a length of 2″ to 3″ can be used.

The correct location of the clip or screw wire is important, since an incorrect position could cause the earring to hang askew or forward, bending the earlobe with its weight.

The patch of the earring back should be soft soldered above the median line of the earring so that the greater weight hangs below the finding. The earring back should be angled so that the wire curve fits the lobe near the junction with the neck.

A flat treatment of single sheets or overlays of metals 20-gauge B and S, or thinner, seldom results in a heavy earring. For more three-dimensional shapes, a forming or repoussé technique in thin gauges would be appropriate.

possibilities in jewelry design

Pendant earrings are usually more complex than button earrings, since an element of mobility must be considered. These earrings are of two parts: the fastening, to which the ear back is soldered, and the pendant form itself. Some craftsmen use a manufactured fastening that is really a part of the earring back.

These earring backs come with a small ring built onto the curved wire from which the pendant is suspended. Some types have bosses—half domes—fixed to the back of the patch itself as a decoration. Unfortunately, these arbitrary machine-produced findings seldom integrate well with the design of the earring itself. It is much better to use a standard earring back and to solder it to a designed form to which the pendant is linked.

For complete mobility, fastening and pendant must be joined in a way that prevents pinching of links or earlobe.

Wire, by itself or combined with sheet, is an ideal material for pendant earrings.

For pierced ears, both button and pendant forms are used.

Findings for button types consist of a fine-threaded rod soldered to a small patch, which, in turn, is soft-soldered to the back of the earring. The rod is inserted through the hole in the earlobe and held in position by a small screw cap. (See Fig. 7–16A.) A simple form consists merely of a small wire rod to which a spring clip is attached. (See Fig. 7–16B.)

Pendant earrings are also suspended directly from thin wire loops that operate

fig. 7–17

on the safety-pin principle. (See Fig. 7–17.)

Some people are sensitive to copper in any form, so pierced-ear wires are often made of high-karat gold wire.

There has been considerable interest in developing new forms of ear decoration. Jewelry has been designed to be worn at various points on the outside of the ear, surrounding the entire ear, or at points within the ear. The problems of developing safe, comfortable, and unobtrusive findings for these new positions are of course greater, but the impact of new uses such as these is often fresh and delightful—as jewelry should be.

• bracelets

After neck ornaments, bracelets for the arm, wrist, or ankle are perhaps the oldest forms of jewelry. Although it is not now the custom in the Western world to wear arm and ankle bracelets, this direction should be explored as a fertile field for innovation.

Wrist bracelets, like necklaces, can be made of one piece, to be clipped on or slid over the hand, or they can be articulated with links or units.

Solid clip-on bracelets are usually made

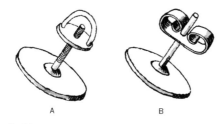

A   B

fig. 7–16

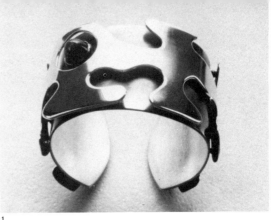

1

2

1 Bracelet, Eleese Brown; silver and amethyst

2 Bracelet, Kay Gonzales; silver

3 Armlet, Paula Stern; silver and copper

4 Armlet; bronze, repousséd and formed

5 Bracelet; bronze

6 Bracelet, Carolyn Barkei; bronze and silver

7 Bracelets; silver

*All student work was done
by undergraduates at
the University of Illinois*

3

4

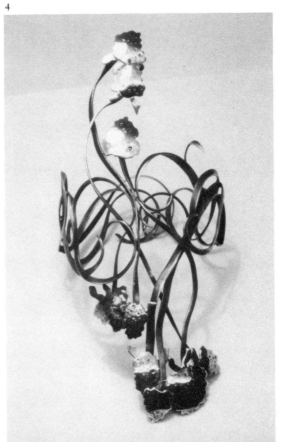

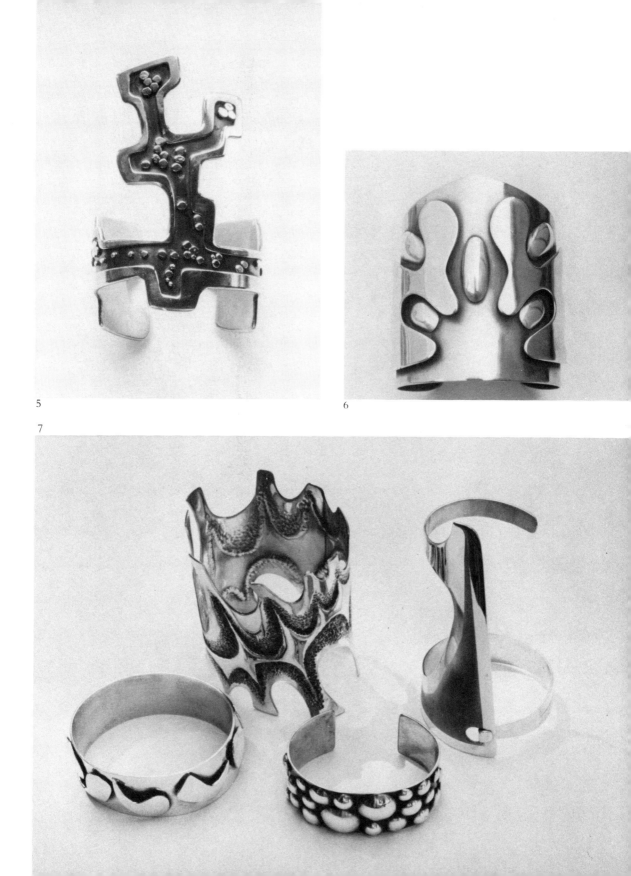

5

6

7

of a thick gauge of metal—12 or 14 gauge—so that the necessary springiness can be maintained. If thinner gauges are used, the constant working of the metal could eventually cause brittleness and cracking. If thin gauges are necessary, it is best to use an overlaid design to reinforce the bracelets where the curve is greatest. If nonmetallic decorations are used, they should be placed where the clipping action will not spring them from their settings.

Clip-on bracelets are difficult to design for general use. Each bracelet should be designed for the individual wearing it if possible. Where this is impossible, a length of 6″, leaving an opening of ¾″ to 1″ for the wrist to enter, is adequate. The ends of the bracelet should always be rounded so that it can be fitted onto the wrist painlessly.

Bracelets that complete a solid circle or oval and through which the hand is slipped should be between 8½″ and 9¼″ in circumference. The bracelet should be measured with a heavy piece of copper or iron wire describing the desired shape. This is most important when designing arm bracelets to be worn above the elbow.

It is a matter of choice whether to solder overlay or other fittings to the bracelet before or after curving it to form.

If soldered before bending, the overlay joins must be absolutely sound or the tension of bending will surely cause parts to lift or break off.

Where delicate forms are to be applied, soldering must be done after bending, since bending usually involves considerable hammering with wood, plastic, or rubber mallets. This hammering could distort or break delicate wire or overlaid forms. Repoussé designs must also be applied after bending, since the raised areas would distort or stretch to breaking if bent too much.

The advantage in bending the bracelet to shape as a final step is that—since all soldering has been completed and no additional heat softening will occur—the bending itself will cause considerable springiness to develop.

When units are to be soldered to the curved bracelet, they must each be prebent or filed to conform perfectly to the surface to which they are soldered.

Large, oval bracelet mandrels are available that help in bending not only the bracelet but also the added forms. Where the bracelet is narrow or constructed of heavy wire, it can most safely be bent to shape by hand. For comfort, it is important to bevel at least all of the inner edges as a matter of course.

Linked bracelets present many of the same construction possibilities and problems described in the section on unit necklaces. Linkages and fastenings are also similar, except that you have more leeway in using tubing for hinges in bracelets. (See Fig. 7–18.)

A hinge can be hidden on the inside of the bracelet or it can be visible between the units.

One of the many ways in which hinges can be constructed is as follows:

1. File the edge of the unit to conform

fig. 7–18

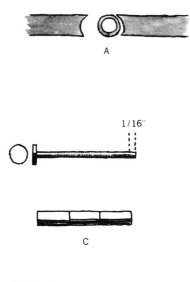

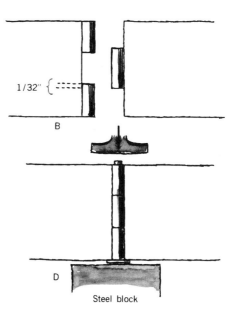

1/32"

B

D

Steel block

fig. 7–19

with the side of the tubing. (See Fig. 7–19a.)

2. Cut a section of tubing ¹⁄₁₆″ longer than the edge of the unit, and again cut it into three equal parts.

3. Solder the two outside sections of tubing to the edge of one unit, allowing the tube ends to be level with the outside edge of the unit. Solder the center section of tubing to the center of the edge of the opposing unit. (See Fig. 7–19B.)

4. Check the fit and carefully file away just enough to form a tight fitting between each of the three sections of tubing. There should be about ¹⁄₃₂″ to file away on the inner ends of each of the outside sections.

5. Use a wire hinge pin just the diameter of the inside of the tubing. This pin should be ¹⁄₁₆″ longer than the combined sections of tubing and should have a disc just the size of the tubing and of 24-gauge metal soldered to one end. (See Fig. 7–19C.)

6. Connect the hinges by inserting the pin through all three tubes and carefully hammering down on the projecting ¹⁄₁₆″ to form a rivet button. (See Fig. 7–19D.)

• rings

Although they are often simple enough to construct, rings present difficulties that do not occur in other forms of jewelry. The main problem is that they must fit comfortably.

Ring sizes range on a scale from No. 0 to No. 13½. Each size differs by 0.032″ in diameter from the next full size. Mandrels are made that are ringed with numbered grooves, each indicating a ring size. A set of graduated ring sizes, each stamped with the number of a full or half size, is useful in determining the diameter of a ring.

A simple band of the correct diameter and shape is often the base for more complex ring designs. The following describes the construction of a simple band, or *shank*.

1

2

3

4

1 Rings, Terry Zimmerman and Asta Sheehan; constructed silver and amber

2 Rings; constructed silver and gold

3 Rings, Patt Markey; constructed 14K gold and opal

4 Rings; constructed silver and bronze

5 Rings, Joyce Moty; silver and copper

6 Ring, Patt Markey; constructed gold, silver and tiger eye

7 Ring, Patt Markey; constructed 14K gold, garnet and jade

8 Rings; constructed silver

possibilities in jewelry design

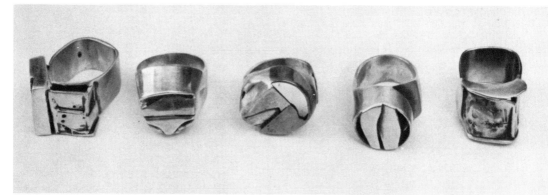

5

6

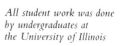

*All student work was done
by undergraduates at
the University of Illinois*

8

7

263

A SIMPLE RING BAND (SHANK)

The gauge of sheet metal or round or rectangular wire for a ring band must be determined by the intended use for the ring (occasional or constant), or the preference of the wearer. Where heavy-duty durability is not most important, appearance becomes the determining factor. In general, a man's ring is two to four gauges thicker than a woman's ring: 18-gauge B and S for a woman's ring and 14- to 16-gauge for a man's ring are average gauge sizes.

The width of the band can be determined only by design principles. Comfort in wearing must be kept in mind while designing a ring. A band that is too broad can cause skin irritations because moisture and dirt collect underneath.

RING-BAND CONSTRUCTION

1. Measure the blank. If you know the ring size in inches, add 1½ times the gauge or thickness of the metal to ensure sufficient length. *Example:* The circumference of the finger is 2″; the metal is 18 gauge; then the total length would be as shown in Fig. 7–20.

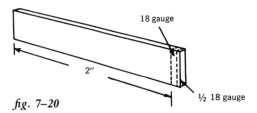

18 gauge

2″

½ 18 gauge

fig. 7–20

2. Circumference can be measured quite accurately by cutting a ¼″ × 3″ strip of heavy paper and curving it around the large *knuckle* of the wearing finger. Make certain that the paper is curved around loosely enough to indicate accurate length. Mark the paper at the overlapping point. Add 1½ times the

gauge of the metal and transfer these dimensions to the metal.

3. Some mandrels are made with a scale on the handle showing ring sizes in inches. Again, be sure to add 1½ times the metal gauge to the total length.

4. After sawing out the shape, do not file more than the ends of the blank. These *must* be true and parallel for a sound solder join.

5. Bend the ring ends together by hand or with ring-forming pliers or a plastic mallet. Do not be concerned with roundness or symmetry at this point. (See Fig. 7–21.)

fig. 7–21

6. By bending the ends back and forth and over and under each other, a spring or press fit develops to hold the ends firmly together. It is not necessary to use binding wire if this has been carefully done. Check to make certain that the ends meet cleanly for the entire length of the join. (See Fig. 7–22.)

7. Prepare the band by propping it on

fig. 7–22

charcoal or pumice pebbles, or by holding it in spring-locking soldering tweezers. The join should face up and should be covered by one piece of *hard* or *I T* solder next to the other along its entire length. It is a good plan to use a bit more solder than usual and to allow the excess to remain until all other soldering has been completed. This helps to prevent the disintegration of the solder seam during future soldering. (See Fig. 7–23.)

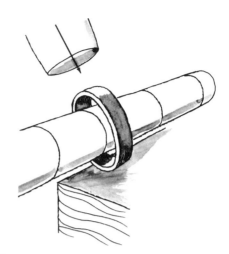

fig. 7–24

fig. 7–23

8. Heat the ring so that both sides of the join absorb equal heat. Unequal heating could attract the melting solder away from the join, and this must be carefully avoided. Heat until the solder has been fused down into the join; check this by examining the under side. Then quench the band in cold pickle or water as quickly as possible.

9. Remove all traces of flux *glass* with hot water. Once again, examine the join and add more solder if necessary.

10. If the join is solid, the ring may be *trued* or made round on the ring mandrel. Using the mandrel as a support, shape the ring into circular form with a wood mallet against the support of the bench. (See Fig. 7–24.)

11. The final truing takes place while hitting the edge of the band lightly with the edge of the planishing hammer. Since the mandrel is tapered, it is important to reverse the ring several times during this process. (See Fig. 7–25.) If the ring is too small, it can usually be enlarged by striking the surface of the ring with the face of the planishing hammer. This tends to thin the gauge

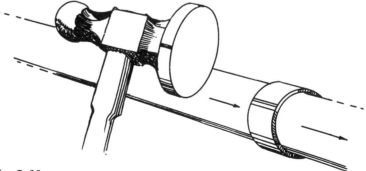

fig. 7–25

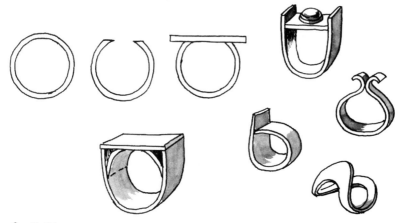

fig. 7–26

of the ring rather quickly, so care should be exercised during this step. If the band is too large after truing, it must have a section cut out (on both sides of the first solder join). Then it can be resoldered as before.

12. Once the band fits well, the necessary filing of inside and outside edges and surfaces can be done. If nothing is to be added, the band can be buffed and polished by hand or, supported safely on a mandrel, with the buffing machine. There are several types of buffing mandrels designed for the inside surfaces of a ring.

13. After the band is thoroughly finished, other parts such as tables, wire appliqué, or bezels can be added, using lower melting solders (*medium* and *easy*).

The basic band can be pierced for positive and negative shapes before bending, or it can be filed on edges and surfaces to bring out relief areas.

For a description of basic bezel construction, see the section "Gemstones" in Chapter 4.

Variations of the basic ring shank can be combined with tables or other forms in the following ways. (See Fig. 7–26.)

Ring bands can be made of wire using various combinations of shapes and gauges. The measurement plan is the same as for sheet. The wires can be soldered together before bending by placing the accurately measured pieces carefully side by side. (See Fig. 7–27.)

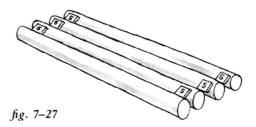

fig. 7–27

Pieces of *hard* solder, enough to fill the entire join between each wire, are placed at one or both ends of the combined wires. If the wire ring is to be formed into a circle, the ends should be filed to angles to make a smooth, strong join. (See Fig. 7–28.) When soldering with *hard* solder, there are often small unmelted lumps left after the join has been filled. These can be

possibilities in jewelry design

fig. 7–28

removed with a fine triangle or barrette needle file and an edged scotch stone.

If two or more wires are to form the base support for a table, they can be soldered easily in the following manner:

1. Construct and solder the individual wires so that they are identical in shape and diameter. (See Fig. 7–29A.)
2. If three rings are used, sand a slight flatness on the side of ring No. 1 by rubbing it on a flat sheet of medium emery paper. After sanding, the edge should touch all around the circumference of the ring when placed on a level steel block.
3. Flatten ring No. 2 on both edges in the same way.
4. Flatten ring No. 3 only on one side.
5. Place ring No. 1, flat edge up, on a smooth charcoal block. Paint half of the circumference with flux and the other half with yellow ocher. Place two or more pieces of *hard* solder at a point farthest away from the first ring join and in the center of the fluxed area.
6. Place ring No. 2, fluxed and painted with yellow ocher, in the same way as ring No. 1, on top of the first ring. Add solder to ring No. 2 and place ring No. 3, also painted with ocher and flux, on top of ring No. 2.
7. Solder the rings together by concentrating the heat on the fluxed side of the rings. The yellow ocher should prevent the solder from flowing completely around the rings. (See Fig. 7–29B.)
8. After pickling and washing, the rings can be pried apart in their unsoldered sections by inserting a knife blade and carefully twisting to the desired width. (See Fig. 7–29C.)
9. The points on the ring bands to which a table can be soldered may be filed level and the band soldered to the table from behind with *easy* or *medium* solder. (See Fig. 7–29D.)

Another basic ring-forming technique forms the band and the table base at the same time, as shown in Fig. 7–30.

Variations of this shape are suggested in Fig. 7–31.

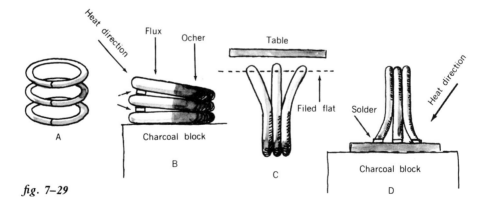
fig. 7–29

267

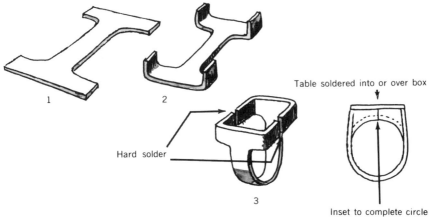

Table soldered into or over box

Hard solder

3

Inset to complete circle

fig. 7–30

4

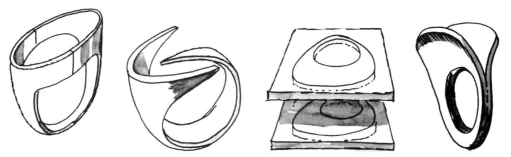

fig. 7–31   *fig. 7–32*

It is difficult to presize a ring of this design, so it often helps to make a model of heavy paper, using the final paper forms as templates for shaping the metal.

A final suggestion on ring forms is to cut the entire ring shape out of two or more sheets of metal and, as in the above design, solder only half of the shank together. (See Fig. 7–32.)

● cufflinks and studs

Cufflinks can be made using wire appliqué or free-standing wire shapes, or they can be formed or cast or constructed of sheet metal. The only real considerations are that they fit well and that they be safe to wear. Many fine designs would not be practical because of sharp projections or thin wire additions. The average cufflink size is a square or circle of 1″ diameter, although the designer has considerable leeway here.

Since the design and construction problems of the face of the cufflink are the same as those for pins, pendants, and earrings, it should be necessary only to describe various fastening possibilities.

On commercial swivel-bar cufflinks, several of which are quite cleanly designed, the distance between the swivel bar and the cufflink face is about ⁹⁄₁₆″, al-

possibilities in jewelry design

fig. 7–33

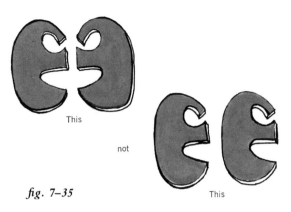

This

not

fig. 7–35

This

though this could be somewhat shorter for women's cufflinks.

Two types of commercial link findings are suitable to fine jewelry. One type has a soft solder patch for use with enamels, and the other, really the better one, has two parts. (See Fig. 7–33.)

Having a separate joint to which the finding is finally riveted allows the use of silver solder. Excess heat on the finding itself would quickly destroy the temper of the spring in the swivel bar. Use a piece of solder ⅛″ square, premelt it where you want the joint to be (usually centered), add the joint, and reheat. The bar of the swivel should be parallel with the horizontal axis of the cufflink design.

Cufflink findings are often constructed by the craftsman, and they can be variations of the designs in Fig. 7–34.

As in earrings, it is often practical to saw and file both cufflinks at the same time by holding two pieces of sheet in a vise or a ring clamp. Remember to oppose the pieces eventually so that the design matches on each cuff. (See Fig. 7–35.)

Also, as in earrings, it is not always necessary to make each half of a pair identical. A meaningful variation on a theme might be far more interesting than absolute uniformity.

● buckles

Buckles, like rings, present the added difficulty of having to fulfill a specific function. They must be simple enough for easy wear, sturdy enough to withstand constant use, and interesting enough to warrant substituting them for perfectly usable, if uninspired, manufactured articles. Fig. 7–36 shows several buckle fastenings.

In Fig. 7–36A the bar to which one end of the belt is sewed can be made of 8- to

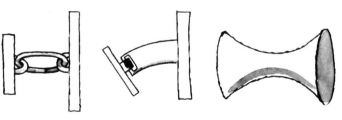

fig. 7–34

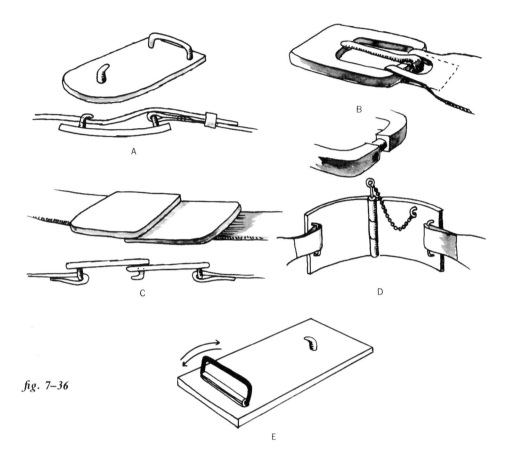

fig. 7–36

10-gauge wire. The curved peg is of the same gauge, but it should be rounded and smoothed. The loose end of the belt slides behind the buckle, the peg enters a hole, and the end is slipped into an inside leather or metal loop.

Fig. 7–36B shows the structure of the conventional buckle, which of course can be varied in proportion and size to any degree desired. The point at which the buckle tongue is bent around the buckle bar should be filed round and notched to prevent the tongue from slipping.

Fig. 7–36C has the two belt ends sewed to 10- or 12-gauge wire loops on the back of each buckle half. The halves are held together by one or more heavy wire hooks

placed through corresponding holes. If the belt is to be adjustable, one belt end might be fastened to a number of snaps.

In Fig. 7–36D a variation of the last buckle described uses tubing for a hinge. This tubing should have a thick wall to withstand the constant opening and closing of the buckle. The removable pin has a ring attached to one end from which a small sturdy chain runs to a loop on the inside of one buckle half. This secures the pin even when the belt is open.

Fig. 7–36E is a variant of Fig. 7–36A using tubing and wire, usually at least 14 gauge, which is bent into a partial flat link and, as a final step, inserted into the ends of the tubing. (See #10, #11, page 37.)

If a buckle is to be made of one thickness of metal, it should be at least 12 gauge to prevent a flimsy appearance. Thickness can of course be built up by layers of overlaid metal, wood, or other materials.

● buttons

Since sewing on a button through holes in its surface could destroy much of its design unity, it is better to fasten it to the cloth from behind by sewing through rings or half-loops soldered to the back. To avoid an unpleasant thinness, the button should be domed and backed with a flat sheet or built up to 8- or 10-gauge thickness. (See Fig. 7–37.)

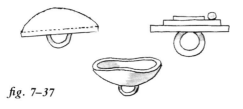

fig. 7–37

● tie bars and tie tacks

There are two general qualifications for tie bars: They must clip well and they cannot be too heavy. Machine-made findings for tie bars, although they may function well, seldom integrate well with the bar itself in shape and design.

Tie bar clips can be made in two basic ways. The clip can be an extension of the bar, bent to shape after all soldering and oxidation has been completed. If overlay forms of sheet or wire are used, they should not be soldered closer than ⅜″ from the point of the beginning curve. (See Fig. 7–38.) It would be difficult to bend a double-thickness at that point without putting a great strain on the solder join.

To maintain as much hardness as possible in the clip—a strong spring is absolutely necessary—all soldering should be done without quenching the work in cold water or pickle. Oxides can be removed by boiling pickle when the work has reached room temperature after soldering.

Before bending, the clip should be carefully planished with a smooth, flat-faced hammer on a smooth, flat stake. The compression of the hammer blows will increase the springiness of the metal.

The second basic construction consists of using two parts: the bar and a separate clip form. In Fig. 7–39A, note that the clip section is as long as the bar itself and that the bottom edge of the squared end is sharply beveled.

In Fig. 7–39B, the clip has been given a sharp bend so that it can be soldered to one end of the bar without having the sol-

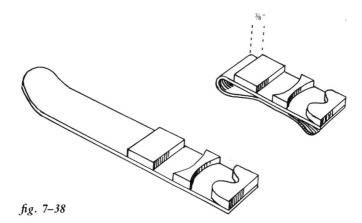

fig. 7–38

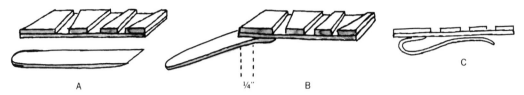

fig. 7-39

der run too far. The bend in the clip should be hidden. Do the bending after all soldering has been completed.

If special hard or half-hard spring sterling silver is used, the clip must be soldered on with lead solder to avoid annealing it.

If standard sterling silver is used, the same pickling procedure as described for Fig. 7-38 should be followed.

Bending the clip often can be done by hand, using a smooth round rod of the proper size to form the curve around. A pair of smooth-jawed bending pliers often helps to work the clip up against the back of the bar. A few careful taps—this *could* distort the bar—with a wooden mallet often help to bend the clip against the bar. The surfaces where the bar and the clip touch can be scored cleanly with a file to supply a better grip. (See Fig. 7-40.)

Most ties are 2″ to 3″ wide, so the bar itself should be about that length. The width depends on the design, and total weight should be considered since a heavy tie bar usually works itself off.

Tie tacks use a pointed peg, which is pressed through both tie and shirt to be fastened from inside the shirt with a clutch catch.

The manufactured findings are usually simple in design and very practical.

The peg is soldered to the base of the design with soft solder. It should be located somewhat above the median line of the design for good balance. (See Fig. 7-41.)

Tie tacks can be made by soldering a pointed peg to the design back and constructing a one- or two-piece clutch catch. If possible, spring silver should be used in constructing tie tack catches. (See Fig. 7-42.)

● photographing jewelry

Photographing small metal forms, whether for color slides or for black-and-white

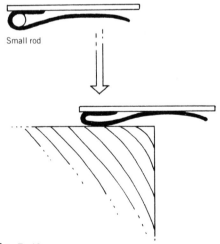

Small rod

fig. 7-40

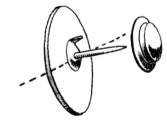

fig. 7-41

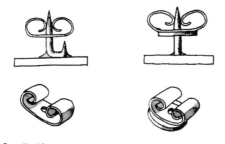

fig. 7-42

prints, requires special lighting arrangements, focusing, and exposure timing.

The conventional way to photograph jewelry is on a dark cloth—black velvet seems to be preferred—but this is perhaps the least effective approach. Each piece of

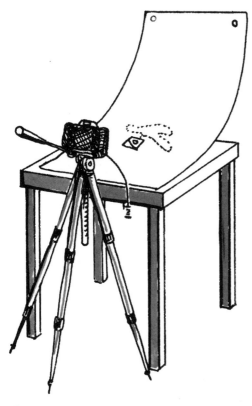

fig. 7-43

lint and dust glows and shows itself in competition with the jewelry.

A much better surface is fabric in a neutral color—gray denim, natural monk's cloth, even fine burlap. The texture of the fabric should be quite fine or the background will appear overly "busy."

Pebbleboard, gray or white illustration board, or even a heavy onionskin paper are all ideal, since texture is fine and large sheets can be curved to form a variety of background effects. In Fig. 7-43, one can see that the cardboard, curved up as it is, will form a disappearing background that can reduce visual confusion when viewing the piece of jewelry. An alternate method is to position the tripod-held camera to view directly down onto the work. Sometimes this is not feasible when photographing large units such as necklaces and chains. For such objects, an angled shot, as in Fig. 7-43, is best.

Dramatic backgrounds such as driftwood, bricks, stones, weathered planks, and so forth, although they may be interesting, tend to be too dynamic for the jewelry scale and can overwhelm it.

CAMERAS

Any still camera can be used, but the easiest type is a 35 mm. single lens reflex unit with added extension rings, tubes, or close-up lenses. Some cameras accommodate a bellows extension that works as well as extension rings. These latter attachments are required, since photographing with the standard 50 to 70 mm. lens results in a large background view and a minuscule piece of jewelry lost in the middle somewhere.

Generally the narrowest (often designated as "No. 1") extension ring is all that is needed to enlarge the object to fill the print or slide adequately. With the narrowest ring it is seldom necessary to adjust exposure time beyond that indicated by a light meter for the film you are using.

273

FOCUS

The advantage of the single lens reflex camera over other types is that you are able to view the object through the lens in exactly the desired position before tripping the shutter. There will be no chopped-off tops or bottoms of work because viewing and shooting lenses are not separate from each other.

It is most advantageous to have a deep depth of focus—all of the object should be clearly defined. This requires a high *f*-stop—as high as *f* 22 if possible—and a correspondingly increased exposure time. Increased exposure time—sometimes as long as two to three seconds—requires that the camera be mounted on a sturdy tripod and

that you use a remote-control shutter-release cable. Attempting to hand-hold a camera at low speeds and high *f*-stops will result in blurring and misfocusing.

LIGHTING

Studio lighting with photoflood lamps or spotlamps tends to be too harsh for photographing polished metal or reflective gemstones. Highlights that are picked up on such surfaces tend to "burn out" much detail in the jewelry and are distracting.

Flood lamps can be used if they are covered with tissue or onionskin paper, or they can be placed to shine through a tent or awning made of light, white cloth. Bed

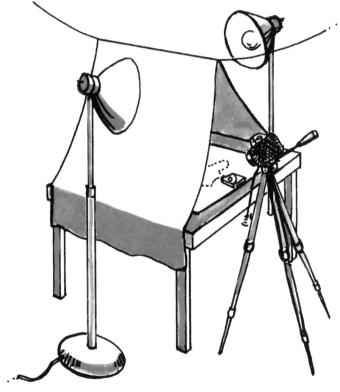

fig. 7–44

possibilities in jewelry design

sheets work well. This filter diffuses the light and excessive highlights are avoided. (See Fig. 7–44.) Similar tents or awnings are effective for shooting work out of doors on sunny days. Overcast days do not make strong reflective highlights and awnings are then unnecessary.

Good photographs can be made indoors near a window with a southern exposure—necessary for brightness. However, it may be necessary to diffuse direct sunlight coming through the window by taping a sheet of tracing paper to the glass.

The most important factors in this process are long exposures at high f-stops. Only in this way can an enlarged view of a small object be photographed in total focus.

8   stimulants for the mind's eye

To instruct in design is, in a sense, a presumption. Nothing is as personal as an individual's design idiom, and to write about the best way of developing a design idiom can result in gross generalities.

Many authors have attempted manuals of design—formulas to successful solutions of the infinite problems of design. Most have failed because they depended too heavily on the generalities and gave too little emphasis to design as a personal development.

Certainly the foundations of design—such as balance, rhythm, and variety—are sound enough, but without suggesting the wealth of visual excitement around us with which to build on these bases, no more than conformity of thinking and style can result.

In the history of art there have been centuries when a style reigned with such absolute uniformity that few artists could conceive of breaking the rules. In many cultural periods the minor changes, the subtle abstractions of natural form, had developed so slowly that eventually the idea source was lost completely and each generation continued in the tradition of the previous generation.

Today, those who live in the highly industrialized countries find the opposite to be the case. Tradition has often been completely replaced by the concept of change for the sake of change. The old ways, simply because they are old ways, are discarded in favor of newness and planned obsolescence—the sources of a happy and successful life. This results in an ever more frantic search for a fresh approach, whether superficial or serious.

Never in the history of art has such pressure been placed on the individual artist-designer. In place of the comforting and absolute knowledge that he or she *exists* within a social cell, today's visual artist may search alone in a landscape without roads and without signposts.

There is a tragic anachronism in this. In museums, galleries, and libraries, on radio, in film, and on television, we have virtually all of the knowledge of the past, the present, and even some of the future at our fingertips. We have an encyclopedic collection of all that man has thought and done. At the same time we move in a traditionless world, or—more exactly—in a world where we can adopt a hundred traditions as our own if we wish. Too many choices can be just as binding to the free imagination as too few.

The artist-designer must therefore come to an agreement within himself. He must become his own critic in all things since society can no longer accurately judge him within the framework of a tradition.

Styles and modes of expression change today much faster than ever before. In the twentieth century each decade—almost each year—has had its fashionable idiom of expression. It would seem impossible for a serious and painstaking artist to anticipate each wave and consistently ride its crest. To do this is not only impossible but is also invalid, since a vogue may or may not have lasting value until it is viewed over distance and time.

The concept of freedom of expression is sound and healthy. The question to be answered is: freedom from what? What unbearable restrictions, what tasteless dogma? Since all is permissible, is there anything to rebel against? Many would say yes. Aesthetic conformity should breed rebellion. Within a small tribe with limited knowledge of other people and their ways, a design conformity was an understandable development. To conform to a successful style of expression today is irrational and superficial, since we do know what others have done and are doing, and we can profit by the thousands of mistakes and successes of the past.

Stated simply, the artist-designer of today must be omnivorous. He must have great curiosity, and above all he must be ever critically aware. He must be as objective about an artifact made three thousand years ago—analyzing its value as an object of creative unity—as he is of the work of his contemporaries. He might even be a little cynical and suspicious of the success of a current mode until he gleans from it that which is universal, exploratory, or stimulating.

Since the artist may strike off in any direction he wishes, he must equip himself with knowledge. It is never enough merely to know how to manipulate materials—*that* sort of knowledge can be taught to anyone. What cannot be taught—and this separates the serious artist from the imitator—is the discovery of stimulation and excitement in form in all its variety, natural, man-made, or accidental.

This the artist-designer must do for himself. He must be an art historian, not to catalogue and describe, but rather to dissect, to analyze, and to explore. He must be a naturalist, discovering for himself the relationships of shape, color, and texture in the natural forms around him. All he sees, all he senses, is stored for future use. The greater the experience of seeing and feeling, the less possible it is for the artist to be caught with only a conventional or trite solution to a design problem.

The artist must above all be an inventor. He must invent his personal analysis of a shape, a color, and a texture. To invent, he must experiment. Each experiment should lead to a conclusion, since to experiment merely for the sake of experimentation is like building on quicksand—nothing solid can result.

• some basic design principles

Design, whether it be for jewelry, sculpture, painting, or any of the many visual art forms, is based on simple universal principles. Although terms of definition may vary, each designer is ultimately concerned with shape, form, surface, and color.

The results of the successful use of these basics can express tension or repose, stability or flux, the minute versus the mammoth, the rhythmic against the unpredictable. Each of these almost emotional responses can be emphasized or understated to make an individual work of art.

The term *design* has, for many, the meaning of balance—even bisymmetrical balance. Although world art is full of many

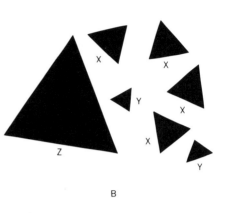

fig. 8–1

handsome examples of bisymmetric balance, it is only one way of arriving at this all-important element in a work of art. In Fig. 8–1A bisymmetric balance is achieved by balancing X with X, Y with Y, and Z in the exact center.

The emotional response to a design of this sort is one of security, lack of surprise, and—after a short while—apathy. The eye quickly recognizes the interrelationships of the shapes and finds no more that is stimulating.

Fig. 8–1B has also arrived at a balance— a dynamic balance, a balance of constant movement over basic stability. The large form—Z—although placed to one side of the center, does not overbalance the rectangle since the X and Y forms flow between the halves and, because of a multitude of angles, create enough stimulation to balance the massive attraction of the large triangle.

In addition, the relationship between each small form and its neighbor is different from every viewpoint. There is no easy prediction of spaces, and therefore no quick apathy. This brings the problem of containment into position.

All visual art forms, with perhaps the exception of mobile sculpture, exist within finite boundaries. A painting lives in its rectangle, a piece of sculpture within its envelope of material, a piece of jewelry within its practical size and shape.

Many sculptural forms send out lines of motion that are not contained by a frame. The rooms or landscapes in which they rest form the limits of shape and form just as well.

The idea is that the eye should be brought back to the subject rather than led constantly and irrevocably out and away. For centuries painters have worked on methods of composing so that the eye remains within the picture, finding all that is necessary there.

In the design of a piece of jewelry it is often helpful to establish an arbitrary limitation. This could, logically, be the maximum size of the object as defined by a circle, an oval, a square, or a rectangle.

Whether the design is an abstraction of a natural form or a nonobjective invention, the discipline of altering shape to a containing limitation often helps to develop unity and compactness.

The concept of compactness in design has its historic basis. Perhaps the most extreme, and successful, example of this is seen in Scytho-Sarmatian art. These people, perhaps as an involuntary reaction to the limitless space of the Asian steppes from which they came, had a strong sense of *horror vacui*—they felt that uninvolved space

fig. 8–2 Scytho-Sarmatian bridle fittings

Although terms vary, there are two fundamental approaches to design: the *abstract* and the *nonobjective*.

The abstract can be defined as the invention of form based on a specific object. To abstract is to alter and reorganize reality. That there is a great range of possibilities within the term abstraction can be recognized when one considers that merely translating objects in the round to a two-dimensional surface, as in painting, is already an abstraction even if the rendition is photographically accurate. The artist has already made important decisions regarding what is to be used and what is to be discarded.

However, within the framework of abstraction one might take considerable liberties with form as it originally exists. An object can be simplified, dissected, and recombined. It can be enriched in shape and surface where, in its original form, these aspects might lack interest.

The principle of showing simultaneous views—the top, bottom, and sides or the inside and the outside of an object—has often been used in abstraction.

Emphasis of existing basic qualities such as the sharpness of projections or the softness of rounded forms can be important in stating the *essentials* of a natural form. Throughout man's creative history, these intellectual or intuitive processes have served to identify the artist with his time and with his environment.

Figs. 8–3, 8–4, and 8–5 demonstrate the above design approaches, even though they vary considerably in time and geography. Surely this indicates that the natural development of abstract imagination is both individual and universal.

It is difficult for one who has not long thought in terms of abstraction to organize form, shape, and texture in a personal way. On the one hand it is all too easy to be influenced by the apparently successful so-

was uncomfortable in their art. Consequently, the design of the culture is known for its compact use of shape. Forms, usually animal subjects, were often distorted to fit compactly into the frame of an object. Figure 8–2 shows how even the simple planes of a reindeer and a goat could be enriched by translating them into parts of other animal forms. Not only are the objects carefully organized, but the space between—the negatives formed by positive form—are carefully planned to create visual variety.

279

Ornamental shield,
Kerema District, New Guinea

Ritual object,
Gaboon, Africa

Pablo Picasso,
20th Century painter

fig. 8–3

Mayan war god,
Yucatan, Mexico

Eskimo dance mask, Alaska

Head of an Apostle,
early 13th Century France

fig. 8–4

Balinese shadow puppet

Zuni dance mask,
S.W. United States

Paul Klee, 20th Century painter

fig. 8–5

1

The author, perhaps because of early interests in drawing and natural history, has found that animal and human subjects, often reflecting delight in the abstractions of earlier times, are the most stimulating of many design directions. Robert von Neumann has long been interested in using a variety of materials and both old and new techniques in the development of his jewelry, feeling that the greater the repertoire of experiences, the more flexible the approach to a design solution can be.

As a personal preference, the author creates only one example of each design though often many variations of a basic idea might be developed. He has a strong conviction that a unique work in precious metal may incorporate all those elements which constitute a serious work of art in painting and sculpture, and, since this is the case, a sound training in a variety of media is of great importance to the contemporary artist-designer in jewelry.

2

1 Earrings; silver, copper, gold

2 "Warrior"; constructed pin, shakudo, copper, silver, gold

3 "The Apartment"; pendant, silver, gold, ivory, with rosewood stand

4 "Bellerophon and Pegasus"; constructed pin, silver, ivory

5 "Owl"; constructed pin, lamination, silver, ivory

3

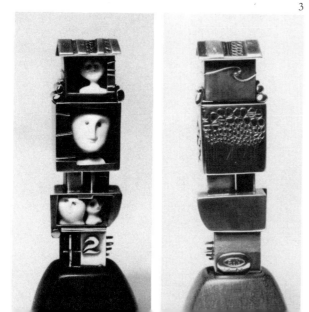

4

5

lutions of other artists, in which case work becomes unnecessarily derivative. The alternative is too often an attempt at an obvious originality—an originality based on extremes of distortion and shock effect. If these extremes are not based on the knowledge of the original subject, they are most often trite in their efforts at novelty.

There is no easy formula for a sound abstract sense. It can only be the natural result of an all-consuming curiosity about the nature of all things. The more you know about an object, the greater the latitude for intelligent interpretation and reorganization. At any point in the abstraction of form, there should be visible the essential truth of the original form. It should be impossible to forget the bone, the muscle, and the sinew that lie beneath the skin. If, in reorganizing the concept of a snail shell, one totally ignores the pure geometry of its convolutions, the essence of the idea of a snail shell is lost.

Fortunately, today we live in an atmosphere of free inquiry. To enable us to delve into the complete knowledge an artist should seek, we have infinite sources of information. The artist must make use of the extensions of the naked eye; the microscope, the camera, the telescope are all extensions that give greater scope to our reality. They allow us to see into, through, and around things that are too small or too complex for the eye alone. Everything that these devices can bring to us is logical to use in creative expression.

The history of man's efforts in constructing meaningful images—his art—is a part of our total knowledge. It can and also should be used. This does not mean that it is valid to repeat the forms of the past—only that it is possible and certainly right to analyze past approaches to abstraction. In the process of analysis, some of the historic solutions become the equipment of the artist in a natural way and can be used when the need occurs. What can be used are the ideas of abstraction, not the actualities of defined form.

Turning one's back on the past just because it is the past discards unthinkingly the logic of development that has caused man to grow with each generation.

Perhaps the best equipment for an artist is a sketchbook for recording daily what intrigues him. The mere act of defining an image or an idea on paper serves to fix these elements permanently in the mind.

● the nonobjective: a definition

The nonobjective direction in design is, if anything, even more purely intellectual than abstraction. By definition, nonobjective forms are *invented* to suit a need. They are the pure expression of emotion or intellect without the obvious starting point of an image (natural form).

An imagination based on the knowledge necessary to abstract is all-important to the invention of nonobjective form.

Because the possibilities of invention in this sense are so limitless, there is always the possibility of choosing the easy solution. The rules of the game are self-imposed and have no social framework. The entire direction is so personal that many artists—who may lack creative depth—cannot work in this direction comfortably. This is probably why so much nonobjective design is anonymous because of its similarity.

As an approach to nonobjective invention, several aspects should be defined.

The accidental form: Often the accident of natural or man-made form suggests the development of personal expression.

The texture of wood grain, the fracture planes of stone, or the silhouette of a hole in a windowpane can suggest a direction of interpretation and development.

An aerial photograph of a river delta or of farmland might suggest interplays of

stimulants for the mind's eye

sinuous or angular shapes to be organized into satisfying images.

This is not to suggest that these photographic images should be translated directly into pictorial or sculptural forms. Rather, the perceptive imagination should be stimulated and fortified by constantly recognizing the suggestions they offer. Again it is a matter of seeing with greater clarity and receptivity.

Once the mind is organized, the emotional-intellectual evolution of nonobjective forms can become both personal and developmental. Equipped in this way, the artist can approach each problem as an exciting exercise in interpretation. Without such organization the result is sure to be eclectic, trite, and repetitive.

Should a form or organization of forms transmit the essence of sharpness, the shapes used by the artist would be the ultimate in sharpness as he sees it.

He may decide that the overall quality will be that of tension and disorganization, and he will employ shape, color, and texture to best express this. A variety of these essential qualities could be combined or exploited separately. Such things as softness, ornateness, simplicity, stability, fluidity, and rigidity could all be the framework over which the expression is built.

All of the basic principles of design—variety, repetition, tension, and relaxation—are needed to make a nonobjective form interesting.

Each form invention in Fig. 8–6 possesses a basic similarity. They are all compounded of curved lines terminating in points, and they also have one or more internal shapes. Some are obviously more pleasing to the eye than others. What causes pleasure in one and a sense of boredom or irritation in another?

In some the sheer variety of all parts creates an interest that is total. The positive—the form itself—is no more compelling than the negative space(s) formed

by the limits or enclosure of the form. Fig. 8–6F is boring because there is not enough variety in proportion to make the surrounding form interesting. In this respect Fig. 8–6E is much more stimulating.

Figs. 8–6A, K, and J, in their essential symmetry, are exhausted of their shape excitement much more rapidly than are Figs. 8–6B, D, and L.

All of the elements within a confined form must relate intelligently to each other. A painful mistake, often seen in beginning shape inventions, is the uncomfortable combination of disparate shapes. In Fig. 8–7 the severe geometry of the haphazard internal shapes has nothing in common with the totally different—and uninspired—surrounding shape. Far from creating an interesting tension, the result is only an unpleasant chaos.

Tensions—the strong contrast of qualities within a single expression—are very important. The inventions seen in Fig. 8–8 demonstrate a number of ways in which such tensions can be intellectually exploited.

Balance is also of utmost importance. If a basically stable, and calm, form has a note of excitement somewhere within the form, this must be placed in such a position that the eye finds it in balance with the total shape. This can be achieved by repetition as well as by single placement. (See Fig. 8–9.)

Another sort of balance is involved with touch, or *tangency*. Since the discipline of containment is so necessary in art—what some artists call *structure*—anything that threatens containment should be intentional and never an accident.

In Fig. 8–10A, the single point tangent to the containing form destroys balance and creates an uncomfortable sense of leakage. In Fig. 8–10B, where several points touch the exterior, the central form interacts with the exterior in a sort of support, or balance.

fig. 8–6

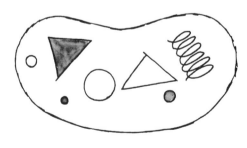

fig. 8–7

stimulants for the mind's eye

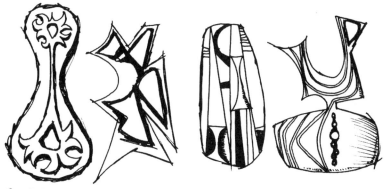

fig. 8–8

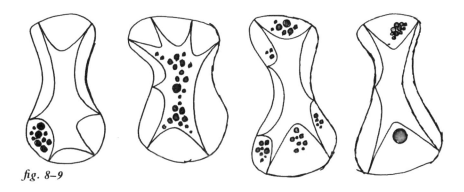

fig. 8–9

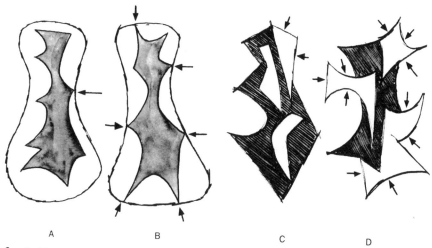

A   B   C   D

fig. 8–10

285

Fig. 8–10C has only one form with a common edge. The eye is drawn to this point irresistibly but without good reason. Fig. 8–10D has a better balance of shapes with a common edge.

The elements of balance and variety are equally important to abstract development and to nonobjective invention. Figs. 8–11, 8–12, and 8–13 illustrate how variety can develop as an idea is reinterpreted many times.

The same search for the essential is nec-essary in abstraction, and without this an abstract form tends to become overly specific. An aspect of cuteness—with all of its transient shallowness—enters into abstraction when the superficial surface becomes more important than the essential identity of the object. As an example, much inexpensive costume jewelry is made in the shape of dogs, cats, clowns, and so forth. Invariably the designer has attempted to be too specific: It had to be an Irish setter, or a Siamese cat, or a Ringling

fig. 8–11

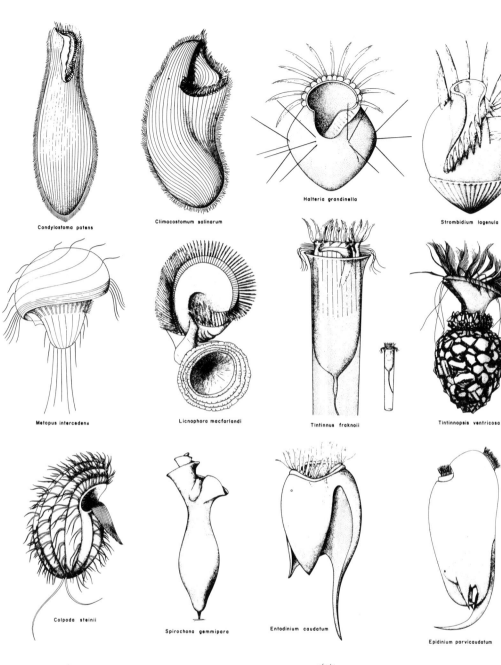

Condylostoma patens

Climacostomum salinarum

Halteria grandinella

Strombidium lagenula

Metopus intercedens

Licnophora macfarlandi

Tintinnus fraknoii

Tintinnopsis ventricosa

Colpoda steinii

Spirochona gemmipara

Entodinium caudatum

Epidinium parvicaudatum

*The shapes of protozoans are often
excellent examples of the balance between
simple, massive form and delicate textural
detail. Seeing how living forms have solve[d]
this design problem, an artist may find
clues to aid him in his own invention.*
Drawings by Alice Boatright

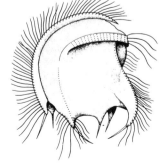

Saprodinium dentatum

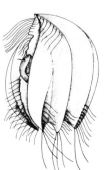

Epalxella mirabilis

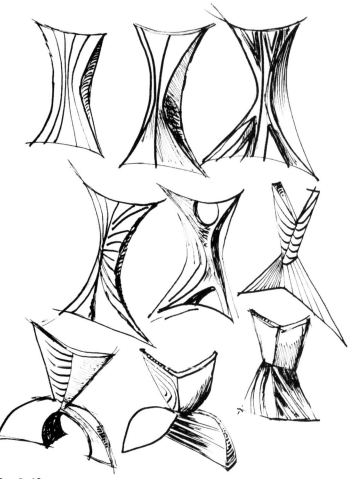

fig. 8–12

clown. In being so specific the designer felt compelled to create an illusion of reality unsuited to the material, even though it was well suited to a mass-production technique. The treatment of these forms is never subtle or exacting enough to bring it off as virtuosity. The result can only be a clumsy aping of nature.

It is of course more fitting to have the material in mind as well as the technique of working the material, and then adapt the form-idea to these truths. Only in this way can an abstraction have meaning, since it must always be a restatement of fact expressed in a language imposed by the tools and the materials used.

Every point made so far could apply to any visual art process. Jewelry, however, has a special function: Jewelry is decoration. Its only function is to enrich the appearance of the wearer. But pure decoration has sometimes been frowned upon in recent years. Perhaps this has been because of the great lack of personality in decorative art in the last century or so. Since decorative art has always had greater

stimulants for the mind's eye

fig. 8–13

currency with the public than have the traditionally more personal forms of art, the decorative artist has too often adjusted his ideas to what he thought the public would want. This has led to a conventional repetition of shape and treatment.

To be decorative, an object need not be ornate or complex. It needs only to capture the attention, then to stimulate curiosity and allow for leisurely contempla-

tion of its uniqueness. It must above all be stimulating enough to bring attention to itself again and again. In this respect, all successful art is decorative—it enriches its environment as well as the visual experience and knowledge of the viewer.

The concept of individual statement is all important in art, and especially so in jewelry. The successful piece of jewelry separates the wearer from the throngs. If

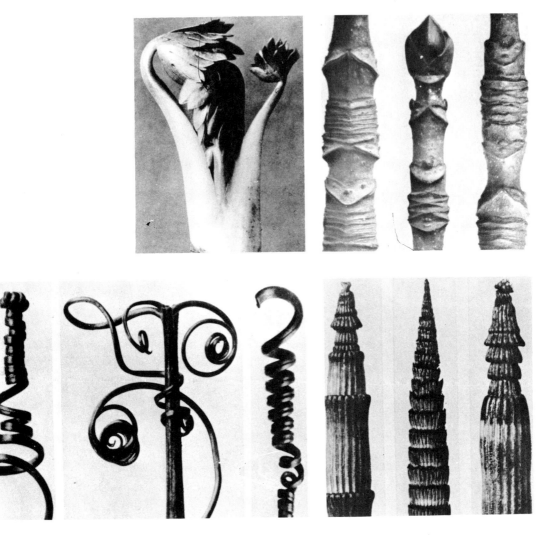

It is often disconcerting to contemporary artists to find that chance in nature has already created an infinite variety of forms. There is no need for feeling so, since, by steeping himself in visual contacts with as many natural forms as possible, the artist may more intelligently evolve personal and better-related forms and shapes in his work. In taking elements of plant forms out of their normal context as specific plants, as in these photographs, a discerning eye discovers an ever-fascinating variety.

stimulants for the mind's eye

291

This random collection of photographs indicates how objects, taken out of context, can become completely satisfying images—often to be used as points of departure by the artist. Once the eye is trained to see the specific—and to abstract from it the general—it can never again be without stimuli, and imagination becomes unlimited. Photos by the author.

1 Peacock feather

2 Granite and shadows

3 Sycamore bark

4 Frost on window

5 Oil drops on water

6 Cactus

7 Old Italian door

8 Red cabbage

9 Shells

10 Algae

11 Chains and saws

12 Tidal flat

stimulants for the mind's eye

6

7

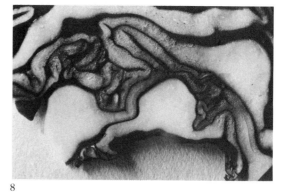

8

9

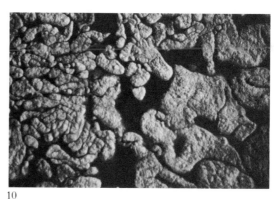

10

11

12

everyone wore the same design, jewelry would soon be discarded.

In jewelry, as in all other art forms, craftsmanship can only implement and support sound design, never supplant it. Craftsmanship alone may well express virtuosity, but never invention and exploration.

Sound design without the support of excellent craftsmanship is equally inadequate, since slipshod appearance forcibly detracts from the total impact of a work of art. A mutual interdependence is not only necessary, it is the reason for all serious art. If possible, this is even more true of jewelry than other art forms. By its nature a piece of jewelry is precious, not only in its intrinsic value as gold or silver or gems, but also because of its smallness and the delicacy of its design and workmanship. Being small, it invites close scrutiny as well as a desire to touch and savor its form and surface. Such close scrutiny makes unthinking and unloving treatments of materials all too evident.

Many of the barriers to sound design have already been mentioned. One point requires additional emphasis. This can be defined as *design honesty*. Perhaps the ultimate sin in any art is to plagiarize ideas without adding something to them. The sin is first against the originator, whether a contemporary or one who lived and worked centuries ago. More important, the sin is against the plagiarist himself. He has diminished his own stature by depending completely on another's idea. He has wasted to some degree his unique ability of decision and selectivity. In using the easy solution he has forfeited his right to pride, satisfaction, and all sense of achievement. This is the tragedy inherent in all how-to-do-it kits and formulated design manuals.

Of course it is impossible to invent form without bringing to the invention some of one's remembered visual experiences. What you have seen you own, and what you own you can use, but to use something exactly as you have seen it—without adding, or even subtracting, from it—deprives you of such ownership, just as a museum copyist of an old master cannot lend his name to a faithful copy without identifying it as such.

There are, however, times when memory moves the hand without conscious acknowledgment of plan or reason. The echo of a former delight makes its sound quickly and quietly as a pencil might move from one point to another in a sketchbook.

It is important to make memory a storehouse holding a multitude of shapes, surfaces, colors, and lines, as well as complete images. If this memory resource is full enough, it will become difficult to depend too greatly on another's ideas. Alternatives replace limitations; confidence replaces the contentment with being merely adequate.

Within the framework of this book it is possible to give only a hint of the many stimuli that could help to develop a design personality. The photographs and drawings on preceding pages indicate the range of resources available, but anyone with a strong sense of curiosity will find it a simple matter to add to the list in variety and depth.

appendix

● comparative weights

1 ounce Avoir. = 0.912 ounce troy = 28.35 grams

16 ounces Avoir. = 14.6 ounces troy = 1 pound Avoir.

1 ounce troy = 480 grains = 31.1 grams

1 ounce troy = 20 pennyweight = 1.1 ounces Avoir.

1 pennyweight (dwt.) = 24 grains = 1.555 grams

1 pound Avoir. = 453.6 grams = 7,000 grains = 16 ounces Avoir.

1 pound troy = 373.2 grams = 5,760 grains = 12 ounces troy

1 dram = 60 grains = 3.888 grams

1 gram = 15.43 grains = 0.032 ounce troy

1,000 grams (1 Kilogram) = 2.2 pounds = 35.26 ounces Avoir.

1 grain = 0.065 gram

100 grains = 6.5 grams

APOTHECARIES' WEIGHT

The grain, the ounce, and the pound of the apothecaries' weight system are the same as for the troy weight system.

● measures of length

1 inch (1″) = 2.54 centimeters = 25.4 millimeters

1 foot (1′) = 0.305 meter = 30.48 centimeters = 304.8 millimeters

1 meter = 39.37 inches

1 centimeter = 10 millimeters

10 centimeters = 1 decimeter = 100 millimeters

100 centimeters = 1 meter = 10 decimeters

● fluid measures

1 ounce = 29.57 cubic centimeters = 1.8 cubic inches

1 dram = ⅛ ounce (0.125 ounce) (fluid)

1 gill = 4 ounces (fluid)

1 pint = 16 ounces (fluid)

1 quart = 2 pints = ¼ gallon = 57¾ cubic inches

1 gallon = 4 quarts = 128 ounces (fluid) = 3.78 liters and 231 cubic inches = 0.134 cubic foot

1 cubic centimeter (cc.) = 16.23 minims

1 liter = 1,000 cc. (a little more than 1 quart U.S.) = 0.264 U.S. gallon

1 cubic foot = 7.481 U.S. gallons = 1,728 cubic inches

1 Imperial gallon = 1.2 U.S. gallons = 4.54 liters = 277.27 cubic inches

● circumference

Diameter (Inches)	Circumference (Inches)	Diameter (Inches)	Circumference (Inches)
3	9⅜	8	25⅛
3½	10⁵⁄₁₆	8½	26¹¹⁄₁₆
4	12⁹⁄₁₆	9	28¼
4½	14⅛	9½	29¹³⁄₁₆
5	15¹¹⁄₁₆	10	31⅜
5½	17¼	10½	32¹⁵⁄₁₆
6	18¹³⁄₁₆	11	34½
6½	20⅜	11½	36⅛
7	21¹⁵⁄₁₆	12	37¹¹⁄₁₆
7½	23½		

• weights

TROY WEIGHT

Used in weighing the precious metals.

```
   24 grains = 1 pennyweight (dwt.)
   20 dwt.' = 1 ounce troy
   12 ounces = 1 pound troy
5,760 grains = 1 pound troy
```

AVOIRDUPOIS WEIGHT

Used in weighing base metals.

```
16 drams (or drachms) = 1 ounce Avoir.
16 ounces = 1 pound Avoir.
16 ounces = 7,000 grains
28 pounds = 1 quarter
 4 quarters = 1 hundredweight (cwt.)
20 hundredweight = 1 ton Avoir.
```

To convert ounces troy to ounces avoirdupois, multiply by 1.09714. To convert ounces avoirdupois to ounces troy, multiply by 0.91146.

GRAM WEIGHT

```
 1 gram = 15.43 grains troy.
 1.555 grams = 1 pennyweight (dwt.)
31.104 grams = 1 ounce troy
28.35 grams = 1 ounce Avoir.
```

CARAT WEIGHT

Used in weighing precious and semiprecious stones. (The term *Karat* refers to the quality of purity in gold.)

```
1 carat = 3 1/16 grains troy.
1 carat = .007 ounce Avoir.
1 carat = 1/5 gram
```

The carat is further divided into *points* for simple measurement:

```
1 carat = 100 points
1/2 carat = 50/100 points
1/4 carat = 25/100 points
1/8 carat = 12 1/2/100 points
```

• mohs scale

The Mohs Scale is a system for classifying the hardness of minerals. Included in parentheses are some common materials for comparison.

Graphite, Talc	1
(Human skin 1½)	
Gypsum (Plaster), Alabaster	2
(Fingernail 2½)	
Calcite, Limestone, Mexican Onyx, Pearl	3
(Copper coin 3½)	
Fluorite	4
(Lead glass 4½)	
Apatite	5
(Window glass 5½)	
Feldspar	6
(Tungsten, chromium, carbon steel 6¾)	
Quartz	7
Tourmaline, Zircon	7½
Topaz	8
Chrysoberyl, Beryl	8½
Corundum (Rubies, Sapphires)	9
Diamond	10

Diamonds vary in hardness with location. In order of hardness: Australia-Borneo, Hardest; South America, India, Africa, Softest

• temperature conversions

To convert degress Fahrenheit (°F) to degrees centigrade (°C), first subtract 32, then take 5/9 of the remainder. To convert degrees centigrade to degrees Fahrenheit, first multiply by 9/5, then add 32.

or

To convert degrees centigrade to degrees Fahrenheit, first multiply by 1.8, then add 32. To convert degrees Fahrenheit to degrees centigrade, first subtract 32, then divide by 1.8.

or

To convert degrees centigrade to degrees Fahrenheit, first multiply the centigrade figure by 9, then divide the obtained figure by 5 and add 32. To convert degrees Fahrenheit to degrees centigrade, first subtract 32 and multiply by 5, then divide the obtained figure by 9.

Each 1°C = 1.8°F. The number 32 represents the difference between the nominal starting points 0 and 32.

A FEW COMPARISONS

°C		°F
1000	=	1832
500	=	932
100	=	212
0	=	32

• converting fractional and decimal inches to millimeters

Fractions	Decimal Inches	Millimeters
1/64	0.0156	0.3969
1/32	0.0313	0.7937
3/64	0.0469	1.1906
1/16	0.0625	1.5875
5/64	0.0781	1.9843
3/32	0.0937	2.3812
7/64	0.1094	2.7781
1/8	0.1250	3.1750
9/64	0.1406	3.5718
5/32	0.1562	3.9687
11/64	0.1719	4.3656
3/16	0.1875	4.7624
13/64	0.2031	5.1593
7/32	0.2187	5.5562
15/64	0.2344	5.9530
1/4	0.2500	6.3499
17/64	0.2656	6.7468
9/32	0.2812	7.1437
19/64	0.2969	7.5405
5/16	0.3125	7.9374
21/64	0.3281	8.3343
11/32	0.3438	8.7312
23/64	0.3594	9.1280
3/8	0.3750	9.5249
25/64	0.3906	9.9217
13/32	0.4062	10.3186
27/64	0.4219	10.7155
7/16	0.4375	11.1124
29/64	0.4531	11.5092
15/32	0.4687	11.9061
31/64	0.4844	12.3030
1/2	0.5000	12.6999

• melting points and specific gravity of principal nonferrous metals

Metal	Melting Point Fahrenheit	Melting Point Centigrade	Specific Gravity
Platinum	3224	1773	21.45
Nickel	2645	1452	8.85
Copper	1981	1083	8.93
Gold	1945	1063	19.36
Silver	1761	962	10.56
Sterling silver	1640	893	10.40
Zinc	787	419	7.14
Lead	621	327	11.37
Tin	450	232	7.29

• ring sizes

Each ring size unit differs 0.032" from the next full size in diameter. The diameter of a ring is measured at the inside diameter at the center of the band width.

Size	Inch	Size	Inch
0	= 0.458" dia.	6½	= 0.666" dia.
¼	= .466" dia.	7	= .682" dia.
½	= .474" dia.	7½	= .698" dia.
¾	= .482" dia.	8	= .711" dia.
1	= .490" dia.	8½	= .730" dia.
1½	= .506" dia.	9	= .746" dia.
2	= .522" dia.	9½	= .762" dia.
2½	= .538" dia.	10	= .778" dia.
3	= .554" dia.	10½	= .794" dia.
3½	= .570" dia.	11	= .810" dia.
4	= .586" dia.	11½	= .826" dia.
4½	= .602" dia.	12	= .842" dia.
5	= .618" dia.	12½	= .858" dia.
5½	= .634" dia.	13	= .874" dia.
6	= .650" dia.	13½	= .890" dia.

• common and chemical names of compounds*

Common Name	Chemical Name	Common Name	Chemical Name
Acetic ether	Ethyl acetate	Blanc-fixe	Barium sulfate
Acid of sugar	Oxalic acid		(artificial)
Aldehyde	Acetaldehyde	Bleaching powder	Calcium chloro-
Alum ⎫	Generally refers to		hypochlorite
Alum flour ⎬	potassium aluminum	Blende	Natural zinc sulfide
Alum meal ⎭	sulfate	Blue copperas	Copper sulfate
		Blue salts	Nickel sulfate
Alumina	Aluminum oxide	Blue stone	Copper sulfate
Alumino-ferric	A mixture of	Blue verditer	Basic copper carbonate
	aluminum and sodium	Blue vitriol	Copper sulfate
	sulfates	Bone ash	Impure calcium
Alundum	Fused alumina		phosphate
Aniline	Phenyl amine	Bone black	Crude animal charcoal
Aniline salt	Aniline hydrochloride	Boracic acid	Boric acid
Antichlor	Sodium thiosulfate	Borax	Sodium tetraborate
Antifebrin	Acetanilide	Bremen blue	Basic copper carbonate
Antimony black	Antimony trisulfide	Brimstone	Sulfur
Antimony bloom	Antimony trioxide	Burnt alum	Anhydrous potassium
Antimony glance	Antimony trisulfide		aluminum sulfate
Antimony red ⎫		Burnt lime	Calcium oxide
Antimony vermilion ⎬	Antimonous oxysulfide	Burnt ocher ⎫	Ferric oxide
Antimony white	Antimonous oxide	Burnt ore ⎭	
Antimony yellow	Basic lead antimonate	"Butter of"	Refers to the chloride
Aqua fortis	Nitric acid		
Aqua regia	Nitric acid and		
	hydrochloric acid	Cadmium yellow	Cadmium sulfide
Argol	Crude potassium acid	Calamine	Zinc silicate
	tartrate	Calcite	Mineral calcium
Arsenic glass	Arsenous oxide		carbonate
Aspirin	Acetyl-salicylic acid	Caliche	Impure sodium nitrate
Azurite	Basic copper carbonate	Calomel	Mercurous chloride
		Camphor, artificial	Pinene hydrochloride
		Cane sugar	Sucrose
		Carbolic acid	Phenol
Bakelite†	Resin from phenol +	Carbonic acid ⎫	
	formaldehyde	Carbonic anhydride ⎬	Carbon dioxide
Baking soda	Sodium bicarbonate	Carborundum†	Silicon carbide
Barium white	Barium sulfate	Carnallite	Magnesium potassium
Baryta	Barium oxide		chloride
Barytes	Barium sulfate (natural)	"Caustic"	Refers to the hydroxide
Bauxite	Hydrated alumina		of a metal
Beet sugar	Sucrose	Ceruse	Basic lead carbonate
Bentonite	Impure aluminum	Chalk	Calcium carbonate
	silicate	Chili niter ⎫	
Benzene	Mixture of low boiling	Chili saltpeter ⎬	Sodium nitrate
	liquid alkanes	China clay	Aluminum silicate
Benzol	Benzene	Chinese red	Basic lead chromate
Bichrome	Potassium dichromate	Chinese white	Zinc oxide
Bitter salt	Magnesium sulfate	Chloramine T	Sodium p-toluene-
Black ash	Impure sodium		sulfochloramide
	carbonate		

*This table reproduced from *Handbook of Chemistry and Physics,* through the courtesy of Robert C. Weast. Pigments named refer to the pure substance and not to mixtures often sold under the same name.

†Trade name.

Common Name	Chemical Name	Common Name	Chemical Name
Chloride of lime	Calcium chloro-hypochlorite	Formalin	40% solution of formaldehyde in water
Chloride of soda	Sodium hypochlorite solution	Formin	Hexamethylene tetramine
Chrome alum	Potassium chromium sulfate	Freezing salt	Crude sodium chloride
Chrome green	Chromium oxide	French chalk	Hydrated silicate of magnesium
Chrome red	Basic lead chromate	French verdigris	Basic copper acetate
Chrome yellow	Lead chromate	Fruit sugar	Fructose
Chromic acid	Chromium trioxide	Fuller's earth	Hydrated magnesium and aluminum silicates
Cinnabar	Mercuric sulfide	Fulminate of mercury	Mercuric fulminate
Cobalt black	Cobalt oxide	Fusel oil	Mixed amyl alcohols
Cobalt green	Cobalt zincate		
Common salt	Sodium chloride	Gasoline	Mixture of low boiling hydrocarbons suitable for use in internal combustion engines
Copperas	Ferrous sulfate		
Corn sugar	Glucose		
Corrosive sublimate	Mercuric chloride		
Corundum	Aluminum oxide		
Cream of tartar	Potassium hydrogen tartrate	Galena	Natural lead sulfide
		Glauber's salt	Sodium sulfate
Cresylic acid	Mixture of o-, m-, and p-cresol	Glucose	Dextrose
Cupferron	Nitrosophenyl-hydroxylamine	Glycerin	Glycerol
		Grain alcohol	Ethyl alcohol
		Grape sugar	Glucose
Dekaline	Decahydronaphthalene	Green verditer	Basic copper carbonate
Derby red	Basic lead chromate	Green vitriol	Ferrous sulfate
Derinatol	Basic bismuth gallate	Gypsum	Calcium sulfate
Dextrose	Glucose		
Dutch liquid	Ethylene chloride	Hartshorn salt	Ammonium carbonate carbamate
		Heavy spar	Barium sulfate
Eau-de-Javelle	Potassium hypochlorite solution	Hexamine	Hexamethylene tetramine
Eau-de-Labarraque	Sodium hypochlorite solution	Horn silver	Silver chloride
		Hypo	Sodium thiosulfate
Emerald green	Copper aceto-arsenite		
Emery powder	Impure aluminum oxide	Indian red	Ferric oxide
		Iron black	Precipitated antimony
Epsom salts	Magnesium sulfate	Iron mordant	Ferric sulfate
Essence of bitter almonds	Benzaldehyde		
Essence of mirbane	Nitrobenzene	Kainit	Double salt of potassium magnesium sulfate and magnesium chloride
Everitt's salt	Potassium ferrous ferrocyanide		
		Kaolin	Aluminum silicate
Feldspar	Potassium aluminum silicate	Kieselguhr	Siliceous earth
		Kieserite	Mineral magnesium sulfate
Ferro prussiate	Potassium ferrocyanide	King's yellow	Arsenous sulfide
Fixed white	Barium sulfate		
Flowers of sulfur	Sulfur		
"Flowers of" a metal	A synonym for the oxide	Lampblack	Impure carbon
		Lanolin	Mixture of cholesterol and esters
Fluorspar	Calcium fluoride		

● common and chemical names of compounds—(continued)

Common Name	Chemical Name	Common Name	Chemical Name
Laughing gas	Nitrous oxide	Oil of wintergreen, artificial	Methyl salicylate
Lemon chrome	Barium chromate		
Levulose	Fructose	Oleum	Fuming sulfuric acid
Lime	Calcium oxide	Olifiant gas	Ethylene
Litharge	Lead monoxide	Orpiment	Arsenic trisulfide
Lithopone	Zinc sulfide + barium sulfate	Osmic acid	Osmic tetroxide
Liver of sulfur	Mixed potassium sulfides	Paris blue	Ferric ferrocyanide
		Paris green	Copper aceto-arsenite
Lunar caustic	Silver nitrate	Pearl ash	Potassium carbonate
Lysol	Cresol soap solution	Permanent white	Barium sulfate
		Petroleum ether	Mixture of hydrocarbons boiling from 40 to 60°C
Magnesia	Magnesium oxide		
Magnesite	Magnesium carbonate		
Malachite	Basic copper carbonate	Phenic acid	Phenol
Manganese black	Manganese dioxide	Phosgene	Carbonyl chloride
Marble	Calcium carbonate	Phosphate rock	Calcium phosphate
Marsh gas	Methane	Picric acid	sym-Trinitrophenol
Massicot	Lead monoxide	Plaster of paris	Calcium sulfate
Methanol	Methyl alcohol	Plumbago	Graphite
Metol	p-Methylaminophenol sulfate	Precipitated chalk	Calcium carbonate
		Prussian blue	Ferric ferrocyanide
Microcosmic salt	Sodium ammonium hydrogen phosphate	Prussic acid	Hydrocyanic acid
		Putty powder	Impure stannic oxide
Milk sugar	Lactose	Pyrites	Ferrous di-sulfide
Milk of barium	Barium hydroxide	Pyroligneous acid	Crude acetic acid
Milk of lime	Calcium hydroxide	Pyroligneous spirit	Methyl alcohol
Milk of magnesium	Magnesium hydroxide	Pyrolusite	Manganese dioxide
Milk of sulfur	Precipitated sulfur		
Minium	Lead tetroxide	Quicklime	Calcium oxide
Mohr's salt	Ferrous ammonium sulfate	Quicksilver	Mercury
		Quinol	Hydroquinone
Molybdenite	Molybdenum disulfide		
"Muriate of" a metal	Chloride of the metal	Realgar	Arsenic disulfide
Muriatic acid	Hydrochloric acid	Rectified spirit	Alcohol 90–5%
		Red antimony	Antimony oxysulfide
Naphtha (Petroleum)	A petroleum distillate	Red lead	Lead tetroxide
Naphtha (Solvent)	A coal tar distillate	Red liquor	Aluminum acetate solution
Natron	Sodium carbonate		
Niter	Potassium nitrate	Red precipitate	Oxide of mercury
Nitro-lime	Calcium cyanamide	Red prussiate of potash	Potassium ferricyanide
Nitrous ether	Ethyl nitrate	Rochelle salt	Potassium sodium tartrate
Nordhausen acid	Fuming sulfuric acid		
		Rock salt	Sodium chloride
Oil of bitter almond	Benzaldehyde	Rouge	Ferric oxide
Oil of garlic	Allyl sulfide		
Oil of mirbane	Nitrobenzene	Saccharin	Benzoic sulfimide
Oil of mustard, artificial	Allyl isothiocyanate	Sal ammoniac	Ammonium chloride
		Salol	Phenylsalicylate
Oil of pears	Amyl acetate	Salt	Sodium chloride
Oil of pineapple	Ethyl butyrate	Salt cake	Impure sodium sulfate
Oil of vitriol	Concentrated sulfuric acid	Salt of amber	Succinic acid

Common Name	Chemical Name	Common Name	Chemical Name
Salt of lemon⎫ Salt of sorrel⎭	Potassium acid oxalate	Tartar emetic	Potassium antimonyl tartrate
Salt of tartar⎫ Salt of wormwood⎭	Potassium carbonate	Tetralin	Tetrahydronaphthalene
		Tin crystals	Stannous chloride
Saltpeter	Potassium nitrate	Tin white	Stannic hydroxide
Salvarsan	3, 3'-Diamino-4, 4'-dihydroxy-arsenobenzene dihydrochloride	T.N.T.	Trinitrotoluene
		Toluol	Toluene
		Trona	Natural sodium carbonate
Satin white	Calcium sulfate	Turnbull's blue	Ferrous ferricyanide
Scheele's green	Copper hydrogen arsenite	Ultramarine yellow	Barium chromate
Schlippe's salt	Sodium thioantimonate	Unslaked lime	Calcium oxide
Silica	Silicon dioxide		
Slaked lime	Calcium hydroxide	Vanillin	Methyl ether of protocatechualdehyde
Soda, washing	Sodium carbonate	Venetian red	Ferric oxide
Soda crystals	Sodium carbonate	Verdigris	Basic copper acetate
Soda lime	Mixture of calcium oxide and sodium hydroxide	Vermilion	Red mercuric sulfide
		Vitriol	Sulfuric acid
Sodium hyposulfite	Sodium thiosulfate	"Vitriolate of"	"Sulfate of"
Soft soap	Potash soap		
Soluble glass	Sodium silicate	Washing soda	Sodium carbonate
Soluble tartar	Potassium tartrate	Water glass	Sodium silicates dissolved in water
Spirit of hartshorn	Ammonia solution	White acid	Hydrofluoric acid and ammonium fluoride
Spirit of salt	Hydrochloric acid		
Spirit of wine	Ethyl alcohol	White arsenic	Arsenous oxide
Stassfurtite	Magnesium borate and chloride double salt	White lead	Basic lead carbonate
		White vitriol	Zinc sulfate
Sugar of lead	Lead acetate	Whiting	Calcium carbonate
Sugar of milk	Lactose	Witherite	Barium carbonate
Sulfuric ether	Diethyl ether	Wood alcohol⎫	
Superphosphate	Impure calcium acid phosphate	Wood naphtha⎬ Wood spirit⎭	Methyl alcohol
Sylvine	Potassium chloride	Xylol	Xylene
Sylvinite	Sylvine with rock salt	Yellow prussiate of potash	Potassium ferrocyanide
Table salt	Sodium chloride		
Talc	Hydrated magnesium silicate	Zinc blende	Mineral zinc sulfide
		Zinc vitriol	Zinc sulfate
Tartar	Crude potassium bitartrate	Zinc white	Zinc oxide

• silver, gold, platinum, and palladium round wire*

WEIGHT IN PENNYWEIGHTS OR OUNCES PER FOOT IN B AND S GAUGE

B & S Gauge	Thick-ness in Inches	Fine Silver Ozs.	Sterling Silver Ozs.	Coin Silver Ozs.	Fine Gold Dwts.	10K. Yel. Gold Dwts.	14K. Yel. Gold Dwts.	18K. Yel. Gold Dwts.	Plati-num Ozs.	Palla-dium Ozs.
1	.28930	4.38	4.32	4.30	161.0	96.2	109.	130.	8.91	4.99
2	.25763	3.47	3.43	3.41	128.	76.3	86.1	104.	7.07	3.94
3	.22942	2.75	2.72	2.70	101.	60.5	68.3	81.5	5.61	3.19
4	.20431	2.18	2.15	2.14	80.3	48.0	54.2	64.6	4.45	2.42
5	.18194	1.73	1.71	1.70	63.6	38.0	43.0	51.2	3.53	1.97
6	.16202	1.37	1.36	1.35	50.5	30.2	34.1	40.6	2.80	1.56
7	.14428	1.09	1.07	1.07	40.0	23.9	27.0	32.2	2.22	1.24
8	.12849	.863	.852	.848	31.7	19.0	21.4	25.6	1.76	.984
9	.11443	.685	.676	.673	25.2	15.1	17.0	20.3	1.39	.780
10	.10189	.543	.536	.533	20.0	11.9	13.5	16.1	1.11	.619
11	.09074	.431	.425	.423	15.8	9.46	10.7	12.7	.877	.491
12	.08080	.341	.337	.335	12.6	7.50	8.47	10.1	.695	.389
13	.07196	.271	.267	.266	9.96	5.95	6.72	8.01	.552	.309
14	.06408	.215	.212	.211	7.89	4.72	5.33	6.36	.437	.495
15	.05706	.170	.168	.167	6.26	3.74	4.23	5.04	.347	1.54
16	.05082	.135	.133	.133	4.97	2.97	3.35	4.00	.275	.154
17	.04525	.107	.106	.105	3.94	2.35	2.66	3.17	.218	.122
18	.04030	.0849	.0838	.0834	3.12	1.87	2.11	2.51	.173	.0968
19	.03589	.0674	.0665	.0662	2.48	1.48	1.67	1.99	.137	.0767
20	.03196	.0534	.0527	.0525	1.96	1.17	1.33	1.58	.109	.0609
21	.02846	.0424	.0418	.0416	1.56	.931	1.05	1.25	.0863	.0483
22	.02534	.0336	.0331	.0330	1.23	.738	.833	.994	.0684	.0383
23	.02257	.0266	.0263	.0262	.979	.585	.661	.789	.0543	.0304
24	.02010	.0211	.0209	.0208	.777	.464	.524	.625	.0430	.0241
25	.01790	.1068	.0165	.0165	.616	.368	.416	.496	.0341	.0191
26	.01594	.0133	.0131	.0131	.489	.292	.330	.393	.0271	.0151
27	.01419	.0105	.0104	.0103	.387	.231	.261	.312	.0214	.0120
28	.01264	.00835	.00825	.00821	.307	.184	.207	.247	.0170	.00952
29	.01125	.00662	.00653	.00650	.243	.145	.164	.196	.0135	.00754
30	.01002	.00525	.00518	.00516	.193	.115	.130	.155	.0107	.00598
31	.00892	.00416	.00411	.00409	.153	.0914	.103	.123	.00847	.00474
32	.00795	.00330	.00326	.00325	.122	.0726	.0820	.0978	.00673	.00377
33	.00708	.00262	.00259	.00258	.0964	.0576	.0651	.0776	.00534	.00299
34	.00630	.00208	.00205	.00204	.0763	.0456	.0515	.0614	.00423	.00236
35	.00561	.00165	.00162	.00162	.0605	.0362	.0408	.0487	.00335	.00188
36	.00500	.00131	.00129	.00128	.0481	.0287	.0324	.0387	.00266	.00149
37	.00445	.00104	.00102	.00102	.0381	.0228	.0257	.0306	.00211	.00118
38	.00396	.000820	.000809	.000806	.0302	.0180	.0204	.0243	.00167	.000934
39	.00353	.000652	.000643	.000640	.0240	.0143	.0162	.0193	.00133	.000742
40	.00314	.000516	.000509	.000507	.0190	.0113	.0128	.0153	.00105	.000587

*Square wire is 1.27324 times as heavy as round wire of the same gauge.

● decimal equivalents of drill sizes

Size	Decimal Equivalent	Size	Decimal Equivalent	Size	Decimal Equivalent	Size	Decimal Equivalent
½	0.500	G	0.261	23	0.154	1/16	0.0625
31/64	.4843	F	.257	24	.152	53	.0595
15/32	.4687	E—¼	.250	25	.1495	54	.055
29/64	.4531	D	.246	26	.147	55	.052
7/16	.4375	C	.242	27	.144	3/64	.0468
27/64	.4218	B	.238	9/64	.1406	56	.0465
Z	.413	15/64	.2343	28	.1405	57	.043
13/32	.4062	A	.234	29	.136	58	.042
Y	.404	1	.228	30	.1285	59	.041
X	.397	2	.221	⅛	.125	60	.040
25/64	.3906	7/32	.2187	31	.120	61	.039
W	.386	3	.213	32	.116	62	.038
V	.377	4	.209	33	.113	63	.037
⅜	.375	5	.2055	34	.111	64	.036
U	.368	6	.204	35	.110	65	.035
23/64	.3593	13/64	.2031	7/64	.1093	66	.033
T	.358	7	.201	36	.1065	1/32	.0312
S	.348	8	.199	37	.104	67	.032
11/32	.3437	9	.196	38	.1015	68	.031
R	.339	10	.1935	39	.0995	69	.029
Q	.332	11	.191	40	.098	70	.028
21/64	.3281	12	.189	41	.096	71	.026
P	.323	3/16	.1875	3/32	.0937	72	.025
O	.316	13	.185	42	.0935	73	.024
5/16	.3125	14	.182	43	.089	74	.0225
N	.302	15	.180	44	.086	75	.021
19/64	.2968	16	.177	45	.082	76	.020
M	.295	17	.173	46	.081	77	.018
L	.290	11/64	.1718	47	.0785	1/64	.0156
9/32	.2812	18	.1695	5/64	.0781	78	.016
K	.281	19	.166	48	.076	79	.0145
J	.277	20	.161	49	.073	80	.0135
I	.272	21	.159	50	.070		
H	.266	22	.157	51	.067		
17/64	.2656	5/32	.1562	52	.0635		

• surface speeds of wheels

IN FEET PER MINUTE [F.P.M.]

Motor or Spindle Speed r.p.m.	2"	4"	6"	8"	10"	12"	14"
1,000	525	1,050	1,575	2,100	2,600	3,100	3,600
1,200	630	1,260	1,950	2,550	3,200	3,750	4,400
1,400	730	1,470	2,250	2,950	3,650	4,400	5,100
1,600	840	1,680	2,550	3,400	4,200	5,000	5,900
1,800	940	1,890	2,900	3,800	4,750	5,650	6,600
2,000	1,050	2,100	3,200	4,200	5,250	6,250	7,300
2,200	1,150	2,300	3,450	4,550	5,750	6,900	8,000
2,400	1,260	2,500	3,750	5,000	6,300	7,500	8,800
2,600	1,360	2,700	4,100	5,450	6,800	8,200	9,600
2,800	1,470	2,950	4,400	5,900	7,400	8,900	10,400
3,000	1,570	3,140	4,700	6,250	7,900	9,400	11,200
3,200	1,680	3,350	5,000	6,650	8,400	10,000	11,900
3,400	1,780	3,560	5,250	7,000	8,900	10,600	12,600
3,600	1,880	3,780	5,600	7,500	9,500	11,300	13,300

supply sources for tools and materials

● precious metals

Allcraft Tool and Supply Co., Inc.
  100 Frank Road, Hicksville, NY 11801
Hauser and Miller
  10950 Linvalle Dr., St. Louis, MO 63123
Swest, Inc.
  10803 Composite Drive, Dallas, TX 75220

● copper, brass, bronze, etc.

Allcraft Tool and Supply Co., Inc.
  215 Park Ave., Hicksville, NY 11801
T. E. Conklin Brass and Copper Co., Inc.
  324 W. 23 St., New York, NY 10011
Revere Copper and Brass, Inc.
  230 Park Ave., New York, NY 10010

● findings

Allcraft Tool and Supply Co., Inc.
  215 Park Ave., Hicksville, NY 11801
C. R. Hill Co.
  35 W. Grand River, Detroit, MI 48208
C. E. Marshall Co.
  1113 W. Belmont, P.O. Box 7737, Chicago, IL
  60657

Swest, Inc.
  10803 Composite Drive, Dallas, TX 75220

● tools

Allcraft Tool and Supply Co., Inc.
  100 Frank Road, Hicksville, NY 11801
Paul Gesswein and Co., Inc.
  235 Park Ave. S., New York, NY 10003
Northwest Pitch Works
  5705 26th Ave., N.E., Seattle, WA 98105
  (excellent repoussé pitch)
Swest, Inc.
  10803 Composite Drive, Dallas, TX 75220

● chemical supplies

The following list is a partial geographic distribution
of chemical supply firms which are able to supply
small amounts of chemicals to individuals.

EAST

Allcraft Tool and Supply Co., Inc.
  100 Frank Road, Hicksville, NY 11801
  (usual chemicals for jewelry making)

Burrell Corp.
2223 Fifth Avenue, Pittsburgh, PA 15219
Howe & French, Inc.
99 Broad St., Boston, MA 02110
New York Laboratory Supply Co.
78 Varick St., New York, NY 10013
Seidler Chemical & Supply Co.
12–16 Orange St., Newark, NJ 07102

SOUTH

W. H. Curtin & Co.
P.O. Box 606, Jacksonville, FL 33033
P.O. Box 1491, New Orleans, LA 70113
Will Corporation of Georgia
P.O. Box 966, Atlanta, GA 30301

MIDWEST

Electro-Glo Company
625 S. Kolmar Ave., Chicago, IL 60624
(For electropolishing)
Harshaw Scientific Co.
1945 E. 97th St., Cleveland, OH 44106
9240 Hubbell Ave., Detroit, MI 48228
Kansas City Laboratory Supply Co.
307 Westport Rd., Kansas City, KS 66111
London Chemical Co., Inc.
240 Foster Ave., Bensonville, IL 60106
(Chemicals for cleaning copper and copper alloys)
Physician's Hospital Supply Co.
1400 Harmon Pl., Minneapolis, MN 55403
Roemer-Karrer Co.
810 N. Plankinton Ave., Milwaukee, WI 53203
E. H. Sargent & Co.
4647 W. Foster Ave., Chicago, IL 60630

WEST

Braun-Knecht-Heimann Co.
2301 Blake St., Denver, CO 80205
1400 16th St., San Francisco, CA 94119
W. H. Curtin & Co.
1812 Griffin St., Dallas, TX 75202
Scientific Supplies Co.
600 Spokane St., Seattle, WA 98104

CANADA

Canadian Laboratory Supplies, Ltd.
403 St. Paul St., W., Montreal 1, Quebec.
3701 Dundas St., W., Toronto 9, Ontario.
Cane & Co., Ltd.
1050 W. 6th Ave., Vancouver, B.C.

• casting equipment and supplies

Allcraft Tool and Supply Co., Inc.
100 Frank Road, Hicksville, NY 11801
The Cleveland Dental Mfg. Co.
Cleveland, OH
The Jelrus Company, Inc.
136 W. 52 St., New York, NY 10019
Kerr Dental Mfg. Co. (Wholesale only. Will
supply addresses of local distributors)
6081–6095 Twelfth St., Detroit, MI 48208
Alexander Saunders & Co.
P.O. Box 265, Coldspring, NY 10516
Swest Inc.
10803 Composite Drive, Dallas, TX 75220
S. S. White Dental Mfg. Co.
55 E. Washington St., Chicago, IL 60602

• electroplating and electroforming supplies

Batavia Chemical Co.
Rt. 25, Aurora, IL 60507
(Plating Chemicals)
Bert Bricker, Inc.
P.O. Box 171, Wilmington, DE 19899
(Silver conductive paint)
Edmund Scientific Co.
42 Edscorp Bldg., Barrington, NJ 08007
(Ammeters, rheostats, etc.)
H.B.S. Equipment Division
3543 E. 16th St., Los Angeles, CA 90023
(Tanks, rectifiers, etc.)
Hoover and Strong
111 West Tupper St., Buffalo, NY 14201
(General Plating Supplies)
Matheson Scientific, Inc.
Elk Grove Village, IL 60007
(Plating Chemicals)
Micro-Circuits Co.
New Buffalo, MI 49117
(Conductive paint)
Technic, Inc.
P.O. Box 965, Providence, RI 02901
(Black Plating and other Plating Solutions)
Tolber Division, Micro Products
220 W. 5th St., Hope, AR 71801
(Micro-Peel and solvent. Stopout for etching,
plating, etc.)
Warner Electric Co., Inc.
1512 W. Jarvis Ave., Chicago, IL 60626
(Conductive paint)
Wornow Products
15051 E. Don Julian Rd., Industry, CA 91744
(Silver ink for silk screen)

Most general suppliers of jewelry-making materials also carry some plating equipment. Farm supply stores often carry cupric sulphate.

• lapidary equipment

Grieger's
  1633 E. Walnut St., Pasadena, CA 91106
M.D.R. Manufacturing Co.
  4853 W. Jefferson Blvd., Los Angeles, CA 90016
Technicraft Lapidaries Corp.
  3560 Broadway, New York, NY 10031
Vreeland Manufacturing Co.
  4105 N.E. 68th Ave., Portland, OR 97213

• gems

Contact local lapidary or "rock hound" clubs. Many lapidary hobbyists are willing and able to cut specific shapes and sizes difficult to find elsewhere.

• enamels

Norbert L. Cochran
  2540 S. Fletcher Ave., Fernandina Beach, FL 32034
  (U.S. Distributor of Schauer & Co. enamels, Vienna, Austria. Excellent quality)
Thomas C. Thompson Co.
  1539 Old Deerfield Rd., P.O. Box 127, Highland Park, IL 60035
Vitrearc Division., Ceramic Coating Co.
  P.O. Box 370, Newport, KY 41072
  (Lead-free enamels)

• domestic and exotic hardwoods

Cotton Hanlon, Inc.
  Cayuta, NY 14824
Craftsman Wood Service Co.
  2727 S. Mary St., Chicago, IL 60608
J. H. Monteath Co.
  2500–08 Park Ave., New York, NY 10000
Youngblood Lumber Co.
  1335 Central Ave., N.E., Minneapolis, MN 55400

• plastics

Amplast, Inc.
  3020 Jerome Ave., New York, NY 10468
Cadillac Plastic and Chemical Co.
  1245 W. Fulton, Chicago, IL 60607
Castolite Co.
  Woodstock, IL 60098
Hysol Epoxikits, Electro-Insulation Corp.
  2535 Clearbrook Dr., Arlington Heights, IL 60005
  (Excellent adhesives)
Rohm and Haas Company
  Independence Mall West, Philadelphia, PA 19105
  (Write for retailers)
Thermoset Plastics, Inc.
  5101 East 65th St., P.O. Box 20049, Indianapolis, IN 46220

• general tools

Brookstone Co.
  Peterborough, NH 03458
Silvo Hardware
  107–109 Walnut St., Philadelphia, PA 19106

bibliography

• jewelry techniques (english language)

Abbey, Staton: *The Goldsmith's and Silversmith's Handbook*, London, Technical Press, Ltd., 1952.

Auld, J. Leslie: *Your Jewellery*, London, Sylvan Press, 1951; Peoria, Ill., Chas. A. Bennett Co. (distributors).

Maryon, Herbert: *Metalwork and Enameling*, New York, Dover Publications, 1955.

Metal Finish Guidebook and Directory, Westwood, N.J., Metals and Plastics Publications, Inc., 1971.

Morton, Philip: *Contemporary Jewelry: A Studio Handbook*, New York, Holt, Rinehart and Winston, 1970.

O'Connor, Harold: *The Jewelers' Bench Reference*, Dunconor Books, Box 2000, Crested Butte, Colo. 81224.

Pack, Greta: *Chains and Beads*, New York, D. Van Nostrand Co., 1952.

Pack, Greta: *Jewelry and Enameling*, 2nd ed., New York, D. Van Nostrand Co., 1953

Rose, Augustus F., and Cirino, Antonio: *Jewelry Making and Design*, Worcester, Mass., Davis Publication Inc., revised, 1946.

Steakley, Douglas: *Holloware Techniques*, New York, Watson Guptill, 1979.

Untracht, Oppi: *Metal Techniques for Craftsmen*, New York, Doubleday, 1968.

Wilson, Henry: *Silver Work and Jewellery*, New York and London, Pitman Publishing Corp., 1902.

• jewelry techniques (foreign language)

Boitet, Alfred: *Traite Pratique du Bijoutier-Joaillier (French)*, Paris, Editions Garnier Fréres, 6 rue des Saints-Péres.

Braun-Feldweg, Dr. Wilhelm: *Metall-Werkformen und Arbeitsweisen (German)*, Verlag Gold und Silber, New York, Stechert-Hafner, Inc., 1975.

Czerwinski, Albert, and Hub, Friedrich: *Die Goldschmiedelehre (German)*, Leipzig, Verlag Wilhelm Diebener, 1931.

Diebener, Wilhelm: *Handbuch des Goldschmieds (German)*, Leipzig, Verlag Wilhelm Diebener, 1929.

Herman, Reinhold: *Elementare Gestaltungslehre für den Goldschmied (German)*, Verlag Gold und Silber, New York, Stechert-Hafner, Inc.

Schwan, Christian: *Die Metalle, Ihre Legierungen und Lote, Die Oberflachen behandlung der Metalle, Rezept und Werkstattbuch für den Gold und Silberschmied (German)*, Verlag Gold und Silber, New York, Stechert-Hafner, Inc.

Wilm, H. J.: *Lebendige Goldschmiedekunst (German)*, Verlag Gold und Silber, New York, Stechert-Hafner, Inc.

• historic technique references

Bergsoe, Paul (English translation by F. C. Reynolds): *The Gilding Process and the Metallurgy of Copper and Lead Among the Pre-Columbian Indians, The Metallurgy and Technology of Gold and Platinum Among the Pre-Columbian Indians (References to granulation and other fusing techniques)*, Copenhagen, Danmarks Naturvidenskabelige Samfund, I Kommission Hos G.E.C. Gad. Vimmelskaftet 32, 1937, 1938.

Cellini, Benvenuto (English translation by C. H. Ashbee): *Treatises on the Arts of Goldsmithing and Sculpture.* 1966

Davidson, Patricia F., and Hoffmann, H.: *Greek Gold*, Brooklyn, The Brooklyn Museum, 1966.

Gunsaulus, Helen: *The Japanese Sword and Its Deco-*

ration, Chicago, Field Museum of Natural History, 1924.

Jisl, Lumir: *Swords of the Samurai*, Knihtisk, Prague, 1767 (English language).

Maryon, Herbert: *Metalwork and Enameling (References to granulation, lamination, inlay, etc.)*, New York, Dover Publications, 1955.

Milliken, William M.: "The Art of the Goldsmith," reprinted from the *Journal of Aesthetics and Art Criticism* 6, no. 4, June, 1948.

Robinson, B. W.: *The Arts of the Japanese Sword*, Rutland, Vt., Charles E. Tuttle Co., 1961.

Rosenberg, Marc: *Geschichte der Goldschmiedekunst (German)*, Vols. I, II, III (*References to niello and granulation*). Out of Print—Library of Congress, Class-NK 7106, Book-R8.

Smith, Cyril Stanley: *A History of Metallography*, Chicago, University of Chicago Press, 1960.

Wilson, Henry: *Silverwork and Jewellery (References to inlay, lamination, and Japanese techniques)*, London and New York, Pitman Publishing Corp., 1902.

Withered, Newton: *Medieval Craftsmanship and the Modern Amateur*, London, Longmans, Green & Co., 1923.

• history of jewelry and related forms

Adair, John: *Navajo and Pueblo Silversmiths*, Norman, Okla., University of Oklahoma Press, 1945.

Alexander, Christine, ed.: *Ancient Egyptian Jewelry, Chinese Jewelry, Greek and Etruscan Jewelry, Jewelry, The Art of the Goldsmith in Classical Times, Medieval Jewelry, Near Eastern Jewelry, Renaissance Jewelry*, New York, Metropolitan Museum of Art.

Bainbridge, Henry C.: *Peter Paul Faberge, His Life's Work*, London and New York, B. T. Batsford, 1949.

Banco de la República Rogotá: *80 Masterpieces from the Gold Museum*, Colombia, Banco de la República, Bogotá, 1954.

Barradas, Jose Perez de: *Orfebreria Prehispánica de Columbia (Spanish)*, (*Excellent examples of Pre-Columbian goldwork*), Colombia, Banco de la República, Bogotá, 1958.

Bradford, Ernle Dusgate Selby: *Contemporary Jewellery and Silver Design (Examples of modern English commercial design)*, London, Heywood & Co., 1950.

Bradford, Ernle Dusgate Selby: *Four Centuries of European Jewellery*, New York, Philosophical Library, 1953.

Burch-Korrodi, Meinard: *Orfevrerie D'Eglise (French)*, (*Contemporary French examples of enameled ecclesiastic objects and jewelry*), Paris, Editions, Alsatia, 1956.

Burger, Dr. Willy: *Abendlandische Schmelzarbeiten (German)*, Berlin, Richard Carl Schmidt & Co., 1930.

Burgess, Frederick W.: *Antique Jewelry and Stones*, New York, Tudor Publishing Co., 1972.

Carli, Enzo: *Pre-Conquest Goldsmith's Work of Colombia*, New York, W. S. Heinman, 1958.

Evans, Joan: *A History of Jewelry, 1100–1870*, New York, Pitman Publishing Corp., 1953.

Gehring, Prof. Oscar: *Josef Wilm, der Gold und Silberschmied (German)*, (*Excellent contemporary work in granulation*), Verlag Gold und Silber, New York, Stechert-Hafner, Inc.

Hald, Arthur: *Contemporary Swedish Design*, Stockholm, Nordisk Rotogravyr, 1951.

Hara, Shinkichi: *Die Meister der Japanischen Schwertzieraten (German)*, (*Examples of Japanese inlay and patination*), Hamburg, Verlag des Museums für Kunst und Gewerbe, 1931.

Hendley, Thomas H.: "Monograph on Indian Jewellery" (*Jewellery of India and Ceylon*), London, *The Journal of Indian Art*, vol. 12, W. Griggs and Sons, 1884–1900.

Jessup, Ronald F.: *Anglo-Saxon Jewellery*, New York, Frederick A. Praeger, 1953.

Jossic, Yvonne Francoise: *1050 Jewelry Designs (Some fine historic examples)*, Philadelphia, Alfred Lampl, 1946.

Kelemen, Pal: *Medieval American Art, vols. I & II (Excellent text and illustrations)*, New York, The Macmillan Co., 1943.

McCarthy, James Remington: *Rings Through the Ages*, New York, Harper & Brothers.

Muller-Erb, Rudolph: *Der Goldschmied Mohler (German)*, Stuttgart, Chr. Belser Druckerei und Verlag, 1941.

Rogers, Frances, and Beard, Alice: *5000 Years of Gems and Jewelry*, Philadelphia, J. B. Lippincott, 1947.

Rossi, Filippo: *Italian Jeweled Arts*, New York, Harry N. Abrams, 1954.

Salin, Bernhard: *Die Altgermanische Thieronamentik (German)*, Stockholm, Wahlstrom & Widstrand, Forlag.

Schweeger-Hefel, Annemarie: *Afrikanische Bronzen (German)*, (*West African designs in metal from Ife and Ashanti areas*), Vienna, Kunstverlag, Wolfrum, 1948.

Steingraber, E.: *Antique Jewelry (Excellent examples of medieval and Renaissance European jewelry)*, New York, Frederick A. Praeger, 1957.

Thoma, Hans: *Kronen und Kleinodien (German)*, Berlin, Deutscher Kunstverlag, 1955.

Ugglas, Carl Gustaf: *Kyrkligt Guld-och Silversmide (Swedish)*, Stockholm, Wahlstrom & Widstrand, Forlag, 1933.

Woodward, Arthur: *A Brief History of Navajo Silversmithing*, Flagstaff, Ariz., Northern Arizona Society of Science and Art, 1938.

• lapidary information

Anderson, B. W.: *Gem Testing for Jewelers*, London, Heywood & Co., 1947.

Drake, Dr. E. H., and Pearl, R. M.: *The Art of Gem Cutting*, Portland, Ore., Mineralogist Publishing Co., 1945.

Gravender, Milton F.: *Fascinating Facts about Gems*, Los Angeles, Gemological Institute of America.

Howard, J. Harry: *Revised Lapidary Handbook*, Greenville, S.C., 504 Crescent St., 1946.

Howard, Henry: *The Working of Semi-Precious Stones*, Greenville, S.C., 504 Crescent St.

Kraus, E. H., and Slawson, C. B.: *Gems and Gem Material*, 5th ed., New York, McGraw-Hill Book Co., 1947.

Shipley, Robert M.: *Dictionary of Gems and Jewelry*, Los Angeles, Gemological Institute of America, 1974.

Sinkankas, A.: *Gem Cutting, a Lapidary's Manual*, New York, D. Van Nostrand Co., 1955.

Sperisen, Francis J.: *The Art of the Lapidary*, Milwaukee, Wis., Bruce Publishing Co., 1950.

Willems, J. Daniel: *Gem Cutting*, Peoria, Ill., Manual Arts Press, 1948.

• enameling techniques and history

Bates, Kenneth F.: *Enameling Principles and Practice*, Cleveland, World Book Co., 1951.

Cunynghame, H. H.: *Art Enameling on Metals*, London, Constable & Co., 1906.

Dalton, O. M.: *Byzantine Enamels in Mr. Pierpont Morgan's Collection (Fine examples of early European cloisonné and champlevé techniques)*, London, Chatto and Windus, 1912.

Day, Lewis F.: *Enamelling*, London and New York, B. T. Batsford, 1907.

Gauthier, Marie-Madeleine S.: *Emaux Limousins Champlevés des XII, XIII et XVI Siècles (French)*, Paris, Gérard Le Prat, 268 Boulevard Saint-Germain, 1950.

Hasenohr, Curt: *Email (German)*, Dresden, Verlag der Kunst, 1955.

Koningh, H. de: *Preparation of Precious and Other Metal Work for Enamelling*, London, The Technical Press, 1947.

Lavendau, Pierre: *Leonard Limousin et Les Emailleurs Française (French)*, Paris, Henri Laurens.

Millenet, Louis-Elie: *Enamelling on Metal*, London, The Technical Press, 1947.

Otten, Mitzi, and Berl, Kathe: *The Art of Enameling*, New York, 1950.

Seeler, Margaret: *The Art of Enameling*, New York, D. Van Nostrand, Reinhold Co.

Thompson, Thomas E.: *Enameling on Copper and Other Metals*, Highland Park, Ill., Thomas C. Thompson Co., 1539 Deerfield Road, 1950.

Untracht, Oppi: *Enameling on Metal*, Philadelphia, Chilton Company, 1957.

• engraving techniques

Bowman, John J.: *Jewelry Engraver's Manual*, New York, D. Van Nostrand Co., 1954.

• plastics techniques

Castolite Company: Descriptive process Bulletins published as *The Castoliter*, Woodstock, Ill., The Castolite Company.

• books of interest in the abstraction of natural forms

Bentley, W., and Humphreys, W. J.: *Snow Crystals*, New York, Dover Publications, 1962.

Bliss, Robert Woods Collection: *Indigenous Art of the Americas*, Washington, D. C., Smithsonian Institution, 1947.

Boas, Franz: *Primitive Art*, New York, Capitol Publishing Co., 1951.

Borovka, Gregory: *Scythian Art*, New York, Frederick A. Stokes Co., 1928 (*out of print*).

Bossert, Helmuth T.: *Alt Syrien (German)*, Tübingen, Ernst Wasmuth, 1951.

Bossert, Helmuth T.: *Art of Ancient Crete*, London, A. Zwemmer, Ltd., 1937.

Einstein, Carl: *Afrikanische Plastik (German)*, Berlin, Verlag Ernst Wasmuth, A. G., 1921.

Elkin, A. P.: *Art in Arnhemland*, Chicago, University of Chicago Press, 1950.

Griaule, Marcel: *Folk Art of Africa*, New York, Tudor Publishing Co., 1950.

Heine-Geldern, Robert von: *Indonesian Art*, New York, The Asia Institute, 1948.

Leenhardt, Maurice: *Folk Art of Oceania*, New York, Tudor Publishing Co., 1950.

Linton, Ralph, and Wingert, Paul S.: *Arts of the South Seas*, New York, Museum of Modern Art, Simon and Schuster, 1946.

Lothrop, Samuel Kirkland: *Cocle, An Archaeological Study of Central Panama*, Cambridge, Mass., Peabody Museum, Harvard University, 1937.

Markman, Sidney David: *The Horse in Greek Art*, Baltimore, Johns Hopkins Press, 1943.

Minns, Ellis Hovell: *The Art of the Northern Nomads*, London, H. Milford, 1944.

Roes, Anna: *Greek Geometric Art*, Haarlem, 1933.

Roth, Edward: "Primitive Art from Benin," *International Studio Magazine*, January 1899.

Schmalenback, Wilhelm: *Die Kunst Afrikas (German)*, Basle, Holbein Verlag, 1953.

Tischner, Herbert: *Oceanic Art*, New York, Pantheon Books, 1954.

● periodicals

American Craft (General Craft Information), American Craft Council, 22 West 55th St., New York, N.Y. 10019

Ceramics Monthly (Sections on enameling), Professional Publications, Inc., Box 12448, Columbus, Ohio 43212.

Crafter's Friend (Sections on enameling), The Potter's Wheel, Inc., 11447 Euclid Ave., Cleveland, Ohio 44106.

Design Quarterly (Two issues on contemporary American jewelry, 1955 and 1959), Walker Art Center, 1710 Lyndale Avenue South, Minneapolis, Minn. 55403.

Deutsche Goldschmiede-Zeitung (German), Rühle-Diebener Verlag, Stuttgart, Olgastrasse 110.

Metalsmith (Excellent for new techniques information), Society of North American Goldsmiths, 8589 Wonderland N.W., Clinton, Ohio 44216.

Gold und Silber (German), Stechert-Hafner, Inc., 31 East 10 St., New York, N.Y. 10003 (distributors).

The Lapidary Journal, Del Mar, Cal.

Index

Page numbers in bold indicate illustrations